ATTENTION DEFICIT DEMOCRACY

ATTENTION DEFICIT
DEMOCRACY

James Bovard

First published 2005 by
PALGRAVE MACMILLAN™
175 Fifth Avenue, New York, N.Y. 10010 and
Houndmills, Basingstoke, Hampshire, England RG21 6XS.
Companies and representatives throughout the world.

PALGRAVE MACMILLAN is the global academic imprint of the Palgrave Macmillan
division of St. Martin's Press, LLC and of Palgrave Macmillan Ltd. Macmillan® is a
registered trademark in the United States, United Kingdom and other countries. Palgrave
is a registered trademark in the European Union and other countries.

ISBN 1–4039–7108–0

Library of Congress Cataloging-in-Publication Data
Bovard, James.
Attention deficit democracy / James Bovard.
    p.   cm.
    Includes bibliographical references and index.
    ISBN 1–4039–7108–0 (alk. paper)
    1. Democracy.   2. Democracy—United States.   3. United States—Politics and
government—2001–   I. Title.

JC423.B757   2006
320.973'09'0511—dc22

                                                                        2005051259

A catalogue record for this book is available from the British Library.

Design by Letra Libre, Inc.

First edition: January 2006
10 9 8 7 6 5 4 3 2 1

Printed in the United States of America

Contents

Credo for
the New American Patriotism

I believe:

That politicians are more honest than they seem;

That government is more competent than it appears;

That government is benevolent, regardless of how much it wastes or how many people it harms;

That citizens must trust the government, regardless of how often it lies;

That democracy is a panacea, regardless of how often it fails;

That freedom is whatever the president says it is, pending revision.

—James Bovard

CHAPTER 1

Introduction

The forms of our free government have outlasted the ends for which they were instituted, and have become a mere mockery of the people for whose benefit they should operate.

—"Americus," 1775[1]

Delusions about democracy are subverting peace and freedom. The American system of government is collapsing thanks to ignorant citizens, lying politicians, and a government leashed neither by law nor Constitution. While presidents and pundits harp on democracy's inevitable spread around the world, it is perishing at home.

Victorious politicians routinely invoke the "will of the people" to sanctify their power. But voters cannot countenance what they do not understand. The "will of the people" is often simply a measure of how many people fell for which lies, how many people were frightened by which advertisements, and which red herrings worked on which target audiences. Rather than the "will of the people," election results are often only a one-day snapshot of transient mass delusions.

Many Americans have little or no idea how government works or who is holding the reins on their lives. The majority of American voters do not know the name of their congressman, the length of terms of House or Senate members, what the Bill of Rights guarantees, or what the government is actually doing in the vast majority of its interventions. A survey after the 2002 congressional election revealed that less than a third of Americans knew "that the Republicans controlled the House of Representatives prior to the election."[2] Recent polls show that almost two-thirds of Americans could not name a single Supreme Court justice and that 58 percent of Americans could not name a single cabinet department in the federal government.[3]

Americans are assured that they are free because rulers take power only with the people's informed consent. What does "informed consent" mean these days? It means knowing the names of the president's pets but not knowing his record on key issues. It means knowing the sexual orientation of family members of candidates for high office, but falling prey to their rewriting of history. It means recalling the phrases the government endlessly repeats, and screening out evidence of government atrocities.

The political ignorance of scores of millions of Americans prevents them from recognizing the consequences or dangers of government actions. The citizenry is increasingly on automatic pilot, paying less attention to each new war, each new power grab, each new dubious presidential assertion.

The rising gullibility of the American people may be the most important trend in U.S. democracy. With each passing decade, with each new presidency, it takes less and less to snooker Americans. And a candidate only has to fool enough people on one day to snare power over everyone for four years.

Attention Deficit Democracy begets a government that is nominally democratic—in which elections are boisterous events accompanied by torrents of deceptive ads and mass rallies. But after the election, the president returns to his pedestal. Attention Deficit Democracy lacks the most important check on the abuse of power: an informed citizenry resolutely defending their rights and liberties.

In 1693, William Penn, the founder of Pennsylvania, wrote what could be the motto for modern American government. "Let the people think they govern, and they will be governed."[4] Rulers endlessly assure people that they are in charge—while creating agency after agency, program after program that people can neither comprehend nor control. Americans' political thinking is becoming akin to the recitation of the Pledge of Allegiance—a series of bromides that sink into the mind and stifle independent, critical thought.

MONARCHICAL MYTHS OF DEMOCRACY

President George W. Bush calls democracy "the most honorable form of government ever devised by man."[5] Americans are taught that the sum of American democracy is vastly greater than its parts. Regardless of how often the candidate withholds information or how many false claims he emits, no matter how deluded the average voter, and no matter what manipulations occur before and during voting—election results are sacrosanct.

The same type of myths have grown up around democracy that long propped up monarchs. In the 1500s, peasants were encouraged to believe that the king was chosen by God to serve His purposes on Earth. Today, Americans are encouraged to believe that Bush's reelection victory is a sign of God's approval of Bush's reign.[6] In the 1600s, English yeomen were told that any limit on the King's power was an affront to God. Today, Americans are told that any restraint on the president's power thwarts the Will of the People. In the 1700s, the downtrodden of Europe were told that their king possessed the sum of all Earthly wisdom. Today, people are encouraged to believe that the president and his top cadre practically know all and see all—their insider information transcends the petty facts unearthed by the CIA, congressional committees, or the 9/11 Commission. In the early 1800s, people were encouraged to believe that their kings automatically cared about their subjects, simply because that was the nature of kings. Now, people are taught that the government automatically serves the people, simply because a plurality of voters assented to one of the politicians the major parties offered them.

As people became more literate and better informed, they lost their faith in monarchs. But new delusions have replaced old superstitions. Democracy multiplies the number of people with a vested interest in delusions about government. Americans are supposed to sit back, confident that voting cures all political evils—as if the process for selecting rulers vaccinated the political system from harm. People are told that as long as they can cast a ballot, they will be safe. In a democracy, people are led to believe that they can easily apply the brakes to government, no matter how unstoppable it becomes.

FABRICATING A RIGHT TO RULE

It is a common saying among political campaign consultants: "In victory, all sins are forgotten." Unfortunately, the sooner citizens forget the lies of the campaign trail, the sooner they will be victimized by new government failures and sacrificed in more unnecessary wars.

Losing a certain percentage of the voters who understand issues or recall facts is now simply a "transaction cost" for a political campaign. The only lies that are unforgivable nowadays are those that repel more voters than they con. And regardless of how brazen a politician's howlers, the media rushes to repaint him as worthy of respect and deference.

The biggest election frauds usually occur before the voting booths open. Bush is upholding a long tradition of presidential deceit. He was reelected in large part due to mass delusions about Iraq. An August 2004 poll found that "among those who wrongly believe that Iraq had Weapons of Mass Destruction, 81% think going to war was the right decision. Among those who correctly know that Iraq had no WMD, just 8% think the war was right."[7] Bush and Cheney successfully inoculated tens of millions of voters against reality, linking Saddam to Al Qaeda and 9/11 and portraying the invasion of Iraq as a necessary part of the war on terrorism. A University of Maryland October 2004 poll analysis concluded, "It is clear that supporters of the president are more likely to have misperceptions than those who oppose him."[8]

For many voters in 2004, Bush's presumed personal goodness was all that they needed to know. When Bush acted like he was incorrigible, many voters hailed his conduct as proof he was steadfast. When Bush refused to admit any mistakes, many voters assumed his record was impeccable. The more Bush boasted of his consistency, the less attention many Americans paid to reality. Bush "almost never entertains public doubt, which is part of the White House design to build a more powerful presidency," the *Washington Post* reported.[9] To breed blind faith in the ruler, people are encouraged to see the president as infallible. When Bush stumbled in the presidential debates, many supporters felt a bond with him as someone also not weighed down by excessive intellectual baggage. Floridian Lynn Farr, a 43-year-old former restaurant owner, explained his vote for Bush: "The guy wears a cowboy hat. He cuts brush. You always see [news] clips of him driving a big ol' Ford truck and working on his ranch. He's one of us."[10]

Bush has proven that a president can get away with far more hokum than previously thought. Unfortunately, this was also the lesson of the Clinton presidency. Even though Americans often recognized that Bill Clinton lied, many still believed him when he promised to "feel their pain."[11] Clinton's case for bombing Serbia in 1999 was as dubious as Bush's case for invading Iraq. But for both Clinton and Bush, their self proclaimed good intentions made unjustified U.S. killings irrelevant.

"Presidents have lied so much to us about foreign policy that they've established almost a common-law right to do so," history professor Leo Ribuffo observed in 1998.[12] From John F. Kennedy lying about the Bay of Pigs debacle in Cuba; to Johnson lying about the Gulf of Tonkin resolution; to Richard Nixon lying about the secret bombing of Cambodia; to Jimmy Carter lying about the Shah of Iran being a progressive, enlightened ruler; to Ronald Reagan lying about terrorism and Iran-Contra; to George H. W. Bush lying about the justifications for the first Gulf War, entire generations have come of age since the ancient time when a president's power was constrained by a duty of candor to the public.

Unfortunately, many citizens' minds are sponges, soaking up whatever government emits. Lies almost always turn out to be duds, as far as detonating any backlash against political abuses. Self-government is vanishing because of black holes in citizens' heads where connections are not made and sparks do not fly.

Ironically, despite the government's long record of deceits, distrust of government is more dangerous than government power itself—at least according to the conventional wisdom of today's Establishment. Private doubts are supposedly a greater threat to America than official lies. Trust in government becomes mass Prozac, keeping people docile and compliant.

BATTERED CITIZEN SYNDROME

The government is exploiting public dread to redefine the relation between rulers and the American people. White House Chief of Staff Andrew Card, in a talk to Republican National Convention delegates in September 2004, praised Bush's role as the protector of the nation and assured them that "this president sees America as we think about a 10-year-old child. I know as a parent I would sacrifice all for my children." Card's comment generated almost no controversy.[13] Yet viewing Americans as young children needing protection makes a mockery of democracy. Is servility now the price of survival?

The more ignorant the populace, the easier it becomes for rulers to frighten people into submission. Bush was reelected in part because his administration, policies, and statements, helped by many dubious alerts and warnings, boosted the number of Americans who feared a terrorist attack during 2004. Each time the feds issued a new warning of a terrorist threat after 9/11, the president's approval rating rose by an average of almost 3 percent.[14]

As long as enough people can be frightened, then all people can be ruled. Politicians cow people on election day to corral them afterward. The more that fear is the key issue, the more that voters will be seeking a savior, not a representative—and the more the winner can claim all the power he claims to need.

We now have the Battered Citizen Syndrome: the more debacles, the more voters cling to faith in their rulers. Like a train engineer bonding with the survivors of a train wreck that happened on his watch, Bush constantly reminded Americans of 9/11 and his wars. The greater the government's failure to protect, the greater the subsequent mass fear—and the easier it becomes to subjugate the populace. The continuing follies and flounders of the war on terrorism were irrelevant compared to the paramount promise of protection. The craving for a protector drops an Iron Curtain around the mind, preventing a person from accepting evidence that would shred his political security blanket.

MESSIANIC MOONSHINE

In recent years, Americans have devoted far more effort to spreading democracy than to understanding it. Bush, echoing Clinton and earlier presidents, says that America is "called" to spread democracy and freedom around the world. Forgetting the warnings by early presidents about the dangers of foreign entanglements, the U.S. government is charging forward to remake the world in its own image.

Americans have been taught to view U.S. intervention abroad as the equivalent of a holy man touching a sick person, instantly healing whatever ails them. Even if the person isn't sick, getting a holy nudge can't but help them. "Fixing" elections is doing a service to foreign peoples since the U.S. government knows what is best for them. And if foreigners object to U.S. interference, that just proves that they are deluded and must be protected from themselves.

In his second inaugural address, Bush issued a revolutionary challenge to every government in the world: "We will persistently clarify the choice before every ruler and every nation: The moral choice between oppression, which is always wrong, and freedom, which is eternally right."[15] Bush is correct that freedom is "eternally right." But that does not confer upon Bush or other U.S. presidents the right to act like the World Pope of Democracy, entitled to appoint rulers in each nation upon Earth. The notion of American uniqueness has gone from a point of pride to a pretext for aggression.

ELECTIVE DICTATORSHIP

President George Washington declared in 1790 that "the virtues and knowledge of the people would effectually oppose the introduction of tyranny."[16] But today's Americans do little to justify the confidence of the nation's first president. The federal government has been rapidly adding new coercive penalties to its statutory arsenal for decades. Americans have acquiesced to politicians and bureaucrats taking over one area of their lives after another.

President Washington may have also been confident that his fellow citizens and their offspring would not forget his warning that "Government is not reason, it is not eloquence—it is force."[17] Unfortunately, as long as recent American presidents continue to praise freedom, they are usually permitted to seize as much power as they please. On November 13, 2001, Bush announced that he had the right to nullify all rights. Bush decreed that he had the power to label as an "enemy combatant" anyone suspected of involvement with terrorism. The president need provide no evidence for such designations; there would be no access to courts to challenge such a label; and people could be detained forever on the president's accusation. And "enemy combatants" need not be combatants. Bush administration lawyers have made clear that even hapless donors to foreign charities can be seized and held without charges if their contribution ends up in the wrong hands. In July 2005, Bush's solicitor general announced in federal court that the entire United States is a "battlefield" upon which Bush has absolute power to have people—including American citizens—seized and detained indefinitely.[18]

In 2002, Bush's top legal advisors informed him that, as commander-in-chief during wartime, he was above all the laws Congress enacted. Bush's legal whiz kids also redefined torture so that CIA agents and U.S. soldiers could brutalize detainees without fear of prosecution. Americans were assured that the Abu Ghraib photos that leaked out in 2004 were the result of "a few bad apples." However, details later emerged that CIA operatives or U.S. soldiers had killed dozens of detainees during interrogations in Afghanistan and Iraq. Reviving a hallowed tradition from the Middle Ages, the administration announced that it could use "evidence" gained from torture to prosecute detainees in its military tribunals. Americans' scant response to the torture scandal signaled their growing tolerance for absolute power—as long as the president promised it would be used to make them secure.

This is the age of Leviathan Democracy. Leviathan was the Biblical term that English philosopher Thomas Hobbes used in 1651 to describe a government absolute and far superior to its subjects, whose task was to obey and, when ordered, die. The United States was an anti-Leviathan at its founding—the first government to be created with strict limitations on its power enshrined into the Constitution to protect citizens from their rulers in perpetuity.

But in recent decades, government power has become unbounded. The U.S. government still has the formal trappings of a democracy—candidates, elections, congressional proceedings, judges draped in long black robes. But we have fallen far from the Founding Fathers' ideal of a Rule of Law. Today, when the president's desires extend beyond legal boundaries, the Constitution and the statute book be damned.

Attention Deficit Democracy begets Leviathan because rulers exploit people's ignorance to seize more power over them. The bigger government becomes, the fewer citizens understand it, the less representative it will tend to be. The contract between rulers and ruled is replaced by a blank check. As long as presidents and their appointees recite the proper phrases and strike the correct poses, they can do as they please.

Democracy unleashes the State in the name of the people. Yet citizens are assured that their government will protect liberty, no matter what. Democracy automatically reins itself in so that it does not gorge on power like a horse eating too many oats, stopping only when it explodes.

Government is an elective dictatorship when voters do little more than select who will violate the laws and Constitution. Bush, like other U.S. presidents, perpetually equates democracy with freedom. But if the purported consent of voters confers upon the winner the right to nullify citizens' rights—they are voting for a master, not a representative. Elections become little more than reverse slave auctions, in which slaves choose their masters.

Voting is now a way of conferring power and honors on politicians, rather than a method of reining in rulers. In the early American Republic, candidates would stress their fidelity to the Constitution. But the Constitution has vanished from the campaign trail, replaced by competing promises of new handouts and new protections against the vicissitudes of daily life.

The Founding Fathers did not design a "Great Leader" democracy. The ultimate principle of the American system of government is strict limits on the power of all branches of the federal government. Yet Bush, like earlier presidents, has swayed many people to view checks and balances as a peril to their personal survival.

Attention Deficit Democracy lulls citizens into thinking that they have nothing to fear from the rising number of sticks and shackles that politicians and bureaucrats can use on them. The peril of rising U.S. government power is stark to foreigners, who see U.S. aggression around the globe. It is stark to many people who hear the president talk of military killings as "bringing justice" to the deceased. It is stark to those who fear the United States may invade their country next. But it is not stark to too many Americans.

THE COMING END OF AMERICAN DEMOCRACY?

The more authoritarian the U.S. government becomes, the louder presidents praise democracy. Unfortunately, *democracy* is a magical word that permits speakers to automatically fog the minds of many listeners.

By what standard could American democracy be considered a success? Simply because referendums on rulers occur without widespread violence? Because most Americans acquiesce to whomever the political system ordains as the winner? Because the majority of people continue obeying, and paying taxes? Simply because there have not been Albanian-style mass violent attacks on government office buildings?

Bogus fears can produce real servitude. Politicians stampede people with one dubious terror attack warning after another; one constitutional right after another is decimated; one barrier against absolutism after another is breached.

Is our era coming to resemble medieval times, when people were so suffused with fear that they formally signed away their rights and pledged fealty to whoever promised to protect them? There is scant glory or dignity in panicky national referendums to choose a Shepherd-in-Chief.

Are Americans free simply because they are permitted a perfunctory choice on who will molest their rights and liberties? How much of a facade of democracy is necessary to placate the public? Is it the "will of the people"—or at least the majority—to be deluded? Does self-government now mean anything more than showing up once every few years to ratify one's rulers? Is the sole question remaining in American politics—how to find a good master for the American people?

It is naive to trust to the ignorant preferences of frightened people to preserve freedom. In America today, all leaders have to do is brazenly deny obvious facts and they become entitled to commit new abuses. Bush has demonstrated how easily tens of millions of people can be conned into contented subjugation and marching lockstep behind a president whose falsehoods have already left thousands of Americans dead and maimed. The more lies that a government gets away with, the more it will assume that it can get away with anything and everything.

People need defenses against democracies as well as tyrannies. The road to political ruin is paved with positive thinking. The issue is not whether democracy is good or evil, but that seeing democracy as an absolute good opens the gates to great evil. Because of Clinton's and Bush's invocations of democracy to consecrate their power and sanctify foreign aggression, it is vital to analyze democracy now.

At this point, the de facto American theory of government consists of trusting to the good intentions of those who hold nearly boundless power over us, trusting that they will not violate any laws that don't really need violating, that they won't bomb any foreign countries that don't really need bombing, and that they won't torture anyone who doesn't really need torturing. And if they do violate laws, bomb foreigners, and torture innocents—then it is all harmless errors and folks should just move along because there is nothing to see here.

This book examines the rising ignorance of the electorate, the fearmongering tactics of the 2004 and other presidential campaigns, the profusion of lying and how it fundamentally changes candidates' relation to citizens, the ways in which contemporary elections are degenerating into a tawdry trading of votes for handouts and subservience, and the current Messianic Democracy push. The ongoing torture scandal will be considered in depth as the arch-example of what happens when the government is permitted to grant itself absolute power, when "due process" consists of nothing more than long delayed coroners' inquests. We will briefly consider popular delusions on the inevitability of democracy and the inevitability of democracies keeping the peace. Finally, we will look at some reforms that can curb politicians' damage and recapture the blessings of representative government for ourselves and posterity.

It would be a mistake to view Bush as an aberration in modern political history. There are far more parallels between Bush and Clinton than either Democrats or Republicans would like to admit. And most of Clinton's abuses followed precedents set by Bush Sr., Nixon, Johnson, and earlier presidents. Bush is more a symptom of the decay of American democracy than a first cause.

To detail current failings is not to idealize the past. There was no Golden Age in America in which all politicians were honest, most citizens were politically savvy, and government strictly obeyed the Constitution. And yet, the deterioration on all fronts in recent years is a fundamental change, not simply a brief pause in the annals of national greatness.

A democratic government that respects no limits on its own power is a ticking time bomb, waiting to destroy the rights it was created to protect. The more people who believe democracy is failsafe, the more likely it will fail. Attention Deficit Democracy produces the attitudes, ignorance, and arrogance that pave the way to political collapse.

This book will deal with democracy as the term is currently understood. Democracy is commonly used to describe a political system that involves regular elections, opportunities for citizen involvement, and purported limits on government power. There are other definitions that are more philosophically pure or intellectually stout. However, it would be a waste to spend hundreds of pages condemning the current system solely for failing to measure up to one abstract definition. Instead, we will examine what democracy in the real world is becoming, using the statements and standards of earlier centuries to vivify how times are changing.

CHAPTER 2

Ignorance and the Mirage of Informed Consent

If once the people become inattentive to the public affairs. . . . Congress and Assemblies, judges and governors shall all become wolves. It seems to be the law of our general nature, in spite of individual exceptions.

—Thomas Jefferson, 1787[1]

Never in history have so many been fooled by so little.

—Harley Sorensen, 2004[2]

Modern democracy is based on faith that the people can control what they do not understand. As government has grown by leaps and bounds, "government by the people" has become one of the great fairy tales of our times. As the Founding Fathers feared, citizen ignorance often brings out the worst in their rulers.

GENERAL IGNORANCE OF VOTERS

Contemporary Americans may be less politically astute than their ancestors. Lord Bryce, a British ambassador to the United States and the author of the classic *American Commonwealth,* commented on Americans in 1921: "Nobody says, as men so often say in France, Germany, and Italy, 'I never trouble myself about politics.'"[3] Bryce declared: "Political opinion is better instructed than in Continental Europe because a knowledge of the institutions of the country and their working is more generally diffused here than there through the rank and file of the native population."[4]

But Bryce's cheery view may have been out of date by the time his book was published. Millions of Americans were profoundly embittered by the government lies and abuses that permeated the First World War and the Prohibition aftermath. By the mid-1920s, many intellectuals were losing faith in voters. In his 1925 book, *Public Opinion,* Walter Lippman commented that the typical citizen "gives but a little of his time to public affairs, has but a casual interest in facts and but a poor appetite for theory."[5] But the political theorists completely ignored this basic limitation. Lippman complained that civics textbooks implied that, to be well-informed, citizens "must have the appetite of an encyclopediast and infinite time ahead of him."[6] University of Kansas sociologist Seba Eldridge, in a 1929 book *The New Citizenship,* lamented that "evidences multiply that [the American citizen] has failed grievously to practice the self-determination imputed to him by the accepted theory of democracy; and grave doubts are raised that he can ever approximate, in practice, the attainment of that ideal."[7] Eldridge, sounding like a contemporary Blue State American, observed, "The enormous influence in political campaigns of grossly misleading propaganda, as in the Presidential campaign of 1924, is further evidence of political unintelligence on the part of a great many voters at general elections."[8] The biggest beef of Eldridge, a self-described socialist sympathizer,[9] seemed to be that voters did not support far greater government power: "The persistence of unsolved problems in all such cases, long after the methods of solving them have been worked out, is due largely to the ignorance, indifference, and inactivity of the citizen."[10]

Most Americans have long been political knowledge lightweights. U.S. government aid to the Nicaraguan Contras was one of the hottest political issues of the 1980s. But polls showed that most citizens—even those who voiced opinions to pollsters—did not know who the Contras were or where Nicaragua was located in relation to the United States.[11] After the Reagan–Gorbachev summit in Geneva in 1986, less than half of Americans polled could name the leader of the Soviet Union.[12] In 1989, only 25 percent of people knew what the FICA deduction on their payroll stub meant—even though the Social Security tax is the heaviest federal tax that most wage earners pay.[13]

Shortly after the 1994 congressional elections, only 39 percent of the public knew of the Republican "Contract with America," even though this was the most prominent issue in a congressional election in decades. A *Washington Post*–Harvard University study revealed: "Four in 10 Americans don't know that the Republicans control Congress; and half either think the Democratic Party is more conservative politically than the GOP or don't feel they know enough to offer a guess."[14] The survey also found that "only 26 percent knew the 6-year term of office of a U.S. senator" and less than half the public knows that a member of the House of Representative is elected to a two-year term.[15] Almost half of Americans "believe that the President has the power to suspend the Constitution."[16] Christopher Shea noted in *Salon* that "On a typical election day, 56% of Americans can't name a single candidate in their own district, for any office."[17]

Voter ignorance was a key factor in the 2000 presidential election—and not just in Florida. The 2000 election was determined by the weather, according to an analysis by Princeton political scientists Christopher Aachen and Larry Bartels. They analyzed climatic readings from 1895 to the present and concluded that "wet or dry conditions in a typical state and year cost the incumbent party seven-tenths of a percentage point, while 'extreme' droughts or wet spells cost incumbents about 1.5 percentage points."[18] Aachen and Bartels observed, "Voters responded to climatic distress in 2000—as they have repeatedly throughout the past century—by punishing the incumbent government at the polls." Aachen and Bartels concluded, "Real voters often have only a vague, more or less primitive understanding of the connections (if any) between incumbent politicians' actions and their own pain or pleasure."[19]

During 2000, the University of Michigan's National Election Survey conducted a comprehensive survey of Americans' political knowledge. George Mason University law professor Ilya Somin analyzed the results and found that only 55 percent knew that Janet Reno was the attorney general, only 15 percent knew the name of any candidate for the House of Representatives from their congressional district, only 11 percent could identify William Rehnquist as the chief justice of the Supreme Court, and only 9 percent knew that Trent Lott was the Senate majority leader.[20]

Surveys of people's knowledge of names, titles, or job descriptions do not reveal if they actually comprehend what government is doing. To expect that knowing the length of a Senate term or the names of Supreme Court justices makes voters competent is like assuming that knowing that cars have four wheels is enough to avoid being conned by a car mechanic. Basic knowledge might aid one in knowing where in the phone book to look to contact a government office, but in an era when government policies and interventions are proliferating like mosquitoes, a few factoids are not enough.

Americans possess far greater knowledge of popular culture than of politics and government. Ten times more Americans knew the name of the host of "Who Wants to be a Millionaire" than knew the name of the Speaker of the House of Representatives in 2000.[21] In the 1992 election, "Eighty-six per cent of likely voters knew that the Bushes' dog's name was Millie; only fifteen per cent knew that Bush and Clinton both favored the death penalty. It's not that people know nothing. It's just that politics is not what they know,"[22] Louis Menand noted in the *New Yorker*.

While the size of government is mushrooming, Americans' understanding of how government works may be shrinking. Michael Delli Carpini, dean of the Annenberg School of Communication at the University of Pennsylvania, noted that "despite an unprecedented expansion in public education, a communications revolution that has shattered national and international boundaries, and the increasing relevance of national and international events and policies to the daily lives of Americans, citizens appear no more informed about politics today than they were half a century ago."[23] More years in government schools have done little or nothing to help citizens understand how government operates. It would be naive to expect politically controlled education to enlighten people about the perils of political power. But, because public schools are largely a sacred cow, this conflict of interest is ignored or rarely discussed in polite company.

Many people believed that the soaring popularity of political talk radio would boost voter literacy. However, "exposure to these programs is not significantly related to even elementary tests of political information," according to a *Journal of Broadcasting and Electronic Media* examination of the knowledge of regular talk show listeners.[24]

Ignorance is thriving in part because Americans are reading less. A National Endowment for the Arts survey estimated that "the number of non-reading adults increased by more than 17 million between 1992 and 2002."[25] Between 1992 and 2002, the number of adults who read a daily paper declined from six in ten to four in ten.[26] Though reading books and newspapers is no guarantee of political literacy, people are far more likely to be able to follow and remember a complex argument when they read about it than when they see politicians blathering bromides on television.

In 1835 Alexis de Tocqueville noted in *Democracy in America* that "to persuade people to take an interest in their own affairs is, I know well, an arduous enterprise. It would often be easier to get them interested in the details of court etiquette than in the repair of their common dwelling."[27] Unfortunately, insofar as people do pay attention to politics, it is increasingly focused on the day-to-day utterances or behavior of the presidents—the triumph of the "Great Leader Democracy." But attention is sporadic even when the topic is titillating. For instance, in 1998 and early 1999, there was vastly more attention given to what Clinton did to the intern than to what the federal government was doing to the American people. And even then, "only about a third of the American public followed media accounts of the Clinton–Lewinsky scandal 'very closely.'"[28] The scandal probably convinced many people that simply getting a religion-invoking, happily married man in the Oval Office would restore decency in Washington.

Long-term deterioration of American political rhetoric is also dulling Americans' minds. Presidential addresses have become little more than "pontification cum anecdotalism."[29] University of Tulsa political scientist Elvin Lim concluded, "The urge to dumb down has been a rare constant in the two hundred year history of the presidency, persisting in spite of the different personalities and ideologies of the 43 men who have held the office."[30] Lim noted that the last century has seen "the intensified de-intellectualization of American presidential rhetoric, which in its modern mode has exhibited an increased tendency to avoid references to cognitive and evaluative processes and states." Presidents have made themselves far more prominent in their official rhetoric, shifting public attention from the government to the supreme leader. Lim found that "keywords of typical republican rhetoric have become unpopular, with references to the once honored words like republic, citizen, character, duty, and virtuous falling significantly."[31] Voters may understand government power less because the topic is vanishing from official addresses: "References to legal and judicial terms have taken a sharp fall since around William Howard Taft, as have references to the tools and forms of formal power."[32] Instead, the message is that the president cares about the voter.

THE EXPERTS VS. MASS IGNORANCE

In 1755, French political philosopher Jean Jacques Rousseau claimed to have "irrefragably" proved that "the voice of the people is in fact the voice of God"[33]—"Vox Populi, Vox Dei." This handy slogan makes mass ignorance no impediment to transmitting the will of God.

However, the prevailing tenets of political science frown on using divine intervention to justify contemporary democracy. Instead, professors offer various explanations why voter ignorance is no threat to popular government. Some professors insist that voters can imbue wisdom via intense feelings. Professor Wendy Rahn declared that "certain kinds of affective experiences . . . help inform the individual about the state of his or her world."[34] Professors George Marcus and Michael MacKuen also argued that "emotion can help uninformed

citizens to learn during presidential campaigns."[35] Apparently, intense feelings
generate a deeper wisdom that transcends mere factual knowledge.

Other defenders of ill-informed citizens rely on what Professor Philip
Converse derisively labeled in 1964 as "the miracle of aggregation."[36] Under
this sanguine view, random errors by ignorant voters will cancel themselves
out, thus permitting informed voters to decide the election.[37] Professor Somin
notes one absurdity of this assumption: "If the argument were correct, elections would have the same outcome if only the ballots of the well-informed
minority were counted."[38]

The only reason to assume that ignorant voters balance out in an election is so political scientists can avoid recognizing this gaping flaw in contemporary democracy. This "miracle of aggregation" is as credible as the
accounting used on Soviet collective farms at the end of the season, which
blamed bad weather for missing bushels of wheat and potatoes. The "miracle of aggregation" presumes that the multiplication of ignorance magically
begets wisdom. This is nothing more than the triumph of hope over experience at the ballot box.

Another defense of voter ignorance relies on celebrating the status quo.
Professor John Mueller, who holds the Woody Hayes chair in National Security Studies at Ohio State University, offered a defense of low expectations in
the *American Journal of Political Science:* "The amazing thing about democracy
is that the selectors and reviewers *are* substantially incompetent, but the
process nevertheless generates able, even superior leaders, and tends to keep
them responsive and responsible."[39] In words unlikely to be quoted in any future State of the Union address, Mueller asserted: "Democracy is really quite
easy—any dimwit can do it—and it can function remarkably well even when
people exhibit little in the way of self-discipline, restraint, commitment,
knowledge, or certainly, sacrifice for the general interest."[40]

The 2004 presidential campaign provided an excellent test for such theories. We will examine how ignorance and delusions have become the dominant
factors in presidential approval—and thus in setting the nation's direction.
The following sections will analyze America's most recent presidential election.

Pollsters in the fall of 2004 reported that most Americans were "very interested" in the presidential race.[41] But pervasive interest did not beget widespread understanding. A pre-election analysis of Tennessee public opinion by
Middle Tennessee State University noted, "On four of the five [domestic
agenda] issues, only about half of a given candidate's supporters hold opinions
consistent with those of the candidate. . . . When quizzed about which candidates hold which positions on the five issues, Tennesseans score an average of
only two right answers—about the same result one could get by merely guess-
ing."[42] Other surveys indicated that Tennesseans were typical of Americans in
2004, as far as their grasp of candidates' positions.

9/11 AND POLITICAL SAINTHOOD

George W. Bush was reelected in large part because he was perceived to be a stronger leader than John Kerry. Much if not most of Bush's image as a strong leader came from his actions and comments after the 9/11 terrorist attacks. The number of Americans who approved of Bush's job performance "climbed from 51% in the Gallup poll of September 10, 2001 to a remarkable 86% in the next poll released on September 15. This was the largest change between consecutive presidential approval polls ever reported by Gallup in more than 65 years," a Cornell University study noted.[43]

One of the great divides in the 2004 election year was between those who viewed 9/11 as Bush's greatest moment—and those who saw the attacks as partly the result of major failures by U.S. intelligence and law enforcement agencies. On 9/11 and in the subsequent weeks and months, Bush and other top government officials assured Americans that the U.S. government had been completely blindsided by the attackers. The vast majority of Americans initially accepted such claims by Bush and team.

However, in May 2002, Americans learned that FBI agents in Arizona and Minnesota had warned Washington about suspicious Arabs in pilot training programs. Americans also got the first hints about a warning of Al Qaeda attack preparations Bush received a month before 9/11. National Security Advisor Condoleezza Rice held a press conference on May 16 to stomp on these proliferating doubts about the administration's credibility. She insisted, "I don't think anybody could have predicted that these people . . . would try to use an airplane as a missile, a hijacked airplane as a missile."[44] Yet intelligence analysts provided many such warnings in the prior years.

As the 2004 campaign progressed and terror alerts multiplied, many Americans forgot about the pre-9/11 attack warnings. Even after several heavily publicized, highly critical 9/11 Commission staff reports, as well as a report by the Senate Intelligence Committee, only 62 percent of Americans believed that "the Bush administration was warned by intelligence reports about possible terrorist attacks in the U.S."[45] The Bush reelection campaign persuaded Americans to start scoring Bush after the terrorist attacks—as if Bush was inaugurated at noon on 9/11, instead of on January 20, 2001. Democratic political analyst Stanley Greenberg observed after the election that the number one reason to vote for Bush was, "obviously, 9/11 and how he responded to that."[46]

THE MYTH OF SADDAM AS THE TWENTIETH HIJACKER

Nowhere was Americans' ignorance more profitable for Bush than on the war with Iraq. Bush and Vice President Dick Cheney were reelected in large part because they inoculated scores of millions of Americans against the evidence of the deceits and failures of the U.S. war in Iraq. They swayed tens of millions of Americans to take their beliefs from their rulers, not from the facts.

Americans may be more gullible on foreign policy in part because of their greater global ignorance. A 2002 survey for *National Geographic* found that "roughly 85 percent of young Americans [aged 18 to 24] could not find Afghanistan, Iraq, or Israel on a map." Almost 30 percent of the young adults surveyed could not locate the Pacific Ocean and 56 percent were unable to locate India.[47] As the old saying goes, "War is God's way of teaching people geography."

In the days after 9/11, when pollsters asked Americans who they thought had carried out the 9/11 attacks, only 3 percent of respondents suggested Iraq or Saddam Hussein as culprits. But Bush and Cheney strove to make Americans believe that Saddam was linked to 9/11 or closely associated with the terrorist group that carried out the attack. The Saddam–Al Qaeda link was the linchpin for exploiting 9/11 to justify preemptive attacks around the globe.

In his official notification of invasion sent to Congress on March 18, 2003, Bush declared that he was attacking Iraq "to take the necessary actions against international terrorists and terrorist organizations, including those nations, organizations, or persons who planned, authorized, committed, or aided the terrorist attacks that occurred on September 11, 2001."[48] Bush tied Saddam to 9/11 even though confidential briefings he received informed him that no evidence of any link had been found. In a speech to troops shortly after Baghdad fell, Bush characterized his attack on Iraq as "one victory in the war on terror that began Sept. 11."[49]

Months of accusations and insinuations by the Bush administration profoundly affected Americans' perceptions of Iraq and the war. A February 2003 poll found that 72 percent of Americans believed that Hussein was "personally involved in the September 11 attacks."[50] Shortly before the March 2003 invasion, almost half of all Americans believed that "most" or "some" of the 9/11 hijackers were Iraqi citizens. Only 17 percent of respondents knew that none of the hijackers were Iraqis.[51]

Throughout 2004, the Saddam–Al Qaeda link was repeatedly officially debunked. A 9/11 Commission staff report on June 16 concluded that there was no evidence of a "collaborative relationship" between Saddam and Al Qaeda. The findings were trumpeted in headlines across the nation. Despite this broad coverage of the report, 55 percent of Bush supporters wrongfully believed that the 9/11 Commission reported that "Iraq was providing substantial support to al Qaeda," according to a University of Maryland Program on International Policy Attitudes poll a few weeks later. A *Wall Street Journal*/NBC News poll asked Americans "whether you agree or disagree with [the 9/11 Commission] finding. . . . Saddam Hussein and the Iraqi government did not collaborate with Al Qaeda in attacking the United States on 9/11."[52] Almost half of the respondents disagreed.

Any lingering doubts on this topic should have been quashed on July 9, when the Senate Intelligence Committee issued a 511-page report on the CIA and Iraq. The report concluded that the CIA "reasonably assessed . . . that these contacts [between Saddam and Al Qaeda] did not add up to an established formal relationship." The report also recognized that the CIA accurately concluded that "to date there was no evidence proving Iraqi complicity or assistance" in the 9/11 attacks.[53] The report noted that the CIA's accurate judgments on Saddam, Al Qaeda, and the non-link to 9/11 "were widely disseminated *[prior to the U.S. invasion of Iraq],* though an early version of a key CIA assessment was disseminated only to a limited list of Cabinet members and some sub-Cabinet officials in the administration." Neither Bush nor Cheney permitted the facts to impede their rhetoric on Iraq (see chapter 5).

Encouraging Americans to believe that Saddam was behind 9/11, and to see the Iraq war as vengeance for 9/11, made it far easier to justify an unprovoked attack on a nation that posed no threat to America. A September 2004 *Newsweek* poll found that 42 percent of Americans believed that Saddam was "directly involved in planning, financing, or carrying out the terrorist attacks."[54] As of mid-October, "75% of Bush supporters continue to believe that Iraq was providing substantial support to al Qaeda, and 63% believe that clear evidence of this support has been found," according to a University of Maryland poll.[55]

The Bush campaign's portrayal of the invasion of Iraq as a necessary part of the war on terrorism saved the president. The 55 percent of voters who said that the war in Iraq is "part of the war on terrorism" went for Bush by a 4 to 1 margin. The 43 percent who said Iraq was not part of the war on terrorism voted for Kerry by an 8 to 1 margin.[56]

WEAPONS OF MASS DECEPTION

The Bush team's invocations of Saddam's purported vast arsenal of weapons of mass destruction convinced Americans that the United States could not afford to wait for the United Nations weapons inspection process to continue. In a March 17, 2003, speech giving Saddam 48 hours to abdicate power, Bush declared, "Intelligence gathered by this and other governments leaves no doubt that the Iraq regime continues to possess and conceal some of the most lethal weapons ever devised."[57] Bush also justified the invasion of Iraq by appealing to UN resolutions that, he said, "authorized" the United States and other governments "to use force in ridding Iraq of weapons of mass destruction."

The constant references to WMD by Bush administration officials burned the issue into Americans' minds. Several months later, almost a quarter of Americans wrongly believed that Iraq had actually used its weapons of mass destruction against American forces during the fighting in March and April 2003.[58]

In the weeks and months after the fall of Baghdad, Bush repeatedly asserted that U.S. forces had discovered WMD or that Saddam had weapons programs. "We found the weapons of mass destruction. We found biological laboratories," Bush declared to journalists on May 29, 2003. Five weeks later, Bush again claimed vindication because "we found a biological lab" in a truck trailer. However, CIA investigators concluded that the trailer had nothing to do with an Iraqi WMD program.

On January 28, 2004, the CIA's David Kay testified to two Senate committees on the result of the almost-finished great WMD hunt. As CBS News noted, "Kay was chosen last year as the Iraq Survey Group leader in part because he was convinced weapons would be found."[59] Kay's group included a thousand people and cost about a billion dollars (on top of the costs of the invasion purportedly motivated by WMD). But Kay announced to the Senate Armed Services Committee that "we were almost all wrong" about Iraq possessing WMD. Kay's tell-tale "almost all wrong" phrase was hyped in front-page headlines across the nation and got massive airtime on television news and talk shows.

Despite the publicity that Kay's comments received, a March 2004 poll by the University of Maryland found that "63% of Bush supporters thought, incorrectly, that [Kay] had concluded that Iraq had at least a major WMD program."[60]

On October 7, Americans heard from the CIA's Charles Duelfer, the chief U.S. weapons inspector chosen by Bush to go to Iraq and complete the work of the Iraq Survey Group. Duelfer's team issued a thousand-page final report that offered literary analysis (speculating on how Hemingway's "The Old Man and the Sea" short story appealed to Saddam Hussein) in lieu of any WMD discoveries.[61] Duelfer's report was widely seen as the final demolition of the Bush administration's original *causa belli*. The report, coming out the day before the second presidential candidates' debate, generated front-page headlines. Yet, a University of Maryland poll taken after the report's release found that 57 percent of Bush supporters incorrectly believed that Duelfer "concluded that Iraq did have either WMD (19%) or a major program for developing them (38%)."[62]

WMD delusions persisted through Election Day. Another University of Maryland poll, shortly before the 2004 election, found that "72% of Bush supporters continue to believe that Iraq had actual WMD (47%) or a major program for developing them (25%)." Fifty-six percent assumed that most experts believed Iraq possessed WMD at the time of the U.S. invasion. Bush supporters also wrongly believed that the invasion of Iraq was welcomed around the world.[63]

Bush supporters' approval of the war depended largely on their delusions. They were asked: "If, before the war, US intelligence services had concluded that Iraq did not have weapons of mass destruction and was not providing substantial support to al Qaeda," what should have been done? "58% of Bush supporters said in that case the U.S. should not have gone to war. Furthermore, 61% express confidence that in that case the President would not have gone to war."[64]

The October 2004 University of Maryland report explained that Bush supporters

> continue to hear the Bush administration confirming these beliefs. Among Bush supporters, an overwhelming 82% perceive the Bush administration as saying that Iraq had WMD (63%) or a major WMD program (19%). . . . Seventy-five percent of Bush supporters think the Bush administration is currently saying Iraq was providing substantial support to al Qaeda (56%) or even that it was directly involved in 9/11 (19%). . . . Interestingly, these perceptions of what the Bush administration is saying are something on which Bush and Kerry supporters agree.[65]

Stephen Kull, director of the University of Maryland's Program on International Policy Attitudes, commented: "To support the president and to accept that he took the United States to war based on mistaken assumptions likely creates substantial cognitive dissonance, and leads Bush supporters to suppress awareness of unsettling information about prewar Iraq."[66] The more information about the war that people suppressed, the easier it became for them to support Bush and to view opponents of the war as unpatriotic, un-American, or otherwise possessed by demons.

Many Americans became deluded on Iraq thanks to television overdoses. The University of Maryland conducted a series of polls in 2003 and found that 60 percent of respondents held one or all of the following erroneous beliefs: that the U.S. troops had found WMD in Iraq, that clear evidence linked Saddam with the 9/11 terrorists, and that most foreigners either supported the U.S. invasion of Iraq or were evenly divided pro and con. Fox News viewers were three times more likely to hold at least one of the mistaken beliefs on Iraq as were people who got their news from National Public Radio or PBS. However, five times as many people cited Fox News Network as their primary news source as those who cited NPR and PBS. Forty-seven percent of those who listed newspapers and magazines as their primary news source held at least one of the three misconceptions.[67] The study warned that close attention to some news programs could induce delusions: "Among those who primarily watch Fox, those who pay more attention are more likely to have misperceptions."[68] Bill O'Reilly, Fox News' most popular talk show host, boasted a few days after the report came out: "I think Fox News Channel was lucky because we were less skeptical of the war, and the war went very well. So we won."[69] Citizens who trusted the media to audit the Bush team's claims were sorely disappointed, since most of the media allied itself with the government instead of the truth. Most of the mainstream media was perennially deferential to the government—even after the Pentagon announced a program to deceive world opinion. (See page 99.)

AN EASY SOVEREIGN CON

Political labeling trumped reality throughout 2004. When public opinion on the Iraq war finally began turning against the Bush administration in the Spring of 2004, the Bush administration responded by hyping plans to formally give sovereignty back to Iraqis. Subsequent announcements and spinning revealed how little it takes to con the American people—at least until the polls close.

On June 28, 2004, Bush's man in Baghdad, Coalition Provisional Authority Chief Paul Bremer, handed a leather-bound document to Iyad Allawi, the former CIA operative placed by the United States at the head of the interim Iraqi government. Because of fears of insurgent attacks during the sovereignty ceremony, the Bush administration secretly conveyed the document two days earlier than planned. At the time, Bush was at a NATO summit in Turkey. National Security Adviser Rice handed him a slip of paper declaring "Iraq is sovereign." Bush jotted "Let Freedom Reign" on a piece of paper and handed it back to Rice. Bush proudly announced to the world, "The Iraqi people have their country back." Some Americans may have thought that this was the same phrase used on the first Independence Day in 1776. But "let freedom ring" is far different than "let freedom reign"—especially when "reign" meant the continued dominance of the U.S. military over a foreign country.

Bush bragged, "Not only is there full sovereignty in the hands of the Government, but all the ministries have been transferred, and they're up and running."[70] However, prior to pseudo-abdicating, the Coalition Provisional Authority dictated that U.S. and British troops would have immunity from prosecution from the new Iraqi government—effectively creating a diplomatic corps of 160,000 people with guns and heavy weapons and no liability for wrongful killings. The sovereignty transfer did not impede the U.S. military from continuing to heavily bomb civilian areas and sweep up vast numbers of innocent Iraqi civilians for interrogation and detention. Bremer's electoral edict also dictated that "one of every three candidates on a party's slate must be a woman." In Bremer's final weeks, he issued a flurry of edicts dictating long-term restrictions on Iraq's new government and decreeing the hiring of more than 20 Iraqis for five-year terms in key positions. The *Washington Post* noted, "As of June 14, Bremer had issued 97 legal orders, which are defined by the U.S. occupation authority as 'binding instructions or directives to the Iraqi people' that will remain in force even after the transfer of political authority."[71]

Bush bragged in a July 13 Wisconsin speech: "Because we acted, Iraq is a free and sovereign nation."[72] But the puppet government was no model republic. One of Allawi's first acts was to issue an edict to give himself dictatorial power "to impose curfews anywhere in the country, ban groups he considers seditious and order the detentions of people suspected of being security risks." The *New York Times* explained that Allawi "wants to show he can rule with an iron fist."[73]

After Bush announced the sovereignty handover, the American media sharply curtailed its coverage of the Iraqi conflict. Americans paid more attention to Bush's bragging about the "sovereignty handover" than to the rising number of dead U.S. soldiers. The average daily number of attacks on U.S. forces in Iraq rose sharply from June through September, as did the average number of U.S. military dead per month.

Sovereignty hoopla convinced millions of Americans that the Iraqi problem had been or would soon be solved. A survey done in the ten days after the sovereignty handover showed that almost twice as many Americans believed that the new Iraq government had at least an equal share of power than believed that the U.S. military was still the supreme power in the country. The poll, by the University of Pennsylvania's Annenberg Center, also found that "fifty percent of the respondents said they thought the number of United States troops in Iraq should be reduced to no more than 'a few thousand' in six months or less."[74] This was a peculiar belief since neither Bush nor Democratic presidential nominee John Kerry were hinting of any such withdrawal. People may have based this expectation on what happened in prior conflicts after the U.S. announced it was formally turning over the reins. CNN polling expert William Schneider concluded: "The handover of authority in Iraq at the end of June apparently had exactly the effect that the White House intended: It made Iraq seem like less of an American problem."[75]

Inattentive voters also helped make U.S. torture in Iraq and Afghanistan non-issues in the presidential race. University of California Professor Mark Danner observed in October 2004: "So far, officials of the Bush administration,

who counted on the fact that the public, and much of the press, could be persuaded to focus on the photographs—the garish signboards of the scandal and
not the scandal itself—have been proved right. This makes Abu Ghraib a pe-
culiarly contemporary kind of scandal, with most of its plotlines exposed to
view—but with few willing to follow them and fewer still to do much about
them."[76] The ephemeral outrage over torture exemplifies Attention Deficit
Democracy—something that momentarily intrudes into people's consciousness
and then quickly fades.

There was probably more attention paid to Kerry's sports gaffes than to
Abu Ghraib during the last seven weeks of the campaign. The fact that Kerry
misstated the name of the Green Bay Packers' stadium and the score from a
Red Sox World Series game received more attention in October than the fact
that White House and Justice Department lawyers had proclaimed that the
president was above the law and could order torture. (This issue will be ex-
plored in-depth in chapter 6.)

A *Washington Post* analysis noted that the Kerry campaign "gambled on
building up the Massachusetts senator's image in the belief that voters were familiar with Bush's weaknesses and the turmoil in Iraq."[77] Professor Ira Chernus noted that one exit poll showed that "ninety percent of Bush voters said
things are going well in Iraq."[78] In contrast, "Eighty-two percent of Kerry voters said things are going badly in Iraq."[79]

Bush and his campaign chief, Karl Rove, masterfully converted public ignorance into presidential adulation. The 2004 presidential race illustrated how
easily Bush's campaign could sweep away his biggest debacles from the minds
of most of his supporters. Flag-waving, slogans and a few smears endlessly repeated and—voila!—by the end of the campaign, Bush could arrive via military helicopter for massive football stadium rallies with the theme song from
"Top Gun" blaring away—reprising the USS *Abraham Lincoln* "Mission Accomplished" photo op from May 1, 2003. Even though the vast majority of
post-war predictions and hopes had crashed and burned, voters still cheered
Bush's military strut.

Bush's appeals to moral values permitted voters to instantly and nobly
transcend their own ignorance. The Bush campaign made mentally negligent
citizens feel morally superior. The president swayed people to view almost
everything as a clash of good versus evil. And once the basic labels had been
attached, then all questions were settled. The *New Republic* commented
shortly after the election: "The president ran on broad themes, like 'character'
and 'morals.' Everyone feels an immediate and intuitive expertise on morals
and values—we all know what's right and wrong."[80] For true believers, "good
vs. evil" trumps hard facts almost every time.

Some Europeans denounced the United States as a "moronocracy" because
of the ignorance of American voters in the 2004 election. Britain's *Daily Mir-*

ror greeted the election results with a banner headline: "How can 59,054,087 people be so dumb?"[81] But the fact that morons vote for a candidate does not make everyone else who voted the same way a moron. Simply because many Bush voters were ignorant or deluded does not negate the fact that many well-informed, intelligent citizens voted for Bush. Many voters had sound reasons to vote for Bush or against Kerry (because of his flip-flopping on the war in Iraq, his long history of championing expanding government, a demeanor often perceived as distant or arrogant, etc.).

Despite claims that the president received a sweeping mandate on November 2, 2004, there was no informed consent from voters for continuing Bush's policies. Considering that roughly 60.8 percent of eligible voters made it to the polls, Bush's 50.8 percent of the vote amounts to 29 percent of eligible voters. Of those 29 percent, how many Bush supporters voted for him while understanding that Iraq had no WMDs, that Saddam was not linked to 9/11, and that the military situation in Iraq was grim? The percentage of Americans who exercised informed consent in casting ballots for Bush was likely less than 15 percent of the electorate. Many of those voters probably embraced Bush as the lesser of two evils—not because they liked his policies. Exit polls on election day showed that "more Americans (55 percent) said they thought the country was 'headed in the wrong direction' than those who said it was headed in the right one, and fewer than half of Americans polled (49 percent) said that they approved of the President's performance in office," the *New York Review of Books* noted.[82] A September 2004 NBC–*Wall Street Journal* poll found that, even though a majority favored Bush, only 9 percent hoped that his second term "would look like his first term." Yet, because more voters signaled a preference for Bush over Kerry, everything Bush subsequently did became "the will of the people."[83]

ENOUGH KNOWLEDGE TO LEASH RULERS?

The conventional wisdom is that Americans know enough to keep the government in line, thus ensuring that freedom is secure. Even though Americans do not know the minutiae of a politician's record, they have still imbibed sufficient wisdom from living in the United States to understand enough about how government operates. This is the fluoridated water theory of citizen competence. But do Americans know enough to prevent their government from trampling their rights?

In August 2005, the American Bar Association (ABA) released a poll purportedly showing Americans' understanding of the doctrine of the separation of powers. The separation of powers is vital to the checks and balances that the Founding Fathers established to protect individual liberty and curb arbitrary power. The issue of separation of powers is crucial to some of the greatest controversies of recent years, including the proliferation of executive orders, the president's power to designate people as enemy combatants and try them before kangaroo court military tribunals, the White House's right to withhold almost any and all information from both Congress and the American people, the demands by Republican congressmen that judges compel continued life support for brain-damaged Terri Schiavo.

According to the ABA, the poll produced mixed tidings. Only 45 percent of respondents chose the correct description of separation of powers in a multiple choice question. Only 55 percent could recognize the three branches of government. Respondents were then asked: "How important is the principle of 'separation of powers' in the federal government?"[84] The possible answers: "Important, not important, not sure what it means." Because 82 percent said "important," the ABA proclaimed victory and issued a press release entitled: "Vast Majorities of American Adults Profess Support for Constitutional Concepts of Separation of Powers and Checks and Balances."[85] ABA President-elect Michael Greco said the poll "shows that the average American understands enough to know that the different branches of government have distinct roles."[86] In reality, the fact that 82 percent assented to "important" is as revealing as a poll showing that most people preferred "good government" to "bad government."

Respondents were asked to answer the following question: "Which of the following best describes what 'separation of powers' means?" The results:

8% Not sure/Decline to answer

45% Congress, the President and the Federal Courts each have different responsibilities.

15% The federal government does some things, like set postage rates, while state governments have other powers, like setting speed limits on state highways.

27% Different federal departments have different powers. For example, the Department of Defense runs the military while the Department of Justice prosecutes crimes.

6% Republicans can do some things, but Democrats can do others.

The question on "separation of powers" was practically Mensa-like compared to the ABA's question on "checks and balances": "Which of the following best describes what 'checks and balances' refers to?"

6% Not sure/Decline to answer

6% Regulation of auditors and the financial services industry by the Securities and Exchange Commission.

8% The decisions by the Federal Reserve Board about interest rates and banking.

15% Negotiations between Congress and the President over a balanced federal budget.

64% A division of power among the branches of federal government that prevents any one of them from going beyond their constitutional authority.

To say that choosing a right answer to such a question reveals an understanding of the American system of government is like saying that knowing that New York is on the east coast proves a mastery of geography. The questions illustrate how polls often overstate Americans' political understanding.

Power grabs by politicians are rarely accompanied by a multiple choice question for the benefit of slow-witted citizens. Instead, when the executive branch is seeking to seize new power, the president can deploy his immense prestige, his top advisors with their focus-group-tested phrases and their Ivy League credentials. The president can address the nation and give speeches in heavily choreographed settings with handpicked audiences guaranteed to applaud. The president can be assured that much, if not most, of the media will defer to almost any utterance he makes. (Journalists who kowtow are far more likely to get the chance for one-on-one presidential interviews that can turbo-charge their careers.) Very few citizens have the knowledge (or the confidence in their understanding) to resist such tidal waves. Even when the government clearly distorts U.S. legal history or court precedents, few citizens know enough to recognize government lies. Many citizens simply lack sufficient mental traction to resist government's claims. Professor Stephen Earl Bennett, one of the nation's leading experts on voter competence, observed, "Anyone who has witnesses a focus group will despair at the platitudinous, impressionistic, and woefully uninformed nature of people's political reasoning."[87] The same could be said of most of the floor debates in the House of Representatives.

When criticism of government swells and politicians feel they must make at least a cosmetic response, public ignorance permits Washington to offer farcical remedies to real problems. Beginning in 2003, petitions and resolutions against the Patriot Act poured into Congress. The ruckus across the nation over the Patriot Act focused on whether the Justice Department and Federal Bureau of Investigation were using the new law to violate rights and privacy. In late 2004, Congress mandated the creation of the Privacy and Civil Liberties Oversight Board. This new board provides grist for an automated response to constituent letters to congressmen complaining about the Patriot Act. But the nature of the new board raised doubts about whether members of Congress understand the "separation of powers"—or whether they simply threw a sop to gullible voters. All the members of the new oversight board are appointed by the president, and the board is located in the White House. The oversight board is totally controlled by the same branch of government committing the abuses. The law obliged the president to appoint five members, but he made no appointments until seven months later. An ABA publication noted that the timing of the appointments "is widely viewed as part of the administration's push to encourage Congress to reauthorize provisions of the USA Patriot Act that expire within the next few months."[88] Bush did not appoint any experts on civil liberties to the board; instead, it was stacked with Republicans who formerly held government positions where they were enforcement zealots. The board has no subpoena power, and Bush has the right to fire any board member at any time. As of August 2005, the board had still held no meetings.[89] Yet, Bush's appointments to the non-meeting board may have helped spur overwhelming congressional support for re-enacting controversial portions of the Patriot Act. Similar charades have been performed by other administrations, and have usually been greeted with similar gullibility.

IGNORANCE AIDING "BIG GOVERNMENT"

The more politically illiterate people become, the easier it is for politicians to seize new powers—all the while denouncing Big Government. During the closing weeks of the 2000 presidential campaign, Americans were assured that: "I'm opposed to big government. . . . I'm for a smaller, smarter government, one that serves people better, but offers real change and gives more choices to our families. . . . I don't believe there's a government solution to every problem."[90] Vice President Al Gore stressed his small government bona fides—at the same time that he called for government subsidies for individual savings, draconian new land-use controls, and more subsidies for seniors' health care. A *Presidential Studies Quarterly* analysis noted that "Gore distanced himself from 'big government' without dropping any of his proposals for government spending."[91] The Republican candidate, George W. Bush, also endlessly assured voters that he was opposed to Big Government—at the same time that he championed a vast increase in federal meddling in local schools, new federal subsidies for churches and other religious entities, and many other government aid programs.

The question of whether a politician opposes Big Government now hinges solely on whether he can accuse an opponent of favoring even Bigger Government. During the 2004 campaign, Bush repeatedly denounced his Democratic opponent, John Kerry, for "proposing a big government health care plan"[92]—even though Bush in 2003 had strong-armed Congress into enacting an expansion of Medicare that will cost taxpayers two trillion dollars in the coming decades.

Bush was following in the footsteps of President Bill Clinton, who famously declared in his 1996 State of the Union address: "The era of Big Government is over."[93] Clinton realized that deriding Big Government would be profitable, especially after the Republican takeover of Congress in 1994. In his second Inaugural address on January 20, 1997, Clinton proclaimed: "Today we can declare: Government is not the problem, and government is not the solution. . . . We need a new government for a new century—humble enough not to try to solve all our problems for us, but strong enough to give us the tools to solve our problems for ourselves."[94] As long as government is merely giving—and controlling—the tools, then presumably it is no threat to anyone. The end of the era of Big Government did not dissuade Clinton from proposing in his 1997 State of the Union address to dictate federal standards for all new teachers, create an "army" of a million volunteers to tutor kids that teachers failed to teach, provide $5 billion for fixing local schoolhouses, declare war on gangs, boost federal spending on the war on drugs, and expand NATO. Apparently, as long as a politician verbally rejects "Big Government," voters approve of him promising them new benefits and more protection. Clinton revealed the practical meaning of his end of Big Government when he bragged that the Small Business Administration "cut its [loan] applications for small business people from an inch thick to one page and give people an answer in 72 hours."[95] Rather than reducing the size of government, this "reform" only makes it easier and faster for uncreditworthy people to bankrupt themselves after receiving government subsidized loans. A 2004 University of Pittsburgh study found Clinton surpassed all other presidents studied in "credit claiming without evidence" of actual achievement in his State of the Union addresses.[96]

A slight variation on this charade is for presidents to claim that they are merely increasing opportunity, thus making rising federal power irrelevant. In his 1992 acceptance speech at the Democratic National Convention, Bill Clinton pledged "a government that expands opportunity, not bureaucracy."[97] During the 2004 presidential campaign, Bush continually declared that "my opponent is running to expand Government. We're running to expand opportunity."[98] The fact that the opportunity supposedly expands as a result of new government programs and edicts is immaterial if the "O word" is invoked.

Citizens' knowledge of government has stagnated. The number of government agencies that can accost, prohibit, penalize, tax, impound, impede, detain, subpoena, confiscate, search, indict, fine, audit, interrogate, levy, wiretap, "cease-and-desist," sanction, and otherwise harass and subjugate the citizen and/or his property and rights has skyrocketed. Yet, most citizens have made no corresponding buildup in knowledge of government rules and procedures and of their legal rights and options. Thus, the imbalance between the State and the citizen has vastly increased. It takes more than invocations of high school civics lessons to rescue a citizen in the bureaucratic cross-hairs.

Thanks to Attention Deficit Democracy, many people no longer realize that creating new programs, expanding the size of government, and enacting new laws will mean that some people will have more power over other people. If the new laws include criminal penalties, this will directly subjugate some Americans to other Americans. If the new programs include new handouts, this will empower politicians and bureaucrats to determine who receives what. The first type of law will spread fear, and the second type will breed servility.

Abuses of government power have become largely non-events, of interest only to the victims and immediate bystanders. Many people have apparently concluded that government poses no threat to them or their families, regardless of how large and intrusive it becomes. As long as the government is only punishing "bad guys," then there is no problem, because they know they are good Americans. In recent decades, new prisons have sprouted like McDonald's across the land and prison guards have been one of the nation's fastest growing employment categories.[99] But there has probably been little or no increase in the number of Americans who recognize that government decrees can wreck their lives.

CONCLUSION

It is a popular saying that people get the government that they deserve. This has rarely been more false than in current times. The fact that most Americans are politically ignorant does not entitle other people to control their lives. The fact that someone does not have fire insurance does not entitle his neighbor to burn down his house. Similarly, the fact that most people are politically negligent does not entitle government to trample their rights. Because individual rights do not come from government, politicians have no right to revoke the rights due merely to people's negligence.

With each election, more and more voters cast ballots with little or no connection to reality. In the same way that dementia patients are prone to exploitation by caregivers and others, ignorant voters are easy pickings for politicians who want to profit from their mental voids. There is an old saying that "the cure for the problems of democracy is more democracy." But what is the cure for the problem of ignorant voters?

The only way that massive ignorance of public policy will not subvert meaningful democracy is if politicians somehow know and respect people's wishes—even if the people themselves are ignorant of their own will. Voter ignorance is irrelevant to democracy only if politicians are automatically all-wise and benevolent. But no such class of politicians has been discovered to exist outside of Washington novels and high school civics textbooks.

The myth of voter competence is vital to the legitimacy of Leviathan. If voters do not know what they are doing, then rulers cannot claim they are following the people's will when they impose new burdens, restrictions, taxes, and punishment on the citizenry. Instead of being a triumph of the people's will, government action becomes old-time exploitation and repression.

Many of the people who are most vocal and adamant about praising contemporary democracy are also champions of Leviathan. They hail democratic processes not because they permit people to restrain government, but because mass ignorance results in nearly unlimited government power. People's ignorance of government makes it easier for government to forcibly improve people's lives.

Voters cannot countenance what they do not understand. There cannot be an honest mandate to power based on the number of citizens who accept the canards of their rulers. Popular ignorance cannot legitimize political absolutism.

CHAPTER 3

Fearmongering and the Battered Citizen Syndrome

With your help on Nov. 2, the people of America will reject the politics of fear.
—President Bush, October 20, 2004.[1]

If George Bush loses the election, Osama bin Laden wins the election.
Rep. Tom Cole (R-Okla.), March 23, 2004[2]

AMERICA IS BECOMING A DEMOCRACY of knocking knees, sweating foreheads, and folks who jump too high at any sound. The 9/11 attacks opened up a vast Yukon Territory for emotional exploitation of voters. The less people understand, the more easily they can be frightened into submission. Americans' attention deficit is a demagogue entitlement program.

Montesquieu, in his 1748 classic *The Spirit of the Laws,* identified fear as the principle of despotic governments. Montesquieu stressed that "fear ought to be the only prevailing sentiment" in such regimes.[3] President Bush made the same point in a March 8, 2005, speech at the National Defense University: "Pervasive fear is the foundation of every dictatorial regime—the prop that holds up all power not based on consent."[4]

But fear is becoming a trademark of modern democracy. H. L. Mencken commented in 1918: "The whole aim of practical politics is to keep the populace alarmed and hence, clamorous to be led to safety—by menacing it with an endless series of hobgoblins, all of them imaginary."[5] And even when the dangers are real, politicians fan the flames—thereby making people more pliable and submissive.

Fearmongering has often permeated American presidential races. On the eve of the 1920 presidential election, Democratic presidential candidate James Cox declared: "Every traitor in America will vote tomorrow for Warren G. Harding!"[6] Cox's warning sought to stir memories of the "red raids" conducted in 1919 and 1920 by Attorney General Mitchell Palmer, during which thousands of anarchists, communists, and suspect foreigners were summarily jailed and, in many cases, deported. The American people rejected Cox and embraced Warren Harding's promise of a "return to normalcy."

President Franklin Roosevelt put "freedom from fear" atop the American political pantheon in his 1941 State of the Union address.[7] But FDR's political legacy—especially Social Security—has institutionalized fearmongering in presidential and congressional races. In the 2004 race, the Kerry campaign ran an advertisement that claimed that Bush had a "plan to privatize Social Security that cuts benefits by 30 to 45 percent." But Bush had made it clear that he did not intend to slash benefits for current recipients or people near retirement.[8]

Kerry's efforts were mild-mannered compared to Bill Clinton's 1996 re-election campaign and its notorious "Mediscare" advertisements designed to make voters believe that a vote for Republican nominee Bob Dole was practically euthanasia. The *Chicago Tribune* described one Clinton ad as showing "a steadily beeping EKG machine monitoring a patient's heartbeat. After a voice described how the GOP wanted to raise Medicare premiums and cut benefits, the machine stopped beeping and went into a monotone. Everyone who watches 'ER' knew what that meant—someone had died."[9]

Whipping up fear was the flipside of Clinton's "feeling your pain" governing style. Clinton fanned people's fear of guns, life without medical insurance, militias and anyone who was vocally anti-government, hot summers, etc. Yet, Clinton also relished promising "freedom from fear," invoking it to justify warrantless searches of the homes of public housing residents, requiring government school children to wear uniforms, and a federal takeover of health care.[10]

Bush has embraced the freedom from fear theme more than any Republican president. In his 2005 State of the Union address, he announced, "We will pass along to our children all the freedoms we enjoy. And chief among them is freedom from fear."[11] But it was vital that Americans not be given freedom from fear until November 2, 2004.

Voter ignorance made possible and profitable the most fear-mongering presidential campaign in modern American history. Voters could choose whether they would be killed by terrorists if they voted for Kerry or whether they would be left destitute and tossed out in the street if they voted for Bush.

Boston University professor Tobe Berkovitz commented: "It's not surprising that both campaigns are looking for the leverage point: scaring the hell out of the American public about what would happen if the other guy wins."[12] Moises Naim, editor of *Foreign Policy*, observed that the Bush campaign was "using the fear factor almost exclusively. This is a highly researched decision with all the tools of public opinion management. It's nothing but a reflection that it works."[13]

TERRORISM PROFITEERING

Bush was reelected in large part because his administration and campaign boosted the number of Americans frightened of terrorism during 2004. In October 2001, 73 percent of Americans feared another imminent terrorist attack. By early 2004, only 55 percent had such fears. But by August 2004, the figure had rebounded to 64 percent.[14] This 9 percent proved vital for Bush. People who saw terrorism as the biggest issue in the 2004 election voted for him by an almost 7 to 1 margin.[15]

Bush's reelection campaign intensified Americans' memories of terrorist carnage. One of the first Bush reelection campaign television ads, in early 2004, entitled "Safer, Stronger," showed firemen carrying a flag-draped corpse from the rubble at Ground Zero. A second ad, showing an American flag in front of the wreckage of the World Trade Center, featured the motto "Tested" and began with a statement from the president—"I'm George Bush and I approve this message." An announcer then informed viewers: "The last few years have tested America in many ways. Some challenges we've seen before. And some were like no others. But America rose to the challenge. . . . Freedom, faith, families, and sacrifice. President Bush. Steady leadership in times of change."[16]

The TV ads were followed by five-alarm terror alerts that spurred even more helpful publicity. On May 26, Attorney General John Ashcroft announced: "Credible intelligence from multiple sources indicates that Al Qaeda plans to attempt an attack on the United States in the next few months. This disturbing intelligence indicates Al Qaeda's specific intention to hit the United States hard. . . . After the March 11th attack in Madrid, Spain, an Al Qaeda spokesman announced that 90 percent of the arrangements for an attack in the United States were complete." He assured one and all that the attack plans had been "corroborated on a variety of levels."[17] Ashcroft also distributed photos of seven Arab terror suspects and urged Americans to "be on the lookout . . . for each of these seven individuals. They all pose a clear and present danger to America. They all should be considered armed and dangerous."

The 2002 law that created the Department of Homeland Security made it the lead agency in assessing and publicizing terror threats. However, Homeland Security Secretary Tom Ridge first learned the details of the Gang of 7's devastating attack plan while watching Ashcroft's televised news conference. A few hours before Ashcroft's fireworks, Ridge appeared on CNN and announced: "America's job is to enjoy living in this great country and go out and have some fun."[18] Homeland Security officials told the media that "there was no new information about attacks in the U.S., and . . . no change in the government's color-coded 'threat level.'"[19]

The Ashcroft warning quickly became a laughingstock—at least to people who followed the news. NBC News reported on May 28 that Ashcroft's primary Al Qaeda source was "a largely discredited group, Abu Hafs al-Masri Brigades, known for putting propaganda on the Internet" that had falsely "claimed responsibility for the power blackout in the Northeast last year, a power outage in London, and the Madrid bombings."[20] One former White House terrorism expert commented: "The only thing they haven't claimed credit for recently is the cicada invasion of Washington."[21] The group's warning consisted of one e-mail sent two months earlier to a London newspaper. *Newsweek* reported that the White House "played a role in the decision to go public with the warning. . . . Instead of the images of prisoner abuse at Abu Ghraib, the White House would prefer that voters see the faces of terrorists who aim to kill them."[22] *Newsweek* also noted that most of the seven terror suspects "have been on the well-publicized FBI most-wanted lists for months, if not years."[23] The feds also had no evidence that most of them had been in the United States in recent years.

Just before the Fourth of July weekend, the FBI notified 18,000 law enforcement agencies of a new terrorism threat: "booby-trapped beer coolers" as well as "plastic-foam containers, inner tubes and other waterborne flotsam." It was unclear whether this warning rallied the redneck vote for Bush.

The Bush administration followed Independence Day with hints that terrorists could cancel the November 2 election. On July 8, Secretary Tom Ridge called a press conference and announced: "Credible reporting now indicates that al-Qaeda is moving forward with its plans to carry out a large-scale attack in the United States in an effort to disrupt our democratic process."[24] Ridge warned: "These are not conjectures or mythical statements we are making. These are pieces of information that we could trace comfortably to sources that we deem to be credible."[25] Ridge added: "I think we have to err on the side of transparency to protect the voting rights of the country." A *USA Today* front page headline blared: "Election Terror Threat Intensifies." The Homeland Security Department formally requested that the Justice Department "analyze what legal steps would be needed to permit the postponement of the election were an attack to take place."[26]

Democrats derided Ridge for firing blanks. Rep. Robert Wexler (D-Fla.) commented: "I am deeply concerned that the Bush administration is copying and pasting old terror alerts that were later found to be fabricated." Rep. Jane Harman (D-Cal.), the senior Democrat on the House Intelligence Committee, condemned Ridge's warning: "Six days ago, the leadership of the House and Senate Intelligence Committees and leadership of the House and Senate were briefed on these so-called new threats. They are more chatter about old threats, which were the subject of a press conference by Attorney General Ashcroft and Director Mueller six weeks ago."[27]

On Sunday, August 1, immediately after the Democratic National Convention, the Bush administration announced "Code Orange" terror alerts for banks and financial institutions in New York, Newark, and Washington, D.C. Ridge, in a press conference that his aides heavily hyped to television news producers,[28] announced that there is "new and unusually specific information about where Al Qaeda would like to attack."[29] Ridge warned that the attacks could involve "weapons of mass destruction" and "biological pathogens." Ridge said the new information was "sobering news, not just about the intent of our enemies but of their specific plans and a glimpse into their methods." A senior Homeland Security official said that this new information was received by the intelligence community "sometime on Friday" and was "so specific they immediately began trying to corroborate it."[30] Ridge announced that "we won't do politics" with terror alerts and then reminded Americans that Bush was personally responsible for saving them: "We must understand that the kind of information available to us today is the result of the President's leadership in the war against terror."[31]

The terror alert resulted in heavily armed, black-clad lawmen being posted outside the stock exchanges and the major banks in both New York and Newark. Truck searches and closures of major roads created huge traffic jams in the Big Apple.[32] The new terror alert reduced the bounce Kerry received from the Democratic convention.

But after the press conference spurred gasps across the land and stole the Democrats' thunder, news trickled out that the alert was based on evidence gathered before 9/11. Two days after his announcement, Ridge conceded that there was "no evidence of recent surveillance" by terrorist suspects of the buildings and areas placed under heightened alert.[33] But he stressed: "I don't want anyone to disabuse themselves of the seriousness of this information simply because there are some reports that much of it is dated, it might be two or three years old."

In his weekly radio address the following Saturday, Bush declared that the "elevation of the threat level in New York, New Jersey, and Washington D.C. was a grim reminder of the dangers we continue to face. . . . We're a nation in danger."[34]

On August 12, the Associated Press reported that a White House official conceded that "the Bush administration has discovered no evidence of imminent plans by terrorists to attack U.S. financial buildings."[35] But the lack of evidence did not prevent them from maintaining a high alert status. One Bush administration official explained that the administration would have issued the terror alerts "even had it known at the time that the surveillance documents did not point to an imminent operation."[36]

On August 27, the FBI, in its weekly bulletin to 18,000 state and local law enforcement agencies, warned: "Recent intelligence suggest that al-Qaeda may still be planning an attack, possibly targeting highly populated public places in large U.S. cities, in the weeks immediately prior to the elections." Predictably, the warning leaked out—helping put Americans in the right frame of mind for the Republican National Convention and its theme of Bush as 9/11 hero.

On September 13, Attorney General Ashcroft held a conference call with all 93 U.S. attorneys around the nation to warn of new terrorist threats. Shortly after the call, Michael Shelby, the Bush administration's appointee as chief U.S. attorney in Texas, reportedly declared at a meeting of the Southern District of the Anti-Terrorism Advisory Council that the conference call revealed "the high probability that a terrorist incident of the magnitude of the 9/11 attacks would occur in the United States within the next 6 weeks."[37] On September 23, Fox News Network, picking up on the reports of the conference call, quoted one law enforcement official's warning that "every day there is new information that raises the level of anxiety."[38]

Making antiterrorism efforts far more visible also fed fears. The *Washington Post* reported on September 27 that "agencies across the federal government are launching an aggressive and unusually open offensive aimed at thwarting terrorist plots before and during the presidential election in November. . . . At the U.S. Capitol, Police Chief Terrance W. Gainer has ordered a number of his officers to wear sophisticated new equipment to protect them from a biological or chemical attack."[39] Photos of such outfits likely spurred the heebie-jeebies in the heartland. The *Post* noted: "By publicizing the government's disruption efforts . . . authorities say they hope to forestall any plans for similar attacks here." But making antiterrorism efforts as visible as pre-9/11 airport security guards would not daunt a sophisticated terror network accustomed to innovating and exploiting obvious gaps in defenses. The *Post* noted that "numerous counterterrorism and law enforcement officials concede that the activity is not based on any new or specific intelligence."[40]

Overhyped terror attack warnings jangled some nerves on Capitol Hill. After Sen. Mark Dayton (D-Minn.) received a closed-door intelligence briefing, he shut down his Capitol Hill office and sent his staff home. Before fleeing, someone posted a sign on his Senate office door, declaring that it was closed "because of a top-secret intelligence report." The rest of the Senate staff continued business as usual.

Dayton got spooked after a joint FBI–CIA terrorism briefing, which one U.S. government official described as "way over the top," describing "fire and brimstone raining down from the skies" and "the continental U.S. [going] up in smoke." D.C. Police Chief Charles Ramsey noted that "there is no credible information about planned attacks—nothing to set off the reaction we saw" from Dayton. But Dayton denounced other senators: "To leave our young staffs there as human shields so we can make a statement, I think, is the height of irresponsibility."[41] While Dayton was ridiculed by some people for his shut-down, almost no one raised questions about the type of hogwash the FBI and CIA were feeding members of Congress.

In early October, a Bush advisor told the *Washington Post* that the president's reelection campaign's strategy aimed to stoke public fears about terrorism.[42] A few days before the election, a video of Osama Bin Laden popped up in which the terrorist leader warned: "Your security is in your own hands. Any nation that does not attack us will not be attacked."[43] A Bush–Cheney campaign official gleefully told New York's *Daily News,* "We want people to think 'terrorism' for the last four days. And anything that raises the issue in people's minds is good for us."[44] A senior GOP strategist, describing the Bin Laden video as a "little gift" for the Bush campaign, added that "anything that makes people nervous about their personal safety helps Bush."[45] The *Daily News* noted that "the new tape . . . makes it difficult for Kerry to keep hammering Bush on the subject without appearing to be capitalizing on terror. Kerry eliminated those lines from his speeches yesterday evening."

After all the alerts and sweating, America miraculously obliterated the terrorist threat on Election Day. Attorney General Ashcroft, in a resignation letter dated November 2 and publicly released a week later, informed Bush: "The objective of securing the safety of Americans from crime and terror has been achieved."[46] After Bush's victory was secure, the feds also canceled the heightened terrorist alerts for New York, Newark, and Washington, D.C. There was no evidence that the risk was lower simply because Ashcroft was relinquishing his grip on power. In the days before Bush's second inaugural, the feds again reduced terror warnings—perhaps seeking to make Republican donors less timid about coming to Washington to express their gratitude to Bush.[47]

Standards for terrorism alerts may have been more lax during election season than in previous years. The *New York Times* derided the Bush administration in late October for having "turned the business of keeping Americans informed about the threat of terrorism into a politically scripted series of color-coded scare sessions."[48] Shortly after resigning in 2005, former Homeland Security Chief Ridge complained that the Bush administration often raised the terrorist alert level based on flimsy evidence. Ridge spoke out to "debunk the myth" that his department was to blame for the frequent alerts. Ridge declared: "More often than not we were the least inclined to raise it. . . . There were times when some people were really aggressive about raising it, and we said, 'For that?'"[49]

Election season terror alerts placed Americans in a psychological cross-fire—warning them again and again, vaguely but ominously, and then implicitly promising that their government would protect them. As the *American Prospect*'s Matthew Yglesias observed: "On terrorism, Bush's incentives are all wrong; the worse he does substantively, the better he does politically. When attacks increase around the world, people are reminded of the threat, they feel less safe in their own homes, and this—or so Bush's aides believe—benefits the president."[50]

Terror alerts might have made the difference on Election Day. Robb Willer, assistant director of the Sociology and Small Groups Laboratory at Cornell University, examined the relationship between 26 government-issued terror warnings reported in the *Washington Post* and Bush's approval ratings. "Each terror warning from the previous week corresponded to a 2.75 point increase in the percentage of Americans expressing approval for President Bush," Willer concluded.[51] Thanks to Attention Deficit Democracy, even though many of the specific terror alerts were later debunked in the media, Bush still profited. The Cornell study also found a "halo effect": Americans' approval of Bush's handling of the economy also rose immediately after the announcement of new terror warnings.[52] Apparently, the more terrorists who wanted to attack America, the better job Bush was doing.

Terror alerts boosted Bush's ratings because few people paid attention to the real news on government antiterrorism programs and policies during the election season. If they had, they would have received the following jolts:

- On August 21, the 9/11 Commission issued a staff report revealing that the FBI had failed to take action against known Al Qaeda fundraisers before 9/11. The report warned that government efforts against terrorist money laundering were continuing to flounder.[53]
- On August 30, Americans learned of more than 750 documented reports of federal air marshals "sleeping on duty, lying, testing positive for alcohol or illegal drugs while on the job or losing weapons," according to the Department of Homeland Security Inspector General.
- On September 9, the Transportation Security Administration announced that it was making a class-action settlement with 15,000 people who had complained about TSA agents looting or damaging their luggage. The settlement, following the indictments of thieving TSA

agents caught on videotape, sparked doubts as to who would protect Americans from their TSA protectors.

- On September 26, an IG report revealed that the FBI had failed to translate more than 120,000 hours of terrorist-related wiretaps and other intercepts. Almost half of all FBI offices had computer snafus that may have caused Al Qaeda–related wiretaps to be deleted before they could be analyzed.[54]
- On the Sunday before the presidential election, news leaked out that the finances of the Homeland Security Department—a vast amalgamation of 22 agencies and 170,000 government workers, and one of Bush's biggest bragging points—were so botched that some antiterrorist agencies were saving money by banning agents from using government cars and even prohibiting photocopying.[55]

Shortly after the election, the feds confessed that the most visible post-9/11 security blanket the government provided was often not worth a wooden nickel. After spending almost $5 billion on new screening devices for airports and other locations, the federal government decided to ditch much of the equipment because it was "ineffective, unreliable or too expensive to operate."[56] Rep. Chris Cox, chairman of the Homeland Security Committee, came to the government's defense: "After 9/11, we had to show how committed we were by spending hugely greater amounts of money than ever before, as rapidly as possible."[57] Government spending, regardless of how wasteful, was assumed to comfort voters.

Bush was never held liable by voters for the antiterrorism boondoggles his administration spawned. If Bush supporters could not grasp that Saddam was not linked to 9/11, it is not surprising that they never linked the president to Transportation Security Administration debacles. Bush's and other officials' continual victory proclamations in the war on terror overwhelmed all the evidence of government failure on the homefront. Voters' response to Bush was not unprecedented, since earlier presidents also reaped ballot harvests from hitting the panic alarm—no matter how badly the government subsequently floundered.

BANNING THE GOOD BOOK

Ever since Thomas Jefferson was portrayed as a crazed atheist who would turn America into Sodom during the 1800 presidential election, religious smears have occurred on the campaign trail. In 1928, the Ku Klux Klan fired up opposition to Catholic Democratic nominee Al Smith in the presidential race. Throughout

American history, many politicians have sought to frighten voters into thinking that their opponent will ravage their most personal beliefs.

In September 2004, the Republican National Committee sent mass mailings to residents of Arkansas and West Virginia warning that the Bible could be banned if liberals won the election. The left side of the flier showed the cover of the Bible with the word "BANNED" across the front. The flier's right side showed a man on his knees, putting a wedding ring on the finger of another male. The flier warned: "Our traditional values are under assault by Liberals and their hand-picked activist judges. They are using the courts to get around the Constitution and impose their radical agenda." The flier warned:

> The liberal agenda includes:
>   Removing "under God" from the Pledge of Allegiance
>   Allowing teenagers to get abortions without parental consent
>   Overturning the ban on the hideous procedure known as Partial Birth
>   Abortion
>   Allowing Same Sex Marriages[58]

The mailing urged West Virginians to "vote Republican to protect our families" and defeat the "liberal agenda."

Kerry had not mentioned anything about banning the Bible, and even some conservative religious groups were offended by the RNC mailings. The Republican National Committee's Christine Iverson defended the flier: "When the Massachusetts Supreme Court sanctioned same-sex marriage and people in other states realized they could be compelled to recognize those laws, same-sex marriage became an issue. These same activist judges also want to remove the words 'under God' from the Pledge of Allegiance."[59] But the fact that some federal judges decreed that the phrase "under God" violates the separation of church and state did not prove Kerry's predatory intent toward the Good Book.

The targeted mass mailings outraged state pride. Sen. Robert Byrd (D-WV) howled: "They must think that West Virginians just bounced off the turnip truck. . . . But the people of West Virginia are smarter than that. We're not country bumpkins who will swallow whatever garbage some high-priced political consultant makes up."[60] A columnist for the *Charleston Daily Mail* bitterly complained, "Why didn't the RNC send the pamphlet to the other 48 states? And why is West Virginia the object of these tricks, political and otherwise, from other groups? Do they think we are really that dumb?"[61] (Bush received 87,000 more votes in West Virginia in 2004 than in 2000, winning the state by a much larger margin.)

FLEECING THE SHEEP

For at least 40 years, American politicians have sometimes used television ads to spur dread. The most famous TV ad of the twentieth century from the pre-Reagan era was the so-called daisy ad. This 1964 Lyndon Johnson campaign spot showed a young girl "picking the petals off a daisy before the screen was overwhelmed by a nuclear explosion and then a mushroom cloud and Mr. Johnson declared, 'These are the stakes.'"[62] The ad did not specifically claim that Barry Goldwater, the Republican nominee, would annihilate the human race, but the subtle hint wafted through. Though this ad only aired once, it instantly became a legend.

During the 2004 campaign, residents of swing states were under constant bombardment by throat-grabbing political ads. In late September, the Bush campaign released a television ad titled "Peace and Security." The *New York Times* described the ad: "A clock ticks menacingly as a young mother pulls a quart of milk out of a refrigerator in slow motion, a young father loads toddlers into a minivan and an announcer intones ominously, 'Weakness invites those who would do us harm.'"[63]

The most memorable Bush ad, released a few weeks before the election, opened in a thick forest, with shadows and hazy shots complementing the foreboding music. A female announcer ominously declared, "In an increasingly dangerous world, even after the first terrorist attack on America, John Kerry and the liberals in Congress voted to slash America's intelligence operations by $6 billion—cuts so deep they would have weakened America's defenses." The ad then focused on a pack of wolves reclining in a clearing. The voiceover concluded "And weakness attracts those who are waiting to do America harm" as the wolves began jumping up and running toward the camera.[64]

At the end of the ad, the president appeared and announced: "I'm George W. Bush and I approve this message." One liberal cynic suggested that the ad's message was that voters would be eaten by wolves if Kerry won. A Bush adviser told ABC News that "the ad was produced and tested months ago. Voter reaction was so powerful that we decided to hold the ad to the end of the campaign and make it one of the closing spots."[65]

The Bush ad spurred protests by the equivalent of the Lobo Anti-Defamation League. Pat Wendland, the manager of Wolves Offered Life and Friendship, a wolf refuge near Fort Collins, Colorado, complained: "The comparison to terrorists was insulting. We have worked for years, teaching people that Little Red Riding Hood lied."[66] Rob Edward of Sinapu, another Colorado "wolf advocacy group," commented: "Wolves don't pose a threat to humans, unlike terrorists. Now we have this huge graphic media buy that associates the maligned species with terrorists."[67] Edward was especially perturbed that the Bush ad was launched during National Wolf Awareness Week.

The ad was as deceptive as it was menacing. The vast majority of viewers likely assumed that "the first terrorist attack" meant 9/11. However, the ad actually referred to a 1993 truck bomb that exploded in the parking garage of the World Trade Center and killed six people.

The accusation that Kerry had slashed intelligence spending was false. Kerry, along with other senators, proposed in 1995 to rein in intelligence spending by 3 to 5 percent. (The total U.S. spy budget is a secret.) But the budget change would not have cut spending since at least one major spy agency was sitting on a huge stash of unspent funds from previous years.[68] At the time Kerry proposed his budget trim, U.S. spy agencies had been expanding for over half a century, largely to defend against the Soviet Union. After the collapse of the USSR—far and away the top threat to American security—it was not extremist to talk of curbing spy budgets.

It was ironic that the Bush campaign tarred Kerry for not recognizing that terrorism was a catastrophic threat after 1993, since the Bush administration was lackadaisical about the threat from January 20 through September 10, 2001. The wolf pack ad was based on a "reverse" seven-year statute of limitation for 9/11: anything that Kerry did since 1995 could be held against him while nothing Bush did in his first 8 months as commander-in-chief could be used against him. Kerry was guilty for not having foreseen 9/11 six years earlier, while Bush was innocent despite not having reacted to the cascading warnings of terrorist attacks before 9/11. Bush, in a 2003 interview, described his attitude prior to 9/11: "I didn't feel a sense of urgency about al Qaeda. It was not my focus; it was not the focus of my team."[69]

The Bush campaign also sought to make Americans dread change. The *Wall Street Journal* noted, "Bush is portraying change as too risky for a country facing the perils that confront America today and focusing his message squarely on the dangers a Kerry administration might pose."[70] The Kerry campaign's top pollster, Mark Mellman, observed after the election: "The Bush campaign used fear very well to make voters risk averse."[71] Bush surrogates also routinely pushed audience's fear buttons. A professional wrestler asked a crowd of tens of thousands of Bush supporters in Orlando in October shortly before the president arrived: "If your babies were left all alone in the dead of night, who would you rather have setting there on the porch— John Kerry and his snowboard or George W. with his shotgun?"[72] A pro-Bush group called Progress for America went one better, running TV ads displaying pictures of Osama Bin Laden and masked terrorists as the announcer asks: "These people want to kill us. Would you trust Kerry against these fanatic killers?"[73]

CHENEY, TERRIFIER IN CHIEF[74]

During the fall campaign, Vice President Cheney rarely missed an opportunity to remind listeners that a Bush defeat could be fatal. A week after the Republican National Convention, Cheney told a handpicked Iowa audience: "If we make the wrong choice [on Election Day], then the danger is we'll get hit again and we'll be hit in a way that'll be devastating from the standpoint of the United States." Cheney warned: "I think that would be a terrible mistake for us."[75] *New York Times* columnist Maureen Dowd commented on Cheney's Iowa pitch: "It is a sign of the dark, macho, paranoid vice president's restraint that he didn't really take it to its emotionally satisfying conclusion: Message: Vote for us or we'll kill you."[76]

A *Washington Post* September 2004 profile noted that Cheney's stump speech was "gloomy and deadly serious. Cheney . . . rallies Republicans on the campaign trail with visions of apocalypse."[77] Cheney warned supporters: "Today, we face an enemy every bit as bent on destroying us as were the Axis powers in World War II. . . . This is not an enemy we can reason with, or negotiate with, or appease. This is, to put it simply, an enemy that we must destroy." The *Post* noted: "The crowds cheered, pumping their fists in the air. While President Bush campaigns with an upbeat message that a second Bush administration will keep Americans safer, Cheney speaks like Darth Vader, as the ticket's voice of fear."[78]

On October 19, Cheney notified voters that a Kerry win could result in their cities being nuked: "The biggest threat we face now as a nation is the possibility of terrorists ending up in the middle of one of our cities with deadlier weapons than have ever before been used against us—biological agents or a nuclear weapon or a chemical weapon of some kind to be able to threaten the lives of hundreds of thousands of Americans."[79] This was not Cheney's first tactical nuclear invocation. On March 17, 2003, on the eve of the U.S. invasion of Iraq, Cheney declared during a "Meet the Press" interview that "we believe [Saddam] has, in fact, reconstituted nuclear weapons."[80]

In the final weeks of the campaign, Bush himself hit the terrorism button harder than ever. On October 18, Bush traveled to New Jersey and draped himself in 9/11. Bush denounced Kerry's positions: "This kind of September-the–10th attitude is not the way to protect our country." In a speech in Marlton, N.J., Bush declared: "While America does the hard work of fighting terrorism and spreading freedom," Kerry "has chosen the easy path of protest and defeatism."[81] The *New York Times* mentioned that Bush's "easy path of protest and defeatism" phrase "evoked Mr. Kerry's statements about Vietnam 34 years ago. His use of terms like 'a policy of weakness,' 'giving up the fight' and 'a strategy of retreat' appeared intended to paint Mr. Kerry as an appeaser at best and a coward at worst."[82] Bush was appealing to the notion—cherished by some diehards—that the United States lost the Vietnam war because of the protests on the streets in America, rather than because of liars in the White House and the Pentagon (see chapter 5).

CRITICISM AS A WEAPON OF MASS DESTRUCTION

Since the 2004 election largely turned on who would be the best protector, the Bush campaign sought to make Americans view criticism of the president as if it were a weapon of mass destruction. Democratic Senator Zell Miller, the keynote speaker for the Republican National Convention, delivered the angriest prime-time speech at a modern political convention. Watched by a national television audience of millions, Miller revealed that political opposition is treason: "Now, at the same time young Americans are dying in the sands of Iraq and the mountains of Afghanistan, our nation is being torn apart and made weaker because of the Democrats' manic obsession to bring down our commander in chief."[83] There was no evidence that such criticism of Bush's foreign policy was ripping America asunder—but trumpeting the accusation made Bush critics appear a pox on the land. Miller denounced Kerry's record on national defense and suggested that he would leave the military armed with only "spitballs." When Miller was pressed for evidence of his charges in a post-speech interview, he angrily talked of challenging MSNBC's Chris Matthews to a duel. Every word in Miller's speech was preapproved by the Bush campaign. In the following weeks, Bush often appeared with Miller at campaign stops, signifying Bush's embrace of his message.

The Zell Miller "criticism-as-treason" theme permeated the campaign. Former New York City Police Commissioner Bernie Kerik, stumping around the nation for Bush, told audiences: "Political criticism is our enemy's best friend."[84] The *Washington Post* noted on September 24 that "President Bush and leading Republicans are increasingly charging that Democratic presidential nominee John F. Kerry and others in his party are giving comfort to terrorists and undermining the war in Iraq—a line of attack that tests the conventional bounds of political rhetoric."[85] When the United States' hand-picked leader of Iraq, Iyad Allawi, visited the White House, Bush declaimed that Kerry's criticisms of his Iraq policy "can embolden an enemy."[86]

Other prominent Republicans jumped on the bandwagon. Sen. Orrin Hatch (R-Utah), chairman of the Senate Judiciary Committee, condemned Democrats for "consistently saying things that I think undermine our young men and women who are serving over there." John Thune, the Republican senate candidate in South Dakota, denounced Senate Minority Leader Tom

Daschle: "His words embolden the enemy."[87] Bush campaign manager Ken Mehlman condemned the Kerry campaign for "parroting the rhetoric of terrorists" and warned: "The enemy listens. All listen to what the president said, and all listen to what Sen. Kerry said."[88]

In the first two debates, Bush repeatedly implied that Kerry's criticisms of his policies in Iraq proved Kerry was unfit to be president. Bush kept coming back to Kerry's use of the phrase "the wrong war in the wrong place at the wrong time" as if Kerry had greatly sinned against the American people by saying such a thing. Apparently, by definition, anyone who criticizes a ruler is unfit to correct that ruler's mistakes.

Each time Kerry talked of Bush's failures in Iraq, Bush claimed that Kerry was attacking U.S. troops, and many citizens believed him. Each Kerry criticism of a specific debacle became further proof of Kerry's lack of patriotism. Following media reports about the looting of an Iraqi ammo dump after its capture by American forces, Kerry criticized the Bush administration for neglecting to secure the explosives, some of which may have later been used to attack U.S. troops. Bush erupted: "Sen. Kerry is again attacking the actions of our military in Iraq, with complete disregard for the facts. Sen. Kerry will say anything to get elected."[89] Bush spokesmen condemned Kerry for criticizing before all the facts were out—at the same time the administration continued withholding facts. The Bush team wanted Americans to believe that anyone who criticized the Iraq war was opposed to defending America.

The expanding concept of treason plugged the president's growing credibility gap. The Democrats were supposedly not allowed to say anything critical about Iraq, and the Bush campaign was not obliged to say anything honest about it. Thus, Bush only needed to perpetuate his wars to perpetually silence his critics.

The demonization of criticism helped anger ill-informed voters, fostering intolerance that helped Bush win reelection. Criticism was apparently inherently more dangerous than perpetuating disastrous policies. This would make sense only if blind obedience provides the equivalent to body armor for the entire nation.

The same "support Bush or betray America" paradigm had helped Republicans capture the Senate in the 2002 congressional elections. In mid-2002, when he was White House political director, Mehlman created a PowerPoint presentation for Republican candidates urging them to "highlight fears of future terrorist attacks."[90] (A copy of the disk with the project was dropped in a park near the White House.) In September 2002, after Democrats balked at some anti-union provisions in the administration's legislation to create a Homeland Security Department, Bush declared his opponents are "not interested in the security of the American people."[91]

Bush's tactics were aided by a coterie of talking heads who portrayed his campaign much more loftily than it was. Republican pollster Frank Luntz asserted two days after the election: "Some will claim that Mr. Bush won on Tuesday because he waged a campaign of fear. The exact opposite was the case. Americans turned to him precisely because they saw him as the antidote to that fear."[92] But this was exactly the point of the Bush campaign strategy—to fan fear and portray Bush as the antidote. Luntz's rewriting of history was perhaps inspired by his work for many Republican politicians and organizations. (In a June 2004 confidential memo to Republican candidates, Luntz urged them to remember: "'9/11 changed everything' is the context by which everything follows. No speech about homeland security or Iraq should begin without a reference to 9/11.")

THE BATTERED CITIZEN SYNDROME

In the same way that some battered wives cling to their abusive husbands, the more debacles the government causes, the more some voters cling to rulers. The good citizen is supposed to always believe, or at least hope, that next time politicians will not abuse them—that there are "signs of a turnaround" in their character and competence, so it is "better just to stick it out."

The more frightened many people became, the more grateful they were toward the president. The more terror alerts, the more loudly people prayed to perpetuate Bush in power. Even as U.S. government aggression abroad created more enemies, many citizens clung more tightly to the government as their only possible savior. Even Bush's chief of the Central Intelligence Agency, Porter Goss, publicly admitted that the Iraq war was spurring terrorism, warning Congress in early 2005 that "Islamic extremists are exploiting the Iraqi conflict to recruit new anti-U.S. jihadists. Those jihadists who survive will leave Iraq experienced and focused on acts of urban terrorism."[93] Yet, this blunt warning did not stop Bush from continuing to claim or imply that the war in Iraq was making Americans safer.

The more an election is about fear, the more the winner will presume to be entitled to all the power he claims to need to combat the threat. The more that fear is the key issue, the more that voters will seek a savior, not a representative.

The more fears government fans, the fewer people will recall the danger of government itself. The more frightened people become, the more prone they will be to see their rulers as saviors rather than as potential oppressors. The continual promises of freedom from fear allowed Bush and his predecessors to boost the number of Americans who fear limits on government power more than they fear government itself. After promising freedom from fear, a politician can simply invoke polls showing widespread fears to justify seizing new power. The more people government frightens, the more legitimate its power grabs become.

CONCLUSION

John Adams, in his 1776 *Thoughts on Government,* observed, "Fear is the foundation of most governments; but it is so sordid and brutal a passion, and renders men in whose breasts it predominates so stupid and miserable, that Americans will not be likely to approve of any political institution which is founded on it."[94] The Founding Fathers hoped that the American people would continue to have the virtues and confidence necessary to perpetuate liberty. Insofar as government is increasingly relying on fear to secure support and submission, government degrades the people. And the more degraded people become, the easier it is for politicians to frighten them into further submission.

The American public and media's response to the post-9/11 fearmongering showed an ignorance of history—as if this was the first time that any politician seized unnecessary power in the wake of a debacle. This was epitomized by derisive references to "September 10th Americans"—folks who did not cast their principles and beliefs overboard when the World Trade Center towers came crashing down. But those who think that terrorism changed everything forget the ancient tradition of politicians frightening people into submission. Nothing the U.S. government did in the wake of 9/11 revealed any fundamental change in how politicians manipulate emotions and perceptions.

The more clearly people perceive reality, the better they recognize the danger of subjugation. Fear is perhaps the ultimate enemy of clear thinking. The Bush administration faced a choice of giving the truth to the American people, or trying to scare them to death. The better people understood the situation in Iraq, the less support they had for Bush. Thus, Bush's best hope was confusion and fear.

After the 2004 election campaign, the clearest mandate is for people to be sheep with the president as their shepherd-in-chief. Once this motif is accepted, quibbling about sheep's rights is pretty silly. The sheep cannot claim rights against their shepherd without risking losing protection. Thus, they had best stay in their place, count their blessings, and bleat on cue.

What rights does a politician acquire from an electoral victory based on frightening voters into submission? Or from persuading enough voters that they will be killed or maimed if the other candidate wins? How can the mass production of bogus fears produce real legitimacy?

CHAPTER 4

Messianic Democracy

With God's help, we will lift Shanghai up and ever up until it is just like Kansas City.
—Senator Kenneth Wherry (R-Neb.), 1940[1]

It is the policy of the United States to seek and support the growth of democratic movements and institutions in every nation and culture, with the ultimate goal of ending tyranny in our world.
—George W. Bush, January 20, 2005[2]

"DOING IT FOR DEMOCRACY" IS THE ULTIMATE EXONERATION for U.S. foreign policy. Presidents brazenly misrepresent U.S. foreign policy, claiming far more idealistic motives than they actually have. Unfortunately, "democracy" sometimes means nothing more than the United States' divine right to impose pro-American governments upon foreign peoples.

Americans' support for democracy has long been exploited by politicians and political operatives to provide a respectable sheen for brutal U.S. interventions. But the honest idealism of the heartland is rarely permitted to impede the appropriations process in Washington. Despite the perennial failure to back up lofty rhetoric with honorable action abroad, the American public blithely continues to support U.S. meddling around the globe.

KILLING IN THE NAME OF DEMOCRACY

The U.S. government's first experience with forcibly spreading democracy came in the wake of the Spanish-American War. When the U.S. government declared war on Spain in 1898, it pledged it would not annex foreign territory. But, after a swift victory, the United States annexed all of the Philippines. As Tony Smith, author of *America's Mission,* noted, "Ultimately, the democratization of the Philippines came to be the principle reason the Americans were there; now the United States had a moral purpose to its imperialism and could rest more easily."[3]

President William McKinley proclaimed that, in the Philippines, the U.S. occupation would "assure the residents in every possible way [the] full measure of individual rights and liberties which is the heritage of a free people substituting the mild sway of justice and right for arbitrary rule."[4] McKinley also promised to "Christianize" the Filipinos, as if he did not consider the large number of Filipino Catholics to be Christians.[5] McKinley was devoted to forcibly spreading American values abroad at the same time that he championed high tariffs to stop Americans from buying foreign products.

The United States Christianized and civilized the Filipinos by authorizing American troops to kill any Filipino male ten years old and older and by burning down and massacring entire villages. (Filipino resistance fighters also committed atrocities against American soldiers.) Hundreds of thousands of Filipinos died as the United States struggled to crush resistance to its rule in a conflict that dragged on for a decade and cost 4,000 American troops' lives. Despite the brutal U.S. suppression of the Filipino independence movement, President George W. Bush, in a 2003 speech in Manila, claimed credit for the United States bringing democracy to the Philippines: "America is proud of its part in the great story of the Filipino people. Together our soldiers liberated the Philippines from colonial rule."[6]

President Woodrow Wilson raised tub-thumping for democracy to new levels. As soon as Wilson took office, he began saber-rattling against the Mexican government, outraged that Mexican President Victoriano Huerta had come to power via military force (during the Mexican civil war that broke out in 1910). Wilson announced in May 1914: "They say the Mexicans are not fitted for self-government; and to this I reply that, when properly directed, there is no people not fitted for self-government."[7] Wilson summarized his Mexican policy: "I am going to teach the South American republics to elect good men!" U.S. Ambassador to Great Britain Walter Hines Page explained the U.S. government's attitude toward Latin America: "The United States will be here 200 years and it can continue to shoot men for that little space until they learn to vote and rule themselves."[8] In order to cut off the Mexican government's tariff revenue, Wilson sent U.S. forces to seize the city of Veracruz, one of the most important Mexican ports. U.S. soldiers killed hundreds of Mexicans (while suffering 19 dead) and briefly rallied the Mexican opposition around the Mexican leader.

In 1916, U.S. Marines seized Santo Domingo, the capital of the Dominican Republic. After the United States could not find any Dominican politicians who would accept orders from Washington, it installed its own military government to run the country for eight years. The previous year, the U.S. military had seized control of Haiti and dictated terms to that nation's president. When local residents rebelled against U.S. rule in 1918, thousands of Haitians were killed. Author Tony Smith observed, "What makes Wilson's [Latin American] policy even more annoying is that its primary motive seems to have been to reinforce the self-righteous vanity of the president."[9]

After Wilson took the nation into World War I "to make the world safe for democracy," he acted as if fanning intolerance was the key to spreading democracy. Wilson increasingly demonized all those who did not support the war and his crusade to shape the post-war world. Wilson denounced Irish-Americans, German-Americans, and others, declaring, "Any man who carries a hyphen about him carries a dagger which he is ready to plunge into the vitals of the Republic."[10] Wilson urged Americans to see military might as a supreme force for goodness, appealing in May 1918 for "force, force to the utmost, force without stint or limit, the righteous and triumphant force which shall make Right the law of the world."[11] As Harvard professor Irving Babbitt commented: "Wilson, in the pursuit of his scheme for world service, was led to make light of the constitutional checks on his authority and to reach out almost automatically for unlimited power."[12]

The deaths of more than 300,000 Americans in World War I did nothing to bring Wilson's idealistic visions to Earth. The 1919 Paris peace talks became a slaughter pen of Wilson's pretensions. One of Wilson's top aides, Henry White, later commented: "We had such high hopes of this adventure; we believed God called us and now we are doing hell's dirtiest work."[13] Thomas Fleming, the author of *The Illusion of Victory*, noted, "The British and French exploited the war to forcibly expand their empires and place millions more people under their thumbs." Fleming concluded that one lesson of World War I is that "idealism is not synonymous with sainthood or virtue. It only sounds that way."

During the 1920s and 1930s, U.S. military interventions in Latin America were routinely portrayed as "missions to establish democracy."[14] The U.S.

military sometimes served as a collection agency for American corporations or banks that had made unwise investments or loans in politically unstable foreign lands. Marine Corps Major General Smedley Butler bitterly lamented of his 33 years of active service: "I spent most of my time being a high class muscle-man for Big Business, for Wall Street and for the Bankers. In short, I was a racketeer, a gangster for capitalism. . . . I helped in the raping of half a dozen Central American republics for the benefits of Wall Street."[15]

Franklin Roosevelt painted World War II as a crusade for democracy—hailing Stalin as a partner in liberation. FDR praised Stalin as "truly representative of the heart and soul of Russia"[16]—as if the lack of bona fide elections in Russia was a mere technicality, since Stalin was the nation's favorite. Roosevelt praised Soviet Russia as one of the "freedom-loving Nations" and stressed that Stalin is "thoroughly conversant with the provisions of our Constitution."[17] Harold Ickes, one of FDR's top aides, proclaimed that communism was "the antithesis of Nazism" because it was based on "belief in the control of the government, including the economic system, by the people themselves."[18] The fact that the Soviet regime had been the most oppressive government in the world in the 1930s was irrelevant, as far as FDR was concerned. It was great that Hitler lost the war, but a catastrophe that Stalin won.

President Eisenhower was no slacker on invoking democracy. In 1957, he declared, "We as a nation . . . have a job to do, a mission as the champion of human freedom. To conduct ourselves in all our international relations that we never compromise the fundamental principle that all peoples have a right to an independent government of their own full, free choice."[19] Eisenhower was perfectly in tune with the Republican Party Platform of 1952, which proclaimed, "We shall again make liberty into a beacon light of hope that will penetrate the dark places. . . . The policies we espouse will revive the contagious, liberating influences which are inherent in freedom."[20]

But Eisenhower's idealism did not deter the CIA, fearing communism, from toppling at least two democratically elected regimes. In 1953, the CIA engineered a coup that put the Shah in charge of Iran. In 1954, the CIA aided a military coup in Guatemala that crushed that nation's first constitutionally based government. The elected Guatemalan government and the United Fruit Company could not agree on the value of 400,000 acres that the Guatemalan government wanted to expropriate to distribute to small farmers. The Guatemalan government offered $1.2 million as compensation based on the "taxed value of the land; Washington insisted on behalf of United Fruit that the value was $15.9 million, that the company be reimbursed immediately and in full, and that [President Jacobo] Arbenz's insistence on taking the land was clear proof of his communist proclivities," as *America's Mission* noted.[21] Yet, at the same time, the federal government was confiscating huge swaths of private land throughout American inner cities for urban renewal and highway projects, often paying owners pittances for the value of their homes. The fact that the U.S. government got miffed over a 1954 Guatemalan government buyout offer helped produce decades of repressive rule and the killings of hundreds of thousands of Guatemalan civilians.

John F. Kennedy's praise for spreading democracy did much to establish his idealistic credentials. In 1956, while he was a U.S. senator, Kennedy urged U.S. support for Vietnam to achieve "a revolution of their own making, for their own welfare, and for the security of freedom everywhere." Kennedy justified U.S. intervention in Southeast Asia with the same terms that President George W. Bush used to justify U.S. intervention in the Middle East almost 50 years later: "Vietnam represents a proving ground for democracy in Asia. . . . Vietnam represents the alternative to communist dictatorship. If this democratic experience fails . . . then weakness, not strength, will characterize the meaning of democracy in the minds of still more Asians. . . . We cannot afford to permit that experiment to fail."[22] Kennedy's devotion to democracy did not deter him from approving the violent overthrow of South Vietnam's president in 1963.

President Kennedy also launched the Alliance for Progress, a massive U.S. aid program for Latin America. At the kickoff speech on March 13, 1961, Kennedy announced to Latin American ambassadors that "our unfulfilled task is to demonstrate to the entire world that man's unsatisfied aspiration for economic progress and social justice can best be achieved by free men working within a framework of democratic institutions." Kennedy proposed that "the American Republics begin on a vast new Ten Year Plan for the Americas, a plan to transform the 1960's into a historic decade of democratic progress."[23] But, after several Latin American countries began tilting toward leftist leaders, "the administration began backing new military dictatorships on anticommunist grounds, an initial tendency that hardened into consistent policy in the Johnson years," as Thomas Carothers, the director of the Carnegie Endowment's Democracy and Rule of Law Project, wrote.[24]

Some Latin Americans got caught in the crosswinds of U.S. policies. As Carothers noted,

In Guatemala, USAID [the U.S. Agency for International Development] funded a large program in the late 1960s and early 1970s to train rural leaders, so as to give rural communities more say in their own development. At the same time, the Defense Department and the CIA were actively supporting the Guatemalan military's counterinsurgency campaign against the small but growing guerilla forces and all organized political opposition. . . . More than 750 of the rural leaders who took part in the agency's earlier program were murdered in the war between the U.S.-backed Guatemalan military and the leftist rebels.[25]

Other Latin American political reformers got the short end of the stick thanks to the U.S. government's Public Safety Program, which trained and bankrolled police forces that routinely tortured detainees and opponents.[26]

On April 28, 1965, President Lyndon Johnson sent U.S. Marines into the Dominican Republic to suppress a popular uprising against the military junta that had deposed the nation's president. Johnson justified the invasion by stating that: "What began as a popular democratic revolution, committed to democracy and social justice, very shortly moved and was taken over and really seized and placed into the hands of a band of Communist conspirators." There was no evidence that the communists were behind the anti-junta protests, but U.S. paranoia of another Castro was sufficient justification. Thirty-one U.S. troops were killed in the fighting, along with 3,000 Dominicans.[27]

The Johnson administration periodically invoked democracy to sanctify its war in Vietnam. On January 12, 1966, President Johnson announced: "We fight for the principle of self-determination—that the people of South Vietnam should be able to choose their own course, choose it in free elections without violence, without terror, and without fear."[28] In early 1967, Johnson informed South Vietnamese generals: "My birthday is in late August. The greatest birthday present you could give me is a national election."[29] The *New York Times* hyped the subsequent election, noting that American officials were "surprised and heartened" by the purported high voter turnout and that the election "has long been seen as the keystone in President Johnson's policy of encouraging the growth of constitutional processes in South Vietnam."[30] However, the election failed to create a government with popular support, and the Tet offensive a few months later revealed the hollowness of the South Vietnamese government.

South Vietnamese democracy (and well-being) was very low on the list of U.S. military priorities. A March 25, 1965, memo from Assistant Secretary of Defense John McNaughton to Defense Secretary Robert McNamara weighted U.S. priorities:

70%—To avoid a humiliating US defeat (to our reputation as a guarantor).
20%—To keep SVN [South Vietnam] (and then adjacent) territory from Chinese hands.
10%—To permit the people of SVN to enjoy a better, freer way of life.
ALSO—To emerge from crisis without unacceptable taint from methods used.[31]

This memo—signaling that the U.S. government had largely given up on South Vietnamese democracy—was written in the same month that the first contingent of U.S. forces designated for combat—3,500 Marines—arrived in Vietnam. (U.S. force totals would eventually exceed 500,000.) Yet, because invoking democracy played well with voters, Johnson and high-ranking government officials pushed this button to justify both U.S. losses and the massive bombing campaign of North Vietnam.

In 1973, the CIA helped overthrow the elected government of Salvador Allende in Chile, bringing in a 15-year period of military rule and subverting one of the oldest democracies in the western hemisphere. The CIA's actions in Chile were not out of character. From the early 1950s through the early-to-mid 1970s, the CIA "engaged in numerous covert efforts to bolster selected political parties, to tilt elections, and otherwise to influence political outcomes," actions sometimes justified "as support for the cause of democracy," Carothers noted.[32]

The Reagan administration perennially invoked spreading democracy to sanctify its Central American policies. The Reagan administration deluged the Honduran government with aid at a time when it was being condemned for committing widespread atrocities. Gen. Gustavo Alvarez, the military strongman who effectively ran the country, was linked to death squad activities that resulted in the killing of masses of Hondurans.[33] John Negroponte, the U.S. ambassador to Honduras at that time, confidentially assured Washington of Alvarez's "dedication to democracy." Negroponte was also the point man for securing more arms for the Nicaraguan Contras based in Honduras and for publicly denying that the Contras were based in Honduras. The *Washington Post,* which obtained confidential government cables from that period, noted in 2005 that "Negroponte's support for Alvarez remained unwavering until March 30, 1984, when fellow officers ousted Alvarez from office, accusing him of corruption and authoritarian tendencies."[34] (Negroponte became the Bush administration's ambassador to the United Nations in 2001 and, later, the president's national intelligence chief.)

One of the biggest Reagan-era democracy interventions was the 1984 El Salvador presidential election, when AID "paid for computers and a voter registration system to help ensure that the elections were credible."[35] Reagan hailed the election victory of Christian Democratic presidential candidate José Napoleon Duarte: "The people of El Salvador have spoken. We, along with other nations committed to a democratic form of government, must heed their courageous action."[36] At the same time that AID aided election mechanics, the CIA covertly bankrolled Duarte "to help ensure the election came out the way the Reagan administration wanted."[37]

GOVERNMENT HANDOUTS FOR FREEDOM

After congressional hearings in the mid-1970s revealed case after case of the CIA's role in subverting foreign governments, manipulating foreign elections, and bribing foreign media, Congress reined in the CIA's subversive activities. The leash on the CIA outraged many American politicians and intellectuals who believed the United States owed it to the world to continue intervening almost any place, any time.

In a speech to the British Parliament on June 8, 1982, President Ronald Reagan declared:

> Let us now begin . . . a crusade for freedom that will engage the faith and fortitude of the next generation. . . . What I am describing now is a plan and a hope for the long term—the march of freedom and democracy which will leave Marxism-Leninism on the ash heap of history as it has left other tyrannies which stifle the freedom and muzzle the self-expression of the people. The objective I propose is . . . to foster the infrastructure of democracy.[38]

The National Endowment for Democracy (NED) was created the following year. Allen Weinstein, the agency's first chief, explained the Endowment's rationale in 1991: "A lot of what we do today was done covertly 25 years ago by the CIA."[39] NED aimed to be cleaner than the CIA—not the loftiest standard.

NED was created because President Reagan believed the federal government was not doing enough to promote democracy abroad despite the fact that the U.S. Information Agency, the Agency for International Development, and various education programs were conducting scores of exchange programs, sending barge loads of publications overseas, and whooping up the American Way around the globe.

NED is based on the notion that its meddling in foreign elections is automatically pro-democracy, because the U.S. government is the incarnation of democracy. NED has always operated on the principle that "what's good for the U.S. government is good for democracy."

NED seeks to provide the U.S. government with deniability for its foreign meddling. NED describes itself as a "private, nonprofit, grant-making organization created . . . to strengthen democratic institutions around the world."[40] In reality, NED is a government agency that launders U.S. tax dollars, removing the taint before foisting them on U.S.-favored groups abroad.

NED was designed to be largely unaccountable. NED is largely a conduit of taxpayer money to the national Democratic and Republican parties (through organizations they created after NED was authorized—the International Republican Institute and the National Democratic Institute), the AFL-CIO, and the Chamber of Commerce. These four organizations have received most of the money NED has distributed, much of which they passed on to consultants, foreign political parties, and other organizations. For many years, NED's board of directors consisted largely of NED grant recipients. The agency was controlled by lobbyists, political hacks, and interest groups on its gravy train, insuring no shortage of "honest graft." Perhaps Congress believed that having a hand in the till is necessary to truly understand the agency and its mission.

NED's second president, Carl Gershman, a former executive director of the Social Democrats USA, a splinter group of the Socialist Party, asserted in August 1984 that direct federal aid to private organizations would allow the United States to "engage in the competition in the world of ideas."[41] Gershman complained that "the word 'democracy' has been appropriated by its enemies"[42] and justified the new agency: "While only Washington can provide adequate funding, the nongovernmental nature of the endowment allows for more flexibility."[43] NED and its advocates talked as if the idea of freedom could not compete without a government subsidy. But people in East Europe were bitterly opposed to Soviet rule not because they received American-subsidized pamphlets, but because they hated being oppressed.

The Endowment quickly begot debacles and backlashes against the United States. Sen. Ernest Hollings (D-S.C.) observed in 1986: "This thing is not the National Endowment for Democracy but the National Endowment for Embarrassment."[44] Rep. John Conyers (D-Mich.) complained: "From its very inception, the National Endowment for Democracy has been riddled with scandal and impropriety."[45]

The General Accounting Office slammed NED in 1985 for improperly diverting $3 million to institutes connected to the Democratic and Republican parties, despite a prohibition of such handouts in a congressional appropriation bill. Rep. Hank Brown (R-Col.) complained: "Congress has made it abundantly clear that it does not want the money it gives to NED to go to the political parties. How can a group that flouts clear congressional intent presume to teach democracy to others?"[46]

The legislation that created NED prohibited the agency from interfering in foreign elections: "Funds may not be expended, either by the endowment or by any of its grantees, to finance the campaigns of candidates for public office."[47] Yet NED intervened in the 1984 Panamanian presidential election, shuffling $150,000 to support Nicholas Ardito Barletta, the candidate favored by the Panamanian military. At that time, the U.S. government opposed military rule in Panama. After NED money financed a huge May Day rally for Barletta, U.S. Ambassador James Biggs wired Washington: "The embassy requests that this harebrained project be abandoned before it hits the fan."[48] Though Barletta won the election, he was later deposed by the military.

The Reagan administration originally justified NED as a way to promote democracy in "totalitarian" states or where "democracy is still fragile."[49] However, one of the first targets of U.S. intervention was France, a nation with almost two centuries of democratic government. Irving Brown, Paris-based director of international relations for the AFL-CIO, explained the use of NED funds: "France . . . is threatened by the Communist apparatus. . . . It is a clear and present danger if the present is thought of as 10 years from now."[50]

The National Inter-University Union, a right-wing French student group, received $575,000 in NED funds. The group had led "numerous anti-government protests, including mass demonstrations [in 1984] against government plans to remove subsidies from private schools."[51] NED never explained why government subsidies for French private schools were a cause worthy of U.S. tax dollars. The grant was justified because the union was a "counterweight to the propaganda efforts of left-wing organizations and professors active within the university system."[52] The *New York Times* noted the student union's "reputed ties to the Service d'Action Civique, an outlawed, extreme-right paramilitary group."[53] The AFL-CIO's Free Trade Union Institute, which funneled NED money to the French group, informed NED's Gershman that the grant was intended to finance "the struggle against anti-democratic forces, the organization of factions teaching organizational techniques, and techniques for staging demonstrations."[54] After a public uproar, Gershman suspended the grant to the French student group "until we clear up questions about its anti-democratic character."[55]

Gershman initially denied that the grant had been secret. However, a memo to Gershman from Eugenia Kemble, director of the Free Trade Union Institute, insisted that NED activities must be kept secret in some countries: "The beneficiaries of these funds would be in danger or in trouble if the financing was made public . . . because repressive governments or groups of communists could use this information against the individuals or the unions that we want to help."[56] A French newspaper reported that "France is on the list of nine countries for which financing is kept secret, along with the Philippines, Chile, Brazil, Nicaragua, Poland, Surinam, Paraguay and others."[57] NED did not disclose details of the grants either in its annual report or in its reports to Congress.[58] (The grants occurred long before American neoconservatives identified France as an enemy of U.S. hegemony.[59])

Another NED target—also a democracy—was Costa Rica. Even though Costa Rica had been a democracy for almost a hundred years, NED money poured into the coffers of the opposition in the mid-to-late 1980s. Almost half a million dollars in NED money was forwarded via the International Republican Institute (IRI) to the Association for the Defense of Costa Rican Liberty and Democracy, widely perceived as a front for the conservative Social Christian Party.[60] (In its previous presidential campaign, the Social Christian Party pocketed $500,000 from Panama's future dictator, Manuel Noriega.) Rafael Angel Calderon, the party's presidential candidate, personally received almost $50,000 in NED funds. Seven Costa Rican legislators complained to the U.S. Congress that the organization "used the [NED] funds to prepare for the 1990 elections."[61] Costa Rican President Oscar Arias Sanchez may have been targeted because he failed to support the Reagan anticommunist agenda in Central America. Rep. Jim Leach (R-Iowa) complained: "I think it's unseemly, both politically and constitutionally. Here you have the Republican Party involved [via the IRI] with the opposition to the government in power, in a country that is the strongest democracy in Latin America and where the head of state won the Nobel Peace Prize" for his peace plan to end the conflict in Nicaragua.[62]

NED's top target in the 1980s was the Sandinista regime in Nicaragua. One Nicaraguan organization, Prodemca, received $400,000 from NED in 1985. The organization proceeded to place full-page advertisements in the *Washington Post, New York Times,* and *Washington Times* urging Congress to vote in favor of giving $100 million in military and other aid to the Nicaraguan Contras.[63]

In late 1988, Reagan requested and Congress approved $2 million "in support of organizations opposing the Sandinistas" in the 1990 elections. Sally Shelton-Colby, a NED director, explained: "There is a lot of Soviet and Cuban money coming into the Sandinistas. This is an attempt to balance that money by helping the democratic forces."[64] The existence of Soviet aid apparently nullified the U.S. statute book.

Toppling the Sandinistas was also a passion of the "kinder, gentler" presidency of George H. W. Bush. When his administration in September 1989 floated a plan to provide $9 million in aid to Violeta Chamorro's campaign, the *Washington Post* noted that "there appears to be strong sentiment now—even among many Democrats opposed to a resumption of covert CIA activities—for making an open, undisguised contribution to Chamorro as a means of demonstrating U.S. support for democracy in Nicaragua."[65] The Associated Press reported that the Bush administration believed that "the U.S. aid would lend credibility to the opposition."[66] Sen. Tom Harkin (D-Iowa) asked: "Do we really want Mrs. Chamorro to be known as the best candidate American money can buy? Do we really want free elections and fair elections in Nicaragua, or do we want an election bought and paid for by the United States government?"[67]

White House press spokesman Marlin Fitzwater justified the $9 million: "It's the only way to help Mrs. Chamorro and the opposition to assure a reasonable shot at free and fair elections."[68] Yet federal law clearly prohibited NED from financing political campaigns. The Associated Press noted, "To reconcile that apparent conflict, endowment officials say they are not helping Mrs. Chamorro but rather Nicaragua's democratic coalition—and that Mrs. Chamorro just happens to be the coalition's candidate to replace Nicaraguan President Daniel Ortega." When the agency gave $100,000 to a paper owned by Chamorro, it claimed the handout was nonpartisan assistance, even though the paper did not offer "equal space" to the Ortega campaign.[69] The U.S. aid went into the coffers of UNO, the coalition of parties and groups supporting Chamorro. Elizabeth Cohn, a professor at Goucher College, noted, "New organizations sprouted in Nicaragua and NED was first on the scene as their primary, sometimes only, funder. NED monies mobilized the opposition and with the enormous amounts of money NED funneled into Nicaragua, they essentially bought the election."[70] NED's Gershman justified the agency's actions: "If we're not going to enter into those situations—supporting democratic groups—we would not be doing our job."[71] NED's supposed "job" counted for far more than mere federal law.

The creation of NED did not deter U.S. presidents from also invoking democracy when invading foreign nations. On December 19, 1989, President George H. W. Bush launched Operation Just Cause, sending 24,000 troops into Panama to depose Manuel Noriega, a dictator whose usefulness to the U.S. government had expired (after more than 15 years on the CIA payroll, during which he was heavily involved in narcotics trafficking). Bush informed the nation: "The goals of the United States have been to safeguard the lives of Americans, to defend democracy in Panama, to combat drug trafficking, and to protect the integrity of the Panama Canal treaty."[72] The U.S. government had previously shown no concern for Panamanian democracy, since the United States propped up dictators and hailed the 1984 election results that were widely criticized as fraudulent. The U.S. invasion resulted in the deaths of 23 U.S. soldiers and up to a thousand Panamanian civilians. Rear Admiral Eugene Carrol of the Center for Defense Information commented that the Panamanian invasion was going to be Bush's "vindication, denial of the wimp factor in spades. So they sent down a force that wasn't going to encounter any effective resistance but simply overwhelm the opposition and . . . cause tremendous peripheral damage, damage to innocent civilians on a wide scale."[73]

RIGGING BEHIND A FALLEN CURTAIN

As communist dictatorships collapsed across East Europe, NED charged into new nations, bankrolling new political parties and favored writers, groups, and others. Soviet dissident Vladimir Bukovsky warned in 1991 that NED aid was undermining freedom of the press: "When the NED, as it does, singles out this or that Emigre magazine or Moscow newspaper to underwrite, it corrupts both the market and the independence of the press; as the prices of paper and printing get pumped up, the unofficial publications find themselves competing for foreign grants, rather than Soviet readers, to survive." Bukovsky noted that the adverse impacts of book subsidies was "a minor annoyance compared to the political corruption being bred by the dollars of the 'promoters of democracy.'" Commenting on NED aid to a Russian Federation judicial commission, he asked, "How many French francs did the Founding Fathers need to write the American Constitution?"[74]

Boasting about U.S.-bought election victories became fashionable in Washington. Sen. John McCain hooted in 1997: "When we provide the democratic opposition in Albania with 12 Jeep Cherokees and they win an election, I'm incredibly proud."[75] Considering the poverty of many nations, even a relatively small intervention by the U.S. government can swing a foreign election.

In Czechoslovakia, NED provided $400,000 to two groups in 1990 that quickly became political parties and benefited from American favoritism (to the dismay of the other 21 political parties). A U.S. government budget document declared that one NED grant to the Civic Forum aimed to "provide the coordinating offices of the Civic Forum in Prague and its regional centers with needed technical equipment, such as facsimile machines, photocopiers and computer systems, in order for them to prepare for the June 8 elections and consolidate their position as Czechoslovakia's premier democratic movement."[76] NED's Gershman insisted the groups were not political parties at the time the agency budgeted the funds: "This process developed after grants were approved and made. It is an evolving situation. It has been our view that we do not side with one party or another."[77] But the groups were political parties by the time they received the first American government handouts.

George Mason University professor Janine Wedel noted in her book *Collision and Collusion,* "In Poland's parliamentary election of 1991, NED funded only the incumbent candidates, who already had an advantage because they had almost exclusive access to the government-owned television, radio and press."[78] A spokesman for the Conference of Independent Poland, a conservative, populist group that helped form Solidarity, testified before Congress: "The idea to support democracy and pluralism is a very good one. But that has nothing to do with using NED funds to bolster leftist groups in Poland while the center and center-right groups receive no funds at all. . . . Leaving all the American assistance in the hand of one political orientation is not acceptable."[79]

The International Republican Institute began pouring NED money into building up a right-leaning Slovakian political party in the mid-1990s. IRI helped pick out a new party leader, Mikulas Dzurinda, and helped draft a political platform entitled "Contract with Slovakia" (modeled after the 1994 Republican "Contract with America"). After Dzurinda won election as prime minister, the cover of the IRI annual report showed a photo of him "pumping his fist in victory." An IRI newsletter bragged that "IRI polls changed the nature of the campaign," and asserted that IRI efforts resulted in "a victory for reformers in Slovakia." [80] In 2002, both the National Democratic Institute and the International Republican Institute were criticized for illegally intervening in Slovak parliamentary elections. The *Slovak Spectator,* the nation's English language newspaper, noted, "The IRI has made no secret about its efforts to influence Slovak politics." [81] The *Spectator* quoted the IRI: "Given that many Slovaks are apathetic and believe all parties to be the same, [the IRI's] efforts will likely play a key role in shaping the election outcome." [82]

VENEZUELA AND THE LIBERATION OF NED

When George W. Bush took office in January 2001, many of his foreign policy advisors sought a far more aggressive U.S. role in the world. At that time, the Venezuelan government of Hugo Chavez was one of the biggest thorns to America in the western hemisphere. Chavez, a demagogue and former paratrooper who led an unsuccessful military coup in 1992, was first elected in 1998 and reelected in 2000. Chavez was repressing free speech, seizing additional power, attacking his enemies, and destabilizing the economy. Even worse, he vigorously opposed U.S. foreign policy.

NED, the State Department, and AID quickly revved up handouts to Chavez's opponents. NED quadrupled its aid to Venezuelan opponents of Chavez in 2001 and early 2002 to almost $1 million. On April 12, 2002, NED grantees were heavily involved in a military coup that left 40 people dead, hundreds wounded, and Chavez deposed. The new government quickly issued decrees dismantling the Congress and the Supreme Court. Bush administration officials rushed to embrace the new rulers. The IRI's Venezuela subsidiary issued an endorsement, saluting the "bravery" of the new rulers and "commending the patriotism of the Venezuelan military." [83] On the day after the coup, IRI president George Folsom proclaimed, "Led by every sector of civil society, the Venezuelan people rose up to defend democracy in their country." [84]

The *New York Times* reported shortly after the coup: "A total of almost $155,000 in NED money was given [via the AFL-CIO] to the Confederation of Venezuelan Workers, the union which led the work stoppages that galvanized the opposition to Mr. Chavez. The union's leader, Carlos Ortega, worked closely with Pedro Carmona Estanga, the businessman who briefly took over from Mr. Chavez, in challenging the government."[85] The IRI received $340,000 for "political party building"[86] in Venezuela—money that heavily subsidized Acción Democrática, a prime coup mover.

The coup fizzled. Many Venezuelans did not accept the story that Chavez voluntarily signed a statement ceding power. Protests erupted and within two days, Chavez was back in command. Six days after the coup's collapse, Secretary of State Colin Powell boldly announced: "We condemn the blows to constitutional order."[87] Two days later, Bush declared, "The administration was very clear when there were troubles on the streets in Venezuela that we support democracy and did not support any extraconstitutional action."[88]

But Powell's and Bush's belated objections did not expunge suspicions of the U.S. government's role in the coup. High-ranking Bush administration officials had met with the coup leaders prior to Chavez's overthrow. One Defense Department official declared: "We were not discouraging people. We were sending informal, subtle signals that we don't like this guy."[89] The *Boston Globe* noted that a NED-funded trip to Washington by Chavez opponents "may have accelerated the events leading to the April 11 uprising."[90] The CIA was aware that the plot to oust Chavez was imminent and alerted dozens of top Bush administration officials. However, after the coup occurred, the Bush administration denied knowing that there would be an attempt to oust Chavez.[91]

Shortly after Chavez's return, NED president Gershman emailed IRI: "By welcoming [the coup]—indeed, without any apparent reservations—you unnecessarily interjected I.R.I. into the sensitive internal politics of Venezuela."[92] This is hilarious—as if NED had not already been hip-deep in Venezuelan politics, bankrolling many of those who became involved in the coup. Was IRI the problem, or was it the briefcases of NED money received by opposition groups? Regardless of the grantees' actions, NED continued full-throttle funding of IRI.

Chris Sabatini, NED's top official for Latin America, declared after Chavez was toppled: "None of our funds in any way were used to support the coup."[93] NED effectively claimed that it was possible to fund the plotters without aiding the plot. A State Department Inspector General report noted that "it is clear that NED's, [the Pentagon's], and other US assistance programs provided training, institution building, and other support to organizations and individuals understood to be actively involved in the events of April 11–14." But the Inspector General stressed that "we found no evidence that this support directly contributed, or was intended to contribute, to that event."[94] This was not an exhaustive investigation. *Nation* noted that the IG "investigators decided not to interview any Venezuelans, and so they heard from no witnesses who could challenge what embassy officials told the IG."[95] Perhaps NED officials believed they must be presumed innocent unless NED wrote checks specifically for "coup-related activities."

After the failed coup, NED continued heavily intervening in Venezuela, pouring a million dollars a year into the coffers of opposition groups and other entities. In 2003, NED gave $53,400 to a Venezuelan organization promoting a recall campaign to remove Chavez from power. (The recall flopped.)[96]

AID is pouring even more money into the Venezuelan opposition—$15 million between mid-2002 and 2005. AID set up an "Office of Transition Initiatives" in the Venezuelan capital, Caracas. *Newsday* noted, "The suggestion in the name was that Venezuela needed to transition to a new government. Although AID officials said the office's purpose was only to help a country in crisis, they posted a job opening on their Web site that described Chavez as 'slowly hijacking the machinery of government.'"[97] AID refuses to disclose who is receiving its windfalls, and the Venezuelan government is prosecuting some NED grant recipients.

Venezuelans are in a hard situation, with a democratically elected leader who is increasingly acting like a dictator. However, as *Newsday* observed in May 2005, the effort by NED and AID to "oust" Chavez was "so poorly implemented that experts say the net result has been to solidify Chavez's hold on power and has led U.S. senators to worry that administration policy could provoke Chavez into suspending oil shipments, which currently account for 15 percent of U.S. imports."[98]

NED's debacle in Venezuela should have permanently branded the agency as incompetent and untrustworthy. Instead, after the U.S. military failed to discover weapons of mass destruction in Iraq, NED garnered even more attention. Bush needed a new rationale for the war with Iraq. Embracing Messianic Democracy helped him idealize his aggression. Bush hailed NED as his intellectual storm troopers in a speech on the twentieth anniversary of NED's creation: "By speaking for and standing for freedom, you've lifted the hopes of people around the world, and you've brought great credit to America. . . . Each of you at this Endowment is fully engaged in the great cause of liberty." Bush evoked the great memories of earlier times: "This very week in 1989, there were protests in East Berlin and in Leipzig. By the end of that year, every communist dictatorship in Central America* had collapsed."[99] The White House press office added the asterisk on the official text, explaining that Bush actually meant Central Europe.

RE-SAVING HAITIAN DEMOCRACY

Haiti is one of the most frequent recipients of democratic salvation from the United States. In the early 1990s, Haiti's elected ruler, Jean-Bertrand Aristide, became increasingly despotic, encouraging his supporters to kill opponents and critics by placing burning automobile tires around their necks.[100] After Aristide was toppled in August 1991, the United States and the United Nations slapped embargos on Haiti, worsening the island's economic misery and spurring more Haitians to flee to Florida in leaky boats.

In September 1994, President Clinton sent 20,000 troops into Haiti in Operation Uphold Democracy, ejecting the military rulers, and restoring Aristide to power. Clinton hailed the efforts of American soldiers: "The work you're doing is helping the Haitian people win their fight for freedom and democracy. It's making possible the return of an honestly elected government. It's proving to the world that the United States will stand up for democracy in our hemisphere."[101] NED and other federal agencies "poured in more than $100 million in democracy aid in the five years following" the U.S. invasion.[102]

Aristide became increasingly brutal and intolerant, though he managed to win reelection. In February 2004, an array of NED-aided groups and individuals played key roles in a coup that left 100 people dead and toppled Aristide. Prior to the coup, the U.S. Embassy in Haiti reportedly protested that the International Republican Institute's partisan efforts were "undermining the official U.S. policy of working with all sides in Haiti."[103]

ELBOWING THE UKRAINE

The U.S. government pulled out all the stops to help a U.S.-favored candidate win a free and fair election in 2004 in the Ukraine. In the two years prior to the election, the U.S. government spent over $65 million "to aid political organizations in Ukraine, paying to bring opposition leader Viktor Yushchenko to meet U.S. leaders and helping to underwrite exit polls indicating he won a disputed runoff election."[104] Bush proclaimed that "Any election [in Ukraine], if there is one, ought to be free from any foreign influence."[105]

The feds exuded the usual sanctimony regarding their Ukrainian foray. State Department spokesman Richard Boucher declared: "Our money doesn't go to candidates; it goes to the process, the institutions that it takes to run a free and fair election."[106] White House Press Secretary Scott McClellan said, "There's accountability in place. We make sure that money is being used for the purposes for which it's assigned or designated."[107] However, Rep. Ron Paul (R-Tex.) complained: "We do not know exactly how many millions—or tens of millions—of dollars the United States government spent on the presidential election in Ukraine. We do know that much of that money was targeted to assist one particular candidate, and that through a series of cut-out nongovernmental organizations—both American and Ukrainian—millions of dollars ended up in support of the presidential candidate, Viktor Yushchenko."[108] NED's proselytizing for Yushchenko could prove costly for American taxpayers. Yushchenko addressed Congress shortly after his victory and appealed for a massive increase in U.S. foreign aid for his country. The U.S. intervention into the Ukrainian election heightened tensions with Russia. Rather than a pillar of freedom, the new Ukrainian government busied itself re-nationalizing factories, expanding state monopolies, imposing price controls, boosting taxes, and unleashing tax police (widely perceived to be lawless).[109]

IRAQ AND OPERATION FOUNDING FATHERS

In a late February 2003 Washington speech, Bush invoked democracy to sanc-tify his pending war. Bush condescended: "The nation of Iraq—with its proud heritage, abundant resources and skilled and educated people—is fully capa-ble of moving toward democracy and living in freedom." Bush then showed how the coming war would be a stepping stone to lasting peace: "The world has a clear interest in the spread of democratic values, because stable and free nations do not breed the ideologies of murder."[110] But Bush's March 18, 2003, memo to Congress, notifying them that he was invading Iraq, mentioned nothing about democracy as a *causa belli*.

In fact, suppressing democracy was one of the first orders of business for the U.S. occupation authorities. Three and a half months after the fall of Baghdad, U.S. military commanders "ordered a halt to local elections and self-rule in provincial cities and towns across Iraq, choosing instead to install their own handpicked mayors and administrators, many of whom are former Iraqi military leaders," the *Washington Post* reported.[111] Many Iraqis were out-raged to see Saddam's former henchmen placed back in power over them. But a sergeant with the U.S. Army Civil Affairs Battalion running the city of Samarra explained that Iraqis must be content with political "baby steps."[112] U.S. viceroy Paul Bremer insisted that there was "no blanket prohibition" against Iraqi self-rule, but added, "Elections that are held too early can be de-structive. It's got to be done very carefully." Bremer feared that the chaos that followed the toppling of both Saddam and Saddam statutes would not be conducive to electing positive thinkers: "In a postwar situation like this, if you start holding elections, the people who are rejectionists tend to win."[113] And the U.S. military presence would likely be one of the first things freely elected Iraqis would have rejected. Moqtada Sadr, a Muslim cleric whose forces would later fight American troops, protested Bremer's action: "I call for free elections that will represent all Iraqi opinion, far away from the influence of those who have intervened."[114]

The early suppression of popular government helped turn many Iraqis against the U.S. occupation. But, as Noah Feldman, the Coalition Provisional Authority's law advisor, explained in November 2003: "If you move too fast, the wrong people could get elected."[115] The repeated delays of elections were partly the result of the Bush administration's lack of enthusiasm for Iraqi self-rule—as well as its fear that pro-Iran Shiites would win an honest election. The Bush administration initially sought to install Washington favorite Ahmad Chalabi, an Iraqi exile whose false statements on WMD helped sway the U.S. government to invade, as Iraq's ruler. University of Michigan history professor Juan Cole, one of the most respected American experts on the Middle East, observed, "If it had been up to Bush, Iraq would have been a soft dictatorship."[116] The Bush administration finally agreed to hold elections after Grand Ayatollah al-Sistani, the most powerful religious leader in Iraq, sent his followers into the streets demanding an opportunity to vote.

The elections that were eventually held on January 30, 2005, had more in common with a Soviet–era East Bloc election than with a New England town meeting. In the weeks before the vote, the U.S. military carried out Operation Founding Fathers. In Samarra, the get-out-and-vote message was broadcast from loudspeakers at the same time American troops, leaping out of Bradley fighting vehicles, raided and searched people's homes. The messages, taped in Arabic, were part of a selection including "Election news," "Freedom to vote," and "Love and family."[117] In Mosul, U.S. troops put up posters on destroyed buildings that declared: "The terrorists did this to the people of Mosul. They will continue to destroy unless you say, 'Enough is enough.'"[118] No posters were created to affix to buildings destroyed by U.S. bombs and tanks.

U.S. military convoys rolled through Mosul neighborhoods shortly after sunrise on Election Day "with speakers blaring messages urging everyone to vote."[119] Soldiers also passed out thousands of sample ballots. As part of the election campaign, U.S. soldiers rounded up tens of thousands of Iraqis; the United States had more Iraqis under lock-and-key by Election Day than even in the months after the invasion. The U.S. military was so desperate for control that they even dictated bedtimes for government workers. *Newsday* reported, "In their preparations for facilitating Iraq's foray into democracy, Americans made sure Iraqi election workers got to bed early on the eve of the vote, demanding they be tucked in by 11 P.M."

Carina Perelli, the top UN election official, condemned the role of U.S. troops, complaining that "the U.S. military have been extremely, I would say, overenthusiastic in trying to help out with this election."[120] Prior to the election, the Bush team portrayed voter turnout as the measure of Iraqi approval of the U.S. invasion. Bush predicted that "millions of Iraqi voters will show their bravery, their love of country and their desire to live in freedom" by voting.[121]

The U.S. military efforts to boost voter turnout coined a bogus seal of legitimacy for the U.S. invasion of Iraq.

In some places, the polling places were kept secret until the last minute. Most of the candidates' names were kept secret, not even listed on the ballot. The vast majority of candidates never publicly campaigned, fearing assassination. There was no open airing of issues in the media, as the Iraqi government suppressed newspaper and television criticism of Allawi and his government's policies. The government sought to blindfold voters before voters passed judgment on the government. Some Iraqis were told they would be denied food rations if they did not vote.[122]

In most cases, voters had the option only of choosing certain lists—a Kurdish list, a Shia list, or similar groupings. As Ken Sanders, an Arizona lawyer and prominent analyst on the Internet, noted, "Iraqi voters were more or less compelled to vote for an ethnic group, national group, or religious faction. The make-up of the ballot essentially prevented Iraqis from voting for a particular person or political party."[123] The so-called Independent Iraqi Electoral Commission, which had been appointed by U.S. viceroy Bremer, had "absolute power to bar any candidate or organization and has done so. Those who have been barred by the Commission received neither due process nor an explanation why. Thus, the U.S., through its proxy, established the rules for the election and determined who could and could not be a candidate therein," Sanders observed.[124]

The fact that votes were counted was supposedly sufficient to make the election results the will of the majority. However, after the voting was finished in Mosul, "American troops loaded ballots and Iraqi election officials into their armored vehicles and drove them inside the walls of an Army camp, where they nudged tired workers to keep counting,"[125] *Newsday* noted.

Bush proclaimed on the day of the vote that the elections were a "resounding success" and that "the world is hearing the voice of freedom from the center of the Middle East."[126] NED's Gershman hailed the Iraqi elections as "one of the great events in the history of democracy." The American media largely parroted the official line. A few days later, in his State of the Union Address, Bush stated that the elections showed that "the Iraqi people value their own liberty." In words that failed to alarm enough viewers, Bush added, "Americans recognize that spirit of liberty, because we share it."[127] The fact that so few questions and criticisms were raised about an election so obviously tainted illustrates how, for most of the American media, "democracy" is simply whatever the U.S. government says it is. The same newspapers that would have denounced similar abuses in an East Bloc regime or in a Third World tinhorn dictatorship embraced and broadcast the Bush administration's ludicrous claims.

Less than six weeks after the Iraqi elections, the U.S. government revealed a new standard for the purity of Middle East elections. On March 8, 2005, Bush declared that "All Syrian military and intelligence personnel must withdraw before the Lebanese elections for those elections to be free and fair."[128] Bush's comment evoked scant ridicule, despite the brazen U.S. military intervention in the Iraqi election.

After the Iraq election was canonized as a great victory for Bush, other details leaked out showing how the U.S. government manipulated the vote. After it became clear by mid-2004 that pro-American parties were going to get clobbered, President Bush signed a secret authorization for the U.S. government to provide covert aid to Iraqi parties and politicians. However, when senior members of Congress were briefed on the plan (as required by law), they hit the roof. House Minority Leader Nancy Pelosi reportedly objected: "Did we have eleven hundred Americans [soldiers] die [as of that time] so they could have a rigged election?"[129] The Bush administration then canceled its formal covert aid plan. However, the administration carried out the covert aid plan anyhow, using back channels and undercover operators that could be kept secret from Congress as well as the American public. Seymour Hersh reported in the *New Yorker* in July 2005 that "the White House promulgated a highly classified Presidential 'finding' authorizing the C.I.A. to provide money and other support covertly to political candidates in certain countries who, in the Administration's view, were seeking to spread democracy."[130] A former high-ranking CIA official confirmed that the Iraq election was a primary target for the aid.[131] Les Campbell, a top official with the National Democratic Institute, observed, "It became clear that Allawi and his coalition had huge resources, although nothing was flowing through normal channels. He had very professional and very sophisticated media help and saturation television coverage."[132] Ghassan Atiyyah, director of the Baghdad-based Iraq Foundation for Development and Democracy, declared that Allawi's 15 percent final election result (compared to his poll numbers of 3 percent or 4 percent before the vote) "was due to American manipulation of the election. There's no doubt about it. The Americans, directly or indirectly, spent millions on Allawi." Atiyyah complained that "as long as real democratic practices are not adhered to, you Americans cannot talk about democracy."[133] (The Shiite parties apparently also cheated.)

National Security Council spokesman Frederick Jones, asked about the Hersh allegations, insisted that the Bush administration "adopted a policy that we would not try to influence the outcome of the Iraqi election by covertly helping individual candidates for office."[134] But Jones would not answer questions regarding "whether any political parties had benefited from covert support," the *Washington Post* noted.[135] The entire U.S. operation was "legal" only in the sense that it occurred as a result of a secret presidential command—not an auspicious start for a foreign would-be democracy.

WASHINGTON VS. BUSH

In his Farewell Address in 1796, President George Washington warned against "the insidious wiles of foreign influence . . . since history and experience prove that foreign influence, is one of the most baneful foes of republican government."[136] Washington did not offer a long list of asterisks to this truth—he did not say that foreign influence would be welcome if it only helped build up political parties, or merely paid for their "get out the vote drives," image consultants for favored candidates, or newspapers to sing the tune of a foreign government.

Washington warned Americans that

> a passionate attachment of one nation for another . . . gives to ambitious, corrupted, or deluded citizens (who devote themselves to the favorite nation), facility to betray or sacrifice the interests of their own country, without odium, sometimes even with popularity. . . . Such attachments are particularly alarming to the truly enlightened and independent patriot. How many opportunities do they afford to tamper with domestic factions, to practice the arts of seduction, to mislead public opinion, to influence or awe the public councils? Such an attachment of a small or weak toward a great and powerful nation dooms the former to be the satellite of the latter.[137]

The current president is not constrained by the principles or prejudices of the first president. On May 18, 2005, Bush, speaking at an International Republican Institute dinner, hailed IRI for two decades of "strengthening political parties" in foreign countries. Bush explicitly portrayed world freedom as dependent on American paternalism: "So we have a great responsibility: We must help these young democracies build the free institutions that will protect their liberty and extend it for future generations."[138] Bush promised that "in the coming years, we will increasingly focus funding on programs to help new democracies after the elections are over." In other words, the United States will perpetually fix foreign elections—in the name of self-government. When the most recent democracy-promoting boom began in the 1980s, many people thought the U.S. government simply intended to provide one-time assistance to formerly oppressed nations. But the policy quickly shifted from offering a single jump-start to claiming the right to impose a tune-up whenever the U.S. government sees fit.

Bush talked as if foreigners could not learn how to tie their political shoes without the aid of a U.S. government expert: "By helping people build these institutions and develop the habits of liberty, you are helping them transform new democracies into lasting free societies." Bush told IRI members and donors: "We need you to help the democratic reformers you have trained make the transition from dissidents to elected legislators—by teaching them how to build coalitions, set legislative agendas, and master unfamiliar skills . . . like constituent service." Since the attendees were carefully pre-screened, no one hooted aloud at the bizarre notion that the U.S. government must teach foreign politicians how to answer letters from local citizens.

Furthermore, Bush declared, "We need you to help businesses in new market economies organize trade associations and chambers of commerce—so they can promote pro-growth economic policies." Perhaps Bush is not familiar with economist Adam Smith's warning that: "People of the same trade seldom meet together, even for merriment and diversion, but the conversation ends in a conspiracy against the public, or in some contrivance to raise prices."[139] In the United States, many trade associations are primarily concerned with restraint of trade—lobbying for tariffs, licensing restrictions, or other government barriers to protect citizens from the curse of competition. The time of the greatest influence of U.S. trade associations—in the 1920s and the 1930s—was also the time when federal and state governments did the most to make consumers into serfs of businesses.

In his IRI dinner speech, the president also revealed that "We need you to teach newly-elected governments the importance of building public support for their policies and programs—as well as how to effectively engage a free news media." Grown men and women don't need lessons on how to tell the truth. But Bush's idea of "effectively engage" is akin to other people's definition of propaganda and cover-ups.

THE TERRORISM FINANCING ANALOGY

Some Americans shrug off the falsehoods that Bush and earlier American presidents have told about spreading democracy as simply "politics as usual." But, for the residents of foreign nations who have been subjugated or exploited as a result of U.S. intervention, these are not harmless throwaway speech lines. Many advocates of Messianic Democracy make a grand distinction between "military intervention" and "money intervention." There is a presumption that merely intervening with buckets of cash is benign. Yet no foreigner supposedly has a right to object to the U.S. government trying to buy an election victory in their nation.

Few Americans concede the same right to foreign governments. For instance, in 1996, the Chinese government was widely suspected of having provided covert financing for the Clinton reelection campaign (the Clinton campaign denied received any such funds). Some Republicans were ready to impeach Clinton on this alone, and the allegations were enough to convince many conservatives that Clinton was guilty of treason.

U.S. aid to foreign political parties is judged by the mirror image of the standard the U.S. Justice Department uses for terrorist financing prosecutions. If a terrorist group claimed it was innocent because it merely sent large contributions to a front group organization later involved in a violent attack, U.S. prosecutors would laugh them out of court and into prison. But the same sleight-of-hand is supposed to be laudatory when done by the U.S. government. The same standard that applies to terrorist financing should apply to political manipulation. This is especially true since many foreign nations view a de facto effort to take over their government the same way that many Americans view a terrorist attack.

The Justice Department has never prosecuted any NED officials or grant recipients for illegally meddling in foreign elections. The ban on financing campaigns of candidates for public office is simply window dressing: a prohibition against meddling proves NED doesn't meddle. Perhaps the Justice Department assumes that as long as U.S. influence grows, the crimes are victimless.

The U.S. government is currently spending roughly $1.5 billion a year on democracy promotion. But the United States is spending far more to buttress repression than it is to spread democracy. Oppressive regimes such as those in Egypt, Pakistan, Uzbekistan, and Turkmenistan are receiving more than $5 billion a year in foreign aid from the U.S. government.[140] The military and financial aid delivered to dictators is a subsidy for suppressing democracy. Yet, merely talking about democracy apparently absolves Bush for propping up dictators (as it absolved presidents Clinton, Bush Sr., Reagan, and Jimmy Carter). It is ironic that Washington debates often turn on the choice between supporting dictators and spreading democracy. It is as if "mind our own business" is not on the official list of options.

HUFFING IN THE NAME OF DEMOCRACY

NED's democracy efforts—along with those of other federal agencies—have never suffered a shortage of hype. Thomas Carothers noted that, from the mid-1980s to the mid-1990s, "U.S. officials hailed almost every political opening, no matter how partial or hesitant, as a 'democratic revolution.' They portrayed the new democracy aid programs as critical boosts to democracy's future in the recipient countries." Carothers commented on the wave of de-mocratization that began in the 1980s: "The fact that in most regions U.S. ef-forts to promote democracy were largely responses to rather than causes of democratic transitions got lost in the excitement. Americans got in the habit in those years of taking far too much credit for the democratic transitions in Latin America, Asia, Africa, and Eastern Europe."[141]

Rep. Major Owens (D-N.Y.) declared in early 2005: "Our great nation is the premium democratic government of the world and we are all proud of that fact."[142] Owens's comment typifies how many politicians and many normal Americans view democracy. Unfortunately, this pride can spur the belief that the United States is innately capable of edifying all nations. This is the same mindset that permeated the Peace Corps. From the 1960s onward, the Peace Corps acted as if growing up in the United States guaranteed that people would have valuable skills to impart to backward foreigners—regardless if someone was an Art History major sent to Upper Volta to help raise chick-ens.[143] Just because foreign peoples are oppressed doesn't mean that Americans have the answer. Democracy promotion suffers the same inherent flaws as other aid programs. The system becomes geared to political bragging rights, rather than foreign results. Carothers noted: "Democracy assistance proj-ects . . . often emphasize high-visibility activities that seem designed less to meet the needs of the recipient countries than to play well in Washington, in particular to satisfy the unrealistic demands of a Congress determined to see an immediate impact for taxpayer dollars spent abroad."[144]

The fact that the current machinations to peddle democracy are portrayed as triumphs of idealism illustrates how degraded most of the nation's political establishment and media have become. NED scorns the law, muddles foreign elections, and taunts the intelligence of both Americans and foreigners (claim-ing to be independent, when almost all its money comes from the federal gov-ernment). And yet—regardless of how brazen the core falsehoods—most of the media and establishment embrace the agency. As New Republic editor Michael Kinsley observed, "What we have here is a pork barrel for intellectuals. Money for study grants, for travel, for conferences, and especially for layers of admin-istration, as the government gives money to the Endowment, which gives it to a Foundation to give it to an Institute to fund a fellowship program."[145]

CONCLUSION

There seems to be a tacit presumption in Washington that if an anti-U.S. can-didate wins a foreign election, the election was flawed. The spread of pro-U.S. regimes is apparently the same as the triumph of the will of the people, since the people are or should be pro-U.S. And, as Rousseau wrote of the wisdom of the people: "The General Will is always in the right, but the judgment which guides it is not always enlightened."[146] Anyone who is not pro-America—or, more accurately, pro-U.S. government—apparently needs U.S. intervention to become enlightened.

Many Americans are enthusiastic about spreading democracy because they believe that common folks everywhere naturally recognize the goodness of the United States and will enthusiastically support U.S. foreign policy goals. U.S. democracy-spreading seeks to remove the political impediments that prevent the United States from being as universally loved as it deserves to be. Thus, spreading democracy will purportedly solve most of the foreign policy challenges that the United States now faces. This is akin to the belief that U.S. troops would be greeted with hugs and flowers when they invaded Iraq.

Many Messianic Democracy advocates do not stoop to deal with the intense anti-American sentiments in so many foreign countries, especially in the Middle East. Many U.S. policymakers and commentators seem unable to recognize that foreigners resent foreign interference—regardless of the nation that is interfering. As Carothers noted, "Partisan [foreign] interventions feed the tendency of citizens in many transitional countries to believe that their political system is controlled by powerful, obscure outside forces and thus devalue their own role in choosing or influencing their government."[147]

The problem is not simply George W. Bush. The problem is a perennial American attitude. Now that the United States is the world's sole military superpower—at least for the time being—this attitude is far more dangerous, because it is easier for Americans and Washington policymakers to blind themselves both to the limits of U.S. power and to foreign hatred caused by U.S. meddling. Instead, policy is driven by the attitude that America is God's gift to the world, and that those who reject American "help" are insulting God, as well as Washington. This is a new form of U.S. manifest destiny—aiming not to militarily conquer foreign lands, but merely install pro-U.S. governments over foreign peoples.

The fact that American presidents have lied so often about spreading democracy does not prove the falseness of current or future presidential assertions. However, it does not stack the deck in favor of credulity. Unfortunately, Americans are more gullible on democracy than on most topics. Irving Babbitt noted in 1924 that democracy is "likely to be idealistic in its feelings about itself, but imperialistic in its practice."[148] The invocations of democracy to sanctify U.S. government foreign interventions profoundly delude many Americans. Insofar as citizens buy into the "good versus evil" storyline, they become unable to recognize U.S. government machinations abroad, or to see why foreigners resent interference just as heartily as do Americans.

Yet, it is a bit misleading to talk about democracy missionary work—since most missionary groups do not engage in wholesale slaughter. The missionary rhetoric is often a front for power politics. And the issue is not whether such invocations deceive informed critics—but whether they provide enough cover on the homefront to perpetuate foreign interventions.

There is no honest way to "fix" foreign elections. Any such interventions will be plagued by mendacity, deceit, and incompetence. Rep. Hank Brown (R-Col.), the most effective early critic of NED, commented in 1984: "It is a contradiction to try to promote free elections by interfering in them. But this is exactly what N.E.D. has done."[149] When the U.S. government picks foreign winners, democracy loses. The United States talks about democracy as if democratic processes are some type of balm that can heal all of a society's problems—and then U.S. interventionists trumpet the notion that the most important thing is who wins.

The greatest gift the United States can give the aspiring democrats of the world is an example that is a shining city on a hill. As University of Pennsylvania professor Walter McDougall observed, "The best way to promote our institutions and values abroad is to strengthen them at home."[150] But there is scant glory for politicians in restraining their urge to "save humanity." The ignorance of the average American has provided no check on "run amok" politicians and bureaucrats.

CHAPTER 5

Lying and Legitimacy

See, in my line of work you got to keep repeating things over and over and over again for the truth to sink in, to kind of catapult the propaganda.
—President George W. Bush, May 24, 2005[1]

The struggle of man against power is the struggle of memory against forgetting.
—Czech novelist Milan Kundera[2]

DOES THE RIGHT TO RULE NOW INCLUDE the right to lie? Is lying simply another perk of the contemporary presidency? Is the president now considered above the truth, the same way that presidents have often acted above the Constitution?

Probably not since Calvin Coolidge has there been a president who appeared more honest at the finish of his term than at the start. And yet, presidential lies are routinely treated as harmless errors, regardless of how many thousand Americans are killed or maimed as a result.

The media routinely responds to political lies as if they were mere unpleasantries or inevitabilities, scarcely more noteworthy than the sun rising in the East. Historian Hannah Arendt noted in 1971 that anyone who considers that "lies have always been regarded as justifiable tools in political dealings . . . can only be surprised how little attention has been paid, in our tradition of philosophical and political thought, to their significance."[3]

It is a grave error to view a politician's lies like other people's lies. There is a big difference between lying about "the check is in the mail" and lying about "their weapons are going to kill us, so we must kill them first." The lies of the ruler are not idle throwaway lines—they are backed by deadly force.

But today, the scant response to official lies implies that people believe that politicians can deceive citizens without wronging them. This is part of the reason why so little serious attention is paid to political lies. It is as if all the traditional warnings about the dangers of lies are waived when it comes to politics and government. Lies are dangerous, unless the liar can destroy you. Or perhaps the more power a person seeks, the more harmless his lies become.

It is only about once a decade, or once a generation, that the issue of political lying leads the news for more than a week or two in a row. Yet, the aberration is in the media focus, not in the quantity of lying. The novelty is that some people decide that other people should get riled about official lies. The difference is that embers are fanned instead of doused.

The contemporary attitude toward lies is far different than that of the Founders' era. Prof. Gordon Wood, in his masterpiece, *The Radicalism of the American Revolution*, noted, "Eighteenth-century Englishmen were preoccupied with moral character of their leaders precisely because leaders were the source of despotism."[4] The nonchalant attitude toward rulers' lies is in large part the result of the nonchalant attitude toward Leviathan. Because of Attention Deficit Democracy, many people have forgotten the danger of nearly boundless power unconstrained by the truth.

This chapter will focus primarily on lies related to wars, as these are the boldest and most costly lies. Lies related to budgets, taxes, and policies could be piled from here to the moon. But it is when the stakes are highest—when blood is on the line—that a president's trampling of the truth becomes most striking.

BIG LIES IN AMERICAN HISTORY

Mendacity is no novelty in American politics. In the mid-1800s, people joked about political candidates who claimed to have been born in a log cabin that they built with their own hands. This jibe was spurred by William Henry Harrison's false claim of such a politically virgin birth in the 1840 presidential campaign. Professor Eric Alterman, in his book *When Presidents Lie*, observed that "presidential deceptions . . . are the presidential rule rather than the exception."[5]

In 1846, President James Polk took Americans to war after falsely proclaiming that the Mexican army had crossed the U.S. border and attacked a

U.S. army outpost—"shedding the blood of our citizens on our own soil." Though Polk refused to provide any details of where the attack occurred, the accusation swayed enough members of Congress to declare war against Mexico.

In 1917, Wilson took the nation to war in a speech to Congress that contained one howler after another. Wilson proclaimed that "self-governed nations do not fill their neighbor states with spies"—despite the role of the British secret service and propaganda operations in the prior years to breed war fever in the United States. Wilson hailed Russia as a nation that had always been "democratic at heart"—less than a month after the fall of the Czars, and not long before the Bolshevik Revolution. Wilson proclaimed that the government would show its friendship and affection for German-Americans at home—but his administration was soon spearheading loyalty drives that spread terror in many communities across the land.[6]

In 1940, in one of his final speeches of the presidential campaign, President Franklin Roosevelt assured voters: "Your president says this country is not going to war."[7] At the time, Roosevelt was violating the Neutrality Act by providing massive military assistance to Britain and was searching high and low for a way to bring the United States into war against Hitler.

In his 1944 State of the Union address, Roosevelt denounced those Americans with "such suspicious souls—who feared that I have made 'commitments' for the future which might pledge this Nation to secret treaties" at the summit of Allied leaders in Tehran the previous month.[8] In early 1945, FDR told Congress that the Yalta Agreement "spells the end of the system of unilateral action and exclusive alliance and spheres of influence." In reality, FDR signed off on Soviet domination of East Europe and the crushing of any hopes for democracy in Poland.

In August 1945, President Harry Truman announced to the world that "the first atomic bomb was dropped on Hiroshima, a military base. That was because we wished in this first attack to avoid, in so far as possible, the killing of civilians."[9] Hiroshima was actually a major city with more than a third of a million people prior to its incineration.

Presidential and other government lies on foreign policy are often discounted because they are presumed to be motivated by national security. But, as Arendt noted in an essay on the Pentagon Papers, during the Vietnam war, "the policy of lying was hardly ever aimed at the enemy but chiefly if not exclusively destined for domestic consumption, for propaganda at home and especially for the purpose of deceiving Congress."[10] CIA analysts did excellent work in the early period of the Vietnam conflict. But, "in the contest between public statements, always over-optimistic, and the truthful reports of the intelligence community, persistently bleak and ominous, the public statements were likely to win simply because they were public," Arendt commented.[11]

The truth never had a chance when it did not serve Lyndon Johnson's political calculations.

Vietnam destroyed the credibility of both President Lyndon Johnson and the American military. Yet, the memory of the pervasive lies of the military establishment did not curb the gullibility of many people for fresh government-created falsehoods a decade or so later. During the 1980s, the U.S. State Department ran a propaganda campaign that placed numerous articles in the U.S. media praising the Nicaraguan Contras and attacking the Sandinista regime. As the *Christian Science Monitor* noted in 2002, the State Department "fed the *Miami Herald* a make-believe story that the Soviet Union had given chemical weapons to the Sandinistas. Another tale, which happened to emerge the night of President Ronald Reagan's [1984] reelection victory, held that Soviet MiG fighters were on their way to Nicaragua." The General Accounting Office investigated and concluded that the State Department operation was illegal, consisting of "prohibited, covert propaganda activities."[12] There was no backlash against the government when the frauds were disclosed. Instead, it was on to the next scam.

President Reagan paved the way for subsequent presidents in immersing antiterrorist policy in fogbanks of falsehoods. In October 1983, a month after Reagan authorized U.S. Marine commanders to call in air strikes against Muslims to help the Christian forces in Lebanon's civil war, a Muslim suicide bomber devastated a U.S. Marine barrack in Beirut, killing 242 Americans. In a televised speech a few days later, Reagan portrayed the attack as unstoppable, falsely claiming that the truck "crashed through a series of barriers, including a chain-link fence and barbed-wire entanglements. The guards opened fire, but it was too late."[13] In reality, the guards did not fire because they were prohibited from having loaded weapons—one of many pathetic failures of defense that the Reagan administration sought to sweep under the table. In 1984, after the second successful devastating attack in 18 months against a poorly defended U.S. embassy in Lebanon, Reagan blamed the debacle on his predecessor and falsely asserted that the Carter administration had "to a large extent" gotten "rid of our intelligence agents."[14] A few days later, while campaigning for reelection, Reagan announced that the second embassy bombing was no longer an issue: "We've had an investigation. There was no evidence of any carelessness or anyone not performing their duty."[15] However, the Reagan administration had not yet begun a formal investigation. On May 4, 1986, Reagan bragged: "The United States gives terrorists no rewards and no guarantees. We make no concessions; we make no deals."[16] However, the Iranian arms-for-hostage deal that leaked out later that year blew such claims to smithereens. On November 13, 1986, Reagan denied initial reports of the scandal, proclaiming that the "'no concessions' [to terrorists] policy remains in force, in spite of the wildly speculative and false stories about arms for hostages and alleged ransom payments. We did not—repeat—did not trade weapons or anything else for hostages nor will we."[17] But Americans later learned that the United States had sold 2,000 antitank weapons to the Iranian government "in return for promises to release the American hostages there. Money from the sale of those weapons went to support the Contras' war in Nicaragua."[18]

Saddam Hussein's invasion of Kuwait in the summer of 1990 provided a challenge for the first Bush administration to get Americans mobilized. In September 1990, the Pentagon announced that up to a quarter million Iraqi troops were near the border of Saudi Arabia, threatening to give Saddam Hussein a stranglehold on one of the world's most important oil sources. The Pentagon based its claim on satellite images that it refused to disclose. One American paper, the *St. Petersburg Times,* purchased two Soviet satellite "images taken of that same area at the same time that revealed that there were no Iraqi troops 'near the Saudi border—just empty desert.'"[19] Jean Heller, the journalist who broke the story, commented, "That [Iraqi buildup] was the whole justification for Bush sending troops in there, and it just didn't exist."[20] Even a decade after the first Gulf war, the Pentagon refused to disclose the secret photos that justified sending half a million American troops into harm's way. Support for the war was also whipped up via congressional testimony of a Kuwaiti teenager who claimed she had seen Iraqi soldiers removing hundreds of babies from incubators in Kuwaiti hospitals and leaving them on the floor to die. President George H. W. Bush often invoked the incubator tale to justify the war, proclaiming that the "ghastly atrocities" were akin to "Hitler revisited."[21] After the United States commenced bombing Iraq, it emerged that the woman who testified was the daughter of the Kuwaiti ambassador and that her story was a complete fabrication concocted in part by a U.S. public relations firm. Dead babies were a more effective selling point than one of the initial justifications Bush announced for U.S. intervention—restoring Kuwait's "rightful leaders to their place"—as if any Americans gave a damn about putting Arab oligarchs back on their throne. (A few months before Saddam's invasion, Amnesty International condemned the Kuwaiti government for allegedly torturing detainees.)[22]

CLINTON'S BLOODY ANTI-GENOCIDE CHARADE

In the last 30 years, the only presidential lie that had sticking power with the American public was Clinton's assertion that "I did not have sex with that woman—Miss Lewinsky." Everything else faded. It was not as if Clinton had a general reputation for honesty prior to 1998. The "did not have sex" lie was preceded by scores, if not hundreds, of other false statements on public policy.[23]

Clinton lied, among other things, about his AmeriCorps program (perennially labeling the paid recruits "volunteers"), about his trade record (portraying almost 200 U.S. dictates restricting foreign textile imports as agreements to remove foreign barriers to American exports),[24] about being "the only president who knew something about agriculture when I got" to the White House,[25] about the burnings of black churches in Arkansas when he was growing up,[26] and about how "the Brady law stopped half a million criminals from getting guns."[27] He also lied when he told a Democratic National Committee dinner that "we abolished assault weapons" (the 1994 law grandfathered in existing so-called assault weapons)[28] and when he claimed that the FBI took "no provocative action" at Waco prior to their final tank-and-gas assault.[29]

Yet, for some citizens, Clinton lying about sex was finally going too far. For others, it seemed as if lying about sex turned him into a martyr. Clinton's approval rating soared at the same time that the percentage of people who thought he was a liar also rose.

But Americans' distrust of Clinton was easily neutered. At a time when Clinton's personal credibility was near its lowest ebb, Clinton revived his political fortunes by launching an unprovoked attack abroad. The American people apparently concluded that although Clinton could not be trusted with an intern in the Oval Office, he could be trusted to judiciously bomb a capital city of a European nation that posed no threat to America. The public recognized that Clinton was a liar in late 1998 and yet supported his war against Serbia, based largely on the unverified assertions by Clinton and his political appointees. The mere creation of a foreign demon magically restored the ruler's credibility.

The U.S. war against Serbia was based on a series of brazen lies that failed to ignite public skepticism.

Lie # 1: Freedom Fighters

Prior to the start of U.S. bombing in March 1999, Clinton administration officials denounced the Kosovo Liberation Army (KLA) for its "terrorist" actions—including the killing of Serb civilians and arson attacks on churches. The KLA was also known to be heavily involved in narcotics trafficking and was originally founded as a communist organization. But once Clinton committed the United States to war, the KLA became "freedom fighters." Some of the leaders that the Clinton administration hailed as "freedom fighters" in 1999 were indicted for war crimes by the UN Tribunal a few years later.[30]

Lie #2: The World at Risk

In announcing the start of the U.S. bombing of Serbia, Clinton declared in a radio address on March 27, 1999: "Through two world wars and a long cold war we saw that it was a short step from a small brush fire to an inferno, especially in the tinderbox of the Balkans. The time to put out a fire is before it spreads and burns down the neighborhood."[31] The Balkans had nothing to do with the start of World War II (Danzig was on the Baltic Sea, not the Adriatic Sea). There was no evidence that the ethnic conflict in the former Yugoslavia threatened to spill over to Europe or the world. But Clinton had to magnify the threat to justify U.S. aggression.

Lie #3: Genocide

Clinton administration officials continually invoked the threat of genocide to justify the killing of Serb civilians. Secretary of Defense William Cohen on April 7 characterized the bombing of Serbia: "This is a fight for justice over genocide, for humanity over inhumanity, for democracy over despotism."[32] On May 13, Clinton declaimed that "there are 100,000 people [in Kosovo] who are still missing"—implying that they might have been slaughtered. After the bombing ended, Clinton boasted that "NATO stopped deliberate, systematic efforts at ethnic cleansing and genocide."[33]

After the war, UN investigators found no evidence of genocide in Kosovo. Searching the land after the war, UN investigators discovered fewer than 3000 civilians who had been killed in Kosovo from 1997 to 1999, including people killed by NATO airstrikes during the liberation bombing campaign. The dead likely include many combatants from both the Serb and the ethnic Albanian side, as well as Serbs murdered by the KLA.[34]

The fact that there was no genocide was either ignored or dismissed as a "harmless error" by the vast majority of the American media and most of the American public (excepting those of Serb origin and handfuls of activists on the left and the right). There was no sense of national disgrace or national dishonor for having launched an aggressive war based on false charges.

Lie #4: Targeting the Serbian Military

On June 11, the day after a cease-fire was negotiated, Clinton bragged at an Air Force base: "Day after day, with remarkable precision, our forces pounded every element of Mr. Milosevic's military machine, from tanks to fuel supply, to anti-aircraft weapons, to the military and political support."[35] In reality, the U.S. bombing campaign was a dismal failure at destroying the Serb military, which made an orderly withdrawal from Kosovo after the bombing stopped. Only 13 of Serbia's 450 tanks were destroyed, and fewer than 500 Yugoslav soldiers were killed. On the other hand, at least 500 civilians were killed in the bombing, according to Human Rights Watch. (The Yugoslav government stated that 2,000 civilians were killed.) From intentionally bombing a television station, Belgrade neighborhoods, power stations, bridges (regardless of the number of people on them at the time), to "accidentally" bombing a bus (killing 47 people), a passenger train, marketplaces, hospitals, apartment buildings, and the Chinese embassy, the rules of engagement for U.S. bombers guaranteed that many innocent people would be killed. Yet, as Fairness and Accuracy in Reporting, a media watchdog organization, observed, "NATO's persistent focus on the 'accidental' nature of the deaths is rarely questioned by the press; the strongest criticism usually comes in discussions of the damage such 'accidents' do to NATO's PR image."[36] British journalist David Ramsay Steele observed, "The NATO bombardment was almost entirely directed against civilian targets, partly because military targets could not be found. NATO did not dare to invade Yugoslavia or even to fly low over Yugoslavia; it could only 'degrade' the lives of the civilian population by bombing from a great height."[37] The 78-day bombing campaign left much of the country's civilian infrastructure in ruins.

Lie # 5: Peace

In a videotape message after the bombing ended, Clinton assured the Serbian people that the United States and NATO agreed to be peacekeepers only "with the understanding that they would protect Serbs as well as ethnic Albanians and that they would leave when peace took hold."[38] In the subsequent months and years, American and NATO forces routinely stood by as the KLA resumed its ethnic cleansing, slaughtering Serb civilians, bombing Serbian churches, and oppressing any non-Muslims. Almost a quarter million Serbs, Gypsies, Jews, and other minorities fled Kosovo after Clinton's promise to protect them. By 2003, almost 70 percent of the Serbs living in Kosovo in 1999 had fled, and Kosovo was 95 percent ethnic Albanian.[39]

Clinton's Kosovo claptrap succeeded in part because most Americans were poorly informed of the facts on the ground. Few Americans showed any remorse for the innocent Serbs killed by U.S. bombing. The president's endless assertions of good intentions for U.S. bombing was the supreme fact for many Americans. Most of the American media behaved like stage props for a presidential morality play. Matt Tiabbi, later hired by *Rolling Stone* as their media critic, observed, "Independently of each other, and without being directly coerced by the U.S. government itself, virtually every major American television network and print publication has allowed the White House to define the terms of all discussion surrounding the bombing."[40]

Clinton's 1999 war against Serbia illustrates how the higher the government raises the stakes, the more gullible many people become. The same people who would disparage or ridicule a president's budget numbers rush to believe him when he attacks a foreign nation. It is as if the more people a president wants to kill, the more credible he becomes.

Shortly after the end of the bombing, Clinton enunciated what his aides labeled the Clinton doctrine—"whether within or beyond the borders of a country, if the world community has the power to stop it, we ought to stop genocide and ethnic cleansing."[41] In reality, the Clinton doctrine was that the U.S. government is allowed to attack foreign nations on false charges. Clinton profited politically despite the frauds upon which the war was based, and despite the ethnic carnage following the war's end. The war against Serbia proved that the U.S. president would still be viewed as a hero—and even a war hero— by many Americans despite all the evidence to the contrary.

RICE PUFFERY

High profile, strategic lies were also vital to the Bush administration in its campaign to exploit 9/11 to sanctify itself and its warring. The Bush administration fought doggedly to block the creation of a 9/11 Commission to investigate the attacks. After Congress mandated the commission, the Bush administration strove to minimize the commission's access to information, and was able to delay and bottle up the inquiry fairly well—until former Bush counterterrorism czar Richard Clarke publicly testified before the commission. Clarke revealed that Bush and his advisers had disregarded warnings of pending terrorist attacks, in part because of their obsession with attacking Iraq (from the first days of the administration). Clarke concluded that the 9/11 attacks could have been prevented if more attention had been paid to the threat.

Clarke's criticisms outraged many Republicans. Senate Majority Leader Bill Frist (R-Tenn.) asserted that Clarke's confidential testimony before a closed Senate hearing in July 2002 differed from his public testimony before the 9/11 Commission, and warned that "Clarke can and will answer for his own conduct"—widely interpreted as a threat of perjury prosecution.[42]

After Clarke's testimony drove the headlines for a few days, the Bush White House relented and announced National Security adviser Condoleezza Rice would deign to testify publicly. The Bush administration argued that requiring her to testify under oath would tarnish the dignity of the presidency, since she would be representing the president. But the commission did not kowtow on this issue.

When Rice testified to the commission on April 8, 2004, she benefited from special rules: no one was permitted to question her for more than ten minutes at a time.[43] Rice exploited the favored treatment by rambling ad infinitum, using her cloak of dignity to smother the pursuit of truth.

The one commissioner who vigorously questioned her was former Watergate prosecutor Richard Ben-Veniste, who asked: "Isn't it a fact, Dr. Rice, that the August 6th [2001] PDB [President's Daily Brief] warned against possible attacks in this country?"[44]

Rice replied: "You said, did it not warn of attacks? It did not warn of attacks inside the United States. It was historical information based on old reporting. There was no new threat information, and it did not, in fact, warn of any coming attacks inside the United States." Rice later declared that "this was a historical memo. . . . not based on new threat information."[45] Her task became more challenging after Ben-Veniste revealed the title of the brief, "Bin Laden Determined to Strike in U.S." (He was prohibited from disclosing the brief's contents.)

Rice was hailed far and wide for her toughness in holding up under questioning. *Chicago Tribune* columnist Clarence Page declared: "Rice successfully diminished the importance of that [PDB] headline by calling the memo's information old, 'historic,' and too vague and general to move President Bush to take specific action. The truth of that remark will be debated in coming days. For now, Rice appears to have controlled the damage."[46] A CNN overnight poll after her testimony found that "43 percent of Americans polled believed Rice, 36 percent believed Clarke and 21 percent were undecided."[47]

Rice testified on a Friday. The next evening, under intense pressure, the Bush administration finally released a redacted version of the August 6, 2001 President's Daily Brief. The memo warned, "Al-Qa'ida members—including some who are US citizens—have resided in or traveled to the US for years, and the group apparently maintains a support structure that could aid attacks." The memo quoted an Egyptian Islamic Jihad source warning that "Bin Ladin was planning to exploit the operative's access to the US to mount a terrorist strike." The memo noted "FBI information . . . indicates patterns of suspicious activity in this country consistent with preparations for hijackings or other types of attacks, including recent surveillance of federal buildings in New York." The brief followed warnings Bush received in earlier months from the CIA of "Bin Ladin planning multiple operations," "Bin Ladin public profile may presage attack," and "Bin Ladin network's plans advancing." The 9/11 Commission reported that the CIA "consistently described the upcoming attacks as occurring on a catastrophic level, indicating that they would cause the world to be in turmoil, consisting of possible multiple—but not necessarily simultaneous—attacks."[48]

The Bush administration may have known that the President's Daily Brief would eventually be released—but they may have assumed that Rice's testimony would get far more coverage than a memo released on a Saturday night.

Rice's claim that the memo did not "warn of attacks inside the United States" could not pass the laugh test.

Though Rice was under oath when she insisted the attack warnings were merely "historical," there was no talk of charging her with perjury for her false statements. Rice boosted the Bush administration's credibility by lying. Her fraud worked because the vast majority of the media focused on her demeanor, not her falsehoods. It was as if the media commentators felt obliged to keep themselves in an intellectual bubble. It was like Olympic judges assessing a skater solely on her spins, and not on how many times she bounced off the ice.

Since sticking to the official Bush storyline is a main qualification for high office, Rice's performance before the 9/11 Commission may have helped her secure a nomination to be Secretary of State the following January. The deferential treatment Rice received from most members of the Senate Foreign Relations Committee during her January 18, 2005, confirmation hearing illustrated the Statute of Limitation for Major Lies in American Politics.

But the hearing was marred by Sen. Barbara Boxer (D-Cal.), who brought charts with large print and recited false Rice statements. Boxer showed how Rice had asserted, denied, and re-asserted an Iraqi reconstituted nuclear program according to the prevailing polls. Boxer concluded: "I personally believe that your loyalty to the mission you were given, to sell this war, overwhelmed your respect for the truth."[49]

Rice offered no defense for the specific false statements Boxer recited. Instead, Rice got righteous. "We can have this discussion in any way that you would like, but I really hope that you will refrain from impugning my integrity," Rice told Boxer. "I really hope that you will not imply that I take the truth lightly." She harrumphed: "I have never, ever lost my respect for the truth."[50]

When a high-profile political appointee invokes the "hope you will not impugn my integrity" line, a Washington critic usually ceases and desists—fearful of losing their own respectability. But Boxer, who was extremely well-prepared, did not cower.

Boxer was shellacked far and wide. Most editorial writers appeared far more offended by her vigorous challenge than by the false statements by Rice advancing a policy that had already left 1,500 Americans dead. A *Hartford Courant* editorial, headlined "Was She Calling Ms. Rice a Liar?," labeled Boxer's criticisms as "the most unpleasant moment of the hearings." The *Courant* declared: "Ms. Rice had a right to be angry. In effect, she had been called a liar. Ms. Boxer's attack was symptomatic of a regrettable degrading of the culture of civility in Washington."[51]

- A *Washington Times* editorial derided Boxer for sounding "an ugly tone with some specious accusations anyone with an Internet connection can prove are unfounded."[52]

- A *Chattanooga Times Free Press* editorial complained of the "very unbe-coming heckling of the president's nominee to be secretary of state, Dr. Condoleezza Rice."[53]
- A *Boston Herald* columnist declared that "to suggest . . . that Rice not only knew the intelligence to be wrong but also willingly lied to the American public about the faulty intelligence—crossed the lines of pro-fessional conduct and descended into the dark and gloomy world of Democratic politics, and the 'baggage of bigotry.'"[54]

The memory of Rice's false testimony before the 9/11 Commission on April 8, 2004, had apparently completely vanished from the heads of most ed-itorial writers and columnists. That testimony should have settled once and for all whether Rice was credible. Subsequently, the only question should have been: "Is she still lying?" Almost none of the pro-Rice commentaries or edito-rials delved into the facts of the matter as revealed by Boxer.

Apparently, as a high-ranking government official, Rice not only deserved an initial benefit of the doubt—she still deserved the benefit after she lied. It was not like her confirmation hearing was her first appearance on the national scene—and yet her defenders acted as if she must be treated like a political vir-gin. But the more respect nominees receive, the less chance that truth will out. Dignity becomes a license to deceive.

Heated words also flew when Rice's nomination reached the floor of the Senate. Sen. Mark Dayton (D-Minn.) complained: "I don't like to impugn anyone's integrity, but I really don't like being lied to repeatedly, flagrantly, in-tentionally. It's wrong; it's undemocratic; it's un-American; and it's very dan-gerous." Sen. John McCain (R-Ariz.), Washington's reigning king of sanctimony, retorted that "to challenge Condoleezza Rice's integrity I think is out of bounds."[55] But placing challenges to a politician's integrity "out of bounds" simply lowers politicians' cost of lying.

THE 2004 CAMPAIGN

There is a growing imbalance between the savvy of campaign masterminds and the somnolence of American couch potatoes. The 2004 presidential cam-paign broke new ground in the use of and tolerance for brazen falsehoods. The 2004 presidential campaign may have been the most dishonest in American history. *Washington Post* White House correspondent Dana Milbank com-mented on the Bush and Kerry campaigns: "I think they've reached a point where they feel you can say anything, and by the time the press catches up with it, it'll be days if not weeks later."[56] Shanto Iyengar, chairman of Stanford University's Communications Department, observed: "In the specifics, you can get away with just about anything. Ninety-five percent of the American public knows very little about the details. The only people who care about it are journalists and pundits."[57]

On November 3, 2004, Bush magnanimously declared: "So today I want to speak to every person who voted for my opponent. . . . I will do all I can do to deserve your trust."[58] It was ironic that Bush would appeal for "trust" after his deceptive reelection campaign. But this is the politicians' usual canard after a shameless victorious campaign. This is the "re-setting of the clock"—attempting to erase the national memory. It is as if the statute of limitation on remembering the lies of politicians expires at the moment that they are proclaimed winners of an election—as if good memories are now *lèse majesté*.

The whitewashing of the 2004 presidential campaign was the prerequisite to the legitimacy of Bush's second term. Perhaps never before has a president been reelected based on his greatest failures. Despite the howlers of the 2004 campaign, a January 2005 CNN poll found that 56 percent of respondents saw Bush as a strong leader who is honest and trustworthy. Bush's ratings were roughly the same as they had been a year earlier. Thus, Bush's conduct on the campaign trail had zero influence on the percentage of Americans who believed he was honest and trustworthy.

CHENEY AS DESIGNATED DECEIVER

The war in Iraq was Bush's greatest vulnerability in his reelection campaign. Bush and Cheney strove to continually link Iraq to 9/11, since that was the surest way to deflect public ire. On December 9, 2001, Cheney appeared on NBC's *Meet the Press* and announced that it was "pretty well-confirmed" that Mohammad Atta, the mastermind of the 9/11 hijackings, had met with an Iraqi intelligence agent in Prague. No evidence was ever found to support this claim.

The 9/11 Commission concluded in June 2004 that there was no evidence of a "collaborative relationship" between Saddam and Al Qaeda and "no credible evidence" linking Saddam to 9/11.[59] The only "relationship" that 9/11 Commission staff, or the CIA, or other investigators found was a message from Al Qaeda requesting assistance to the Iraqi government in 1994 and which Saddam spurned.

Amazingly, the Bush administration declared victory. The White House e-mailed political allies a statement headlined: "9/11 Commission Staff Report Confirms Administration's Views of Al Qaeda/Iraq Ties."[60] Bush announced that his administration's statements had been "perfectly consistent with what the September 11th commission talked about in their report yesterday."[61]

Cheney appeared on CNBC and declared that the "evidence is overwhelming" that Saddam cooperated with Al Qaeda—the exact opposite of the commission's conclusion. Cheney insisted that "we don't know" whether Iraq was tied to the 9/11 attacks. On the Mohammad Atta meeting in Prague, Cheney insisted: "We've never been able to confirm or to knock it down"—even though everyone else gave up this ghost long ago.[62] When Cheney was asked about his claim that the meeting was "pretty well confirmed," he adamantly declared: "No, I never said that."[63] Cheney even insisted that he was privy to confidential information that the 9/11 Commission did not see. (Commission Chairman Thomas Kean publicly rebutted this assertion.)[64] Cheney denounced the media coverage of the 9/11 Commission Report as "outrageous," "lazy," "malicious," and "irresponsible."[65]

Cheney continued flaunting the spurious link like some hustler waving a bogus religious relic before crowds of slow-witted believers. As the *Washington Post* noted in September 2004, the vice president constantly invoked the Great Red Herring on the campaign trail: "In making the case for the administration's decision to go to war, Cheney gives no ground on his long-held views that Hussein had ties to al Qaeda. . . . At every stop, he tells crowds that the Iraqi leader 'gave safe harbor and sanctuary' to al Qaeda terrorists." The *Los Angeles Times* noted in early October 2004: "The phrases vary. Some days, Vice President Dick Cheney says Saddam Hussein had 'long-established' ties to Al Qaeda. Other days, he says the former Iraqi dictator 'had a relationship' with the terrorist group. But the underlying message remains unchanged— Cheney plants the idea that Hussein was allied with the group responsible for the terrorist attacks of Sept. 11, 2001."[66]

In his opening comments during the vice presidential debate with Democratic nominee John Edwards on October 5, 2004, Cheney declared that Saddam "had an established relationship with al Qaeda" and mentioned that CIA director George Tenet once mentioned a relationship between Saddam and Al Qaeda during congressional testimony. Edwards criticized Cheney: "There is no connection between the attacks of September 11th and Saddam Hussein. The 9/11 Commission has said it. Your own secretary of state has said it. And you've gone around the country suggesting that there is some connection. There is not."[67]

Cheney snorted: "The senator has got his facts wrong. I have not suggested that there's a connection between Iraq and 9/11."[68] Cheney was permitted the ultimate bait-and-switch—permitted to make the assertion in almost all his stump speeches, and then permitted to deny making the assertion in his most heavily televised appearance of the entire campaign.

Later in the debate, Cheney rattled off a litany of statistics on Edwards missing Senate hearings to set up the most carefully planned knockout punch of the debate: "Now, in my capacity as vice president, I am the president of Senate, the presiding officer. I'm up in the Senate most Tuesdays when they're in session. The *first time I ever met you was* when you walked on the stage tonight."[69]

In reality, Cheney and Edward had met at least several times, including a 2001 prayer breakfast where Cheney mentioned Edwards by name, an April 8, 2001, taping of NBC's *Meet the Press,* and the January 8, 2003, swearing in of fellow North Carolina Senator Elizabeth Dole.[70]

As presidential biographer Richard Reeves noted, "You do not forget meeting people who are after your job."[71] Washington and Lee University journalism professor Edward Wasserman observed of Cheney's "ridiculous" assertion: "Cheney is a smart guy with the world's best support staff. They planned to use this zinger. They had to know it wasn't true."[72]

The Bush campaign's response to the exposure of Cheney's falsehood squelched any doubts about whether it was accidental:

- Bush campaign spokesman Steve Schmidt told the *Washington Post:* "The fact is that the vice president has never seen John Edwards at work. . . . He's never met John Edwards at work in the U.S. Senate. The vice president meets thousands of people and he's had three casual encounters with John Edwards. . . . I think most people understand that a casual encounter—a breakfast, Elizabeth Dole's swearing-in—is different from John Edwards showing up at work."[73]
- The *Los Angeles Times* noted that Schmidt "described the prayer breakfast photo as evidence of an 'inconsequential meeting.'"[74]
- Cheney Spokeswoman Anne Womack declared: "While the vice president may have passed the senator in the hall or been at the same event at some point in the past 3 1/2 years, the fact is that Sen. Edwards has one of the worst attendance records in the U.S. Senate. It's no surprise that Sen. Edwards failed to make a lasting impression on the vice president."[75]
- The *Baltimore Sun* noted: "The Bush campaign did not dispute the Cheney-Edwards encounters. Instead, Cheney's wife, Lynne, said voters should focus on Edwards' absences from the Senate—not on what her husband said in the debate."[76]
- Knight Ridder News Service noted: "Cheney aides said Wednesday that his comment wasn't misleading. It pointed up a larger truth, they said: that Edwards has often been absent from his Senate duties, busy running for president."[77]

But this "larger truth" directly contradicted Cheney's "first time I ever met you" assertion.

Apparently, the rule now is to never admit a lie—no matter how brazen, or how incontrovertible the evidence. It is as if Clinton's standard for denying he had sex with Monica Lewinsky is now the Law of the Land. (Clinton explained to his lawyer, Robert Bennett, that Monica had sex with him, but he had not had sex with her.)

The Cheney "never met you before" declaration is one of the most pristine examples of a bold, calculated lie easily verifiable as false. Cheney's falsehoods did nothing to undermine his credibility with Republicans and conservatives. Instead, his adulation rose in proportion to his deceptions. It was as if lying is now a sign of political valor—a sign of courage in refusing to be intimidated by mere facts.

THE RIGHT TO LIE FOR 72 HOURS

Political lies are like snake bites: unless their poison is speedily removed, remedial efforts may be of interest only to coroners and historians. As long as the lies are not exposed in the same news cycle, the refutations may as well be done in a different century, as far as most TV viewers are concerned. But, according to the Bush reelection campaign, lies cannot be exposed until after people's attention wanders.

As the Bush campaign's whoppers multiplied, the *New York Times* ran an article entitled "In His New Attacks, Bush Pushes the Limits on the Facts,"[78] highlighting distortions Bush made of Kerry's record and other issues. The Bush campaign was outraged. Bush campaign spokesman Steve Schmidt bitterly complained: "The Bush campaign should be able to make an argument without having it reflexively dismissed as distorted or inaccurate by the biggest papers in the country."[79] It was as if anyone who exposed the president's lies violated his prerogative. Perhaps the Bush campaign felt entitled to a Brady Act waiting period—a delay of 72 hours before journalists were permitted to disarm a presidential lie.

Often, all that is necessary is to cast aspersions on the motives of critics to insulate a liar with his base of supporters. The Bush campaign vigorously attacked the news media through the fall. The *New Republic* noted that some of the Republican National Committee attacks were "unusually personal and included unflattering pictures of the men, the kind that candidates dig up of their opponents, not of journalists. . . . The fact that the RNC is now devoting a good deal of its time to attacking reporters speaks volumes about how much Bush is relying on negative, unchecked distortions to secure a second term."[80]

The Bush team sought to make the real issue the *victimization of the president.* The doctrine of a liberal media bias preemptively cleansed the president of his falsehoods. The less credibility the media has, the easier it becomes for the president to lie. This spurs a two-front strategy: simultaneously telling lies and attacking the media. This was the same tactic that Hillary Clinton used when she appeared on the NBC Today show in late January 1998 and denounced the allegations of her husband's fling with an intern as a slander by a "vast right wing conspiracy."

Politicians' lies are often shrugged off as harmless puffs of rhetoric. But without falsehoods by Bush, Cheney, and other top officials, Americans would not have supported the Iraq war. The lies on weapons of mass destruction were not "harmless errors" for American families whose father or mother is now dead or maimed, or for the families of Iraqis and others killed in U.S. bombings or at U.S. checkpoints. Memories of the Johnson administration's lies on the Gulf of Tonkin resolution or Clinton's lies on Kosovo did nothing to undermine credulity during Bush's road to war with Iraq.

A senior Bush administration official dismissed a journalist's criticisms of false Bush statements prior to invading Iraq: "The President of the United States is not a fact checker."[81] But Bush never made the slightest apology or admission of his falsehoods or accepted an iota of personal responsibility for misleading the American public. The *Washington Post* reported in July 2003 that Bush's communications director, Dan Bartlett, said "that Bush was not angry to learn the charge [that Iraq was seeking to acquire nuclear bomb material in Niger] was based on flawed information."[82] This is perhaps the most important precedent of the Bush administration: a president can lie a nation into war and suffer no consequences—unless the war does not turn out well.

To permit the "didn't know any better" defense is to absolve rulers of guilt for most falsehoods. To insist that a politician knows that he is uttering a falsehood before he can be labeled a liar is to reward gross negligence: it makes his ignorance a moral bulletproof vest. There will be times when presidents, like other human beings, make inaccurate statements based on erroneous information or erroneous assumptions. Journalist David Corn observed: "An untruth that might have been spoken accidentally becomes a lie if a president and his aides permit it to stand."[83]

THE GOVERNMENT'S ENABLER

Politicians "regenerate" honesty like a salamander growing back a lost tail. The media often treats a president as if he has another "moral rebirth" within hours of his latest lie. As long as the politician can go for one or two speeches in a row without Times Square–sized neon deceits, the press again slips into treating the common politician like a statesman-in-the-making.

The media is usually more devoted to bonding with than exposing the commander-in-chief. Clinton benefitted from a press corps that often treated his falsehoods as non-events—or even petty triumphs. *Newsweek* White House correspondent Howard Fineman commented that Clinton's "great strength is his insincerity . . . I've decided Bill Clinton is at his most genuine when he's the most phony. . . . We know he doesn't mean what he says."[84] In 1936, *New York Times* White House correspondent Turner Catledge made a similar observation about FDR, observing that his "first instinct was always to lie."[85] But the Washington press corps covered up FDR's dishonesty almost as thoroughly as they hid his use of a wheelchair in daily life.

Flora Lewis, a *New York Times* columnist, writing three weeks before 9/11, commented in a review of a book on U.S. government lies on the Vietnam war that "There will probably never be a return to the discretion, really collusion, with which the media used to treat presidents, and it is just as well."[86] But, within months of her comment, the media had proven itself as craven as ever. The *Washington Post's* Dana Milbank, who did some of the best exposes of Bush falsehoods in his first term, noted that it was not until July 2002 that "the White House press corps showed its teeth" in response to administration deceptions. Even the exposes of FBI and CIA intelligence failures in May 2002 did not end the "phase of alliance" between the White House and the press, as political scientist Martha Kumar observed.[87]

Deference to the government is now the trademark of the American media—at least at times when the truth could have the greatest impact. The media was grossly negligent in failing to question or examine Bush's claims on the road to war. When journalists dug up the truth, editors sometimes ignored or buried their reports. *Washington Post* Pentagon correspondent Thomas Ricks complained that, in the lead-up to the U.S. invasion of Iraq, "There was an attitude among editors: 'Look, we're going to war, why do we even worry about all this contrary stuff?'"[88] *New York Times* White House correspondent Elisabeth Bumiller explained the press's conduct at a Bush press conference just before he invaded Iraq: "I think we were very deferential because . . . nobody wanted to get into an argument with the president at this very serious time."[89] After the war started—and after Bush's claims turned out to be false—it was often treated as a one-day story, buried in the back of the front section or on the editorial page. Afterward, most papers quickly returned to printing the president's proclamations as gospel. Alterman, author of *When Presidents Lie*, observed, "Virtually every major news media outlet devoted more attention to the lies and dissimulations of one *New York Times* reporter, Jayson Blair, than to those of the president and vice president of the United States regarding Iraq. Given that these two deceptions took place virtually simultaneously, they demonstrate that while some forms of deliberate deception remain intolerable in public life, those of the U.S. commander in chief are not among them."[90]

The media's docility to the Bush administration repeated the pattern established during the first Gulf War (and during much of the Vietnam War). Chris Hedges, who covered the 1990–91 Gulf War for the *New York Times,* later explained: "The notion that the press was used in the war is incorrect. The press wanted to be used. It saw itself as part of the war effort." Hedges noted that journalists were "eager to be of service to the state," which "made it easier to do what governments do in wartime, indeed what governments do much of the time, and that is lie."[91]

Far from being irate about presidential lies, the media often enjoys sharing a laugh with the commander in chief over such technical inaccuracies. On March 24, 2004, President Bush performed a skit for attendees at the Radio and Television Correspondents annual dinner in which he showed slides of himself crawling around his office peaking behind curtains while he quipped to the crowd: "Those weapons of mass destruction have got to be somewhere . . . Nope, no weapons over there . . . Maybe under here?"[92]

Bush's comic bit got one of the biggest laughs of the night. The *Washington Post* Style section hailed the evening's performance with a headline—"George Bush, Entertainer in Chief." The media dignitaries (including many print media luminaries) made no fuss over the comments—until a mini-firestorm erupted a few days later, spurred by criticism by Democrats and soldiers who had fought in Iraq. Greg Mitchell, the editor of *Editor and Publisher,* labeled the press's reaction as "one of the most shameful episodes in the recent history of the American media, and presidency."[93]

The character of the Washington press corps also shone bright in its non-response to the Downing Street Memo. On May 1, 2005, the London *Times* printed a memo from a British cabinet meeting on July 23, 2002, that reported the findings of the visit by Britain's intelligence chief to Washington to confer with CIA chief George Tenet and other top Bush administration officials. The memo quoted the intelligence chief: "Military action was now seen as inevitable. Bush wanted to remove Saddam, through military action, justified by the conjunction of terrorism and WMD. But the intelligence and facts were being fixed around the policy."[94] The fact that the top level of the British government was aware that the Bush administration was fixing—i.e., manipulating and contriving—intelligence and facts to justify going to war was a bombshell in the United Kingdom. The decision to "fix" facts was illustrated by the torrent of false accusations and statements that Bush and his top officials made against Iraq in the following months. Throughout 2002, Bush continued to speak of how he hoped to avoid going to war with Saddam. In his State of the Union address in late January 2003 and in his subsequent speeches, Bush talked about the United States as a victim, repeatedly asserting that "if war is forced upon us, we will fight."[95] Bush had long since decided to attack, regardless of how many UN weapons inspectors Saddam permitted to roam Iraq.

Yet, the memo was almost completely ignored by the American mainstream media for the first month after its publication in Britain. As Salon columnist Joe Conason commented, "To judge by their responses, the leading lights of the Washington press corps are more embarrassed than the White House is by the revelations in the Downing Street memo."[96]

Hurricane Katrina provided an opportunity for the media to ritually renounce its servility. As the non-response and pervasive debacle became undeniable and the death count soared over a thousand, many talking heads pointed out the government's failures and proudly showed their indignation. A New York Times headline summed up the broadcast media's change in tone: "Reporters Turn From Deference to Outrage." One BBC commentator observed, "Amidst the horror, American broadcast journalism just might have grown its spine back, thanks to Katrina," which he suggested could provide an antidote to the "timid and self-censoring journalistic culture that is no match for the masterfully aggressive spin-surgeons of the Bush administration."[97] NBC Nightly News anchor Brian Williams explained: "By dint of the fact that our country was hit [in 2001] we've offered a preponderance of the benefit of the doubt [to the government] over the past couple [sic] of years. Perhaps . . . this is the story that brings a healthy amount of cynicism back to a news media known for it."[98] But such periodic affirmations of independence are as credible as an alcoholic, regaining consciousness after tumbling down the stairs, piously announcing the end of his boozing days. There will be other bottles—and other stairs.

The pursuit of respectability in Washington usually entails acquiescing to government lies. Many if not most members of the Washington press corps are government dependents. Few Washington journalists have the *will* to expose government lies. This requires placing one in an explicitly adversarial position to the government. It is not that the typical journalist is intentionally covering up government lies, but that his radar is not set to detect such occurrences. Lies rarely register in Washington journalists' minds because they are usually supplicants for government information, not dogged pursuers of the truth. Raising troublesome questions will not help you get any silver platter stories.

The vast majority of the media have docilely repeated Bush's claims throughout his presidency. Television networks likely devote a hundred times as much air time to peddling government falsehoods than to exposing them. The constant barrage of falsehood drowns out the occasional blips of truth. The government only needs the number of people who recognize their lies to be small enough that its latest power play will not be thwarted. The goal is not to prevent well-informed citizens from being nauseated or disgusted by the president's lies. Instead, it is to neutralize the mass reaction to presidential falsehoods, even those that have catastrophic consequences.

PATERNALISM AND NOBLE LIES

Political mendacity is also rarely a concern for most academics and friends of Leviathan. Many contemporary statists believe politicians can be trusted to be benevolent even when they cannot be trusted otherwise.

Lies are sometimes portrayed as something politicians tell to indulge voters, not to deceive those they seek to rule. Economist John Maynard Keynes wrote in 1921: "It is the method of modern statesmen to talk as much folly as the public demands and to practice no more of it than is compatible with what they have said."[99] Keynes even referred to the "obligation" of "Cabinet Ministers to sacrifice veracity to the public weal."[100]

Political lies are sometimes treated as salutary lies. Political lies are the cost of keeping the peace—i.e., keeping folks subdued. Despite the historical record, politicians are presumed to only deceive people for their own good. And the government is still a democracy regardless of how often it deceives citizens, because the rulers are doing it "for the people."

This doctrine of rulers' right to deceive is a hallmark of the followers of Leo Strauss, who profoundly influenced some Bush appointees during his decades as a professor of philosophy at the University of Chicago. Strauss is known as the "philosopher of the noble lie"—based on the assumption that truth is only for the elite. Many of the most effective advocates of attacking Iraq were Straussians, including Paul Wolfowitz, who studied under Strauss. One of the primary sources of the "information" that spurred the U.S. invasion of Iraq was a newly created Pentagon office called the Office of Special Plans. The director of the office, Abram Shulsky (who received his doctorate under Strauss), cowrote a 1999 essay that declared that Leo Strauss "alerts one to the possibility that political life may be closely linked to deception. Indeed, it suggests that deception is the norm in political life."[101] Professor Shadia Drury, author of *Leo Strauss and the American Right*, notes that Strauss believed that "those who are fit to rule are those who realize there is no morality and that there is only one natural right—'the right of the superior to rule over the inferior.'"[102] Strauss's views purportedly heavily influenced neoconservatives, including many of the most vociferous advocates of U.S. aggression, such as Senior Pentagon Advisor Richard Perle, Pentagon Undersecretary for Policy Douglas Feith, Vice President Cheney's top aide Lewis Libby, and media commentators such as William Kristol, William Bennett, David Frum, and Max Boot. The Straussian "noble lies" doctrine illustrates how dissimulation may now be the name of the game, at least for some of the most avid champions of greatly increased federal power—the power to launch preemptive wars against almost any nation on Earth.

LIES AND LEVIATHAN

Big government requires Big Lies—and not just on wars, but across the board. The more powerful government becomes, the more abuses it commits, and the more lies it must tell. Interventions beget debacles that require cover-ups and denials. The more the government screws up, the more evidence the government is obliged to bury or deny. The government becomes addicted to the growth of its own revenue and power—and this growth cannot be maintained without denying or hiding the adverse effects of government power. Likewise, rulers become addicted to prestige and adulation—and these often cannot survive honest accounts of their actions.

Lies propelled Leviathan's growth. Social Security is the single largest government aid program and the Big Lie of domestic politics. From the start, the Roosevelt administration deceived Americans about the nature of the program. Americans were endlessly told that it was an insurance program that would give them vested rights akin to a private contract. But, in a 1937 brief to the Supreme Court, the Roosevelt administration conceded that Social Security "cannot be said to constitute a plan for compulsory insurance within the accepted meaning of the term insurance" and characterized Social Security as a "public charity" program under the "general welfare" clause of the Constitution. On the day in 1937 that the Supreme Court declared Social Security constitutional precisely because it was a welfare system and not an insurance system, the Social Security Administration changed the name of the program from "old age benefits" to "old age insurance." The Brooking Institution's Martha Derthick observed, "In the mythic construction begun in 1935 and elaborated thereafter on the basis of the payroll tax, Social Security was a vast enterprise of self-help in which government participation was almost incidental."[103] In a 1960 Supreme Court case, the U.S. solicitor general stated that Social Security "must be viewed as a welfare instrument to which legal concepts of 'insurance,' 'property,' 'annuities', etc. can be applied only at the risk of a serious distortion of language." New groups were continually dragooned into the system partly as a result of the state's "power to use funds raised by compulsory means to make propaganda for an extension of this compulsory system," as economist Frederich Hayek noted.[104] When a group like the Amish objected on principle and refused to pay Social Security taxes, federal agents swept down and seized their cows, buggies, and other property. Social Security

Commissioner Stanford Ross, after he announced his resignation, conceded in 1979 that "the mythology of Social Security contributed greatly to its success. . . . Strictly speaking, the system was never intended to return to individuals what they paid."[105] If FDR and subsequent politicians had been forthright with Americans—informing them that they were becoming ensnared in a welfare system that quickly became a war chest for incumbents' vote-buying—far more citizens would have opposed the system.

Government aid programs perpetually deceive the public on their batting average. Politicians and bureaucrats are renowned for hyping dishonest job placement numbers. Sen. Dan Quayle (R-Ind.), who parlayed his role as chief author of the 1982 Job Training Partnership Act (JTPA) into the vice presidency, claimed that the Job Training Partnership Act "has a job placement rate . . . for the young people around 70 percent." However, this statistic was actually based not on jobs but on "positive outcomes"—which included learning how to make change from a dollar and demonstrating "effective non-verbal communication with others."[106] The Job Corps, the flagship of Lyndon Johnson's War on Poverty, padded its success claims by counting Corps trainees as employed simply by confirming that they had one job interview.[107] The U.S. Employment Service, which bankrolls state employment services around the country, was long notorious for cooking its books. A 1977 General Accounting Office study found that the Employment Service exaggerated the number of its job placements by 75 percent.[108] These false claims have allowed federal agencies to distract attention from numerous studies that show that federal job training is often worse than useless, undermining the work ethic and employability of people the programs purported to help.[109]

Government education programs are notorious for using deceptive statistics to lull parents about the quality of schooling their children receive. School test data have been manipulated to allow "all 50 state education agencies to report above-average scores for their elementary schools, with most claiming such scores in every subject area and every grade level," as former Education Department official Larry Uzzell stated in 1989.[110] Pervasive statistical shenanigans at local and state levels helped inspire the Bush administration's No Child Left Behind Act, which purported to bring honesty to education. President Bush declared in July 2003 that the new act "essentially says . . . there is going to be high standards and strong accountability measures to every State in the Union."[111] But the new law itself has become another fount of scams. The No Child Left Behind Act spurred states to slash their learning standards so that they could claim "adequate progress" in the following years, thereby complying with the new law and continuing to receive federal subsidies. Such false claims on the achievements of public schools have been vital to defending government's de facto monopoly of education.

Deceit has long since become institutionalized in some government oper-ations. In February 2002, the *New York Times* reported that a new Pentagon operation, the Office of Strategic Influence, was "developing plans to provide news items, possibly even false ones, to foreign media organizations as part of a new effort to influence public sentiment and policy makers in both friendly and unfriendly countries."[112] Federal law prohibits the Pentagon from con-ducting propaganda operations within the United States (except for recruiting operations).

The proposal was widely derided as a *1984*-style Ministry of Truth. When Bush was asked about the new endeavor, he denied any intent to deceive and declared: "We'll tell the American people the truth."[113] The administration speedily backtracked. Rumsfeld bitterly announced the shutdown of the new office, and the media quickly returned to treating the pronouncements of Pen-tagon officials as gospel truth.

Nine months later, Rumsfeld notified the press corps that though the Of-fice of Strategic Information was gone, its controversial activities were contin-uing: "You can have the name, but I'm gonna keep doing every single thing that needs to be done and I have." Rumsfeld's comments were ignored by all the major media outlets.[114] The de facto revival of the Office of Strategic In-formation was part of a massive redesign of how the government seeks to ma-nipulate domestic and world opinion. *Los Angeles Times* columnist William Arkin noted that Rumsfeld's redesign of military operations "blurs or even erases the boundaries between factual information and news, on the one hand, and public relations, propaganda and psychological warfare, on the other."[115] Under the new regime, the Air Force's "information warfare now includes con-trolling as much as possible what the American public sees and reads."[116] Arkin foresaw that "while the policy ostensibly targets foreign enemies, its most likely victim will be the American electorate."[117]

POWER AS THE HIGHEST TRUTH

In Washington, power is the highest truth. Credibility depends on titles, not veracity. The rules of probability are suspended once a person reaches a certain "pay grade." Blind deference might not be surprising if one is talking about semi-literate peasants in some mountain hollow. But it is more of a problem with the academic elite, the media, and the rest of the establishment.

Harvard professor William James is one of the patron saints of Washing-ton. James, the most influential philosopher of pragmatism, offered a defini-tion that has warmed the hearts of generations of politicians: "'The 'true' . . . is only the expedient in the way of our thinking."[118] James also defined truth as ideas in "agreement . . . with reality." Regardless of the realism of James's theory, pragmatism is routinely invoked in Washington to justify ignoring hard facts and proceeding as if government actually functioned as politicians claimed. Truth is whatever serves their party or their interest at any given moment. There are few vigorous challenges to the official lies in Washington except when some political party or strong political faction can profit from the challenge or the exposing. It is almost always pragmatic to go along with the official story.

When it comes to what people in Washington serve, few sign up for slavish devotion to petty details. A strict devotion to mere facts is a poor way to pay a mortgage on a high-toned townhouse in Georgetown or a mansion in Great Falls, Virginia. The question in Washington is not, "What are the facts?" but, "How do I benefit?" Truth is what serves one's ideology, one's faction, one's patrons. We may be seeing the return of the spirit of the 1930s, in which "truth" is defined as those facts or claims that support the One True Ideology.

Perhaps even more than James, German philosopher G. W. F. Hegel set the standard for Washington. Hegel wrote, "Men are as foolish as to forget, in their enthusiasm for liberty of conscience and political freedom, the truth which lies in power."[119] German philosopher Ernst Cassirer, who fled the Third Reich, commented, "These words, written in 1801, contain the clearest and most ruthless program of fascism that has ever been propounded by any political or philosophy writer."[120] Hegel's philosophy was sufficiently idealistic that it equated government and truth: "For Truth is the Unity of the universal and subjective Will; and the Universal is to be found in the State, in its laws, its universal and rational arrangements."[121]

Bush and some of his top aides may be Hegelians without knowing Hegel—like the guy in Moliere's play who was surprised to learn that he had been speaking prose all his life. According to author Ron Suskind, a senior Bush adviser explained that critics like him are "in what we call the reality-based community"—people who "believe that solutions emerge from your judicious study of discernible reality. That's not the way the world really works anymore. We're an empire now, and when we act, we create our own reality. And while you're studying that reality—judiciously, as you will—we'll act again, creating other new realities. . . . We're history's actors . . . and you, all of you, will be left to just study what we do."[122] Perhaps the White House would invoke the president's prerogative to define and redefine reality—to determine facts—not just perceptions.

Some Americans may assume that presidents naturally inherit the same attitude toward truth that George Washington reputedly showed after chopping down the cherry tree. But, in today's Washington, lying for a president may be the ultimate proof of trustworthiness. Bush chose Elliot Abrams as his deputy national security adviser in charge of democracy promotion, even though Abrams had pled guilty to two counts of withholding information from Congress (Bush's father pardoned Abrams in December 1992) in the Iran-Contra scandal. Bush put John Poindexter in charge of the Pentagon's Total Information Awareness surveillance network, not withstanding Poindexter's five felony convictions, including two perjury counts—overturned on appeal. Bush appointed Henry Kissinger as the first chairman of the 9/11 Commission, despite Kissinger's legendary record of duplicity. John Negroponte was appointed first as UN Ambassador and then as the national intelligence director, despite his falsehoods regarding the Nicaraguan Contras during the time he was ambassador to Honduras in the early 1980s.

Professor Alterman reaches an optimistic conclusion, as far as politicians paying for their sins. He asserts that "presidents cannot lie about major political events that have potentially serious ramifications—particularly those relating to war and peace—with impunity. These lies inevitably turn into monsters that strangle their creators."[123] But lies usually catch up with a politician only in children's fairy tales. The vast majority of lies go unexposed, and the vast majority of liars get reelected. Most government cover-ups succeed. The dicta that "the truth will out" is null and void within the District of Columbia, as well as most government bureaus across the land. It is nonsense that people will be told—or will soon learn—what the government has done. This illusion only makes people submissive to continued lying.

Because presidential lying is countenanced, it would be naive to expect government agencies to be more honest than the White House. When top politicians have the right to tell big lies, government agencies inherit the right to lie to people who fall under their sway. Contempt for the public spreads almost by osmosis.

"Truth" is often simply what the government can no longer prudently deny. In many cases, the official version of an event depends strictly on political calculation. Politicians and/or bureaucrats confer and decide exactly how much they must disclose (often because of leaks or information that is no longer deniable) and how much information they can safely withhold. "Truth" is the sheer minimum of disclosure necessary to achieve or maintain credibility, while throttling or openly lying about details that could spur a collapse of faith in government policy or agency or administration.

GOVERNMENT DECEIT VERSUS SELF-GOVERNMENT

Is there some magic about democracy that lets people make wise decisions even though the government deludes them on the major issues of the day?

Does democracy automatically rise above all the mendacity of the rulers? Are we to presume that no matter how much hokum government feeds the people, the people's judgment will be sound—"Garbage in, Vox Dei Out"?

Elections increasingly confer nearly boundless power in part because of citizens' tolerance for lying candidates. Elections let people pick their grand deceiver. If the president has the right to lie as much as he pleases on any issue, "representative government" merely means having a choice of who subsequently deludes you.

The pervasiveness of lies goes to the heart of whether Leviathan can be reconciled with democracy. How much can the people be deceived and still purportedly be self-governing? Arendt wrote of the "most essential political freedom, the right to unmanipulated factual information without which all freedom of opinion becomes a cruel hoax."[124] But any such right has become more scarce since her time. Even when much of the public becomes convinced that the government has lied, there is still little or no pressure on Congress or from Congress to force executive agencies to disclose facts, and not even a whiff of legal liability for those whose falsehoods shed other people's blood. Instead, people shrug and hope that the government will not be as dishonest next time.

Government lying is not simply a result of character defects in politicians, political appointees, and bureaucrats. Instead, it is often the result of a systemic bias against admitting systemic failures. The larger government becomes, the more the deck is stacked against honesty in public affairs. People in government and in power have far more tools and stronger incentives to deceive than the average citizen's incentive and ability to discover the truth about government. It would be naive to expect a few Sunday School–type lectures from the Oval Office to change the situation. Arendt noted that "the lie did not creep into politics by some accident of human sinfulness; moral outrage, for this reason alone, is not likely to make it disappear."[125]

In criminal cases, when a suspect or "person of interest" refuses to disclose everything the government demands, he is sometimes charged with "obstruction of justice." But what corresponding charge is available for American citizens to bring against their government when their rulers refuse to disclose how they are using their power? Political lying is routinely the equivalent of "Obstruction of Self-Government"; but instead of a crime, this is standard operating procedure.

Lies unleash Leviathan. Lies disable the brakes on the expansion and abuse of political power. Lies aim to silence the early warning sirens to the abuse of power—to the trampling of citizens' rights—to the loss of freedom. Lies sway people to lower their political guard.

Leviathan depends on pervasive deceits to maintain public support—or at least to sap public opposition. The more honest the rulers are about the nature of government power and the failures of government programs, the less support citizens have for big government.

Lies are often preemptive strikes on the limits of government power. Thus, Bush seeks to persuade Congress to enact legislation giving government new surveillance powers by vastly exaggerating the number of "terrorists" who have been convicted thanks to the Patriot Act.[126] Bush's proclamations on the Patriot Act successes dominated a few news cycles, and the vulgar facts to the contrary followed too far in the dust to blunt the impact of the false claims. The Bush administration also relied on deceit to railroad the Patriot Act into law in the weeks after the 9/11 attacks. The federal government was portrayed as a helpless giant with scant means to thwart violent conspiracies—despite scores of thousands of federal law enforcement agents and a statute book that already criminalized almost everything except breaking wind in public. Politicians rarely rescind edicts even after the exposure of the scams by which power was seized.

People are encouraged to doubt themselves when they doubt their rulers. People are lulled into delaying passing judgment on lying politicians until it is too late to stop them. "Lying until after the *fait accompli*" is far more pernicious than it appears—since it is extremely difficult to reverse government policies or overturn laws. "Repeal" is an unnatural act for most legislators in most countries. It is especially difficult to repeal bombs already dropped.

The falsehoods on the road to the war with Iraq illustrate how deceit has become ritualized in U.S. foreign policy. From 2002 onwards, the White House Iraq Group spewed out false information that the *New York Times* and other prominent media outlets routinely accepted without criticism or verification. After many of the assertions were later discovered to be false, the White House and much of the media treated the falsehoods as irrelevant to the legitimacy of the U.S. invasion. The lack of attention paid to political lies is itself symptomatic of the bias in favor of submitting to rulers regardless of how much people are defrauded.

Because Bush as president has the right to use power as he pleases, the reasons he provided the American people for the war are practically irrelevant. This is the "Inherent Absolute Power" defense of presidential lying—as if the people should be satisfied with whatever crumbs of truth their leaders choose to brush off the table. The government does no injustice when it deceives because citizens have no right to know how their dollars are spent or their rights are violated.

To accept that politicians have a right to lie to people is to award them the right to abuse. Because what else is a lie that is used to seize new power, to seize more money and property, or to violate rights? The vast majority of presidential lies do not involve interns.

Politicians routinely justify themselves by invoking polls indicating pub-lic support for their actions. But in an age of the Big Lie, public opinion polls become little more than a gauge of the success of government propaganda. The more deceptive government becomes, the more corrupted public opin-ion will be. Lies subvert democracy by crippling citizens' ability to rein in gov-ernment. The percentage of people who supported attacking Iraq was largely the measure of how many people the Bush team deceived. Public opinion cannot sanctify government policies when the opinion is created by govern-ment lies.

The profusion of lies vivifies a contempt for consent. The greater the politician's obligation to the citizens, the more his lies delegitimize his power. Only if we assume that people consent to being lied to can pervasive govern-ment lies be reconciled with democracy. And if people are content to be de-ceived, elections become little more than patients choosing who will inject their sedatives.

FIREWALLS, MENTAL DUDS, AND WET BLANKETS

If a businessman knowingly made false claims for a product and the resulting carnage killed over a thousand people who purchased his goods, the clamor for stringing him up would be near universal. Yet, when a politician does the same thing, millions of Americans hail the malefactor as a strong leader.

Why do people fail to draw adverse inferences from the lies of their rulers? This is one of the biggest mysteries in contemporary democracy. A politician can be caught lying time and again. Yet because they are presumed benevolent, their lies are treated as if they were benign.

The key in contemporary democracy is not whether a president's lies are ex-posed—but whether the evidence has traction with the bulk of the citizenry. Why do lies not detonate in listeners' minds? Is it because people can no longer remember enough to recognize the lies—or that they are so desperate to believe that they discount all evidence that would undermine faith in their saviors?

A *Time* magazine poll in late September 2004 found that only 37 percent of registered voters believed that Bush had been "truthful in describing the sit-uation" in Iraq, while 55 percent said the "situation is worse than Bush has re-ported."[127] Ironically, exit polls on Election Day showed that "Voters who cited honesty as the most important quality in a candidate broke 2 to 1 in Mr. Bush's favor."[128] (Neither presidential candidate was consistently honest in the 2004 campaign.)

In 2004, many voters apparently concluded that Bush was trustworthy de-spite his false statements and misrepresentations on Iraq. It was as if there was a firewall in voters' minds to prevent the damage from specific Bush lies from spreading and engulfing his reputation for honesty. This is the key to modern paternalism: specific lies no longer undermine general trust. As a result, every presidential assertion that has not been specifically and categorically debunked must be presumed correct.

Clinton benefited from similar popular scoring. Professor Stephen Earl Bennett noted, "National Election Studies show that between 1996 and 1998, assessments of whether Clinton was 'moral' and 'honest' fell substantially, while perceptions that he 'provides strong leadership,' 'really cares about people like you,' and is 'knowledgeable' were essentially unchanged."[129]

Even when grave lies on issues of life and death, war and peace are exposed—and even when the lies continue—there is little or no backlash. It is as if each lie is an isolated phenomenon, regardless of how many lies preceded it. Every lie is an "exception that proves the rule" that government is fundamentally trustworthy—and people must continue obeying or else chaos will result.

Perhaps with the growing attention deficit of so many citizens, politicians' lies are no longer as active in their minds as they once were. Perhaps there is a shorter "shelf-life" in people's brains for any non-video-game-related information. Perhaps because people are bombarded by images around the clock, their ability to recall atrophies. Lies often require a slight mental effort, adding two plus two, to recognize.

On the other hand, the type of images the modern White House pump out require no mental exertion. Typical television news consumers see vastly more images of a president invoking democracy, wrapping himself in the flag, and visiting U.S. troops than they hear or see of a president's falsehoods. The only things that penetrate are what government and their media lackeys continually hammer in.

It is as if inductions are now unpatriotic. There has been a concerted effort to stifle Americans' natural reflex to distrust political liars. The result is the defusing of political lies. It is as if tens of millions of wet blankets have been installed in people's heads, preventing any conflagrations from the sparks from Washington.

It is not so much that the Establishment and the media try to make people think that politicians as a class are honest. Instead, people are lulled into thinking that politicians' lies have little or no consequence. Government lies are portrayed as part of the natural order, the same way people once viewed common pestilences. Lies are simply facts of political life—"nothing to see here folks, just move along."

It is not surprising that most intellectuals would treat political lies as harmless since that is the same way they view government power. The nonchalance about presidential lies is part of a general disdain for political damage control.

Too much attention on political lies could end the mass docility which is prerequisite to government raising the people.

In recent decades, federal, state, and local regulators have become far more aggressive about banning and prosecuting private commercial fraud—especially in dealings with average consumers. Making fraudulent claims is apparently more dangerous when selling a refrigerator than when selling a war. It is a hundred times more difficult to get a "refund" as a result of an election stolen by politicians' lies than to get a refund for a purchase based on a business's false representations. There is no political equivalent of the disputed charge resolution process that American Express provides cardholders.

ARE AMERICANS CORRIGIBLE?

Lies are sometimes portrayed as a breach of trust between the government and the people. But the analysis almost always stops at this point—or, at most, it implies that the selection of a new set of rulers will automatically restore legitimacy.

President Clinton's statements were sufficient to persuade conservatives that he was a pathological liar who could not be trusted with any power. Bush's statements have persuaded many liberals that Bush is an incorrigible liar who cannot be trusted with power. America will likely have a 16-year stretch—practically an entire generation—of two presidents who had only the most distant relation with veracity. And yet, the baseline—that Americans can expect truth from their rulers—remains.

Neither conservatives nor liberals seem to reason beyond the immediate case. Few people seem to be raising questions about a political system that automatically vests one individual with vast power. But the more arbitrary power the U.S. presidency possesses, the more it will attract the type of politician who will not hesitate to lie to capture office.

What will restrain the lies of the rulers? No one has a good answer for this. It is something that is rarely discussed in polite company. Instead, we are supposed to assume that the system will correct its own mistakes. And why assume that? Because it has not yet collapsed or brought ruin to America. We are obliged to assume that the lies are relatively harmless—up until the moment when the damage is beyond repair.

If the citizenry does not punish liars, then it cannot expect the truth. To base political theories and expectations on the assumption that tomorrow's rulers will be morally superior to contemporary rulers is not idealism—unless one assumes that an overdose of Quaaludes is idealistic. It is simply escapism—people unable or unwilling to face the facts of the profound and lasting corruption of the political machine they have permitted to take over much of their lives. Will future historians say of today's Americans that "truth was unimportant and entirely subordinate to tactics and psychology," as Nazi propaganda minister Joseph Goebbels wrote in 1941?[130]

Lying is part of the larger problem of deference to the government. If people were not trained to genuflect to their rulers, politicians could not afford to tell so many lies. The more deference, the more deceit. The following chapter will illustrate what happens when government officials feel entitled to absolute power and above any duty to be honest with the American people.

CHAPTER 6

Torture and Absolute Power in Contemporary Democracy

The United States is committed to the worldwide elimination of torture, and we are leading this fight by example. I call on all governments to join with the United States and the community of law-abiding nations in prohibiting, investigating, and prosecuting all acts of torture and in undertaking to prevent other cruel and unusual punishment.

—George W. Bush, June 26, 2003[1]

I always knew the Americans would bring electricity back to Baghdad. I just never thought they'd be shooting it up my ass.

—a young Iraqi translator, November 2003[2]

WHAT SORT OF DEMOCRACY DO AMERICANS NOW LIVE UNDER? The Founding Fathers preached the Rule of Law—strict limits on government power through the higher law of the Constitution. However, our progressive times have long since abandoned such archaic notions. The torture scandal of recent years symbolizes how the federal government now is both above the law and above the truth. The proliferation and perpetuation of U.S. torture vivifies the elimination of all limits on the power of Bush and the U.S. government.

The torture scandal shows how little it takes to sway masses of Americans to supporting—if not demanding—behavior that for centuries has been equated with barbarism. Revulsion to torture was part of what separated modern times from Medieval darkness. Torture has long been officially proscribed in almost all respectable nations (though torture still occurs more often than citizens know). American courts have long refused to accept confessions gained via coercion.

The abuses of recent years are certainly not the first time that the U.S. government has been involved with torture. During the Vietnam war, torture of Viet Cong was ritualized—including the threatening and throwing of prisoners from low-flying helicopters.[3] In the early 1980s, the CIA was distributing its *Human Resource Exploitation Training Manual* to friendly Latin American governments. The manual stressed that when a "new safehouse is to be used as the interrogation site . . . the electric current should be known in advance, so that transformers or other modifying devices will be on hand if needed." The CIA acknowledged that this "referred to the application of electric shocks to interrogation suspects."[4]

The Bush administration is unique, though, in proclaiming its right to torture. Bush, his team, and their apologists continually portray the torture scandal as problems caused by a "few bad apples" or simply the equivalent of college-fraternity hazing. In reality, the abuses range from the endless high-volume repetition of a "Meow Mix" cat food commercial at Guantanamo, to tearing out toenails in Afghanistan, to compulsory enemas for recalcitrant prisoners, to beating people to death in Iraq and kicking them to death outside Kabul, to illegally sending detainees to foreign governments to be tortured by proxy and creating a system of "ghost prisoners" worthy of a banana republic. More people may have been killed during U.S. interrogation sessions in recent years than the total number of American civilians killed by international terrorists in any single year of the 1990s.[5]

Though some people thought the torture scandal might sink Bush after it first erupted, the administration exploited ignorance, patriotism, a cowardly media, and secrecy to contain the damage. The Bush team continually denied reality, and got enough of the Republican Party, the conservative movement, and national media to go along that the truth was quarantined until long after the initial shock and anger had subsided.

The interrogation doctrines, the torture abuses, the official cover-ups, and the sham investigations vivify what the U.S. government has become. The government claimed absolute power—and this claim has still received little or no effective challenge.

DIGITAL PHOTO BLUES

Shortly after 9/11, the Bush administration secretly changed the official policies on interrogations. The *Washington Post,* on the day after Christmas 2002, quoted a U.S. government official who supervised the capture and transfer of accused terrorists, who declared: "If you don't violate someone's human rights some of the time, you probably aren't doing your job." The *Post* interviewed ten U.S. national security officials and reported, "While the U.S. government publicly denounces the use of torture, each of the current national security officials interviewed for this article defended the use of violence against captives as just and necessary."[6] The *Post's* revelations about the routine use of torture by the United States generated scant controversy.

As 2003 drew to a close with no redeeming discovery of Iraqi weapons of mass destruction, Saddam Hussein's history of torture became far more important. Bush routinely portrayed the war as motivated by human rights concerns. On December 14, 2003, the day after Saddam was nabbed by the U.S. military, Bush said, "For the vast majority of Iraqi citizens who wish to live as free men and women, this event brings further assurance that the torture chambers and the secret police are gone forever." On the first anniversary of the U.S. invasion, March 19, 2004, President Bush demanded to know: "Who would prefer that Saddam's torture chambers still be open?"[7]

However, at the time of Bush's pious rhetorical question, a scandal over U.S. torture at Abu Ghraib—Saddam's most infamous prison—was already barreling down the tracks. On April 28, CBS broadcast photos of graphic abuse in Iraq, including bloodied prisoners, forced simulation of masturbation and oral sex, the stacking of naked prisoners with bags over their heads, mock electrocution via a wire connected to a man's penis, guard dogs on the verge of ripping into naked men, and grinning U.S. male and female soldiers celebrating the degradation. Three days later, the *New Yorker,* in an expose by Seymour Hersh, published extracts from a March 2004 report by Major General Antonio Taguba that catalogued U.S. abuses at Abu Ghraib prison, including "Breaking chemical lights and pouring the phosphoric liquid on detainees; pouring cold water on naked detainees; beating detainees with a broom handle and a chair; threatening male detainees with rape . . . sodomizing a detainee with a chemical light and perhaps a broom stick, and using military working dogs to frighten and intimidate detainees with threats of attack, and in one instance actually biting a detainee."[8] On the day after Hersh's article was posted on the internet, Gen. Richard Myers, chairman of the Joint Chiefs of Staff, admitted in a television interview that he had not yet bothered to read the Taguba report.

The Bush administration quickly portrayed the leaked photos as aberrations resulting from a handful of deviant National Guard members. However, a government consultant informed Hersh that the Abu Ghraib photos were specifically intended to be used to blackmail the prisoners abused, "to create an army of informants, people you could insert back in the population."[9] Hersh noted that "the notion that Arabs are particularly vulnerable to sexual humiliation became a talking point among pro-war Washington conservatives in the months before the March, 2003, invasion of Iraq."[10]

The Abu Ghraib photos were only the tip of the iceberg. Far more incriminating photos and videos of abuses existed, which Pentagon officials revealed in a slide show for members of Congress. However, the Bush administration slapped a national security classification on almost all the photos and videos not already acquired by the media. Rumsfeld told Congress that the undisclosed material showed "acts that can only be described as blatantly sadistic, cruel, and inhuman." Highlights included "American soldiers beating one prisoner almost to death, apparently raping a female prisoner, acting inappropriately with a dead body, and taping Iraqi guards raping young boys," according to NBC News.[11] Suppressing this evidence enabled the Bush administration to persuade many people that the scandal was actually far narrower than the facts would later show.

On May 5, Bush granted an interview with Alhurra Television, an Arabic language network owned and controlled by the U.S. government. Bush stressed: "We have nothing to hide. We believe in transparency, because we're a free society. That's what free societies do. They—if there's a problem, they address those problems in a forthright, upfront manner. And that's what's taking place." A minute later, Bush announced what the results of the investigation would be: "We're finding the few [U.S. troops] that wanted to try to stop progress toward freedom and democracy."[12] Three days later, in his weekly radio address, Bush assured Americans that the abuses had been committed by "a small number of American servicemen and women."

On May 7, Defense Secretary Rumsfeld informed the House and Senate Armed Services Committees that he was taking "full responsibility" for "the terrible activities that occurred at Abu Ghraib" and was personally appointing a commission to investigate the problem. Rumsfeld urged members of Congress to recognize the real victims: "If you could have seen the anguished expressions on the faces of those of us in the Department upon seeing the photos, you would know how we feel today." Rumsfeld complained that "people [in Iraq] are running around with digital cameras and taking these unbelievable photographs and then passing them off, against the law, to the media, to our surprise, when they had not even arrived in the Pentagon." Rumsfeld, like Bush, stressed the idealistic upside: "Judge us by our actions. Watch how

Americans, watch how democracy deals with wrongdoing and scandal and the pain of acknowledging and correcting our own mistakes and, indeed, our own weaknesses."[13]

On May 15, Pentagon Deputy Assistant Secretary for Public Affairs Lawrence Di Rita revealed that newspaper editorial writers are as abominable as the soldiers who rampaged at Abu Ghraib. Di Rita declared that the *Washington Post*'s criticisms of Bush administration detainee policies put its editorial page "in the same company as those involved in this despicable behavior in terms of apparent disregard for basic human dignity."[14]

The Republican Party quickly exploited Abu Ghraib to portray Democrats as anti-American and unpatriotic. Republican National Committee Chairman Ed Gillespie accused Sen. John F. Kerry (D-Mass.) of exploiting the scandal as a fund-raising method and declared that Democrats "do not see the reprehensible images from Abu Ghraib Prison as the isolated, aberrant acts of a few soldiers who should be brought to justice. . . . These hasty calls for [Rumsfeld's] resignation reflect a cynical political ploy, or an inaccurate and sadly unfortunate view of the honor of our Armed Forces."[15] Yet, Kerry specifically commented that the prisoner scandal did not reflect "the behavior of 99.9 percent of our troops."[16] This did not dissuade Bush-Cheney campaign chairman Marc Racicot from denouncing Kerry for having suggested that all U.S. troops in Iraq are "somehow universally responsible" for the Abu Ghraib abuses.[17] Many Republicans and much of the conservative media convinced themselves that the torture scandal was a fabrication of the liberal media and of the "hate America" crowd. At a Senate Intelligence Committee hearing on May 10, 2004, Sen. James Inhofe (R-Okla.) fumed: "I'm probably not the only one up at this table that is more outraged by the outrage than we are by the treatment" the Abu Ghraib prisoners received.[18]

On May 16, *Newsweek* published a leaked copy of a memo by White House counsel Alberto Gonzales and other confidential material signaling the administration's support for far more aggressive interrogation methods. In early 2002, Bush issued a ruling to prevent the War Crimes Act from applying to many actions taken by U.S. officials against Al Qaeda and the Taliban. The War Crimes Act, passed by Congress in 1996, applied to all Americans and defined war crimes in part as acts that would be "grave breaches" of the Geneva Conventions on the treatment of prisoners. White House counsel Alberto Gonzales advised Bush: "The nature of the new war places a high premium on other factors, such as the ability to quickly obtain information from captured terrorists and their sponsors in order to avoid further atrocities against American civilians. In my judgment, this new paradigm renders obsolete Geneva's strict limitations on questioning of enemy prisoners and renders quaint some of its provisions."[19] Bush decreed that the Al Qaeda and Taliban forces did not have protection under the Geneva Conventions.

One of the most novel arguments the Bush team used to justify waiving torture prohibitions was the notion that Afghanistan was a "failed state."[20] According to the Bush legal team, if the United States labeled Afghanistan a "failed state," that meant that Afghanistan was not a party to the Geneva Conventions, and thus that U.S. government employees could not be prosecuted for violating the rights of captured Taliban fighters. Attorney General Ashcroft, in a memo to Bush, explained that a presidential determination decreeing Afghanistan a "failed state" "would provide the highest assurance that no court would subsequently entertain charges that American military officers, intelligence officials, or law enforcement officials violated Geneva Convention rules."[21] The practical effect of this doctrine is that if the U.S. government does not approve of a foreign government and labels it a "failed state," the U.S. military and CIA receive a blank check to violate the rights of the residents of that state. There is no reason that Bush or subsequent U.S. presidents could not decree that all non-democracies are by definition "failed states."

On May 25, the Bush administration responded to the growing PR debacle by bringing seven Iraqis whose hands had been chopped off at Abu Ghraib during the Saddam era to the White House for a meeting and photo session with President Bush. (The men received new mechanical hands thanks to private donors in Texas.)[22] The White House subsequently touted the get-together as the "President's Meeting With Tortured Iraqis."[23]

In a May 28 interview with *Paris Match,* Bush was asked: "Do you feel responsible in any way for this moral failure in Iraq?" Bush replied: "First of all, I feel responsible for letting the world see that we will deal with this in a transparent way, that people will see that justice will be delivered. And what I regret most of all is that the great honor of our country has been stained by the actions of a few people." Bush reminded the Frenchman that "America is a great and generous and decent country."[24]

On June 3, Sen. Trent Lott (R-Miss.), who had been Senate majority leader until being pushed out of the job in December 2002, sneered at those who complained about Abu Ghraib. Lott explained to a Mississippi television interviewer: "Hey, nothing wrong with holding a dog up there, unless the dog ate him." Lott explained: "This is not Sunday school; this is interrogation; this is rough stuff." Lott pointed out that some of the Abu Ghraib detainees "should not have been prisoners in the first place, probably should have been killed."[25]

A few days later, another memo leaked out—this one written by the Justice Department Office of Legal Counsel at the request of White House Counsel Alberto Gonzales.[26] The August 1, 2002, memo, which redefined U.S. torture policy, became known as the Bybee memo, after Jay Bybee, the head of the Office of Legal Counsel. Deputy Assistant Attorney General John Yoo was co-author of the memo. The memo was titled "Standards of Conduct for Interrogation under 18 U.S.C. §§ 2340–2340A" (the U.S. anti-torture act) and was "akin to a binding legal opinion on government policy on interrogations."[27]

Rather than a strict interpretation of the law, the Bybee memo was a Torturers Emancipation Proclamation. Violating the anti-torture act carries a penalty of up to 20 years in prison. If the victim dies, the torturer can receive a death sentence. However, the Justice Department revealed that vigilante interrogators had little or nothing to fear from the law.

The memo began by largely redefining torture out of existence. It then explained why even if someone died during torture, the torturer might not be guilty if he felt the torture was necessary to prevent some worse evil. The memo concluded by revealing that the president has the right to order torture because he is above the law, at least during wartime (even if Congress has not declared war).

The Bush-appointed lawyers showed that interrogators can easily be innocent of a torturous intent:

> Because Section 2340 requires that a defendant act with the specific intent to inflict severe pain, the infliction of such pain must be the defendant's precise objective. . . . If the defendant acted knowing that severe pain or suffering was reasonably likely to result from his actions, but no more, he would have acted only with general intent. As a theoretical matter, therefore, knowledge alone that a particular result is certain to occur does not constitute specific intent. . . . Thus, even if the defendant knows that severe pain will result from his actions, if causing such harm is not his objective, he lacks the requisite specific intent even though the defendant did not act in good faith. Instead, a defendant is guilty of torture only if he acts with the express purpose of inflicting severe pain or suffering on a person within his custody or physical control.[28]

The memo offered the following illustration: "In the context of mail fraud, if an individual honestly believes that the material transmitted is truthful, he has not acted with the required intent to deceive or mislead." Mailing dubious herbal medicine brochures thus helped set the standard for government employees who club prisoners to death. The memo assured would-be torturers and torture supervisors: "A good faith belief need not be a reasonable one."

The Justice Department tapped all the highbrow wisdom of its upper echelon to show why the requirement that torture inflict "severe" pain or suffering is liberating for interrogators: "The adjective 'severe' conveys that the pain or suffering must be of such a high level of intensity that the pain is difficult for the subject to endure." The memo then referenced health care policy to shore up a definition of "severe pain," which, for U.S. torture purposes, means "the level that would ordinarily be associated with a sufficiently serious physical condition or injury such as death, organ failure, or serious impairment of body functions."

The memo stressed that mere garden-variety torment posed no legal problem for interrogators. "For purely mental pain or suffering to amount to torture . . . it must result in significant psychological harm of significant duration, e.g., lasting for months or even years." And it is easy to dodge the charge of mental torture, since "if a defendant has a good faith belief that his actions will not result in prolonged mental harm, he lacks the mental state necessary for his actions to constitute torture. A defendant could show that he acted in good faith by taking such steps as surveying professional literature." Thus, as long as a torturer subscribes to respectable medical journals (S&M magazines presumably wouldn't count), he can immunize himself.

Other good news for interrogators included the fact that courts rarely categorize any single twist by an interrogator as torture: "There are no [court] decisions that have found an example of torture on facts that show the action was isolated, rather than part of a systematic course of conduct."

The memo recited the damage of 9/11 in order to justify the presumption that torture would prevent similar carnage: "Given the massive destruction and loss of life caused by the September 11 attacks, it is reasonable to believe that information gained from al Qaeda personnel could prevent attacks of a similar (if not greater) magnitude from occurring in the United States." But the Justice Department's top lawyers offered no evidence of the efficacy of torture (which both the FBI and U.S. military experts dispute).

The Justice Department stressed that even intentionally killing people during an interrogation might be okay:

> The *necessity defense* may prove especially relevant in the current circumstances.
>
> First, the defense is not limited to certain types of harms. Therefore, the harm inflicted by necessity may include intentional homicide, so long as the harm avoided is greater (i.e., preventing more deaths).
>
> Second, it must actually be the defendant's intention to avoid the greater harm. . . .
>
> Third, if the defendant reasonably believed that the lesser harm was necessary, even if, unknown to him, it was not, he may still avail himself of the defense. . . .
>
> Clearly, any harm that might occur during an interrogation would pale to insignificance compared to the harm avoided by preventing such an attack, which could take hundreds or thousands of lives.

The Justice Department preemptively exonerated U.S. government officials who violate the Anti-Torture Act: "If a government defendant were to harm an enemy combatant during an interrogation in a manner that might arguably violate Section 2340A, he would be doing so in order to prevent further attacks on the United States by the al Qaeda terrorist network." The Justice Department did not explain why preventing a catastrophic attack is the only reason why a suspect might be maimed during interrogation.

The Justice Department declared that the president may effectively exempt government officials from federal criminal law, noting that "Congress cannot compel the President to prosecute outcomes taken pursuant to the President's own constitutional authority. If Congress could do so, it could control the President's authority through the manipulation of federal criminal law."

The memo's most revolutionary revelation was that federal criminal law does not apply to the president:

> Even if an interrogation method arguably were to violate Section 2340A, the statute would be unconstitutional if it impermissibly encroached on the President's constitutional power to conduct a military campaign. . . . The demands of the Commander-in-Chief power are especially pronounced in the middle of a war in which the nation has already suffered a direct attack. . . . Any effort to apply Section 2340A in a manner that interferes with the President's direction of such core war matters as the detention and interrogation of enemy combatants thus would be unconstitutional.

The memo stressed the uniqueness of the post-9/11 world: "The situation in which these issues arise is unprecedented in recent American history. . . . These attacks were aimed at critical government buildings in the Nation's capital and landmark, buildings in its financial center." But President James Madison did not announce that the U.S. government was obliged to start torturing people after the British burned down Washington in 1814.

The memo's absolutism would have brought a smile to despots everywhere: "As the Supreme Court has recognized . . . the President enjoys complete discretion in the exercise of his Commander-in-Chief authority and in conducting operations against hostile forces. . . . we will not read a criminal statute as infringing on the President's ultimate authority in these areas." Thus, the "commander-in-chief" label automatically swallows up the rest of the Constitution.

The Bybee memo profoundly influenced U.S. interrogation policy. Bush rewarded Bybee for this and other efforts by appointing him to a federal appellate judgeship. The Senate, not knowing of the torture memo, confirmed Bybee by a vote of 74 to 19.

Also in early June, the Pentagon's *Working Group Report on Detainee Interrogations in the Global War on Terrorism; Assessment of Legal, Historical, Policy, and Operational Considerations* leaked out.[29] This March 6, 2003, report—drawing heavily on the Bybee memo—helped establish interrogation policies for U.S. military personnel in Iraq, Afghanistan, Guantanamo Bay, and elsewhere.

The Pentagon report encouraged government officials to unchain themselves from the statute book: "Sometimes the greater good for society will be accomplished by violating the literal language of the criminal law." The report stressed that "the necessity defense can justify the intentional killing of one person to save two others." Thus, invoking the 9/11 casualty count can almost automatically banish any concerns about collateral damage during interrogations.

Like the Justice Department, the Pentagon brandished the "medical journal subscription" exemption to the Anti-Torture Act: "A defendant could show that he acted in good faith by taking such steps as surveying professional literature."

The Pentagon insisted that unless Congress specifies in a law that the president will be banned from committing specific crimes, the president is presumed to be exempt from any limitation during war time: "In light of the President's complete authority over the conduct of war, without a clear statement otherwise, criminal statutes are not read as infringing on the President's ultimate authority in these areas."

The Pentagon report noted: "As this authority [to torture] is inherent in the President, exercise of it by subordinates would be best if it can be shown to have been derived from the President's authority through Presidential directive or other writing." In other words, prudent torturers will possess a presidential authorization to immunize them for the pain they inflict. (Shortly before the Pentagon report leaked out, the FBI's "On Scene Commander—Baghdad" e-mailed senior FBI officials stating that U.S. military officials in Iraq told him that a secret "presidential Executive Order" permitted them to use extreme interrogation techniques considered illegal by the FBI including "sensory deprivation through the use of hoods," stress positions, and military dogs.[30] The White House denied that Bush had issued such an order.)

The Pentagon updated American military morality, explaining why the principles of the Nuremberg war crimes trials may not apply if soldiers claim that were "following orders."

Interrogators who were ordered to use force would

certainly raise the defense of obedience to orders. The question then becomes one of degree. While this may be a successful defense to simple assaults or batteries, it would unlikely be as successful to more serious charges such as maiming, manslaughter, and maiming.[sic] Within the *middle of the spectrum* lay those offenses for which the effectiveness of this defense becomes less clear. Those offenses would include conduct unbecoming an officer, reckless endangerment, cruelty, and negligent homicide. [italics added]

The fact that the Bush team placed "negligent homicide" in the "middle of the spectrum" of offenses hints at the rigor of interrogations under the new guidelines.

The report stressed that "the defense of superior orders will generally be available for U.S. Armed Forces personnel engaged in exceptional interrogations except where the conduct goes so far as to be patently unlawful." But this is immunity-via-tautology—since the Justice Department's redefinition of torture excludes almost everything except killing and permanently maiming.

The Pentagon also disposed of the danger of U.S. torturers being nailed for violating the Bill of Rights: "An examination of the history of the [Eighth] Amendment and the decisions of this [Supreme] Court construing the proscription against cruel and unusual punishment confirms that it was designed to protect those convicted of crimes." Thus, regardless of what happened during interrogation, detainees could not "successfully pursue a claim regarding their pre-conviction treatment under the Eighth Amendment." This is the type of argument that would have gotten laughed out of court—but the Bush team never had to publicly make such a case. Because the political appointees of the Bush administration effectively silenced the legal experts within the military and elsewhere, the doctrine was presented as credible.

The Pentagon report did cite one risk from the new guidelines: "Should information regarding the use of more aggressive interrogation techniques than have been used traditionally by U.S. forces become public, it is likely to be exaggerated or distorted in the U.S. and international media accounts, and may produce an adverse effect on support for the war on terrorism."[31] The Pentagon feared bad press more than dead detainees.

Every argument made in the Bybee and Pentagon memo against the Anti-Torture Act not limiting the president's power also applies to the War Crimes Act. Yale Law School Dean Harold Koh observed: "If the president has commander-in-chief power to commit torture, he has the power to commit genocide, to sanction slavery, to promote apartheid, to license summary execution."[32] The *Wall Street Journal,* which first published excerpts from the Pentagon report, noted: "A military lawyer who helped prepare the report said that political appointees heading the working group sought to assign to the president virtually unlimited authority on matters of torture—to assert 'presidential power at its absolute apex.'"[33]

DENIALS AND VALUES PILE UP

On June 9, the Bush administration's effort to portray Abu Ghraib as a sadistic novelty took a hit. The *Los Angeles Times* reported that Rumsfeld's legal counsel ordered military intelligence officers in late 2001 to "take the gloves off" while interrogating John Walker Lindh, the American who fought with the Taliban and was captured in Afghanistan. Lindh was deprived of food and sleep and "propped up naked and tied to a stretcher in interrogation sessions that went on for days, according to court papers." He was also "often held for long periods in a large metal container."[34] As Dave Lindorff noted on *Counterpunch,* "Shot in the leg prior to his capture, and already starving and badly dehydrated, Lindh unconscionably was left with his wound untreated and festering for days despite doctors being readily available."[35] According to his attorneys, Lindh requested to speak to a lawyer but interrogators denied his request and did not inform him for 54 days that his father had hired defense lawyers for him. Lindh was repeatedly threatened with death. In a practice that would be repeated at Abu Ghraib, "soldiers took photos and videos of themselves smiling next to the naked Lindh."[36] When Lindh sought to reveal the abuse he suffered in captivity, the Justice Department persuaded a docile federal judge to slap a gag order on him.[37]

On June 10, Bush was asked by a British journalist whether torture can ever be moral. Bush replied: "The instructions went out to our people to adhere to law. That ought to comfort you. We're a nation of law. We adhere to laws. We have laws on the books. You might look at those laws, and that might provide comfort for you. And those were the instructions out of—from me to the Government."[38] But the Bush administration's definition of torture is comforting only to interrogators. And the administration continued refusing to disclose what Bush actually ordered.

On June 17, Defense Secretary Rumsfeld, at a Pentagon press conference, portrayed the government as victim and blamed the news media: "The implication is that the United States government has, in one way or another, ordered, authorized, permitted, tolerated torture. Not true. And our forces read that, and they've got to wonder, do we?"[39] Rumsfeld added: "I have not seen anything that suggests that a senior civilian or military official of the United States of America . . . could be characterized as ordering or authorizing or permitting torture or acts that are inconsistent with our international treaty obligations or our laws or our values as a country."[40] Yet, in December 2002, Rumsfeld personally authorized "the use of techniques including hooding, nudity, stress positions, 'fear of dogs' and physical contact with prisoners at the Guantanamo Bay base." And, as the *Washington Post* noted, Rumsfeld admitted in the same news conference "that he had personally approved the detention of several prisoners in Iraq without registering them with the International Committee of the Red Cross. This creation of 'ghost prisoners' was described by Maj. Gen. Antonio M. Taguba, as 'deceptive, contrary to Army doctrine and in violation of international law.'"[41]

On June 22, Bush responded to criticism: "Let me make very clear the position of my government and our country. . . . The values of this country are such that torture is not a part of our soul and our being."[42] Instead of the issue being Bush's orders, the issue was the American "soul and being." Repeating largely meaningless denials and invocations satisfied most Bush supporters. On the same day, White House counsel Alberto R. Gonzales announced that some parts of the Bybee memo were being formally disavowed, calling it "irrelevant and unnecessary to support any action taken by the president." Gonzales stressed the PR problems caused by the memo: "It was harmful to this country in terms of the notion that we may be engaged in torture."[43] Gonzales talked of his "quaint" memo and other advocacy of vigorous interrogation methods as mere "documents . . . generated by government lawyers to explore the limits of the legal landscape as to what the Executive Branch can do within the law and the Constitution as an abstract matter." Gonzales made it clear that the Bush administration was not disavowing its claim to absolute power: "I must emphasize that the analysis underpinning the President's decisions stands and are not being reviewed. The *Commander-in-Chief override power* discussed in the opinion is, on its face—on its face—limited to our conflict with al Qaeda. There is no indication that it applies to our conflict in Iraq."[44] His qualifying phrases "on its face" and "no indication" reserved the Bush administration's options. This "override power" is something that exists in the minds of conservative absolutists, not the Constitution.

On June 23, Democratic senators sought to issue a subpoena for Bush administration documents on detainee abuses. Republicans defeated the measure by a largely party line vote, 50-to-46. The "talking points" issued to Republicans by the Senate Republican Policy Committee warned: "Because of an out-of-control media and widespread hysteria, the White House and Pentagon have been forced to reveal secret interrogation techniques just to prove our men and women in uniform aren't torturers and murderers. . . . The forced disclosure will now complicate efforts to get information from terrorists who will train to withstand these techniques. . . . It's high past time we remember who [our] enemies are."[45] Sen. John Cornyn (R-Tex.) condemned Democrats' criticism of Bush torture policies as "not only false—they dangerously undermine troop morale, put our troops at risk, and impede our efforts to win the global war against terrorism."[46]

In a June 24 session with Radio and Television Ireland, a petite female interviewer told Bush that most Irish people are "angry over Abu Ghraib. Are you bothered by what Irish people think?" Bush replied: "Listen, I hope the Irish people understand the great values of our country. And if they think that a few soldiers represents the entirety of America, they don't really understand America then."[47]

On June 26, in his annual proclamation on the UN International Day in Support of Victims of Torture, Bush assured the world that "the American people were horrified by the abuse of detainees at Abu Ghraib prison in Iraq. . . . They were inconsistent with our policies and our values as a nation. . . . The United States will continue to lead the fight to eliminate [torture] everywhere."[48]

After the Abu Ghraib torture scandal had percolated for six weeks, the *New York Times* and CBS News polled people on whether "members of the Bush Administration are telling the entire truth, are mostly telling the truth but are hiding something, or are mostly lying" on their statements on Abu Ghraib. Only 15 percent of respondents said the administration was telling the "entire truth"; 52 percent said they were "hiding something"; and 27 percent said they were "mostly lying."[49]

On July 22, the 9/11 Commission's final report called for the U.S. government to do more to wage the "struggle of ideas" against Islamic radicalism. The commission proclaimed: "We should offer an example of moral leadership in the world."[50]

On the same day, the Pentagon re-exonerated itself on the Iraqi torture scandal. A 300-page report from the Army Inspector General, Lt. Gen. Paul Mikolashek, announced that the Abu Ghraib prison abuses were "unauthorized actions taken by a few individuals." A Pentagon press release issued on the day of a congressional hearing on the report declared: "A few 'bad apples' and a lack of proper supervision—not a failure in military training, doctrine or policy—were responsible for detainee abuses in Afghanistan and Iraq." Army Secretary Les Brownlee testified that "we were unable to identify systemwide failures that resulted in incidents of detainee abuse."[51] Army Chief of Staff Gen. Peter Schoomaker assured senators that "the inexcusable behavior of a few is not representative of the courageous and compassionate performance of the majority of our soldiers."[52] Sen. Jim Talent (R-Mo.) praised the report for "vindicating our leaders and our soldiers."[53]

Though the Pentagon insisted that there were no "systemic" failures, the report cited 94 cases of confirmed or possible abuse, including 20 cases in which prisoners were killed or may have been killed. Perhaps the Pentagon concluded that the number of Iraqi dead was negligible in a country of 25 million people. The Inspector General's team did no original investigation but merely looked at reports from previous investigations, many of which were whitewashes. And the new report effectively repudiated the courageous earlier report by Major General Antonio Taguba. A *Washington Post* editorial, "An Army Whitewash," derided the report: "The Army's attempt to hold itself accountable for the abuse of foreign prisoners is off to a terrible start."[54]

While most Americans had suspected a coverup in late June, the issue soon lost its bite. A poll released in late July by the University of Maryland

Program on International Policy Attitudes (PIPA) found that Bush's "handling of the detainee issue made 37 percent say they were less likely to vote for him, while 22 percent said it made them more likely."[55] PIPA research director Clay Ramsay commented that the reports on detainee abuses "are perceived as a sign the administration is trying to do its job right now, trying to do its best to clean up the mess. They are at worst a wash for the president and possibly a little beneficial." Ramsay noted: "We found little sign . . . that people were directly connecting these circumstances to Bush as a person and a leader. We also found that a majority did not connect it very directly to even the secretary of Defense."

At the Democratic National Convention in Boston at the end of July, Abu Ghraib was barely mentioned. Though the torture scandal had sparked fury and protests in America and around the world, the Democratic Party largely ignored the issue in a convention that celebrated the theme of former Navy officer John Kerry "reporting for duty." The Democrats may have been intimidated from mentioning it after the harsh Republican attacks in the preceding months following any criticism of Abu Ghraib or Iraq.

Two more Pentagon reports came out the week before the Republican National Convention. At an August 25 Pentagon press conference announcing the results of his "Investigation of the Abu Ghraib Detention Facility and 205th Military Intelligence Brigade," Maj. Gen. George Fay declared, "There were a few instances when torture was being used." While the Pentagon had previously stressed that a small number of wayward National Guard members were to blame for Abu Ghraib, Fay reported that 27 Military Intelligence personnel "allegedly requested, encouraged, condoned or solicited Military Police personnel to abuse detainees and/or participated in detainee abuse" during interrogations. The Pentagon released only 177 pages of the more than 3,000-page report.

Fay reported that the abuses at Abu Ghraib "spanned from direct physical assault, such as delivering head blows rendering detainees unconscious, to sexual posing and forced participation in group masturbation. . . . What started as nakedness and humiliation, stress and physical training, carried over into sexual and physical assaults by a small group of morally corrupt and unsupervised soldiers and civilians." Fay noted how abusive practices migrated from Guantanamo and Afghanistan to Abu Ghraib: "The techniques employed in [Guantanamo] included the use of stress positions, isolation for up to thirty days, removal of clothing and the use of detainees' phobias (such as the use of dogs)."[56] Similar practices were used by U.S. forces in Afghanistan, with the result that U.S. "interrogators in Iraq, already familiar with the practice of some of these new ideas, implemented them even prior to any policy guidance" from Iraq commanders. One part of the report that the Pentagon suppressed—yet still leaked out—noted that "policies and practices developed and approved for use on Al Qaeda and Taliban detainees who were not afforded the protection of the Geneva Conventions, now applied to detainees who did fall under the Geneva Conventions' protections."[57] Absolute power became addictive.

The report summarized the treatment one detainee received, noting that it is "highly probable" that his allegations "are true."

DETAINEE–07 was left naked in his cell for extended periods, cuffed in his cell in stressful positions ("High cuffed"), left with a bag over his head for ex-tended periods, and denied bedding or blankets. DETAINEE–07 described being made to "bark like a dog, being forced to crawl on his stomach while MPs spit and urinated on him, and being struck causing unconsciousness." . . . On yet another occasion, DETAINEE–07 was forced to lie down while MPs jumped onto his back and legs. He was beaten with a broom and a chemical light was broken and poured over his body. . . . During this abuse a police stick was used to sodomize DETAINEE–07 and two female MPs were hitting him, throwing a ball at his penis, and taking photographs.[58]

"Doggy dance" described the response U.S. interrogators got from Iraqi detainees from threats or lurches or unmuzzling of the guards' canines. The Fay report noted that one soldier dog handler said "that he had a competition with another [dog] handler to see if they could scare detainees to the point that they would defecate. He mentioned that they had already made some de-tainees urinate, so they appeared to be raising the competition." The contest may have sparked an incident "when a dog was allowed in the cell of two male juveniles and allowed to go 'nuts.' Both juveniles were screaming and crying with the youngest and smallest trying to hide behind the other juvenile." The Fay report noted: "When dogs are used to threaten and terrify detainees, there is a clear violation of applicable laws and regulations." Ethnic profiling spurred canine abuse. The report observed: "Interrogations at Abu Ghraib were influ-enced by several documents that spoke of exploiting the Arab fear of dogs."

Stripping prisoners was a key method of punishment and degradation. The Fay report noted: "The use of nudity as an interrogation technique or in-centive to maintain the cooperation of detainees was . . . imported and can be traced through Afghanistan and GTMO [Guantanamo]. . . . The use of cloth-ing as an incentive (nudity) is significant in that it likely contributed to an es-calating 'de-humanization' of the detainees and set the stage for additional and more severe abuses to occur." Detainees were left naked in their cells and de-nied blankets during severe cold weather.[59]

At the press conference at which his report was released, Fay complained that the CIA, widely perceived as being more "aggressive" in its interrogation methods than the Army, had stonewalled his investigation. Fay's report condemned the

CIA for Iraqi detention and interrogation practices that "led to a loss of account-ability, abuse, reduced interagency cooperation, and unhealthy mystique that . . . poisoned the atmosphere" at Abu Ghraib.

In the same week, the Pentagon also released the *Report of the Independent Panel to Review DoD Detention Operations.* This commission was lauded by the media as "independent" because Defense Secretary Rumsfeld inde-pendently picked his friend James Schlesinger to run the show. Schlesinger's reputation as a friend of government goes back a long way. Schlesinger had been appointed as CIA chief by President Nixon after his predecessor, Richard Helms, refused to block the Watergate investigation. On his first day as CIA chief, Schlesinger reportedly announced to the CIA staff: "I'm here to make sure you don't screw Richard Nixon."[60] Nixon later appointed him as secretary of defense, and President Gerald Ford made him his secre-tary of energy. (Rumsfeld was Ford's White House chief of staff.) Schlesinger was also an outspoken advocate of "trust in government." Three years ear-lier, in a speech to the American Society for Public Administrators, Schlesinger lamented that the recent decline in trust in government had re-sulted in "decades of political campaigning which disparage both govern-ment and government servants."[61]

Schlesinger's devotion to government may have exceeded his devotion to fact finding. When Schlesinger was asked whether Rumsfeld should be axed for the abuses that occurred at Abu Ghraib, Schlesinger replied that firing Rumsfeld "would be a boon to all of America's enemies."[62] Schlesinger, blur-ring all standards, testified that "what constitutes 'humane treatment' lies in the eye of the beholder."[63]

At the press conference at which the report was released, Schlesinger min-imized the Abu Ghraib problem as "Animal House on the night shift." Yet, the report noted that at least five people died "as a result of abuse by U.S. person-nel during interrogations."[64] Schlesinger's report showed how the abuses flowed from Bush's own edicts. The report noted that "interrogators and lists of techniques circulated from Guantanamo and Afghanistan to Iraq." On Sep-tember 14, 2003, Lt. Gen. Ricardo Sanchez, the top commander in Iraq, "signed a memorandum authorizing a dozen interrogation techniques be-yond" the standard Army practice under the Geneva Conventions, including "five beyond those approved for Guantanamo."[65] The Schlesinger Report ob-served that Sanchez was "using reasoning from the President's Memorandum of February 7, 2002," which he believed justified "additional, tougher meas-ures."[66] Yet, Schlesinger insisted that there was no policy "that encourages abuse."[67] Despite the clear path from the Oval Office to Abu Ghraib, Schlesinger exonerated Bush, Rumsfeld, and everyone else in the Greater Washington Metropolitan Area.

PRE-ELECTION TACTICAL SECRECY

Many key documents on the torture scandal could have been released in 2004 with no damage to national security. At a September 9 Senate hearing, Sen. Lindsay Graham (R-S.C.) complained that the Pentagon "inappropriately" classified memos that "suggest that those interrogation techniques that were being proposed by civilian authorities [in the White House, the Justice Department, and in Rumsfeld's office] were way out of bounds; that they violated the Uniform Code of Military Justice, they violated international law and they would get our people in trouble."[68] At the same hearing, Pentagon officials claimed to have almost finished a report on how the illegal interrogation methods spread far beyond Guantanamo, but no such report was released before the election. After FBI director Robert Mueller testified to the Senate Judiciary Committee in May regarding FBI views on Bush administration interrogation practices at Guantanamo and Iraq, the FBI compiled a 300-page response to senators' follow-up questions. But the Justice Department, which has jurisdiction over the FBI, locked up the report until after the election.[69]

On September 14, U.S. military authorities proudly unveiled Camp Liberty, a new tent compound to house Iraqi detainees next to Abu Ghraib. Major General Geoffrey Miller, the camp commander, declared that Camp Liberty and other changes in the treatment of Iraqi prisoners are "restoring the honor of America."[70] The camp was used for Iraqis cleared of wrongdoing who were on the verge of being released. The *New York Times* noted that, as detainees were released, a soldier would give them "$25, in the form of a crisp new $20 bill and a $5 bill, and a 12-page glossy pamphlet on Iraq's interim government, 'Iraq. Development.'"[71] The Bush administration's use of the word liberty to try to expunge Abu Ghraib atrocities illustrated how all limits were waived on degrading the American political vocabulary. This was the second re-christening, since Pentagon officials had speedily christened part of the Abu Ghraib complex Camp Redemption in May, when the photos were first rattling the world.

Despite the scandal, Bush ran for reelection as the anti-torture candidate. In a July 20 campaign speech in Missouri, Bush denounced Saddam: "For decades he tormented and tortured the people of Iraq. Because we acted, Iraq is free and a sovereign nation."[72] It was as if torture subverts freedom only if done on a dictator's orders, not when inflicted by the greatest democracy in the world. In the closing weeks of the campaign, Bush constantly reminded audiences: "Think about how far that country has come from the days of torture chambers and mass graves. Freedom is on the march, and America and the world are better for it."[73] Bush never muttered a single sentence fragment to correct his earlier false statements about the narrow extent of the torture scandal.

There were no independent probes into the torture scandal during 2004. All the investigators were under the thumb of the Pentagon. The investigations were all carefully designed to look only downward—with no authority to pursue wrongdoing to the highest branches of the Pentagon and the White House.[74] The multitude of investigations were designed to produce an appearance of thoroughness, and perhaps fatigue people who might conclude that the subject had already been flogged to death. Each additional stage-managed investigation helped the Bush administration block a bonafide independent investigation.

Some apologists exonerated the Abu Ghraib excesses by portraying all detainees as killers or would-be killers. In a January 17, 2004, radio address, Bush declared, "in Iraq, the enemies of freedom are being systematically routed from their holes and rounded up."[75] But the round ups were often only "close enough for government work," and U.S. policies guaranteed that many, if not most, Iraqis detained would be innocent. The Fay report noted that "as the pace of operations picked up in late November–early December 2003, it became a common practice . . . to round up large quantities of Iraqi personnel [i.e., civilians] in the general vicinity of a specified target as a cordon and capture technique.[76] A Red Cross report explained how such raids worked:

> Arresting authorities entered houses usually after dark, breaking down doors, waking up residents roughly, yelling orders, forcing family members into one room under military guard while searching the rest of the house and further breaking doors, cabinets and other property. They arrested suspects, tying their hands in the back with flexi-cuffs, hooding them, and taking them away. Sometimes they arrested all adult males present in a house, including elderly, handicapped or sick people. Treatment often included pushing people around, insulting, taking aim with rifles, punching and kicking and striking with rifles.[77]

U.S. military intelligence officers told the Red Cross that between 70 and 90 percent of detainees in Iraq were "deprived of their liberty . . . [and] had been arrested by mistake."[78]

The "cordon and capture," "sweep and keep" approach turned the U.S. military effort into a numbers game as fraudulent as the body counts of the Vietnam war. Military units were evaluated based on how many Iraqis they brought in, not on whether those nabbed were guilty. The soldiers bringing in the suspects had no obligation to provide evidence that detainees were complicit in anything aside from living in an area unlucky enough to be targeted by a U.S. raid. No effort was usually made to screen detainees to determine who might have valuable information. Instead, the population was treated as if all Iraqi adult males were collectively guilty for the actions of the insurgents. Detainees in Abu Ghraib were routinely held for six months based on no evidence—simply as a result of delays in their release.

As the presidential election entered the final weeks, the *Los Angeles Times* reported that an Army criminal investigation implicated 28 U.S. soldiers involved in the case of two Afghan detainees beaten to death in December 2002. The *Times* noted that some of soldiers were in "the military intelligence unit that later transferred to Iraq and was involved in the Abu Ghraib" debacle. The *Times* revealed that the Army was continuing to investigate credible allegations that a U.S. Special Forces unit abused Afghans with "repeated beatings, immersion in cold water, electric shocks and prisoners being hanged upside down and having their toenails torn off."[79] The *New York Times* earlier reported that two men held at the Bagram air base declared "that they were tortured and sexually humiliated by their American jailers; they said they were held in isolation cells, black hoods were placed over their heads, and their hands at times were chained to the ceiling."[80] The reports had no visible impact on voters.

LEGAL COMPLICATIONS

The ACLU and other organizations filed a Freedom of Information Act (FOIA) request on detainee abuses in October 2003. By law, the government was obliged to respond within 20 business days. But the Pentagon effectively ignored the request, notifying the ACLU that nothing in the material requested involved "questions about the government's integrity which affect public confidence." The Pentagon also declared that the request did not involve "breaking news" and that delaying the response would not "endanger the life or safety of any individual." The ACLU also filed FOIA requests with other federal agencies. However, six months after the requests, the only information the feds had disclosed was "about a dozen pages of talking points prepared for [State Department] press officers concerning the detentions at Guantanamo."[81]

On September 15, 2004, federal judge Alvin Hellerstein rapped the feds' knuckles, rejecting the Bush administration's "national security" claim to justify withholding the information. Hellerstein gave the feds a 30-day deadline to comply. Late the following month, the feds began disgorging thousands of pages regarding detainee abuses and investigations.

On November 30, excerpts of a confidential report given by the International Committee of the Red Cross to the Bush administration in mid-summer splashed the front page of the *New York Times*. The Red Cross complained that methods used on detainees were increasingly "more refined and repressive." Red Cross experts, who spent much of June 2004 at Guantanamo, concluded that practices there "cannot be considered other than an intentional system of cruel, unusual and degrading treatment and a form of torture." The report also divulged grave concerns about the role of medical staff: "Doctors and medical personnel conveyed information about prisoners' mental health and vulnerabilities to interrogators." The report criticized the "apparent integration of access to medical care within the system of coercion."[82]

It is unclear who leaked the report summary to the *New York Times*. But, the report proved that the Bush administration had grossly misrepresented the information the Red Cross provided it. The *Times* noted, "Antonella Notari, a veteran Red Cross official and spokeswoman, said that the organization frequently complained to the Pentagon and other arms of the American government when government officials cite the Red Cross visits to suggest that there is no abuse at Guantánamo."[83]

The Pentagon debunked the Red Cross report by revealing that military personnel sent to Guantanamo "go through extensive professional and sensitivity training to ensure they understand the procedures for protecting the rights and dignity of detainees."[84] White House spokesman Scott McClellan commented: "We strongly disagree with any characterization that suggests the way the [Guantanamo] detainees are being treated is inconsistent with the policies that the president outlined." Unfortunately, Americans still had little or no information on what interrogation methods Bush may have secretly authorized. Bush administration officials continued to portray the criticism as a greater sin than the torture. And the vast majority of Americans remained oblivious.

On December 3, the Bush administration revealed that it had overcome a prejudice that had hampered the speedy administration of justice for hundreds of years. Deputy Associate Attorney General Brian Boyle announced in federal court that the Bush administration could use evidence gained by torture for prosecuting and perpetually detaining alleged enemy combatants. Boyle declared that if military commissions were to "determine that evidence of questionable provenance were reliable, nothing in the due process clause [of the Constitution] prohibits them from relying on it."[85] Boyle's comment symbolized the rapid devolution of American legal and ethical thinking: instead of being barbaric, torture is now merely something of "questionable provenance," akin to hearsay evidence. The military can use evidence gained by torturing detainees because people labeled enemy combatants "have no constitutional rights enforceable in this court," Boyle explained.

On December 14, the ACLU released the first batch of material received under court order, confidential government documents revealing that "Marines in Iraq conducted mock executions of juvenile prisoners last year, burned and tortured other detainees with electrical shocks."[86] An FBI agent had complained to FBI headquarters in June 2004 after seeing U.S. forces involved in "numerous serious physical abuse incidents of Iraqi civilian detainees . . . strangulation, beatings, placement of lit cigarettes into the detainees' ear openings." One FBI agent, back from Guantanamo, complained that "a female U.S. military interrogator stroked and applied lotion to a shackled male prisoner, yanked his thumbs back, causing him to grimace in pain and then grabbed his genitals."[87] *Newsweek* reported that "the U.S. military had originally investigated the case of the genital-grabbing female interrogator at the time it occurred, resulting in a month-long suspension for 'sensitivity training.'"[88]

Wrapping Muslims in Israeli flags was another way the U.S. military tormented its detainees. One FBI agent commented: "I saw another detainee sitting on the floor of the interview room with an Israeli flag draped around him, loud music being played, and a strobe light flashing."[89]

"Sleep management program" was the term for keeping someone awake for days, by beating them if they fell asleep, throwing them under cold showers, or banging on their cell door and yelling at them. One FBI agent noted seeing one Abu Ghraib detainee "handcuffed to a railing with a nylon sack on his head and a shower curtain draped around him, being slapped by a soldier to keep him awake."[90]

Another FBI agent informed FBI headquarters in an August 2, 2004, e-mail:

> On a couple of occasions I entered interview rooms [at Guantanamo] to find detainees chained hand and foot in a fetal position to the floor, with no chair, food or water. Most times they had urinated or defecated on themselves and had been left there for 18, 24 hours or more. . . . On another occasion, not only was the temperature unbearably hot, but extremely loud rap music was being played in the room, and had been since the day before with the detainee chained hand and foot in the fetal position on the tile floor.[91]

As early as December 2002, FBI agents were professing disbelief at Guantanamo interrogation methods. An FBI official at Guantanamo complained in December 2003 that military officers who conducted abusive interrogations were claiming to be FBI agents.[92] The agent said he was told that Deputy Defense Secretary Paul Wolfowitz approved both the ruse and the rigorous interrogation techniques.[93] Pentagon spokesman Di Rita responded to the latest brouhaha: "We've held a number of individuals accountable. . . . And we will continue to pump out documents."[94]

Also in December, congressional leaders bowed to intense White House pressure and deleted a clause from a military appropriations bill that would prohibit torture or inhumane treatment of detainees. The provision, which the Senate passed by 96-to–2, would have also required the CIA and Pentagon to inform Congress about the interrogation methods they were using. The Pentagon protested to Congress that the provision was "unnecessary," and National Security Advisor Condoleezza Rice complained to congressional leaders that the provision "provides legal protections to foreign prisoners to which they are not now entitled under applicable law and policy." One congressional Democrat said that the White House's position gave the impression "that the administration wanted an escape hatch to preserve the option of using torture." The *New York Times* noted that "the final version of the legislation included only nonbinding language expressing a sense of Congress that American personnel should not engage in torture."[95]

On January 1, 2005, the *New York Times* published new revelations on Guantanamo abuses provided by military intelligence officials and interrogators.[96] The *Times* noted: "Military officials have gone to great lengths to portray Guantánamo as a largely humane facility for several hundred prisoners, where the harshest sanctioned punishments consisted of isolation or taking away items like blankets, toothpaste, dessert or reading material." In reality, prisoners would be blasted for days in a row by an audio tape that mixed baby's wailing with meowing from a cat food commercial.[97] Detainees who did not spill their guts were sometimes forcibly given enemas. The *Times* revealed that interrogators used "a Behavioral Science Consultation Team, known as Biscuit, comprising a psychologist or psychiatrist and psychiatric workers. The team was used to suggest ways to make prisoners more cooperative in interrogations."[98] Later that week, the *New England Journal of Medicine* revealed that Guantanamo "military doctors became arbiters, even planners, of aggressive interrogation practice, including prolonged isolation, sleep deprivation and exposure to temperature extremes. . . . Not only did caregivers pass clinical data to interrogators, physicians and other health professionals helped craft and carry out coercive interrogation plans."[99]

From the first days of the scandal, Bush administration officials had assured the public that the wrongdoers would be brought to justice. Perhaps coincidentally, Bush-approved investigations seemed only to discover criminal culpability at the lowest ranks. In January, the court martial hearing of Army Corporal Charles Graner, Jr., was held at Ford Hood, Texas. Graner was widely seen as the ringleader for the National Guard members involved in many of the abusive photos from Abu Ghraib. Graner's lawyer, Guy Womack, insisted that compelling naked Iraqi detainees to form a pyramid was "no big deal" because "Cheerleaders all across America form pyramids every day, and it doesn't hurt people." Trial testimony revealed that "prisoners there were kept naked much of the time, with hoods over their heads, and often chained to the bars in painful 'stress positions.' . . . Army guards regularly beat the prisoners with fists or iron rods, forced them to eat food from a toilet, confronted them with un-muzzled police dogs, and made them wallow naked in the mud outside in near-freezing temperatures."[100] Shortly after some of Graner's worst abuses of prisoners, he was notified in writing by a superior officer: "You are doing a fine job. . . . You have received many accolades from the chain of command and particularly from Lt. Col. Jordan" (the chief intelligence officer at the prison). Graner was found guilty and sentenced to ten years in prison. Graner, in a two-hour statement to the court after he was convicted, declared that he had been ordered to "terrorize" inmates in order to make interrogations easier.[101] Graner's defense was hamstrung because the judge, Army Col. James Pohl, "refused to allow witnesses to discuss which officers were aware of events in cellblock One-Alpha, or what orders they had given," as the *Washington Post* noted.[102]

THE GONZALES CONFIRMATION CHARADE

Bush nominated White House Counsel Alberto Gonzales to replace John Ashcroft as Attorney General, despite Gonzales's role in the torture scandal. Gonzales' planned stint at the Justice Department was widely seen as a step-ping stone to eventually installing him in the Supreme Court.

On the night before New Year's Eve—on the weekend before Gonzales' confirmation hearing to be attorney general—the Justice Department quietly posted a memo on its website redefining torture. The new guideline conceded that an interrogation can become torture "even if it does not involve severe physical pain" and nixed the "didn't specifically intend to torture" defense for interrogators.[103] The timing of the policy revision raised doubts about whether Bush administration policymakers had looked deeply within their hearts at year's end and seen the error of their ways.

The hearing offered a splendid opportunity for the Senate Judiciary Com-mittee to redeem itself after years of largely ignoring U.S. government atrocities. Democrats sought copies of memos that Gonzales had written on interrogation, but the White House spurned the requests. The January 6, 2005, hearing had overtones of a royal visit to parliament. Most of the senators were deferential to Gonzales, as if his right to additional power was long since established—perhaps by his birth. (Gonzales was nominated to the highest cabinet position yet held by a Hispanic.) Sen. Arlen Specter (R-Penn.), the chairman of the committee, opened by asking: "Do you condemn the interrogators' techniques at Abu Ghraib shown on the widely publicized photographs?"[104]

Gonzales waffled, saying that "as someone who may be head of the de-partment, I obviously don't want to provide any kind of legal opinion as to whether or not that conduct might be criminal." But the level of depravity and abuse in the photos had already been instantly condemned as illegal by many former government officials, and the military was prosecuting several enlisted personnel for the conduct. Gonzales also dodged commenting on the criminality of similar abuses at Guantanamo. Specter, speaking as a former prosecutor, pointed out that Gonzales' pretext for ducking the question was not plausible.

Sen. Richard Durbin (D-Ill.) asked what, in most hearings, would have been considered a slow-pitch question: "Do you believe there are circumstances where . . . the War Crimes Act would not apply to U.S. personnel?"

Gonzales responded as if he had been asked to solve the riddle of the Sphinx: "Senator, I don't believe that that would be the case. But I would like the opportunity—I know I want to be very candid with you and obviously thorough in my response to that question. It is sort of a legal conclusion, and I would like to have the opportunity to get back to you on that."

Durbin later asked: "Can U.S. personnel legally engage in torture under any circumstances?" Gonzales again struggled: "I don't believe so, but I'd want to get back to you on that and make sure I don't provide a misleading answer." Torture was obviously going to be the hottest topic of the confirmation hearing, and yet Gonzales repeatedly sounded as if it was a novel topic that he would need to visit a law library to learn about before forming an opinion.

Gonzales kept all interrogation options open. Sen. Patrick Leahy (D-VT) asked him: "Does the president have the authority, in your judgment, to exercise a commander-in-chief override and immunize acts of torture?" Gonzales ducked and fogged: "With all due respect, Senator, the president has said we're not going to engage in torture. That is a hypothetical question that would involve an analysis of a great number of factors." Thus, there could be a "great number" of factors that might justify a president immunizing torturers. Seven months earlier, Gonzales had boldly proclaimed a "commander-in-chief override" regarding torture.

Though Gonzales was a mere 49 years old, he appeared to have the same memory problems that plague geezers on the witness stand. Gonzales pleaded memory failure on point after point, including whether he asked for the Bybee memo, which was addressed to Gonzales and begins: "You have asked for our Office's views regarding the standards of conduct under the Convention Against Torture." Gonzales eventually bravely declared: "I accept responsibility that the memo was addressed to me."

Sen. Ted Kennedy (D-Mass.) asked Gonzales about the FBI's role in interrogation controversies. Gonzales brushed away the dozens of reports of abuses that FBI agents sent to FBI headquarters "and with respect to FBI involvement, the recent reports about these FBI e-mails about abuses at Guantanamo, quite frankly, surprised and shocked me, because it's certainly inconsistent with what I've seen." Gonzales concluded: "And what I'm suggesting is, if confirmed, I need to have the opportunity to go into the department and the FBI and just try to ascertain the facts." After Gonzales was confirmed—and after the FBI fell under his control—there would be no more such pesky e-mails undermining the official story. Many of the FBI agents who had complained about abuses in Iraq and at Guantanamo were experts on counterterrorism and interrogation; unlike Gonzales, they did not spend most of the war on terrorism behind a comfortable desk in the White House.

Gonzales' evasions had the Democrats begging for mercy. Sen. Joe Biden (D-Del.) groveled, "We're looking for you, when we ask you a question, to give us an answer, which you haven't done yet. I love you, but you're not being very candid so far." Biden announced that he would be voting to confirm Gonzales, regardless of Gonzales' contempt for the Judiciary Committee.

Gonzales may have daunted would-be critics by continually referring to the people vigorously interrogated at Abu Ghraib as "terrorists"—despite the stark evidence that the vast majority of detainees there were not terrorists. The Bush administration assumed that anyone who the U.S. government vigorously interrogated is by definition a terrorist—or else they would not have been tortured. Applying the "terrorist" label to victims allowed the Bush team to portray critics of its policies as enemies of American safety.

Gonzales harped at the hearing on how the Justice Department's new torture guideline made the Bybee memo an irrelevant historical relic. However, a week later, the *New York Times* reported: "A cryptic footnote to the new document about the 'treatment of detainees' referred to what [Bush administration senior] officials said were other still-classified opinions. The footnote meant, the officials said, that coercive techniques approved by the Justice Department under the looser interpretation of the torture statutes were still lawful even under the new, more restrictive interpretation."[105] Thus, the new Justice Department opinion may be binding only in situations in which government officials feel torture is not really necessary.

In written responses to senators' questions after the hearing, Gonzales revealed that Bush's 2002 promise of humane treatment of prisoners and a congressional ban on cruel, unusual, or inhumane treatment did not apply to how the CIA acted overseas.[106] Gonzales' response spurred all the Democrats on the Senate Judiciary Committee to vote against his confirmation as Attorney General. The Committee approved Gonzales on a party-line vote, 10-to–8, and he was approved by the full Senate by a vote of 60–36.

In a January 26 press conference, Bush was asked whether the Gonzales statement reflected administration policy—whether Bush had approved a loophole for "cruel, inhumane and degrading treatment . . . so long as it's conducted by the CIA and conducted overseas." Bush replied, "Al Gonzales reflects our policy, and that is: We don't sanction torture."[107]

John Yoo, one of the prime architects of the Bush torture policy, declared in early 2005 that Bush's reelection and Gonzales' confirmation were the equivalent of public acceptance of Bush's interrogation policies. In an interview with the *New Yorker*, Yoo declared that Bush's reelection and the "relatively mild challenge" to Gonzales from the Democrats was "proof that the debate is over. The issue is dying out. The public has had its referendum."[108]

In late February, the ACLU released a batch of classified documents that proved that not all Army officers ignored abuse allegations. Greg Ford, an Army intelligence sergeant, complained in June 2003 to his superior after the other three members of his counterintelligence team in Samarra abused detainees with "asphyxiation, mock executions, arms being pulled out of sockets, and lit cigarettes forced into detainee's ears while they were blindfolded and bound."[109] Ford warned his captain that detainees could be killed during interrogation and urged that the counterintelligence team be transferred elsewhere. Ford said that the captain gave him "30 seconds to withdraw my request or he was going to send me forcibly to go see a psychiatrist." Ford would not withdraw the request, and the captain ordered his weapon confiscated and placed him under 24-hour surveillance. The captain then pressured a military doctor—who initially found Ford stable—to re-examine him, declaring: "I don't care what you saw or heard, he is imbalanced, and I want him out of here."[110] As *Salon* reported, "According to both Ford and a credible witness [Sgt. 1st Class Michael Marciello], Ford was strapped to a gurney and bundled off to a mental ward on the basis of a coerced diagnosis for an indefinite period of time, all before any investigation was even started, much less completed."[111] Ford was then quickly shipped off to a military hospital in Germany—even though no formal medical evacuation order existed. U.S. military doctors there again certified him as in stable mental health but he was returned to the United States for his own "safety," according to Ford's recollection of the doctor's comment.[112]

In early March, the Pentagon coughed up documents on "Ramadi Madness," a DVD made by Florida National Guard soldiers deployed near Ramadi. The DVD, perhaps modeled after "Spring Break Madness" videos of collegiate hijinks, featured "a bound and wounded prisoner sprawled on the ground, and showed his bullet entry and exit wounds. At one point, a U.S. soldier kicked the prisoner in the face." One soldier at the scene told Army investigators that he "thought the dude eventually died. We weren't in any hurry to call the medics.'"[113] Another scene showed soldiers moving the arm of an Iraqi truck driver who had just been shot and killed to make him appear to be waving to the camera. After the video was discovered on a soldier's computer, military lawyers proposed charging the culprits with assault and battery. But the case was dropped after it was "determined that the detainee who was kicked was not abused."[114] The *Washington Post* noted, "The unit's commander told Army investigators he was concerned about the images becoming public and promised to take steps to 'minimize the risk of this and other videos that may end up in the media.'"[115]

CHURCH BLESSINGS

In early March, Washington was treated to another torture exoneration, this one from a panel headed by the former Inspector General of the Navy, Vice Admiral Albert Church III. On the morning the report's executive summary was released, the *Washington Post* revealed that the confidential report "is extremely complimentary of the U.S. operation in Cuba, calling it a model for detention operations, combining strict command oversight, adequate resources, and its isolation from a combat. [Church] reports that of more than 24,000 interrogation sessions, there were just three substantiated cases of abuse, all involving assault."[116] Rumsfeld appointed Church, who was director of the Navy staff, "to identify and report on all interrogation techniques 'considered, authorized, employed or prohibited' in the global war on terror."[117]

Church appeared before the Senate Armed Services Committee on March 10, the day the 21-page summary report was released. Church announced: "My key findings said clearly there was no policy, written or otherwise, at any level that directed or condoned torture or abuse. There was no link between the authorized interrogation techniques, and the abuses that, in fact, occurred."[118] Church conceded that there were "missed opportunities" to have done things better.

The hearing, like Church's investigation, provided another opportunity to hail the wonderful American system of justice. Sen. James Inhofe (R-OK) bragged that, because of the multitude of investigations, "We have shown the world we are a nation of laws, and that we will not tolerate abusive, inhumane behavior by members of our armed forces." Sen. John Warner (R-VA), the chairman, declared, "I think it's to the credit of this great nation that there have been ten reports on this very distressing chapter in our military history—otherwise a military history that is envied by the whole world." Sen. Jim Talent (R-Mo.) proved that terrorists had attacked the United States *because* the U.S. government does not torture: "We have the best military in the world. I don't need an investigation to tell me that there was no comprehensive or systematic use of inhumane tactics by the American military, because those guys and gals just wouldn't do it. . . . That's why the terrorists are attacking us, because we're not the kind of society that would do that." Talent also boasted of the number of investigations: "It's a great country we have, in part because we sweat so much over this stuff." Talent made his own priorities clear: "If our guys want to poke somebody in the chest to get the name of a bomb maker so they can save the lives of Americans, I'm for it."[119]

But rather than ten separate investigations, American taxpayers paid for reruns of the same investigation. The *Washington Post* noted that "the review largely summarizes previous military reports about Defense Department detention operations."[120] Church later declared that "we worked hand-in-glove with the Schlesinger panel." Church's investigation largely ignored the revelations of abuse in the FBI memos.

The Pentagon touted the Church investigation as "very comprehensive,"[121] leaving no stone unturned. Sen. Jack Reed (D-RI) asked Church whether he had interviewed Paul Bremer, the chief of the Coalition Provisional Authority, who was in charge of Defense Department and other U.S. operations in Iraq. Church explained: "Ambassador Bremer, as I understood it, worked for the Department of State."

This remark brought the house down, as Bremer was a Pentagon employee and thus directly in the military chain of command. Church then justified not bothering to speak to Bremer: "There was one or two things I was trying to determine in terms of what Ambassador Bremer knew about potential abuses at Abu Ghraib. . . . I talked to his military assistants, I talked to all those who—a number of those who were at the daily meetings, to try to determine if there was any indication—early indication that he had of abuses that he passed to General Sanchez."

Reed derided the non-interview as a "stunning omission," declaring, "To simply stop with his military assistants to see if they might have gleaned something in a meeting or a conversation seems to be woefully inadequate, with all due respect." (Church was not asked to find Iraq on a map during the Senate hearing.)

Church concluded: "Even in the absence of a precise definition of 'humane' treatment, it is clear that none of the pictured abuses at Abu Ghraib bear any resemblance to approved policies at any level."[122] This was peculiar, since many of the most shocking pictures from Abu Ghraib included specific tactics that Rumsfeld and other top Pentagon officials had personally approved, including the use of dogs to frighten prisoners, nudity as a punitive policy, and the practice of hooding detainees. For Church to invoke the photographs to exonerate the government, at the same time the government continued withholding more gruesome photos and videos, is typical of the bait-and-switches by which the government continually proves its innocence.

Church stressed: "We have six deaths of those who were detainees. . . . We looked at all these deaths, all the detainee deaths to ensure that anything that looked problematic was further investigated." But, the week after Church's summary was released, the Pentagon admitted that 26 detainees in Iraq and Afghanistan had been killed in what was or appeared to be criminal homicides—more than four times as many homicides as Church recognized. The *New York Times* noted, "Only one of the deaths occurred at the Abu Ghraib prison in Iraq, officials said, showing how broadly the most violent abuses extended beyond those prison walls."[123]

Church denied that his report was an exoneration, despite the title of the press release from the Pentagon—"Admiral Issues Report: 'No Policy Condoned Torture, Abuse.'" Church defended his investigation: "We asked for every piece of paper that existed and made a couple of trips to Guantanamo Bay." But Church did not bother interviewing Rumsfeld, or any FBI agents, or any detainees. Instead, he and his investigators talked to the authorities, and then produced an authoritative report exonerating them. When he was pressed to explain why he did not specifically inquire into the roles of Rumsfeld and other top players, Church replied, "I was not tasked to assess personal responsibility at senior levels."

When asked to respond to a human rights group that had derided his report as a "whitewash," Church retorted: "Well, first of all, no one has read my report, so I would challenge you." As long as the Pentagon kept the vast majority of the 368-page report secret, no one could condemn it. Church declared: "But after 800 interviews . . . , several thousand pages of documents that we reviewed over nine months, many under sworn—many were sworn-to interviews, all senior deputy secretary of Defense, the vice chairman—no one—I don't believe anybody can call this a whitewash."[124] This is Washington logic at its best: Truth is a factor of the number of pieces of paper looked at and the number and rank of people listened to.

Church was the perfect Bush administration investigator, showing total deference and zero curiosity. The Church report clarified how much hokum the Bush administration believed it could get away with. All that was necessary was to issue another press release and then have all the Bush supporters in Congress and in the media chant their approval. Both the *New York Times* and the *Washington Post* derided the Church report.[125]

NOT DROWNED, THUS NOT ABUSED

The CIA rarely answered questions about its covert activities in the war on terror. One exception occurred on March 17, when CIA Director Porter Goss testified to the Senate Armed Services committee. Goss stressed that "torture is not—it's not productive. That's not professional interrogation. We don't do torture." Sen. John McCain (R-Ariz.) pushed Goss about the CIA's use of waterboarding, "an interrogation technique in which a detainee is strapped to a board and pushed underwater to make him think he might drown," according to the *Washington Post*.[126] Goss balked at McCain's question, explaining: "You're getting into, again, an area of what I will call professional interrogation techniques."[127] As long as the detainees did not die from "mock" drownings, they have received professional treatment. Waterboarding was explicitly approved in a confidential Justice Department 2002 memo.[128]

When pressed about the conduct of CIA interrogators, Goss declared: "At this time, there are no 'techniques,' if I could say, that are being employed that are in any way against the law or would meet—would be considered torture or anything like that." But this carefully phrased denial could have meant simply that CIA interrogations were suspended for the day of Goss's congressional testimony. When asked whether the CIA had violated the legal ban on torture since 9/11, Goss replied, "I am not able to tell you that."[129] Later that day, after the media requested clarification, the CIA "issued two statements, but no official would agree to be named because of the highly classified subject matter," the *New York Times* noted. One CIA spokeswoman declared: "The agency complies with the laws of the United States, and the director's testimony consistently stated that. None of his comments were intended to convey anything otherwise."[130] It is not encouraging when government spokespeople refuse to be named when they are merely denying that the government breaks the law.

On March 25, the ACLU released documents revealing that the Army had been informed of torture at a U.S. military detention center near Mosul at the same time that the Abu Ghraib scandal was beginning to erupt. One Army investigator concluded, "There is evidence that suggests the 311th MI [Military Intelligence] personnel and/or translators engaged in physical torture of the detainees." An Army investigator concluded that detainees "were being systematically and intentionally mistreated" and that the Geneva Convention was being violated.[131] Soldiers in one case were instructed to "take the detainees out back and beat the fuck out of them."[132] This evidence did not dint the efforts of Bush administration and Pentagon officials to portray the scandal as solely one shift at one prison.

On March 30, a military hearing resumed in Colorado on whether Chief Warrant Officer Lewis Welshofer, Jr., who ran prisoner interrogations at Qaim prison camp in Iraq, would be prosecuted for the death of an Iraqi general who had voluntarily turned himself in to American forces for questioning. Welshofer stuffed the general "upside down in a sleeping bag, binding him in wire, sitting on his chest and covering his mouth."[133] The general had been badly beaten by other soldiers prior to suffocating to death. Maj. Jessica Voss, commander of the 66th Military Intelligence Unit (which had jurisdiction over the interrogation), testified that the "sleeping bag technique" was approved by senior officers.[134] Welshofer was defiant: "I did my job." Acting presidential, he invoked his own goodness to trump all other evidence: "If you ask anyone who knows me, they will tell you I'm actually a pretty nice guy."[135] By the definition that the Bush administration established for torture in 2002, this assertion by itself might almost be enough to prove his innocence. The military sought to close the hearings but a vigorous challenge by the *Denver Post* got the doors open. Details of the abuses by Welshofer and his cohorts were largely ignored outside of Colorado.

On April 19, the ACLU released documents detailing how abuses proliferated in Iraq because Army intelligence officials sent around "wish lists" of their preferred interrogation methods, seeking to use low-voltage electrocution, "phone book strikes," and dogs and snakes on detainees. The wish lists were compiled as a result of requests by U.S. military headquarters in Baghdad. An interrogator with the 501st Military Intelligence Battalion protested to headquarters about the new proposed methods: "It comes down to standards of right and wrong—something we cannot just put aside when we find it inconvenient. We are American soldiers, heirs of a long tradition of staying on the high ground. We need to stay there."[136]

On April 25, the Pentagon announced that the Army Inspector General had completed a review of interrogation processes in Iraq and that the top four commanders were officially cleared of all charges of wrongdoing. A fifth commander, Brig. Gen. Janis Karpinski, the military police commander at Abu Ghraib, was recommended for an administrative reprimand. The report exonerated Lt. General Ricardo Sanchez. When Sanchez had appeared before a congressional committee a year earlier, he had been asked by Sen. Jack Reed (D-R.I.) about an article in that morning's *USA Today* that "reported that you ordered or approved the use of sleep deprivation, intimidation by guard dogs, excessive noise and inducing fear as an interrogation method for a prisoner in Abu Ghraib prison." Sanchez declared that "I never approved any of those measures to be used within CJTF-7 [Coalition Joint Task Force-7] at any time in the last year."[137] Yet, in a September 2003 memo, Sanchez explicitly authorized "the use of 29 techniques for interrogating prisoners being held by the United States. These included stress positions, 'yelling, loud music and light control' as well as the use of muzzled military dogs in order to 'exploit Arab fear of dogs,'" as an ACLU press release noted. The ACLU urged Attorney General Gonzales to investigate Sanchez for perjury, to no avail.[138] The Pentagon signaled that this was its final investigation into the interrogation abuses. A *Washington Post* editorial denounced the failure of the government to investigate Rumsfeld, CIA chief George Tenet, and Gonzales: "That the affair would end in this way is even more disgraceful for the American political system than the abuses themselves."[139]

In late April, controversy exploded over how the Bush administration out-sourced interrogations by seizing suspects and taking them to foreign nations notorious for torture. This process, known as "renditioning," violates both the Geneva Conventions and U.S. law. The Italian government was outraged at a CIA operation that seized a Muslim cleric from the streets of Milan and flew him to Egypt, where he was severely tortured. During an April 28 press conference, Bush was asked how renditioning could be justified under U.S. law, and "would you stand for it if foreign agents did that to an American here?" Bush dismissed the second question as a "hypothetical" and then riffed on the evil of terrorists: "The United States government has an obligation to protect the American peo-ple. . . . I'm not going to let them down by assuming that the enemy is not going to hit us again. We're going to do everything we can to protect us."[140] The evil of the terrorists apparently made irrelevant whatever crimes or abuses the U.S. government committed.

In a May 5, 2005, interview with a Dutch television network, Bush was asked about "prisoner abuse." He leaped to set the record straight, claiming that "all Americans, including me, reject Abu Ghraib. That was an aberration. That's not what America stands for. And if people are concerned about the tac-tics, I understand that, but the goal is peace. And now is the time to work to-gether to achieve peace."[141] Thus, the end justifies the means—even if the means, by stirring up great hatred, assures that the end is not achieved. Label-ing Abu Ghraib an "aberration" revealed that Bush had not been closely fol-lowing the long series of FBI and military documents released by the ACLU.

On May 20, Bush was asked at a press conference how he reacted "to the continuing reports about mistreatment of prisoners held by American military around the world." Bush didn't miss a chance to trumpet American values: "I think the world ought to be—pay attention to the contrast between a society which was run by a brutal tyrant in which there was no transparency and a so-ciety in which the whole world watches a government find the facts, lay the facts out for the citizens to see, and that punishment, when appropriate, be de-livered." Bush then rewrote history: "There have been over, I think, nine in-vestigations, eight or nine investigations by independent investigators that have made the reports very public. I'm comfortable that we're getting to the bottom of the situation and I know we're doing so in a transparent way."[142] The Schlesinger panel was the only investigation that even bothered to feign independence; all the others were conducted by the military and programmed to avoid examining the responsibility of superior officers, political appointees, or presidents. Even though most of the findings of the investigations remained secret, Bush's false claims generated no public ire.

After the Abu Ghraib debacle, the U.S. military reportedly lightened up on its interrogation methods. However, the Iraqi military and security forces have ramped up and are spreading terror among the Iraqi people. An official of the Iraqi Human Rights Ministry complained in July 2005 that "up to 60% of the estimated 12,000 detainees in the country's prisons and military compounds face intimidation, beatings or torture that leads to broken bones and sometimes death."[143] U.S. and British forces helped put some of Saddam's torturers back in business "pulling out [detainees'] fingernails, burning them with hot irons or giving them electric shocks," according to Iraqi officials.[144] In early July, ten Sunni Muslim men and youth suffocated to death in police custody.[145] Even though the U.S. government is aware of such abuses, it continues bankrolling and propping up Iraqi operations. Apparently, torture is barbaric or humane depending solely on the type of government that inflicts the pain.

On May 25, Amnesty International's William Schulz declared that the United States had become "a leading purveyor and practitioner" of torture, and compared Guantanamo Bay to the "gulag." The administration quickly shot back, with Rumsfeld denouncing the charge as "reprehensible," something that "cannot be excused."[146] Cheney, appearing on CNN's Larry King, sneered: "For Amnesty International to suggest that somehow the United States is a violator of human rights, I frankly just don't take them seriously. Frankly, I was offended by it."[147] Cheney effectively declared that no abuses had occurred at Guantanamo, declaring that "allegations of mistreatment . . . come from somebody who had been inside and released to their home country and now are peddling lies about how they were treated."[148]

The following day, Bush was asked about the Amnesty charge in a press conference. Bush draped himself in American moral greatness: "I'm aware of the Amnesty International report, and it's absurd. The United States is a country that promotes freedom around the world. . . . It seemed like [Amnesty International] based some of their decisions on the word and allegations by people who were held in detention, people who hate America, people had been trained in some instances to disassemble [*sic*]—that means not tell the truth."[149] Apparently, anyone who had been detained at Guantanamo could not possibly be an objective, reliable source—unlike U.S. government spokesmen. All that was necessary was for Bush and Cheney to attack the motives of torture victims in order to satisfy much of the American public and media. Prior to invading Iraq, the Bush administration repeatedly cited Amnesty International as a reputable source—at least on Saddam Hussein's villainies.

As the summer of 2005 waned, the Bush administration continued to pretend that the scandal did not exist. In an August 26 press briefing, chairman of the Joint Chiefs of Staff General Richard Myers disparaged any suggestion that the torture problem was widespread: "If it was only the night shift at Abu Ghraib, which it was, it was only a small section of the guards that participated in this, it's a pretty good clue that it wasn't a more widespread problem."[150]

The following month, Americans learned of the complaints of three 82nd Airborne Division soldiers about army cooks and other off-duty troops, for amusement and sport, routinely physically beating Iraqi detainees being held near Fallujah. One sergeant explained: "We would give [detainees] blows to the head, chest, legs and stomach, and pull them down, kick dirt on them. This happened every day." The sergeant said that there were no problems as long as no detainees "came up dead. . . . We kept it to broken arms and legs."[151] Captain Ian Fishback of the 82nd Airborne repeatedly sought to get guidance from superiors on the standards for lawful and humane treatment of detainees. He, like other officers, never received clear guidelines. Fishback publicly complained: "I am certain that this confusion contributed to a wide range of abuses including death threats, beatings, broken bones, murder, exposure to elements, extreme forced physical exertion, hostage-taking, stripping, sleep deprivation and degrading treatment."[152] Tony Lagouranis, a former army interrogator at Abu Ghraib and member of a special intelligence team in Iraq, told PBS *Frontline* in October: "It's all over Iraq. The infantry units are torturing people in their homes. They would smash people's feet with the back of an axhead. They would break bones, ribs."[153] The ACLU released internal military documents that revealed that "officers and NCO's at point of capture engaged in interrogations using techniques they literally remembered from movies." Thus, soldiers' memories of Hollywood war films—*Rambo* or others—helped determine how Iraqis were treated. The documents also revealed cases of poorly trained soldiers unnecessarily killing Iraqi detainees.[154]

Many of the officers involved in the Abu Ghraib scandal have been promoted. In mid-June 2005, the *New York Times* reported that the Pentagon believed that "the Abu Ghraib scandal has receded enough in the public's mind" that Rumsfeld could safely award a promotion to Lt. Gen. Ricardo Sanchez.[155] Maj. Gen. Barbara Fast, the top intelligence officer in Iraq (with responsibility for Abu Ghraib), was appointed commander of the U.S. Army Intelligence Center and School in March 2005.[156] Even Gitmo interrogators who were reprimanded for abuses still found good government gigs afterwards. When Staff Sgt. Jeannette Arocho-Burkart interrogated the prisoners at Guantanamo, she allegedly wore "skimpy clothing to make Muslim men uncomfortable during questioning" and "allegedly smeared red ink on a detainee's face, saying it was her menstrual blood," according to a report in the *New York Daily News*. Arocho-Burkart was reportedly reprimanded for her conduct. After she left the service, she was hired by the Defense Intelligence Agency to teach "strategic debriefing" at the Army Intelligence School where Fast was in command.[157]

Bush's torture policies mortified many of the military's top legal experts. Three days before Gonzales's confirmation hearing, Rear Adm. John Hutson, along with other military experts and former Judge Advocate Generals (JAGs) sent a letter to the Senate Judiciary Committee complaining that Gonzales' memo "fostered great animosity toward the United States, undermined our intelligence-gathering efforts, and added to the risks facing our troops serving around the world."[158] After the summary of the Church report was released, retired Army Gen. John Johns commented that the "hypocrisy of the Pentagon will not only erode our moral standing, it will erode the moral fiber of our nation in general and our military in particular."[159] Details emerged in the summer of 2005 of how the JAGs had vigorously opposed many of the new interrogation methods from the start; political appointees scorned their concerns.

CONGRESS OF CONTEMPT

Democracy is floundering in America in part because the political atmosphere has become profoundly surreal. The torture scandal vivifies how the federal government—and Washington—now operate. The system of checks and balances has almost completely collapsed. The government has apparently been engaged in torture for three years or longer, yet Congress has no will to stop them, or even to inquire about the abuses. Instead, the people's representatives seem terrified of being criticized by the White House.

Rather than providing checks and balances on torture, Congress has usually groveled at the administration's feet. *Washington Post* cartoonist Tom Toles perfectly captured the relationship between the different branches of government in a sketch appearing on the day of Gonzales' Senate confirmation hearing. The cartoon, imitating one of the most famous Abu Ghraib photos, showed a naked body cowering in a corner with a bag labeled "Senate" over his head and his arms up to guard his face saying, "Um . . . Mr. Gonzales, we have this formality called a confirmation process." Gonzales is sitting in a comfortable chair in a spiffy business suit, holding the leash on three snarling attack dogs splashing saliva and hungry for a bite, tugging toward the bag person. Gonzales replies genteelly to his hooded victim: "How very quaint." Toles's ridicule did nothing to awaken the self-respect of most members of Congress.

Instead of seeking facts, many members of Congress out-cravened administration officials. The Chairman of the House Armed Services Committee, Rep. Duncan Hunter (R-Cal.), declaimed, "The inmates in Guantanamo have never eaten better, they've never been treated better . . . the idea that we are somehow torturing people in Guantanamo is absolutely not true, unless you consider eating chicken three days a week is torture." Duncan proved that there had been no human rights abuses at Gitmo by passing out to reporters a copy of an inmate menu which featured lemon chicken.[160]

In the spring of 2005, Congress showed vastly more enthusiasm for investigating steroid use by baseball players than torture by the U.S. government. Congressmen were more concerned about the sanctity of home run records than they were about the CIA or military interrogators killing innocent people. In August 2005, the House Government Reform Committee opened a perjury investigation of a baseball player who had testified to the committee that he did not use steroids but tested positive for steroid use a few months later. Committee Chairman Tom Davis (R-VA) piously announced that "we have an obligation to look at this."[161] Perhaps this obligation to scrutinize private misconduct is the flipside of their obligation to ignore government atrocities.

NO STONE OVERTURNED

Attention Deficit Democracy spurs people to view each government action in isolation—to presume that there is no trend in power and thus that there is no reason to fear government going too far. Many Americans have shrugged off the torture abuses as arcane quibbles about how to make foreign bad guys confess the plans for the next attack. But there is no reason to assume that torture, like other abuses, will not become habit-forming for the feds. The *Washington Post* noted:

> As Mr. Gonzales confirmed at his [January confirmation] hearing, U.S. obligations under an anti-torture convention mean that the methods at Guantanamo must be allowable under the Fifth, Eighth and 14th amendments of the U.S. Constitution. According to the logic of the attorney general nominee, federal authorities could deprive American citizens of sleep, isolate them in cold cells while bombarding them with unpleasant noises and interrogate them 20 hours a day while the prisoners were naked and hooded, all without violating the Constitution.[162]

The Bush administration has a record of first claiming that it is merely seizing absolute power over foreigners, and later revealing that it possesses the same power over Americans. When Bush first decreed his prerogative to label people as enemy combatants, nullify all their rights, and incarcerate them indefinitely without trial, administration spokesmen stressed that this would apply only to foreigners captured on foreign battlefields. Then, in June 2002, the government announced that Jose Padilla, an American citizen, had been arrested in Chicago, labeled an enemy combatant, and was being held in a military brig. Instead of individual rights being "inalienable," as the Declaration of Independence proclaimed, they can be nullified by a secret presidential ruling. Once the government decrees that someone has no rights, it is a small step to declare that there will be no limits on how the government treats that person.

Torture follows naturally from de-humanizing detainees. An annex to the Taguba report noted that a contributing factor to Abu Ghraib abuses was "soldiers' immersion in an unfamiliar 'Islamic culture' and the 'association of Muslims with terrorism,' which created 'misperceptions that can lead to the fear or devaluation of a people.'"[163] Fundamentalist Islamic practices enraged some soldiers. Marine Lt. Gen. James Mattis explained in early 2005, "You go into Afghanistan, you got guys who slap women around for 5 years because they didn't wear a veil. You know, guys like that ain't got no manhood left anyway. So it's a hell of a lot of fun to shoot them."[164] Perhaps torturing such people would be even more fun than shooting them.

Abu Ghraib illustrates how the government buries scandals. The Bush team postpones the facts until they have zero kick, rationing the truth until it loses almost all its fizzle. If all of the information disclosed from late 2004 onward as a result of the federal judge's order had come out at the time of the initial Abu Ghraib photos, the impact might have been politically lethal. Instead, the Bush administration succeeded in isolating the photos, issuing wave after wave of denials and false statements to blunt their impact. The only context that the Abu Ghraib photos had for many Americans was the words of Bush, Rumsfeld, and other administration and Pentagon spokesmen. Danner, author of *Torture & Truth*, noted that "the key strategy of the defense is both to focus on the photographs and to isolate the acts they depict—which, if not the most serious, are those with the most political effect—from any inference that they might have resulted, either directly or indirectly, from policy."[165] If Americans had known the policies and doctrines that had already been established by early 2004—the photos would have almost certainly torpedoed Rumsfeld, and might have even nerved the Democratic Party to make a major issue of torture in the presidential campaign.

CONCLUSION

The American tolerance for torture is one of the greatest shocks of the new century. The scandal indicates the feebleness of American bulwarks against tyranny. What does it take to abolish the legal and constitutional limits on the power of the U.S. government? "The important thing here to understand is that the people that are at Guantanamo are bad people," declared Vice President Cheney in a June 12, 2005 interview.[166] Unfortunately, that is all that many Americans need to know to acquiesce—if not cheer—U.S. government barbarism.

George Orwell wrote in 1945 that "the nationalist not only does not dis-approve of atrocities committed by his own side, but he has a remarkable ca-pacity for not even hearing about them."[167] Any government abuse or atrocity can be "swept away" from the minds of tens of millions of Americans simply by denouncing the liberal media, or by repeated denials that become more ab-surd each passing month. As long as Bush and team are consistent in their ver-bal declarations, all the evidence in the world is naught. Even the FBI memos did not dent the Bush "deny everything and praise American values" defense.

It is understandable that many Americans would be frightened of terror-ism and would favor vigorous government policies to protect the citizenry. But the abuses of detainees created a torrent of hatred. It is very likely that the practices shown in the photos from Abu Ghraib may have gotten more Amer-icans killed than were saved by any intelligence beaten out of detainees.

Many Americans have remained oblivious to the impact that the Abu Ghraib photos and other torture reports have on foreigners. How would Americans have responded if the roles had been reversed? Consider the case of Jessica Lynch, the 20-year-old blond, blue-eyed, attractive West Virginian Army supply clerk captured after her supply convoy was attacked during the invasion of Iraq. The Pentagon and the *Washington Post* trumpeted grossly de-ceptive accounts of her capture and rescue that were later exposed as frauds (and which Lynch disavowed). What if Americans had seen photos of Lynch with blood running from cuts on her thighs, cowering before attack dogs lurching at her? What if Americans saw photos of a hooded Lynch with wires attached to her body, looking like she was awaiting electrocution? What if Americans saw videos of Lynch screaming as she was being assaulted by Iraqi captors? Such evidence would likely have swayed millions of Americans to support dropping nuclear bombs on Iraq. And yet many Americans refuse to recognize how similar evidence inflames Arabs' attitudes toward the United States.

The only thing necessary for a successful coverup is for the president first to continually proclaim that everything will be investigated, and then, months later, to proclaim that everything has already been investigated. Anyone who still criticizes or demands the truth "hates" America. The Big Lie defense works because so many Americans are hellbent on believing their rulers, be-cause much of the media will deferentially trumpet whatever the government claims, and because many Americans are automatically convinced of the de-pravity and guilt of anyone the government chooses to abuse.

Bush's moral invocations appear to have inoculated all policymakers. Bush sways people to view the world through his own "moral" lens—which at times totally blacks out what Bush does not want people to see. Bush talks about America's lofty values, and that satisfies his supporters that the United States could not possibly have committed torture. Proclaimed good intentions somehow confer absolute power over everything and everyone in the world. Simply reminding Americans how wonderful they are negates the evidence of horrendous abuses.

Most of the "investigations" of the torture scandal illustrated how, if government officials deny wrongdoing, the issue is settled—at least for the government. Even where there is information from other government officials that contradicts the proclamations, truth is determined solely by rank. Thus, a general's assertions negate whatever facts are reported by lowly FBI agents.

It is a marvel that the government continues to retain any credibility on this subject. Regardless of how many of its "explanations" blow up in its face like a trick cigar, people still believe. The government is trusted to investigate itself in a way that no private institution would ever be, given similar circumstances. After the Abu Ghraib scandal broke, there was no reason to trust the Bush administration or the Pentagon or the CIA to conduct honest investigations—and yet Congress and the public acquiesced. Even the perennial appearance of a coverup did not disqualify the Bush administration from investigating itself.

The torture scandal shows what happens when politicians and political appointees are permitted to redefine barbarism out of existence. If the government can effectively claim a right to torture, then all other limits on government power are practically irrelevant. What would it take to make the public acquiesce to the torture of Americans? Would simply applying an "odious" label (such as "cult member" at Waco, or "Muslim" with John Walker Lindh) to the victims be sufficient? There certainly was little or no outcry about the brutalizing of John Walker Lindh.

Since U.S. government torture failed to hold most Americans' attention, perhaps anything short of genocide will be shrugged off. But if the government decides it is prudent to kill large numbers of people, politicians could redefine genocide as they redefined torture. Rather than calling it genocide, it would be labeled something like Preemptive Protection of Americans Via Broad-Based Threat Elimination (PPAVBBTE)—or some such tripe. Thus, regardless of what the U.S. military government did abroad, the president would still be able to publicly proclaim that he had ordered them not to commit genocide and that genocide was opposed to American values, and that anyone who accused the United States of genocide has been "trained to disassemble."

Gonzales' confirmation as attorney general also symbolizes the de facto embrace by Congress, the Republican Party, and the conservative movement of torture as a proper instrument of public policy.

Much of the media coverage of the torture scandal was itself a scandal. Regardless of how much proof of torture came out, most of the media remained diffident. At every stage in the torture scandal, the Bush administration issued flat and sweeping denials that later were proven false. And yet, the media continued to respectfully report the denials. There has been no penalty for any government official who made a false public statement on the scandal, from Defense Secretary Rumsfeld to public affairs people to George Bush.

The Bush administration has shown what it takes for the U.S. government to get away with torture: almost nothing—or just some happy talk about the spread of democracy and freedom. The torture scandal exemplifies an Attention Deficit Democracy that has totally failed to restrain government power; a democracy that is incapable of reacting or reining in the rulers even when they are committing abuses that disgrace the nation in the eyes of the world and breed new enemies. The torture scandal apparently spurred few Americans to ask questions about the nature of their government. The lack of reaction by most Americans is almost as damning as the torture itself.

CHAPTER 7

Trusting Government at Any Cost

God save me from him I trust.

—French proverb[1]

A patriot must always be ready to defend his country against his government.

—Edward Albee[2]

SINCE IT HAS NOT BEEN POSSIBLE TO NEUTER POLITICAL POWER, citizens' thinking on government has been neutered instead. Fear of government is portrayed as a relic of less civilized, unrefined times. There is a concerted effort to make distrusting the government intellectually unacceptable, a sign of bad taste or perhaps ill breeding, if not downright ignoble.

The greater the public ignorance, the more government actually rests on blind trust in the goodness of the ruling elite. Blind trust becomes a substitute for informed consent. But mass trust in government compounds the political damage brought about by pervasive ignorance.

Many citizens react to their rulers like little kids who recognize that a stranger is acting suspiciously and may be up to no good—but then decide whether to trust the man depending on the type of candy he pulls from his pockets. It is as if a Reese's Peanut Butter Cup trumps the beady eyes, sweaty forehead, and out-of-season trench coat. Likewise, adults may be wary about a politician—but if the guy promises free prescription drugs or more housing subsidies, many take the bait.

Folks are schooled to believe that their rulers are benign, regardless of the number of lies they tell or abuses they commit. The bias in favor of trusting government brings out democracy's worst tendencies. The normal defenses that people would have against alien authority are undermined by a chorus of politicians and government officials continually reminding people that government is themselves, and they cannot distrust the government without distrusting themselves.

Why should people trust with power individuals who cannot be trusted with the facts? Why do people trust with power people they recognize as liars? Why assume that their perfidy is limited to their false public statements—and not also their conduct? And yet, the issue of trust in government is often treated like a clinical psychology topic—something best solved by putting tens of millions of Americans on the couch and finding out what their damn problem is.

How should people think about their rulers? This is a question that is rarely asked. Instead, it is preemptively squelched by myths pummeled into people's heads from a very early age.

The central mystery of modern political life is: Why are people obliged to presume that politicians and government are more trustworthy than they seem? The question is not, Why do people distrust government? The question is, Why do people follow and applaud politicians who they recognize are lying to them? The mystery is not that politicians lie, but that citizens believe. It is not a question of giving rulers *one* benefit of the doubt—but of giving such benefits day after day, year after year, ruler after ruler.

THE HISTORICAL BASELINE

America is perhaps the first nation founded on distrust of government. Checks and balances were included in the Constitution because of the danger of vesting too much power in any one man or one branch of government. The Bill of Rights was erected as a permanent leash on the political class. As Rexford Tugwell, one of FDR's Brain Trusters and an open admirer of Stalin's Soviet system, groused, "The Constitution was a negative document, meant mostly to protect citizens from their government."[3]

The Founding Fathers issued warning after warning of the inherent danger of government power. John Adams wrote in 1772: "There is danger from all men. The only maxim of a free government ought to be to trust no man living with power to endanger the public liberty."[4] Thomas Jefferson wrote in

1799, "Free government is founded in jealousy, not confidence. . . . In questions of power, let no more be heard of confidence in men, but bind him down from mischief by the chains of the Constitutions."[5] The term "politician" was in disrepute practically from 1776 onward (thanks to the antics of Congress during the Revolutionary War, and the conniving of some of the state legislators after 1783).

Many of the initial curbs on federal power were maintained for most of the first century of this nation's history in part because Americans often had a derisive attitude toward government—especially the federal government. Wariness toward government was one of the most important bulwarks of American freedom. Representative government worked partly because people were skeptical of congressmen, presidents, and government officials across the board. However, beginning in the early 1900s and accelerating in the New Deal, government was placed on a pedestal.[6]

DISTRUST OF GOVERNMENT AS MENTAL ILLNESS

Since the 1960s, it has been common for academics, politicians, and others to label those who distrust the government as mentally ill. This diagnosis was first popularized by Columbia University professor Richard Hofstadter, an early advocate of politically correct thought on government. Hofstadter was one of the most respected twentieth-century American historians. Inspired in part by the 1964 Barry Goldwater presidential campaign, he encouraged people to presume that staunch anticommunists and antisocialists were deranged. Ironically, Hofstadter himself was a former member of the Communist party.[7]

Hofstadter's *The Paranoid Style in American Politics* was first published in 1965 and quickly became canonized by the academic and political establishment; the book was republished in 1996 by Harvard University Press.[8] Hofstadter noted that "the term 'paranoid style' is pejorative, and it is meant to be; the paranoid style has a greater affinity for bad causes than good."[9] He wrote that "What interests me here is the possibility of using political rhetoric to get at political pathology." In Hofstadter's view, distrust of government was amongst the worst political pathologies imaginable.

Hofstadter's condescension toward average Americans was sometimes breathtaking: "Deficit spending is vehemently opposed by great numbers of people in our society who have given no serious thought—*indeed, are hardly equipped to do so*—to the complex questions bearing on its efficacy as an economic device."[10] Apparently, anyone who believed that government should not spend more money than it collected in tax revenue was by definition unfit to judge government policy. Hofstadter dismissed conservative criticisms of the Welfare State economic policies, noting that "*every informed person* recognizes that we have become much richer doing all these supposedly wrong and unsound things than we were when we had hardly begun to do them."[11] Thus, since the gross national product had expanded, no criticism of government economic policies deserved a hearing.

Hofstadter derided the legitimacy of the modern right-wing movement—scorning it as a "pseudo-conservative revolt." Hofstadter observed, "The pseudo-conservative is a man who, in the name of upholding traditional American values and institutions and defending them against *more or less fictitious dangers,* consciously or unconsciously aims at their abolition."[12] Because Hofstadter believed that the threat of government was "fictitious," everyone who feared government was deluded. But this diagnosis derived largely from Hofstadter's presumption that people had nothing to fear from their rulers.

It is worthwhile to recall the political landscape at the time Hofstadter sought to ostracize the beliefs of scores of millions of Americans. The pseudo-conservative, according to Hofstadter, "believes himself to be living in a world in which he is spied upon, plotted against, betrayed, and very likely destined for total ruin. He feels that his liberties have been arbitrarily and outrageously invaded."[13] At that time, the Federal Communications Commission was striving to torpedo right-wing radio. Bill Ruder, Kennedy's assistant secretary of commerce, later declared: "Our massive strategy was to use the Fairness Doctrine to challenge and harass right-wing broadcasters and hope that the challenges would be so costly to them that they would be inhibited and decide it was too expensive to continue."[14] The Internal Revenue Service was carrying out the Ideological Organizations Audit Project to harass and destroy conservative organizations.[15] J. Edgar Hoover's Federal Bureau of Investigation conducted an extensive surveillance operation at the 1964 Democratic National Convention to prevent embarrassing challenges to President Lyndon Johnson.[16] A top Johnson aide also requested that the FBI investigate the campaign staff of Republican challenger Barry Goldwater for "evidence of homosexual activity."[17] In 1965, the FBI kindly did background checks on dozens of people who had sent Johnson telegrams opposing his Vietnam policy.[18] The FBI was also running its COINTELPRO program at that time, including thousands of covert operations to incite street warfare between violent groups, to wreck marriages, to get people fired, to smear innocent people by portraying them as government informants, to sic the IRS on people, and to cripple or destroy left-wing, black, communist, white racist, and other organizations.[19] One FBI internal newsletter encouraged FBI agents to conduct interviews with antiwar activists to "enhance the paranoia endemic in these circles and further serve to get the point across that there is an FBI agent behind every mailbox."[20]

Hofstadter first published his essay on political paranoia in *Harper's* just two months after the Gulf of Tonkin resolution. While Hofstadter ridiculed those who distrusted government, President Johnson's and Defense Secretary Robert McNamara's lies and misrepresentations led to the deaths of scores of thousands of Americans and a million Vietnamese. If Americans had been less credulous, the Johnson administration might not have succeeded in railroading the nation into a futile war.

Hofstadter's doctrine rested on his near-boundless faith in the wisdom and benevolence of the ruling class: "American politics is run mainly by professionals who have developed over a long span of time an ethos of their own, a kind of professional code [that] for all its limitations, is an American institution embodying the practical wisdom of generations of politicians."[21] Hofstadter offered no proof of the wisdom of politicians; instead, it was a self-evident truth. The American establishment embraced Hofstadter's doctrine in part because it glorified them.

In 1964, when Hofstadter's essay was published, three quarters of the public trusted the federal government to do the right thing most, if not all, of the time. By the mid-1990s, only about a quarter of Americans had such trust in government.[22] Distrust of government has gone from being a fringe illness to being a mass psychosis of modern Americans—at least according to the Hofstadter paradigm.

Hofstadter's disdain for opponents of Big Government leads to the Catch–22 of modern Statism: anyone who fears government by definition becomes unfit to judge government. Thus, only Friends of Leviathan can be permitted to chart the course of political progress. Hofstadter remains an icon on campus, despite his profound failure to recognize or admit the danger posed by government.

TRUST AS THE GREAT WHITEWASHER

Trust in government is sometimes demanded most vociferously after some horrendous government blunder or abuse. Such was the case in the aftermath of a federal Alcohol, Tobacco and Firearms deadly no-knock raid and an FBI tank-and-toxic gas assault on the home of the Branch Davidians in Waco, Texas, in 1993 which ended with 80 dead men, women, and children. The Washington establishment almost instantly closed ranks around the federal government, canonizing Attorney General Janet Reno—the person who approved an FBI plan to destroy the Davidians' home to bring the siege to an end—as a hero.[23]

The FBI proceeded at Waco confident that it would receive the benefit of the doubt from the media and the public, regardless of how aggressive it became. In November 1994, Republicans captured control of Congress and, in the summer of 1995, held the first substantive hearings on Waco—much to the dismay of the Clinton administration and its allies in Congress. Even before the hearings began, Democrats sought to delegitimize any criticism of federal law enforcement. White House Chief of Staff Leon Panetta denounced proposals for the hearings as "despicable."[24] Treasury Secretary Robert Rubin warned journalists that federal action at Waco "cannot be understood properly outside the context of Oklahoma City."[25] Rubin did not explain how a 1995 truck bomb provided expo facto exoneration for a 1993 tank assault. Critics of government were portrayed as possible instigators of mass murder. Treasury Undersecretary Ron Noble warned that extremists might view the hearings "and decide to blow up some other building."[26] President Clinton, in a speech to directors of federal law enforcement agencies, denounced Republicans: "It is irresponsible for people in elected positions to suggest that the police are some sort of armed bureaucracy acting on private grudges and hidden agendas. That is wrong, it's inaccurate, and people who suggest that ought to be ashamed of themselves."[27] The president condemned the hearings as part of a Republican "war on police." Clinton sounded like the reincarnation of 1960s right-wingers who blanketed the nation with "Support Your Local Sheriff" bumperstickers.

Throughout the hearings, Democratic congressmen vociferously attacked those who doubted the government's story. Rep. Tom Lantos (D-CA) sneered that "the lunatic fringe still clings to the notion that there was a gigantic government conspiracy that brought about this nightmare. . . . It is difficult to see how any rational human being subscribes to such a notion."[28] But, as the hearings progressed, many government explanations self-destructed. The government's version of events always hinged on the notion that the Branch Davidians intentionally burned themselves to death, and thus that the feds had no culpability for their deaths. Rep. Chuck Schumer (D-NY) derided the notion that the flashbang grenades the FBI threw into the Davidians' home could have done any harm: "Anyone who knows anything about these things knows they can't" inflict fatal harm.[29] Yet, flashbangs have killed numerous people and have also ignited fires. Democrats insisted that the CS gas that the feds pumped into the Davidians' home was basically harmless—even though the same gas had killed dozen of children when used in the Gaza Strip. (The use of CS gas on enemy soldiers was prohibited by an international treaty the U.S. government signed, but the treaty did not prohibit governments from gassing their own subjects.) Attorney General Reno testified and sought to exonerate the government and heap blame on the Davidians. The highlight of her testimony was her assertion that the 54-ton tank that repeatedly smashed into the Davidians' home should not be considered a military vehicle—instead it was just "like a good rent-a-car."[30] Because the media was docile, Reno's comment excited almost zero controversy.

Though the Democrats' demands that people trust the government helped stifle Waco controversies, further revelations trickled out in the late 1990s that reignited the issue. After news leaked out in the summer of 1999 that the FBI covered up the fact that its agents fired incendiary tear gas cartridges into the Davidians' home prior to a fire erupting, Janet Reno was forced to appoint a special counsel to investigate. Reno chose former Republican Senator John Danforth, a stalwart of the Washington establishment. Danforth returned the favor by sending Reno a letter praising her and declaring that she did "exactly the right thing" at Waco.[31] (Reno disclosed the letter during her campaign to become governor of Florida.) Danforth's sweeping judgment clashed with many of the government experts who subsequently reviewed the steps leading up to and including the final assault. His report largely exonerated the feds. At one point during his purported investigation, Danforth complained that the FBI sought to stonewall his investigation and refused to turn over key evidence. But he assured the *Washington Post* that, regardless of whatever evidence the FBI withheld, "there is no chance that it would have any effect on our findings because the evidence is so overwhelming."[32] In the most revealing passage of the final report, Danforth declared his hope that his findings would "begin the process of restoring the faith of the people in their government and the faith of the government in the people."[33] In Danforth's view, government officials had been wrongfully victimized by public distrust—regardless of how many government claims collapsed or how many times the FBI, ATF, or Justice Department revised their Waco stories. Perhaps, after half a lifetime of "service" in Washington, Danforth had forgotten who had used tanks on whom on April 19, 1993.

FANNING TRUST

Encouraging more trust in government has become a major industry. In 1983, the Council for Excellence in Government was created, stocked with former government officials who believed that government deserves more respect. By the late 1990s, half its annual budget came from government contracts and federal agencies. But taking government funds did nothing to undermine the organization's ability to accurately assess the government—at least in the eyes of the media. The Council's proclamations are often hailed as oracles from Delphi. The Council believes that popular distrust of government arises because people are misinformed, not misgoverned.

The Council, along with the Ford Foundation, launched a spinoff in 1997—the Partnership for Trust in Government—to "celebrate government's success." A press release proclaimed that the new organization would "counter 'government bashing' and restore the balance between public cynicism and trust." Girl Scouts can now earn a "Partners for Trust in Government patch" for identifying "local government programs that benefit their communities." There are no patches awarded for girl scouts who expose government coverups.

The trust cause was also championed in books from the most respectable sources. Harvard University Press in late 1997 published *Why People Don't Trust Government,* a production of Harvard's Kennedy School of Government. The political scientists struggled mightily to grasp why so many people failed to recognize so much government benevolence.

Britain's *Times Higher Education Supplement* published an interview with Joseph Nye, the book's senior editor and dean of the Kennedy School.[34] The *Times* reported that "the book, and its subject matter, are being taken seriously in the highest political circles on both sides of the Atlantic. Nye was among a group of American experts led by Hillary Clinton who recently came to Britain for a seminar on the book attended by, among others, Tony Blair, who left clutching a copy."[35] The book—and Nye's move from the Clinton administration to Harvard—was prompted by the 1995 Oklahoma City bombing. Nye explained: "I was preoccupied that people could become so anti-government that they were capable of an act like that."[36] *Why People Don't Trust Government* had no mention of Waco. Nye lamented: "All the evidence is that government and politicians are at least as honest as they were in the past, but that isn't the impression people are getting."[37] Three days after the interview was published, a *Washington Post* banner headline heralded the start of the Monica Lewinsky scandal.

The tone of disbelief in *Why People Don't Trust Government* is at times almost comical. Harvard professor Gary Orren wrote: "The public has not only lost faith in the ability of government to solve problems, but it has actually come to believe that government involvement will just make matters worse."[38] Orren blamed the media for the myth of government incompetence: "People have less direct experience with the federal government and are therefore more reliant on the news media—and the increasingly negative coverage of government—for their impressions."[39] An essay by Harvard emeritus professor Richard Neustadt observed that "we Americans are well advised to mitigate mistrust all we can."[40] The academics were more concerned about criticism of government than about government abuses.

The concluding essay by Nye and co-editor and Harvard professor Philip Zelikow stresses that the problem with Americans' attitude toward government "is a function of *perceived* performance."[41] Nye and Zelikow puzzled over the "apparent contradiction between subjective opinion and objective performance"[42]—between public distrust of government and government's wondrous achievements.

Among the other dangers of distrust of government, tax dodging was high up on the list. Nye warned: "If people believe that government is incompetent and cannot be trusted, they are less likely to provide *such crucial contributions as tax dollars.* . . . Without these resources, government cannot perform well, and if government cannot perform, people will become even more dissatisfied and distrustful."[43] There is nothing like a tax revolt to kill the goose that lays Leviathan's golden eggs. Nye did not explain why citizens would "become even more dissatisfied" if government seized less of their income.

In 2000, a year after Clinton's Senate impeachment trial, Simon & Schuster published *A Necessary Evil: A History of American Distrust of Government,* by Pulitzer Prize–winning professor Garry Wills, one of the most respected popular historians in America. Wills explained that he began the book "in 1994, when the fear of government manifested itself in the off-year election of a Republican majority to Congress" that sought to "cut government subsidies . . . to farmers," among other extremist notions. Wills explained how distrust of government blights American society:

> Many people find themselves surprised at the sympathy they can feel for even outrageous opponents of government—as was demonstrated when popular support blossomed for the anti-government forces holed up with David Koresh at Waco Texas, or with Randy Weaver, who defied the FBI at Ruby Ridge Idaho. . . . But the real victims of our fear are not those faced with such extreme action. . . . The real victims are the millions of poor or shelterless or medically indigent who have been told, over the years, that they must lack care or life support in the name of their very own freedom. Better for them to starve than to be enslaved by "big government." That is the real cost of our anti-government values.[44]

Wills maintained the pro-government high ground by ignoring or distorting some of the cases that stirred the most distrust of government in the 1990s. In an aside about Ruby Ridge, Wills commented, "Federal agents had . . . killed a religious extremist's wife in a raid on his home. This man, Randy Weaver, was a member of the antisemitic 'Christian Identity' movement, and he had defied a court summons. But that hardly seemed a reason for the military assault on his home."[45]

Wills did not mention that the court had sent Weaver an incorrect date to show up for his hearing. Even though a federal agent knew that Weaver had been wrongly informed, he still persuaded the court to issue an arrest warrant for Weaver. And it was not a "raid" or a "military assault" on Weaver's home.

An FBI sniper hiding more than 200 yards away had gunned down Weaver's wife as she stood holding her baby in the cabin door—moments after he had shot Weaver in the back after he stepped out of his cabin. Randy Weaver never fired a shot at the feds, nor even brandished a weapon in their direction. The day before, U.S. marshals had trespassed on Weaver's land and shot his son in the back and killed him after ambushing the boy and a family friend. (A U.S. marshal was killed in the firefight, possibly shot by a fellow marshal.)[46]

Distrust of government may be as likely to provoke violence by government agents as to provoke citizens' attacks on government. Weaver, a white separatist, spouted a lot of nonsense about government conspiracies—but he was a loner living on a northern Idaho mountaintop. Yet, in its indictment of Weaver after the killing of his wife and son, the Justice Department bizarrely claimed that the fact that Weaver had moved from Iowa to Idaho in 1983 and took steps to "purchase, develop and maintain a remote mountain residence/stronghold"[47] proved he was conspiring to have a violent confrontation with the government. Gerry Spence, Weaver's lawyer, observed, "The cabin was built with sticks and plywood so fragile a wolf could have blown it down."[48] The feds included this absurd charge so that they could build a case based on Weaver's anti-government ideology—and thereby shift attention away from the government's actions. The FBI snipers were ordered to shoot to kill any adult male seen carrying a gun—regardless of whether they posed a threat. A 1997 federal appeals court decision condemned the FBI rules of engagement as "a gross deviation from constitutional principles and a wholly unwarranted return to a lawless and arbitrary wild-west school of law enforcement."[49]

Waco and Ruby Ridge, two cases that excited the most distrust in the 1990s, both involved profound government wrongdoing followed by falsehoods and coverups. Regardless of how many times the government was forced (by leaks, court defeats, or other circumstances) to amend its story, the Establishment still disdained almost everyone who invoked either incident to warn of the danger of government power. While many people in the heartland invoked Ruby Ridge and Waco to see the peril of boundless federal power, the Establishment saw such criticisms as proof that many Americans were intellectually unwashed. After each revelation that debunked previous government "truths," the media and establishment would, at worst, emit a few editorials and sighs and then return to the regularly scheduled championing of Leviathan.

9/11 AND TRUST IN GOVERNMENT

The precedents established by one political party are routinely exploited for totally different ends by their opponents. During the 1990s, liberals were in the vanguard, preaching the need to trust government. After 9/11, it was Bush who exploited boundless trust to expand government power in ways that mortified many liberals. The Bush administration could exploit 9/11 because Americans were predisposed to see credulity and obedience as paramount virtues.

The number of Americans who trusted the federal government to do the right thing more than doubled in the weeks after the attack. By the end of September 2001, almost two-thirds of Americans said they "trust the government in Washington to do what is right" either "just about always" or "most of the time."[50]

Amazingly, the attacks even boosted Americans' confidence that government will protect them against terrorists. The *Washington Post* asked respondents in late September 2001, "How much confidence do you have in the ability of the U.S. government to prevent further terrorist attacks against Americans in this country?" From 1995 through 1997, the results consistently showed that only between 35 percent and 37 percent of people had "a great deal" or "a good amount" of confidence that the feds would deter such attacks. In hindsight, the public was far more prescient than Washington policymakers, however, who largely ignored threats of homeland terror attacks. In the aftermath of the attacks, confidence in government's ability to deter terrorist attacks soared to 66 percent.[51]

Many of the most respected and prominent media commentators saw 9/11 as the Great Sanctifier of government power. The *New York Times'* R. W. Apple announced: "Government is back in style."[52] *Wall Street Journal* columnist Al Hunt proclaimed: "It's time to declare a moratorium on government-bashing."[53] *Los Angeles Times* columnist Ronald Brownstein declared on September 19: "At the moment the first fireball seared the crystalline Manhattan sky last week, the entire impulse to distrust government that has become so central to U.S. politics seemed instantly anachronistic."[54] Harvard University political scientist Robert Putnam effused: "I think there is the potential that September 11 will turn out to be a turning point for civic America. . . . There could be some good coming from it if it causes us to become . . . more open-minded about the role of government."[55]

As the months passed and the shock of 9/11 subsided, and as details leaked out of the government muffing or snubbing pre-9/11 attack warnings, public trust in government receded. At the end of May 2002, the Brookings Institution's Center for Public Service issued a report entitled "Opportunity Lost." Center director Paul Light bewailed: "Unfortunately, Americans' trust in government appears to be returning to normal." The co-author of the study, G. Calvin Mackenzie, declared, "September 11 created a government moment, a time for citizens to recognize and appreciate the services that government provides, and the skill with which it performs."[56] Mackenzie, who was the staff director of a National Academy of Public Administration study on trust in government, declared, "There was a *silver lining to the dark cloud of September 11th,* that maybe this was one of those cathartic moments in history" that could "maybe establish a bond of faith that hadn't been there before."[57] MacKenzie stressed: "When the government is trusted, it has broad latitude to take bold action." And if trust in government is low, MacKenzie warned, "Everything is a harder sell for leaders in government. So the level of trust in government matters very substantially in terms of what the instant capabilities of government are at any point in time." But, when rulers are dishonest, government "instant capabilities"—i.e., the ability to quickly seize more power—are among the greatest perils citizens face.

The 9/11 attacks produced many such summons to elevate and glorify government. Yet it was U.S. government foreign policies that stirred up the hornet's nest, breeding hatred that led to the attacks themselves. After two skyscrapers collapse and the Pentagon is in flames, the government is hailed for failing to protect Americans from the enemies its policies helped create. The 9/11 attackers were mass murderers who had no right to kill Americans. But to pretend that the attacks originated out of nowhere or out of hatred of freedom fraudulently exonerates the U.S. government.

The Bush administration did all it could to exploit 9/11 to promote presidential and governmental greatness. However, a 2002 Senate Intelligence Committee investigation found a vast array of federal intelligence and law enforcement failures prior to the attack.[58] Because the Bush administration often stonewalled the Senate investigation, 9/11 widows and widowers pressured Congress to create an independent commission to investigate the attacks. Bush and Republican and Democratic congressional leaders stacked the commission with former congressmen, high-ranking government officials, and others entwined in the Washington establishment. Beverly Eckert, a 9/11 widower and activist, complained: "We wanted journalists, we wanted academics. . . . We did not want politicians."[59]

Philip Zelikow was appointed executive director of the commission. Zelikow, the co-editor of *Why People Don't Trust Government,* had worked closely with National Security advisor Condoleezza Rice and had co-authored a book with her in 1999. Zelikow had also been in charge of the Bush White House transition team on national security matters, had been involved in numerous transition briefings on the subject of terrorism, and was called as a witness before the commission. Zelikow rescued himself from the commission hearing at which Rice testified. Rice was the one government official who perhaps most deserved perjury charges from her testimony, yet there was not a single word of criticism of her in the commission's final report.

The 9/11 Commission became the Bush administration's most famous faith-based initiative. The commission appeared far more concerned with restoring trust than in revealing truth. Bush and Cheney were allowed to testify without a transcript and not under oath. Americans never heard what they said. Instead, the commission offered a synopsis of their comments—as if it would have been impious to quote them directly. The White House was allowed to edit the final version of the commission's report before it was publicly released.

The commission's final 568-page report quickly became a bestseller, widely praised in part because it assiduously avoided judgment. There was no mention in the final report of how Bush and Cheney exploited falsehoods about 9/11 to lead the nation to war against Iraq. But, as Amherst professor Benjamin De-Mott noted in *Harper's*, the report was useless to historians because of a "seeming terror of bias."[60] DeMott was especially appalled that the commission accepted without challenge Bush's assertion that the August 6, 2001, President's Daily Brief was "historical in nature." Demott observed: "There's little mystery about why the Commission is tongue-tied. It can't call a liar a liar." DeMott noted: "The ideal readers of The 9/11 Commission Report are those who resemble the Commission itself in believing that a strong inclination to trust the word of highly placed others is evidence of personal moral distinction."[61]

The 9/11 Commission report provided a litany of government missteps while carefully avoiding raising any ire against the government. The failures often appeared to be more an act of God than failings by specific identifiable individuals. The report strived for a balance of criticism between the current and prior administrations, and between the two political parties. Thus, there was nothing to be done except count our blessings, celebrate our two-party system, and go whip the terrorists.

The 9/11 Commission also compiled ample evidence of government lies. Yet the commission effectively ignored or "rose above" all the falsehoods. There was no sense that the lies of the most powerful officials in the land posed any threat to America. Instead, there were "communication problems" between government agencies.

The establishment aided the government by heaping derision on nonbelievers. The *Washington Post,* in an October 2004 article headlined, "Conspiracy Theories Flourish on the Internet," examined the problems of those who had not accepted the government's latest version of 9/11. The *Post* noted sympathetically, "The ready and growing audience for conspiracy theories about the Sept. 11, 2001, attacks has been particularly galling to those who worked on . . . the bipartisan panel known as the 9/11 commission."[62] In Washington, "bipartisan" is the ultimate test of credibility—as if there was no chance that both parties would ever conspire against the truth. Zelikow bemoaned: "We discussed the theories. When we wrote the report, we were also careful not to answer all the theories. It's like playing Whack-A-Mole. You're never going to whack them all. They satisfy a deep need in the people who create them."[63]

The *Post* turned to a Syracuse University political scientist, Michael Barkun, for psychological insights into nonbelievers: "Conspiracy theories are . . . usually wrong, but they're psychologically reassuring. Because what they say is that everything is connected, nothing happens by accident, and that there is some kind of order in the world, even if it's produced by evil forces." The *Post* never ran any articles on the psychological maladies of people who insisted on believing the government's statements on 9/11 despite the contradictions, or who insisted on clinging to earlier government claims after the government revised the facts.

Zelikow, who was hired by Rice as her top counsel at the State Department a few months after the *Post* article appeared, commented: "The hardcore conspiracy theorists are totally committed. . . . That's not our worry. *Our worry* is when things become *infectious,* as happened with the [John F. Kennedy] assassination. Then this stuff can be deeply corrosive to public understanding. You can get where *the bacteria can sicken the larger body.*"[64] (If the government was so forthright in its investigation of the Kennedy assassination, why were the Warren Commission records sealed for 75 years?)

Not a single one of the top 300 American newspapers or magazines archived on the Lexis-Nexis database commented on Zelikow's "bacteria" and "infectious" characterization of disbelief in the government's version of 9/11. Yet his comment sounded as if the 9/11 Commission saw itself as America's mental health czar. Private doubts are the bacteria, and government assertions are presumably the disinfectant. As long as people believe what the government says, no one will get sick.

The *Washington Post* never portrayed government officials who put out false statements about 9/11 in the same light as it did the private conspiracy buffs. Despite the fact that private citizens have no power over other Americans and that they have no authority to coerce them or drag them into an unnecessary war, their false statements are presented as a greater threat than those of government officials. The obsession with private lies is misplaced, when the real danger is the government lie—a lie embraced and disseminated by a subservient media, vested with all the prestige and aura of the State, and protected by an iron curtain of government secrecy. And regardless of how many times the government changes the official story, people who continue to distrust the government are delirious.

Some of the allegations regarding 9/11—such as the charge that no plane had hit the Pentagon—were easily verifiable as false. *New American,* the magazine of the John Birch Society, ran an article harshly criticizing some of the

9/11 conspiracy theories, though carefully avoiding embracing the government.[65] Yet, as with Waco, the Establishment invoked outlying loons in order to seek to undermine the credibility of all criticism of the government. But the existence of conspiracy nuts does not make the government honest.

SECRECY AND TRUST

In ancient Rome, the consul Scipio was challenged in front of the Senate on his management of one of the Roman territories. Scipio responded by pulling from his robes the accounts documenting his dealings—and then tore them to shreds in front of the audience. Scipio's reputation was so impeccable that he was confident of the audience's embrace, regardless of the destruction of the evidence.[66]

Unfortunately, this is what the federal government does to the American people on a daily basis. Citizens are obliged to trust the government—even when government withholds the evidence that would permit citizens to judge.

The federal government has become far more secretive in recent years. The Freedom of Information Act was severely weakened in 2001, making it far more difficult for citizens to discover federal abuses.[67] A Bush executive order effectively bars public access to far more presidential papers.[68] Almost twice as many documents (15.6 million) were classified by the federal government in 2004 as in 2001.[69] At the same time, the government has slashed the rate of declassifying older documents. The federal government currently spends more than twenty times as much—$7 billion a year—keeping secrets (classifying material) as it does in disclosing information to citizens and others who file Freedom of Information Act requests. The mania for secrecy often goes above and beyond the call of duty, or reason. William Leonard, former director of the federal Information Security Oversight Office, observed, "I've seen information that was classified [by federal agencies] that I've also seen published in third-grade textbooks."[70] Thomas Blanton, director of the nonprofit National Security Archive at George Washington University, said the Bush administration "viewed public access to information as encroaching on executive power."[71]

Government secrecy breeds lies the same way dampness breeds rot. Yet, the media often treats official secrecy as a question of administrative procedures or partisan political squabbles. Regardless of how much information the government hides, citizens should not assume that their rulers are up to no good.

Citizens are obliged to trust the government even after the government trumpets its right to lie to citizens. Bush's solicitor general, Theodore Olson, informed the Supreme Court in 2002 that the federal government had the right "to give out false information . . . incomplete information and even misinformation" whenever it deemed necessary.[72] Olson helpfully explained: "It's easy to imagine an infinite number of situations where the government might legitimately give out false information."[73] But it is difficult to imagine an infinite number of situations in which the government would be honest with citizens in ways that did not serve the government's interest.

Comments such as Olson's are almost always ignored or relegated to the dust bin (or back pages) by respectable media. This is part of the reason why proclamations about the government's right to lie never register in the minds of most Americans. Of course, the fact that the government is entitled to lie does not absolve the citizen of his duty to believe.

POLITICIANS' TRUST BUTTON

Trust is one of the most overused terms in American politics. Politicians invoke "the people's trust" even more often than they proclaim their own humility. On the campaign trail, politicians perennially promise to restore faith and trust in government and in themselves. In his acceptance speech at the 1968 Republican National Convention, Richard Nixon proclaimed: "Let us begin by committing ourselves to the truth—to see it as it is, and tell it like it is—to find the truth, to speak the truth, and to live the truth."[74] Nixon's subsequent conduct indicated that this standard was more of an aspiration or abstract ideal, rather than a strict guide for day-to-day conduct. Nixon became renowned as the most paranoid president of modern times, and his lies on Watergate and other subjects helped dig his political grave.

When he announced his candidacy a few months after Nixon's resignation, Jimmy Carter declared, "There is a simple and effective way for public officials to regain public trust—be trustworthy!"[75] But Carter's presidency did more to stimulate political humor than trust in the government.

When George Bush launched his presidential campaign in July 1999, he declared, "We will show that politics, after a time of tarnished ideals, can be higher and better. We will give our country a fresh start after a season of cynicism."[76] The fresh start did not survive the fracas over the Florida election results. Bush did not help matters when he declared shortly after the Supreme Court effectively crowned him that "If this were a dictatorship, it would be a heck of a lot easier."[77]

In 2004, Democratic presidential candidate John Kerry hit the same theme: "I will restore trust and credibility to the White House." Hitting the same subject, Bush, in his second inaugural address, declared: "The leaders of governments with long habits of control need to know: To serve your people you must learn to trust them."[78]

Yet the more Bush trusts the people, the more he wants to spy on them. Bush's trust did not dissuade his administration from seeking to build the Total Information Awareness network, a system to track every purchase, trip, or phone call that people make; getting congressional approval for the FBI's Carnivore wiretapping system to cannibalize the nation's e-mail without the bother of obtaining a search warrant; launching Operation TIPS—the Terrorist Information and Prevention System—to recruit millions of informants to report on their neighbors and others; and unleashing FBI agents to infiltrate churches, mosques, and political groups even when there is no suspicion of criminal wrongdoing—effectively permitting government agents to go almost anywhere and search almost anything.[79] The Homeland Security Department epitomized the Bush administration's "trust" of Americans when it warned 18,000 local and state law enforcement agencies to keep an eye on anyone who "expressed dislike of attitudes and decisions of the U.S. government."[80] Perhaps Bush simply trusts people not to object when the feds destroy their privacy.

Bush was following in Clinton's footsteps. Clinton, like Bush, continually assured Americans that he trusted them. This did not dissuade the Clinton administration from pushing for the mandatory installation of Clipper Chips in new computers to provide a red carpet for federal spy agencies; attacking creators of private encryption software that would block prying eyes; pushing technology standards to permit a hundredfold increase in wiretaps; championing warrantless searches against public housing residents; converting cell phones into involuntary tracking devices for law enforcement; and pushing for a mandatory government database on citizens' medical records.[81]

The word "trust" spawns fog banks behind which politicians do as they please. The more that politicians talk of trusting the people, the more people take such words as proof the politician himself is trustworthy. The more that trust is invoked, the easier it becomes for government to slip its leash.

THE DANGER OF EXCESSIVE TRUST

Blind trust in government is often portrayed as a harmless error—as if it were of no more account than saying prayers to a pagan deity that didn't exist. However, the notion that rulers are entitled to trust is the most expensive entitlement program of them all. "Follow the leader" has often been a recipe for national suicide. Throughout history, people have tended to trust most governments more than rulers deserved.

Blind trust of government has resulted in far more carnage than distrust of government. The more trust, the less resistance. It was people who believed and who followed orders who carried out the Nazi Holocaust, the Ukrainian terror-famine, the Khmer Rouge blood bath, and the war crimes that characterize conflicts around the globe. It is not just a question of acquiescence but of breeding a docile attitude toward political events and government actions. Docility is a far greater danger than blind fanaticism, at least in Western societies. It is the mass docility that permits fanatics to seize power and wreak havoc. The more people who unconditionally trust the government, the more atrocities the government can commit. All that the government need do afterward is to label and blame the victim.

The history of the United States after 9/11 vivifies the danger of excessive trust in government. The foreign policy response to 9/11 would have been far more targeted if scores of millions of Americans had not written George Bush a blank check. The adulation and deference that Bush received in the immediate aftermath of 9/11 encouraged federal officials to believe that they could do practically whatever they pleased. Top administration officials were laying plans to attack Iraq within days after the Twin Towers collapsed,[82] regardless of zero evidence linking Iraq to the attacks. Less than two weeks after 9/11, senior Bush administration officials were already claiming that the attacks gave the U.S. government carte blanche to attack anywhere in the world. Deputy Assistant Attorney General John Yoo sent White House Counsel Alberto Gonzales a memo on September 25, 2001, suggesting that "an American attack in South America or Southeast Asia might be a surprise to the terrorists," since they were expecting the United States to target Afghanistan.[83]

Excessive trust in government breeds attention deficits. People assume they do not need to keep an eye on government and politicians because government is no threat to them—because their government tells them so. Ignorance combined with blind trust produces citizens pliable for practically any purpose the ruler decrees.

INTELLECTUAL PASSIVE OBEDIENCE

Americans have been schooled to ignore political frauds. Many Americans interpret election campaigns and elections like an investigator assessing commercial fraud solely by examining the signatures on a sales contract. As long as the salesman's and purchaser's signatures are bona fide, then the contract is binding—regardless of how many false representations the salesman made, how many contract provisions the salesman deletes after the contract is signed, or how much the salesman boosts the price after the ink is dry. This is an absurd way to define fraud—and yet this is the standard by which people acquiesce to their rulers.

Believing government lies is the new version of passive obedience. In the 1660s, after the English Civil War and the restoration of the monarchy, preachers hectored the English people that they could never rightfully resist the king. The king was God's chosen and must be obeyed, regardless of how depraved and abusive he or his agents became. As one 1660 English pamphlet warned, "Were not the King a God to man, one man would be a wolf to another."[84] Some of the contemporary discussions on the duty to trust the government resemble those old church sermons.

Passive intellectual obedience means preemptively quieting one's doubts about the statements of one's rulers. It means abstaining from any conscious effort to evaluate the honesty or believability of official statements. It means deferring to government officials even when one's own instincts and understanding points to a different conclusion. It means abstaining from adding two and two, if the sum might cause problems. It means abstaining from planting any seeds of doubts in others' minds. Intellectual passive obedience means accepting the "us versus them" paradigm that politicians exploit to frighten people into obedience. It means viewing political (and all other) reality through a moral lens supplied by one's rulers. And no matter how many lies the rulers tell, the citizens are still obliged to believe—if not actively, then at least to go through the motions and muffle doubts.

The term "intellectual passive obedience" doesn't fit for many citizens, since there is nothing vaguely intellectual about their obedience or about their political views. "Intellectual" implies at least a pretense of effort to comprehend reality. Instead, more and more citizens are simply passive recipients of whatever the media or the government dumps into their stream of consciousness. There is little or no effort to reconcile contradictions, or even to assimilate the fleeting impressions that enter their minds. It may be merely a question of not remembering—of having the scattered and contradictory impressions pushed out of his mind by the latest presidential proclamation—or the latest terror alert.

The earlier version of passive obedience was buttressed by the doctrine of divine right. What is the similar buttress for the new Passive Obedience? The will of the majority? But the people cannot be presumed to have willed their own abuse. The necessity of progress? The epochs when mankind advanced were not characterized by unquestioning submission to whoever got themselves accepted as an authority.

Yet, no matter how many lies the government tells, it can never go morally bankrupt. Government is credible solely because it is government. Intellectual passive obedience results in people permitting the government to exclude practically whatever information or facts it chooses. The government takes broad leeway to define the issues—and thus preemptively doom resistance. Permitting politicians to define issues will minimize the number of citizens who recognize how government power imperils them.

Attention Deficit Democracy, especially when supplemented with a trusting attitude, ensures that citizens will learn little from the perennial failures of their rulers. Instead, fixing political problems, fixing the system becomes as simple as finding a good man to put at the top. Citizens are supposed to assume that a change in the name of the ruler, or a switch in the party in charge, automatically suspends the laws of political probability. This is part of the source of the "honeymoons" for politicians who win elections. But the history of recent decades shows that merely changing ruling parties sometimes accomplishes little aside from re-arranging the chairs at Washington dinner parties.

Good citizens must assume that the fact that someone lied last year, last month, and last week is irrelevant to gauging whether they are honest today. After each new lie, the citizens' minds should "reboot" and return to the default setting, waiting starry-eyed for the next political promise. Each specific claim by a president or government must be treated as credible until it is proven otherwise. And after it is proven false, it is irrelevant because it is an aberration.

When people blindly assume that their leaders are trustworthy, the biggest liars win. To believe the lie is almost to guarantee submission. To accept a false statement from one's rulers is to submit to a lie—to intellectually submit. And submission is habit forming. Politicians do not need to promulgate a duty to submit because as long as people believe, most will submit to almost anything. After people lower their mental defenses, political perfidy is half way home. If people are trained not to doubt—politicians need only continue lying and denying until all barricades that guard individual rights have been smashed, one by one.

DIFFERENT STANDARDS

People are encouraged to judge government by different standards than they use for any other earthly institution. But what is "trust of government in itself"? What does this come down to in the final realm? Simply a presumption that those who are able to capture political power are inherently superior to other human beings. Elected officials have far more power to suppress the evidence of their lies. It is as if the more facts politicians can suppress, the more truth they will tell.

Judging from the comments of politicians and editorial writers, the issue is not whether government is trustworthy, but what will happen if people are permitted to doubt. Some commentators seem spooked by fear of a peasant revolt. The question is not whether the peasants have legitimate grievances—but of the catastrophic results of permitting them to get out of control. Today's elite seems to view trust in government like some of the 1920s elite viewed Prohibition—as something necessary to keep dangerous things out of the hands of common people.

Ironically, the standard for permitted doubts about government is largely set by the mainstream media—a group that tends to be government fed, if not permanently "embedded" in the federal government. Many of the same people who pass judgment on private distrust also make a good living retailing government lies. The same media outlets that ignored Waco and trumpeted the presidential lies that took the nation to war against Serbia and Iraq now sit as arbiters of how far good citizens may be permitted to doubt the government.

Much of the American public appears to separate the issues of trust and power—as if a person's character is irrelevant to how much additional power he should be permitted to capture. For instance, regardless of the number of people who believed that Clinton was a liar, Clinton's proposals to expand federal power to protect people or to give them specific new benefits generally had high levels of popular approval (excepting his 1993–94 health care plan). Public support for vesting more power in an untrustworthy ruler is a sign of how few Americans still understand the nature of government. Many Americans seem to believe that government programs automatically do what politicians promise they will—and nothing more.

The greatest political paradox of our age is that government and rulers are often considered *dishonest yet trustworthy.* Perhaps not "trustworthy" in the sense of deserving a Boy Scout Medal of Honor—but trustworthy enough to be permitted to seize more power over other Americans. Trustworthy enough to be entitled to obedience, regardless of their lies. Trustworthy enough to be obeyed, regardless of how badly things worked out the last time they received deference.

Democracy is far more effective at reducing citizens' fears than limiting Leviathan. Democracy breeds gullibility. Lord Bryce observed in 1921 that "State action became less distrusted the more the State itself was seen to be passing under popular control."[85] The rise of democracy makes it much easier for politicians to convince people that government poses no threat because they automatically control its actions. The result is that the brakes on government power become weakest at the exact time that politicians are most dangerous.

In the same way that power corrupts, blind trust corrupts. To say that people should not blindly trust the government is not to call for anarchy or for violence in the streets or the torching of city halls across the land. It is not a choice of trusting the government or refusing to drive on the right side of the road. Instead, it is a call for people to cease deluding themselves about those who seek to control them.

Politicians who violate their oath to uphold the Constitution have proven themselves unworthy of trust. What is the case for trusting people who have proven themselves untrustworthy? Should people be proud to trust politicians in a way that they would consider foolish regarding any other profession?

Just because government appears to be a necessary evil does not oblige people to trust it. We face a choice of trusting government or trusting free-dom—trusting overlords who have lied and abused their power, or trusting in-dividuals to make the most of their own lives.

Those who insist that people still have a duty to trust the government should explain: At what point will people be released from this duty? Or are they obliged to continue trusting government until their rulers have gotten them or the entire society destroyed? Is the duty of trust irrevocable—or only semi-irrevocable? If the duty to trust is irrevocable, how did free citizens be-come sacrificial offerings for their rulers? And if the trust is revocable, then how can anyone still preach the duty to trust after all the government false-hoods of recent decades?

Attention Deficit Democracy disables the political alarm systems in many citizens' heads. Yet, trust in a dishonest government is true escapism—an eva-sion of responsibility for one's own life and liberties. Deference to lying rulers is self-betrayal. The burden of proof must be on those who insist that lying po-litical candidates automatically become trustworthy elected officials.

CHAPTER 8

Elections as
Reverse Slave Auctions

Anyone who incites violence, other than those elected, will have to face the law.
—Ethiopian Minister of Information Bereket Simon[1]

ONCE THE IGNORANCE OF MOST VOTERS IS RECOGNIZED, maintaining faith in the electoral system requires a reliance on mysticism. Instead of believing that election results are an expression of the latent wisdom of the majority, elections are assumed to protect and serve the citizenry by the equivalent of some type of divine intervention. Election results are providential despite the ignorance, negligence, and greed of many, if not most, voters.

But political mysticism, as usual, provides little more than a pretext to subjugate and exploit. We will consider what elections are and are becoming in the age of Leviathan Democracy.

At the time of the American Revolution, elections were seen as a means for people to protect themselves against rulers—kings, ministers, or any other official wrongdoer. Edmund Burke characterized the role of Parliament: "It was not instituted to be a control *upon* the people. . . . It was designed as a control *for* the people."[2] The people's representatives were to be "a check to insolent, licentious ministers, a terror to ambitious statesmen, a defense against corruption in high offices, and against the violent temper of a prince aiming at arbitrary power," according to one 1782 pamphleteer.[3] Law professor John Phillip Reid, author of *The Concept of Representation in the Age of the American Revolution,* observed, "Eighteenth-century representation was primarily an institution of restraint on governmental power."[4] Representatives had a sacred duty "to take care, that all the executive powers of Government are kept within the Limits of the law," according to one 1769 friend of liberty.[5] As Reid noted, "A constitution became legitimate when the representative element provided a balance to government, checking its authority to an extent sufficient that people were not subject to arbitrary command."[6]

But elections lost their classic function of a defense against government because people supposedly need no defense against themselves. Instead of seeking representatives to safeguard their rights, people now seek strong leaders or saviors to redeem their lives and protect them from all harm, 24/7. In the United States, elections have become largely a question of the two major parties taking turns trampling rights and plundering the Treasury. The glory of democracy is lost when election days become little more than a chance for voters to choose their personal leash-holder.

THE MEANING OF ELECTIONS

Politicians strive to make Americans view elections as sacrosanct. Challenges to election results are portrayed as heresies that threaten to damn the entire republic. After the 2004 presidential election, many Democrats went on the warpath over alleged voter fraud and manipulation in Ohio and elsewhere. The Constitution requires Congress to certify the electoral college voters for each state before a president is officially elected. A handful of Democratic members of Congress formally challenged the seating of the Ohio electors when Congress reconvened in early January 2005. Though the debate in the House of Representatives lasted barely two hours, many Republicans feared raising the topic had derailed the nation and the march of history.

Rep. Stephanie Tubbs Jones (D-Ohio) explained the purpose of the Democratic challenge: "This objection does not have at its root the hope or even the hint of overturning the victory of the President; but . . . We as a body must conduct a formal and legitimate debate about election irregularities. I raise this objection to debate the process and protect the integrity of the true will of the people." Ms. Tubbs Jones, like Republicans who made similar invocations that day, did not define "the true will of the people." She deftly removed any doubts about the wisdom of the challenge: "While some have called our cause foolish, I can assure you that my parents, Mary and Andrew Tubbs, did not raise any fools."[7]

Many Democrats were wary of possible shenanigans from computerized systems. Rep. Maxine Waters (D-Cal.) complained that many states used "more sophisticated technology" for lottery tickets than for elections: "Incredibly even in those few jurisdictions that have moved to electronic voting . . . we do not require a verifiable paper trail to protect against vote tampering. If an ATM machine can give each user a receipt that that user can reply upon, then a voting machine should also be able to give a receipt."[8] But while local and state governments around the nation had ample funds to pay for sports stadiums and foreign jaunts for governors and their aides, they claimed poverty when it came to validating voting.

Republicans went ballistic at the challenge. Rep. Rob Portman (R-Ohio) declared: "This is not the time, ladies and gentlemen, to obstruct the will of the American people."[9] Rep. David Hobson (R-Ohio) bewailed that "this is, in all the years I have been in politics, one of the most base, outrageous acts to take place."[10]

Rep. Roy Blunt (R-Mo.), the House Majority Whip, declared that "We also need to understand that every time we attack the process, we cast that doubt on that fabric of democracy that is so important." Blunt did not specify if the "fabric" was a cover sheet. He sought to put the entire government above questioning: "It is the greatest democracy in the history of the world and it is run by people who step forward and make a system work in ways that nobody would believe until they see it produce the result of what people want to have happen on Election Day."[11] And anyone who doubted the result was an enemy of democracy.

Rep. J. D. Hayworth (R-Ariz.) commented: "The problem we confront with this debate is that it serves to plant the *insidious seeds of doubt* in the electoral process. But to disrupt the Electoral College, to say in effect, hey, we just want to shine light on this problem, is not *the proper use of the people's time*."[12] Invoking "the people's time" implies that every moment that the congressmen were on the floor was sacred. But if the people's time is so sacred, why did most House members leave town immediately after this vote and not return for almost two weeks? (These were the first of more than 15 weeks of paid vacation they were scheduled to receive in 2005.) Similarly, Rep. Steve. Chabot (R-Ohio) declaimed: "This is nothing more or less than an attempt to sow doubt on the legitimacy of this President. It is an attempt to weaken President Bush, and it is unfortunate because we have much work to do in this House and in the Senate putting this country on the right track."[13] Chabot's complaint implied that Congress was on the verge of fixing the nation's ills. The debate did not displace any substantive legislative work scheduled for that day. At the worst, it may have delayed when members of Congress arrived at donors' receptions, or when they caught planes out of Washington after another grueling three-day work week.

Democrats who questioned the election results automatically became terrorist supporters, or at least sympathizers. Rep. David Dreier (R-Cal.), chairman of the House Rules Committee, proclaimed: "We are in the midst of a global war on terrorism and the people who are leading that war on terrorism clearly have no confidence whatsoever in the process of self-determination. And that is why I think that this exercise which we are going through today clearly emboldens those who would, in fact, want to undermine the prospect of democracy." Drier did not specify how many thousands of people around the world would perish as a result of the Democratic maneuver. Dreier warned: "It has been said that democracy still represents the best hope for mankind. Sowing seeds of doubt about a legitimately decided election threatens to unnecessarily dim that hope."[14] Merely questioning some procedures in one election could doom mankind to perpetual tyranny.

Rep. Tom Price (R-Ga.) lamented: "Political grandstanding during this vital electoral college ballot count is shameful and reprehensible. . . . To raise an objection for which many speakers on the other side have said they will oppose—only feeds unfounded discontent in the veracity of our great democracy."[15] Price did not explain how simply raising questions suddenly can make democracy dishonest. The election results must be above reproach not because there was no funny business, but because no one should be permitted to question them.

House Majority Leader Tom DeLay (R-Tex.) put the Democrats' motion in perspective: "It is an assault against the institutions of our representative democracy. It is a threat to the very ideals it ostensibly defends. . . . It is a crime against the dignity of American democracy, and that crime is not victimless." DeLay declared that the Democrats' complaints *"poison our democratic processes."*[16] (On the other hand, the three censures that DeLay received from the House Ethics Committee were a healthy tonic for popular government.)

People are supposed to believe that, regardless of how many fabrications are told on the campaign trail, the election itself is sacrosanct—even though politicians and political appointees are ultimately in charge of counting the votes. Even though the co-chairman of the Bush reelection campaign in Ohio happened to be the same person in charge of vote counting in Ohio—Secretary of State Kenneth Blackwell—any suspicion of wrongdoing was scurrilous.

What senior members of the House of Representatives saw as a grave threat to democracy and the future of humanity failed to hold the attention of the U.S. Senate. The Senate held no debate over the objection. Instead, a handful of senators stood up and made brief comments to the TV cameras and a largely empty floor. Twenty-five senators did not even bother voting on the challenge to the Ohio electors.

Sen. George Voinovich (R-Ohio) vindicated his home state: "As a Republican from Cleveland who has been reelected as a Republican from Cleveland, elected to Federal, State, county, and municipal offices, I am living proof Ohioans know how to count ballots and, more importantly, we count fairly."[17] Voinovich assumed that since it was well-known, if not universally admitted, that he was beyond reproach, his election victories proved that all Ohio elections are impeccable.

Sen. Mitch McConnell, the second-ranking Republican in the Senate and a man renowned for aggressive fund-raising practices, was the designated Wailer in the Senate. He denounced the Democrats: "They should not trample on the proud republican government our Founding Fathers bequeathed us. They should not mock the beautiful concept that sovereignty lies with the people, while our troops are fighting and dying to plant that concept in the soil of Iraq."[18]

Such blather should not be dismissed as merely self-serving emissions. These comments go to the heart of how politicians think about government and their own power—and about citizens' duty to accept unquestioningly whatever election results the politicians proclaim. Citizens are supposed to believe in that magical moment of uplift that occurs when election results are officially certified—expunging all the verbal flim-flams of the campaign itself. The Republicans' comments sounded as if there is a grave danger in letting people even start to think about how the whole process works—as if Republicans were terrified of any questions or challenges that would decrease people's submissiveness to the government.

The "debate" in Congress illustrated how elections are now about consecration, rather than representation. Elections have become something for rulers to shroud themselves in, rather than leashes used by the people. Politicians are obsessed with maintaining the purported dignity of their class, not in resolving doubts about honest vote counting.

AUTOMATIC REMOTE CONTROL

Elections are sometimes portrayed as practically giving people automatic "remote control" on the government. Elections kindly provide a chance for people to pre-program the government for the following years. The government will be based on the popular will, regardless of the ignorance of the populace or the duplicity of the government.

President Lyndon Johnson declared in 1965 that "The vote is the most powerful instrument ever devised by man for breaking down injustice and destroying the terrible walls which imprison men because they are different from other men."[19] But the fact that voting rights helped undermine Jim Crow restrictions on blacks did not prevent the government from ladling new restrictions and burdens on all citizens. During the election campaign the prior year,

Johnson had promised: "We are not about to send American boys 9,000 or 10,000 miles away to do what Asian boys ought to be doing to protect themselves."[20] The fact that parents could vote for or against Johnson did nothing to stop him from betraying his promise and sending their sons to die.

In his 1989 farewell address, President Ronald Reagan asserted, "'We the People' tell the government what to do, it doesn't tell us. 'We the people' are the driver—the government is the car. And we decide where it should go, and by what route, and how fast."[21] But the American people did not choose to "drive" into Beirut and get hundreds of Marines blown up, choose to run up the largest budget deficits in American history, provide thousands of antitank weapons to Ayatollah Khomeni, or have a slew of top political appointees either lie or get caught in conflicts of interest or other abuses of power or ethical quandaries between 1981 and 1988.

On the eve of his 1992 election debacle, President George H. W. Bush told a Texas audience: "And tomorrow, you participate in a ritual, a sacred ritual of stewardship. . . . With your vote, you are going to help shape the future of this, the most blessed, special nation that man has ever known and God has helped create. And so, look at your vote—especially the young people—look at your vote as an act of power, a statement of principle."[22] Yet, few of the people who voted the following day were making a statement of principle in favor of permitting the president to deploy troops (or additional troops) abroad on his whim (as Clinton did in Somalia, Haiti, Bosnia, Kosovo, and elsewhere), permitting the government to waive the Posse Comitatus Act and use military equipment against American civilians (as happened at Waco), or permitting the government to vastly increase its surveillance of the American people. Yet voting in the 1992 election was still "a statement of principle," regardless of how much the winner scorned the voters' principles.

Two days after his 2004 reelection victory, President George W. Bush declared: "When you win, there is a feeling that *the people have spoken* and embraced your point of view . . . and the people made it clear what they wanted."[23] But did voters on November 2 "consent" to the destruction of Fallujah in the following weeks? Did they consent to the nomination of a Homeland Security czar who was openly hostile to any criticism of politicians? Did Bush's National Rifle Association supporters consent to his nominating an individual for attorney general who advocates far more federal restrictions on gun ownership?[24] Did voters consent to the illegal wiretapping of the chief of the UN International Atomic Energy Agency, as the Bush administration sought to discredit and remove an impediment to a U.S. war on Iran?[25] If Bush had made "ending tyranny everywhere via preemptive U.S. military attacks" the theme for his fall 2004 campaign, he likely would have lost the election. Instead, Bush downplayed this notion—until his second inaugural address.

The only way voters consented to such government actions is to assume they granted Bush boundless power to use as he sees fit. But this is the type of consent given by people who forfeit their rights and accept a court-appointed guardian to run their lives.

Politicians routinely invoke elections as absolutions. Shortly before his second inauguration, a journalist asked Bush: "Why hasn't anyone been held accountable, either through firings or demotions, for what some people see as mistakes or misjudgments" on Iraq? Bush replied: "Well, we had *an accountability moment,* and that's called the 2004 election. And the American people listened to different assessments made about what was taking place in Iraq, and they looked at the two candidates, and chose me, for which I'm grateful."[26] An election victory becomes an old-time papal indulgence, expunging all abuses from the official record. Unfortunately, the more ignorant and negligent the citizens, the easier it becomes for winners to invoke their election victories to shroud their abuses.

In the aftermath of the November 2004 election, the refrain from both politicians and editorial pages was that the result of the voting showed the "will of the people." But was it the will of the people to have to choose between George W. Bush and John Kerry, or between Al Gore and Bush, or between Bill Clinton and Bob Dole? (Third-party candidates provided good protest votes but could not block career politicians from office.) This is like saying that it was the will of the Bulgarian consumer in communist times to choose between an unreliable, ramshackle Trabant from East Germany, or an unreliable ramshackle Skoda car from Czechoslovakia. Many American voters felt as frustrated by their choice of presidential candidates as did East Bloc car shoppers in the 1980s. The fact that voters expressed a preference for Bush or Kerry proves nothing about either candidate being the will of the individual voter.

French King Louis XIV declared: "Kings are absolute lords and naturally enjoy the full and free disposal of all the possessions of their subjects."[27] The only way that the 2004 election could exonerate all of Bush's first-term actions is if voting levers are naturally vested with absolute power over everything. Voting levers cannot legitimize violations of rights unless voters and election winners—like King Louis XIV—have the right to use and abuse everything in the nation.

The average American voter had no recourse on November 2, 2004, to make the federal government obey the Constitution or keep the peace. But this was the same situation the voters faced on November 7, 2000, November 5, 1996, and November 3, 1992. Instead, each voter was merely asked to personally consecrate the continued violations of the highest law of the land by whoever won. The current system of government is structured so that voters effectively have to vest near-absolute power in someone. This is simply how the rulers and the Establishment have fixed the game. Any choice that would deny nearly boundless power to the rulers is kept out of the sunlight by the Powers That Be.

French historian Marc Bloch noted that, during the Middle Ages, "the notion arose that freedom was lost when free choice could not be exercised at least once in a lifetime."[28] The only freedom many people sought was to pick whose "man" they would become. Medieval times included elaborate ceremonies in which the fealty was consecrated. With current elections, people are permitted to choose whose pawns they will be. Voting is becoming more like a medieval act of fealty—with voters bowing down their heads—and promising obedience to whoever is proclaimed the winner.

What if being permitted to choose a master once every four years is the primary "freedom" left? Are citizens merely choosing whose vassal they will be? Many citizens today behave akin to slaves who spent their time wishing for a good master, rather than scouting up information on runaway routes.

REVERSE SLAVE AUCTIONS

Have elections become largely therapeutic exercises to comfort people who have ceased even attempting to understand or control their rulers? American presidents perennially equate democracy with freedom. But if victory confers upon the winner the right to nullify all of the voters' rights, it is voting for a master, not a representative. The more unlimited the power of the winners, the more an election resembles a slave auction. But not a normal auction—a reverse auction, with the slaves voting on whom they will be worked by and sacrificed for.

Citizens enter the voting booth with visions of the candidates' latest bids for their votes in mind—and usually cast their ballot for the person who promised the most, either in handouts, "security," world dominance, or some special interest. Then, after the election, the winner claims absolute power over the voters and disposes of much of their paychecks and many of their lives as he sees fit.

Elections are reverse slave auctions in that people are permitted a nominal voice in choosing who will exercise ownership rights over them. But once the winner is sworn into office, the candidate's campaign promises do nothing to curb his power. The moment the bidding ends and a winner is declared, the illusion that the slaves are running the show vanishes.

Elections are akin to slave auctions based on the concept of slavery that helped spur the American Revolution. The Supreme Court relied on this concept of slavery in an 1886 decision: "The very idea that one man may be compelled to hold his life, or the means of living, or any material right essential to the enjoyment of life, at the mere will of another, seems intolerable in any country where freedom prevails, as being the essence of slavery itself."[29] Early Americans equated boundless power with slavery; thus, the danger of England "enslaving" America was constantly invoked to justify armed resistance against King George.

Bush's "enemy combatant" decree fits the classic concept of political slavery. After the 9/11 attacks, Bush decreed that he possessed absolute, unchecked power over anyone in the world *suspected* of being a terrorist, an "enemy combatant," or a supporter of terrorism.[30] The president's executive order supposedly nullified all of the judicial procedures and protections developed since 1789. The administration is adamant that it need provide no evidence to support perpetual detainment of alleged bad guys. The Justice Department informed a federal court in 2002 that no court has the right to scrutinize how the Bush administration labels such suspects: "A court's inquiry should come to an end once the military has shown . . . that it has determined that the detainee is an enemy combatant. The court may not second-guess the military's enemy-combatant determination."[31] The Supreme Court, in a bevy of rulings in late June 2004, explicitly limited the president's power in the case of American citizen Yaser Hamdi, though it ducked the key issue on Jose Padilla on procedural grounds. The Bush administration has largely ignored the Supreme Court rulings and numerous defeats in federal courts.

At a December 2004 court hearing, federal judge Joyce Hens Green asked whether a "little old lady in Switzerland" who mailed a contribution to an Afghan orphanage could be seized as an enemy combatant if, unbeknownst to her, some of her donation was passed on to Al Qaeda. Deputy Associate Attorney General Brian Boyle replied, "She could. Someone's intention is clearly not a factor that would disable detention." Boyle stressed that the U.S. government's power to label someone an enemy combatant "is not limited to individuals who carried a weapon and shot at American troops." Judge Green asked whether a resident of England who taught English to the child of an Al Qaeda leader could be jailed as an enemy combatant. Boyle affirmed that this was indeed the case because "al-Qaida could be trying to learn English to stage attacks there." Boyle explained that teaching English in such a case could be like "shipping bullets to the front."[32] Boyle did not reveal whether the conviction of such an English teacher would depend on which vocabulary words he taught, or whether a reputation for proffering expertise on irregular verbs would be sufficient to damn a suspect. The fact that the Justice Department would brazenly admit that the government's power extends this far—and this solely upon a presidential decree, not on any act of Congress upheld by the courts—epitomizes the new order in America.

With each passing year, the Bush administration's absolute power becomes a more deeply entrenched precedent. In early 2005, the administration proposed an expansive definition of enemy combatant. The definition would be based on the State Department official lists of terrorist organizations, and "anyone detained that is affiliated with these organizations will be classified as an enemy combatant." Thus, there would be no requirement that a person be a combatant before being classified as a combatant and deprived in perpetuity of all rights. The lists upon which such designation would be based have serious flaws. As Human Rights Watch commented:

> They have been criticized, and indeed challenged in the courts, for being vague, overbroad, and for there being no transparent criteria for listing entities on the lists or removing entities from the lists. The list contains generalized names and aliases (for instance, "Mohammad Zia" and "Abdullah Ahmed") that are shared by tens of thousands of persons worldwide. The lists also name entities that are neither at war with nor engaged in terrorism against the United States; for example, the Basque separatist group Euzkadi Ta Askatasuna (ETA), the Sword of David or American Friends of the United Yeshiva Movement; and the Real Irish Republican Army.

Even if a person has no affiliation with terrorist organizations, they can still be classified as an enemy combatant, based on the whim of U.S. officials. The proposed standard is that, for individuals not affiliated with formally labeled terrorist organizations, "guidance should be obtained from higher headquarters."[33] Bush has repeatedly referred to people locked up at Guantanamo as "illegal non-combatants."[34] But the presidential label "enemy combatant" is still sacrosanct even when the president effectively admits it makes no sense. They are "illegal" simply because the president says so.

Nor is there any geographical limit to this power to nullify all rights. The Bush administration's chief lawyer, Solicitor General Paul Clement, declared in a federal appeals court in July 2005 that the entire United States was a "battlefield" where Bush is entitled to order that people be seized.[35] Thus, the president has absolute discretion to declare what the battlefield is—and his power is absolute upon any and all such battlefields. (Clement made this assertion to justify continuing to deny José Padilla access to federal courts, even though he was arrested in the United States and had been held in U.S. military brigs for more than three years.)

This is not the only area in which the president's power is nearly boundless. The president already acts entitled to dispose of the lives of U.S. soldiers for his moral crusades abroad. He also effectively claims ownership rights over former military personnel—compelling them to rejoin and go fight in Iraq. The president's ownership rights over Americans will become starker if the military draft is revived (as many experts predict, especially if Bush was serious about the promises in his second inaugural address). If military conscription is re-imposed, elections will permit citizens to choose who will send them to die in foreign lands in wars based on mass deceptions.

Bush's reelection symbolizes how the Constitution is now far less of a restraint on presidential powers. The torture scandal, the power to nullify all rights via the enemy combatant label, and other gross abuses of power were not major issues in the 2004 presidential campaign. Thus, the first-term abuses become the starting line for the second-term abuses. Bush's reelection made clear that a president's proclaimed goals can exonerate his methods— thus largely obliterating many of the safeguards built in by Founding Fathers. But elections based on the winner receiving unlimited power are based on far different principles than are elections in which winners remain subservient to the Constitution and the law. This is the difference between voting for a master and voting for a chief law enforcement officer. America is far closer today to what the Founding Fathers dreaded—"slavery by constitutional forms."[36]

Either the Constitution leashes the rulers, or the rulers leash the people. There is no middle way: there is no such thing as modified absolute power. Instead, there are only temporary pauses in additional power grabs by the political class. The fact that politicians rarely publicly proclaim themselves absolute and above the law should provide no comfort. The early Roman emperors often stressed their fidelity to the ancient Roman ways. Tiberius, one of the most blood-stained and violence-crazed early emperors, lectured the Senate on the need to obey the laws, warning, "Rights are invariably abridged, as despotism increases: nor ought we to fall back on imperial authority, when we can have recourse to the laws."[37] What matters is not whether rulers curtsy to accepted procedures and protocols, but whether they seize absolute power when they choose. It is not enough if a ruler obeys the Constitution most of the time. This is like certifying as a peaceful citizen someone who only commits homicides on bank holidays.

The slave auction concept of elections is actually too tepid to describe the reality in some of the new democracies arising around the world. When Ethiopia held a hotly contested vote in May 2005, angry protests occurred after the government refused to disclose the election results. The Ethiopian military slaughtered unarmed demonstrators, leaving 38 dead and scores wounded. Ethiopia's Information Minister, Bereket Simon, announced: "Anyone who incites violence, other than those elected, will have to face the law."[38] (The results of the election were finally disclosed in July 2005.) This comment captures the classic definition of government as possessing a monopoly on legal violence. But, in order to be legitimate, politicians are not allowed to use violence against voters until *after* the election. The fact that a government permitted an election somehow gave it the right to kill anyone who protested the non-release of the election results.

DEPENDENCY AND THE DEATH OF DEMOCRACY

In the era of the Founders, few things were more dreaded than "dependency"—not being one's own man, not having a truly independent will because of reliance on someone or something else to survive. One of the glories of America was the possibility that common people could become self-reliant with hard work and discipline. John Philip Reid summarized eighteenth-century political thinking: "Property was independence; lack of property was servility, even servitude. . . . A man without independent wealth could easily be bought and bribed. A man of property had a will of his own." This was part of the reason why many of the states initially required a property qualification for voters. Sir William Blackstone, whose work on the English constitution profoundly influenced Americans, observed that a property qualification for suffrage was necessary because if the property-less "had votes, they would be tempted to dispose of them under some undue influence or other."[39] Thomas Jefferson warned: "Dependence begets subservience and venality, suffocates the germ of virtue, and prepares fit tools for the designs of ambition."[40]

But in modern times, dependency is the highest political good—at least for politicians. Since the 1930s, politicians have striven to leave no vote unbought. Government aid programs have been endlessly expanded, and the government has sought to maximize the number of people willing to accept handouts. Government aid has become redefined as a symbol of self-actualization.

Americans' dependency on government is soaring. Federal social programs have continued expanding in recent decades despite bipartisan rhetoric about rolling back government spending. The Heritage Foundation created an Index of Dependency to measure the rising number of Americans reliant upon government. The index gauges "the pace at which federal government services and programs have been growing in areas in which private or community-based services and programs exist or have existed to address the same or nearly the same needs." The index is based on housing aid, healthcare and welfare assistance, retirement income, and subsidies for college and other post-secondary education. While private programs were judged by how much they actually helped people, the "success" of government programs "is frequently measured by the growth of the aid program rather than its outcome." The Index has a benchmark of 100 for 1980; by 2005, the index reading had risen to 212, signaling more than a doubling of overall dependency on the federal government over the prior quarter century.[41] As a result of the expansion of government "aid" programs into one area after another, subservience rather than initiative is becoming the ticket to prosperity. Now, roughly half of all Americans are dependent on the government, either for handouts, pensions, or paychecks.[42] Government dependents are often an invincible voting bloc. Politicians respond by giving them a perpetual lien on other people's paychecks.

Most voters no longer seem concerned about leashing government. Instead, many if not most are primarily concerned with directing the sludge of government benefits in their direction. Voters want to unleash politicians to give *them* more benefits. When government is viewed as a fount of benefits, limits on government power will appear to be self-deprivation. The more people expect from government, the more biased they become against limiting government power. This was stark in the 1980s debates over a constitutional amendment to balance the federal budget. The most vehement opponents were organized groups representing senior citizens, government employees such as teachers, and others who rely on government checks to pay the bills.

The key question for many voters is: How much is the candidate offering for my vote? Elections routinely degenerate into "advanced auction of stolen goods," in H. L. Mencken's apt phrase. There is vastly more interest during election campaigns in Social Security handouts and policies than in Justice Department and FBI abuses.

Sums spent on government vote-buying usually dwarf all private campaign expenditures. Incumbents perennially use the machinery of state to bombard voters with government handouts, often on the flimsiest pretexts. President Clinton turned the Federal Emergency Management Agency into a permanent part of his reelection campaign.[43] FEMA now routinely blankets residents of swing states with lavish checks for dubious claims for damage from hurricanes and other bad weather.[44] Florida was a key swing state in the 2004 election, and thanks to FEMA and four hurricanes and storms, Florida residents received more FEMA handouts than any state in history. The inspector general revealed in May 2005 that FEMA used a standard that would make a drunken sailor blush. If someone called in and claimed their bed was damaged by a FEMA-recognized adverse weather incident, FEMA insisted on sending them a check to buy an entire new large bedroom suite. FEMA did not require any evidence that a person actually sustained losses. Instead, anyone who called deserved a check. FEMA shoveled out $31 million in the Miami/Dade County area in the months before the election to compensate people from damage from one storm whose winds never exceeded 45 miles per hour.[45] More than 4,000 people received over $8 million to rent temporary housing— even though they had not requested aid and often had suffered little or no home damage. FEMA's handout standard is the mirror image of that used by the Internal Revenue Service, which has never set up toll-free numbers for people to call and nullify their tax obligations merely by asserting they have zero taxable income.

FEMA vote purchases are bargains compared to other ways incumbents purchase their job security. During his 2004 reelection campaign, Bush often bragged about having gotten Congress to enact a new prescription drug subsidy for the elderly—which is now estimated to cost more than $2 trillion over the next 20 years. Clinton had campaigned for reelection in 1996 by hawking a similar benefit, but had not been able to deliver the goods through a Republican Congress.

Prior to Bush's Medicare expansion, the record for the most costly reelection campaign may have been held by Richard Nixon, who railroaded a 20 percent hike in Social Security benefits through Congress and then made sure that each senior citizen received a personal letter from Nixon along with the new higher benefit check a few weeks before the 1972 election.[46] Nixon also destroyed economic freedom in order to perpetuate his pro–free enterprise administration. In August 1971, Nixon imposed wage and price controls that throttled inflationary pressures. At the same time, the Federal Reserve flooded the money supply with new dollars—creating the appearance of an economic boom while federal controls delayed the evidence of inflation. Nixon's policies helped cause international financial crises and the worst U.S. recession since World War II.

LEVIATHAN VS. "FREE AND FAIR" ELECTIONS

The more powerful rulers become, the lower the odds for "free and fair elections." The bigger government becomes, the more votes it can buy. The number of levers, bribes, and penalties that can be exploited by incumbents has multiplied. The expansion of government is a major reason why the House of Representatives in most elections has a lower turnover rate than the Soviet Politburo had in its glory days. The U.S. Census Bureau in 1996 contacted all the offices of all the members of Congress and offered them free data to help them "target your mailing, locate the most advantageous area to hold your town meetings, or profile your congressional district to assess your constituents' needs."[47] Ninety-eight percent of incumbents are routinely reelected—in part because the profusion of federal programs provides tools for incumbents to buy support and gratitude. Congressmen enact laws and fund agencies that snare citizens in one spider's web after another—and then congressmen receive credit for helping citizens get untangled from the web. Former congressman Vin Weber observed: "We create the government that screws you, and then you're supposed to thank us for protecting you from it."[48]

How can "free" elections occur when pervasive unfairness via political decrees and finagling is the order of the day? How can the playing field be level when politicians have entitled half the potential voters to live off the other half? How can there be free elections in an increasingly unfree society?

Confining the power of the State is one of the best ways to ensure "free and fair" elections. Yet, in elections in recent decades, regardless of who loses, Leviathan always wins. There has been no significant discussion of limiting federal power in any presidential election since 1980, when Ronald Reagan was the Republican nominee. Reagan began his first term by clearly stating that government is an enemy of freedom. Yet, once in power, Reagan often abandoned his limited government mantra and launched one moralistic crusade after another, including reviving a war on drugs that was the primary source of a fourfold increase in America's prison population in the following decades. Reagan did little or nothing to curb Internal Revenue Service Agents' abuse of American citizens.[49] The Justice Department pioneered sweeping new interpretations of the racketeering law that criminalized new forms of white-collar behavior. It also swayed the Supreme Court to define down the Fourth Amendment to give federal agents far more leeway to invade private land without a warrant.[50] The Environmental Protection Administration reamed thousands of businesses for cleanup bills under Superfund—even though many, if not most, of the companies had little or no blame for the pollution.[51] From 1981 to 1989, the federal government became far more intrusive, punitive, and arbitrary. Yet, Reagan claimed after leaving office that, thanks to his rule, government was no longer a threat to the American people. In a 1994 Washington conservative gala for his eighty-third birthday, Ronald Reagan bragged that, at the time of his 1981 inauguration, "the reach of government had become intolerable. . . . So together we got the government off the backs of the American people."[52] Washington conservatives cheered Reagan's absurd assertion about getting government "off the backs" in part because his presidency and his rhetoric had been very profitable and gratifying for them.

In almost every election, the current extent of government power is taken as the starting bid. The purpose of the election is to wrangle over how it will be expanded and who will be sacrificed and who will be subsidized.

MASS ASSENT IN LIEU OF INFORMED CONSENT

Elections increasingly provide merely the chance for the people to give their assent to the rulers—to signify through gestures (increasingly meaningless) that they consent to continue placing their lives, rights, and liberties at the disposal of whoever got their name on the ballot.

In ancient times, mobs of Romans would cheer the emperor as he rode down the street in his chariot, and the emperor would afterward invoke the crowd's hurrahs to prove his legitimacy. Today, rulers claim their legitimacy from polling results. The process is more dignified than the howls of Roman mobs, but the difference between the end results is narrowing. While democracy boosters talk about a semi-divine process wherein the people knowingly choose the person that will best carry out the general will, the reality is that voters in 2004 were merely permitted to choose which Yale "Skull 'n' Bones" member would hold sway over their lives. Or, as in 2000, to choose which millionaire political family offspring would rule them. Or, as in 1996, 1992, and 1988, to choose which career politician would take their leash.

Rather than a republic, we increasingly have an elective dictatorship. A government is an elective dictatorship when the people are permitted to choose who will violate the laws and the Constitution.

The original Constitution included both severe limits on government power, and specifications on how that power could be acquired and used. The American people understood that claiming power in violation of the limits set in the Constitution and the Bill of Rights was illegitimate. Yet, less than a decade after the first Congress convened, President John Adams' Federalist Party passed a Sedition Act that authorized prison sentences for any person who "shall write, print, utter or publish . . . any false, scandalous and malicious writing or writings against the government of the United States, or either house of the Congress of the United States, or the President of the United States, with intent to defame the said government" or "bring them . . . into contempt or disrepute."[53] This was an explicit revocation of the First Amendment of the Bill of Rights, which declared that "Congress shall make no law . . . abridging the freedom of speech, or of the press." This power grab spurred Thomas Jefferson to write a resolution enacted by the Kentucky legislature which proclaimed that the doctrine "that the general government is the exclusive judge of the extent of the powers delegated to it [is] nothing short of despotism; since the discretion of those who administer the government, and not the Constitution, would be the measure of their powers."[54] (The opposition to the Alien and Sedition Acts was a key reason why voters tossed out Adams and elected Jefferson in 1800.)

But today, we are encouraged to believe that the sole test of legitimacy is popular support of the government. Yet this is the same type of legitimacy that most dictatorships have claimed throughout history. To make public opinion the sole test of legitimacy is to reward official deceit and fearmongering.

As people become more politically ignorant, their attention often narrows to the question of who is to be the supreme ruler—as if that is all that matters. The less people understand about how government works, the easier it is to get them to focus on promised results, rather than actual procedures. Due process becomes a mere phrase, or even a pointless distraction in the pursuit of a Great Protector. This is reflected by the tacit acceptance by many Americans that an election victory entitles a politician to "do what he thinks right." Yet, politicians are the class of people least deserving of such trust—as if lifelong frenetic pursuit of power somehow proves benevolent intent.

Support for elective dictatorship also increasingly permeates U.S. foreign policy. Thomas Carothers of the Carnegie Endowment for International Peace noted that during the Clinton years, when judging "a transitional country" such as Russia, U.S. policymakers routinely "equate a particular leader with democracy and assume that steadfast support for that leader is the best means of promoting democracy. Through such policies the U.S. government often gives too little support to the systemic reforms that are needed for real democratization, alienates other political forces in the society, and holds onto leaders in decline long after they have been discredited domestically."[55] Often the measure of success of U.S. foreign policy is not the procedures foreign nations follow, but the photo opportunities provided for U.S. rulers when they visit abroad or when foreign chieftains visit Washington.

The more power the winner of an election receives, the less he will be obliged to respect voters' preferences or rights. The sheer quantity of government power insulates an election winner from the citizenry: it is as if he has entered a giant fortress on an impregnable hill after winning. And though he may look down benevolently, the people can do little more than petition for mercy—or hire lobbyists with insider contacts who promise to deliver their petitions.

Politicians are the class of people defined by their drive to ascend into positions of power over other people. Politicians are those who are willing to pay the highest personal price to place their hands upon the levers of government coercion. Citizens who wish to be free cannot afford delusions on the nature of government or the character of those who pursue power to dictate how others must live. The issue is not whether the rulers smile and feign sympathy when cracking the whip.

VOTING LEVERS AS BOGUS KEVLAR

It has been over a generation since excessive federal power was a burning issue during a presidential election. At best, liberals have loudly warned about the danger of permitting conservatives to have power, and conservatives have railed about the danger of putting liberals in power. But the notion that the government has amassed more power than any leader or party can be trusted with rarely arises in polite society.

A government can safely handle only a finite quantity of power. The Bill of Rights is the fuse box of the American system of government. Violating constitutional rights is the equivalent of blowing fuses. If fuses are blown often enough, and if warnings of overloaded wiring are perpetually ignored, eventually the entire building goes up in flames.

The more power that voting levers confer, the more unreliable elections become as a mode of governance. Elections, rather than antibiotics for the body politic, become simply another quack cure.

The more expansive the government's power, the more absurd voting levers become as a means of citizen self-defense. Vastly more weight is placed these days on voting levers—as if they were made of titanium instead of plastic. Citizens are assured that no matter how big government becomes, one vote is all a person needs to defend himself against it. But once the power of the rulers passes a certain point, relying on voting levers is like shooting blanks at a charging Grizzly bear.

Because of Attention Deficit Democracy, voting levers are more likely to sanctify abuses than safeguard citizens. Official deceits and mass ignorance have combined to erode citizens' constitutional constraints on government. With the current trend, voting will soon be little more than an opiate of the masses.

CHAPTER 9

Democratic Delusions on Peace and Inevitability

See, free nations are peaceful nations. Free nations don't attack each other. Free nations don't develop weapons of mass destruction.
—George W. Bush, October 3, 2003[1]

Ultimately, the best strategy to ensure our security and build a durable peace is to support the advance of democracy. Democracies do not attack each other. . . .
—President Bill Clinton, January 25, 1994[2]

DRIVEL ABOUT DEMOCRACY HAS LONG THRIVED in Washington. As soon as democracy is idealistically invoked, it is as if the laws of probability have been suspended. The "standards of proof" in Washington debates are often as low as one can find outside an elementary school cafeteria room. Mere assertions repeated *ad nauseum* and flaunted by dignitaries trump almost anything, depending on who is spouting. History exists only to be selectively invoked to vindicate further seizures of power, or new incursions abroad.

Two of the biggest contemporary political delusions are the notions that democracies inevitably beget peace and that the spread of democracy around the globe is inevitable. Each of these beliefs will be examined, noting how they arose and how they have been exploited to sanctify political power and military aggression.

THE DEMOCRATIC PEACE FRAUD

The doctrine of "democratic peace" now provides vital camouflage for the American war machine. Michael Novak, a theologian with the pro-war American Enterprise Institute, observed, "Democracy is the new name for personal dignity. Democracy is the new name for peace." The idea that democracies never fight wars against each other has become axiomatic for many scholars. Professor Jack Levy commented in 1989 that the democratic peace is "as close as anything we have to an empirical law in international relations."[3]

This doctrine has long proven handy for presidents seeking the high moral ground for U.S. artillery. When President Woodrow Wilson asked Congress to declare war on Germany on April 2, 1917, he proclaimed, "The world must be made safe for democracy. Its peace must be planted upon the tested foundations of political liberty." Wilson said nothing about making democracy safe for the world. Wilson assured America that "A steadfast concert for peace can never be maintained except by a partnership of democratic nations. No autocratic government could be trusted to keep faith within it or observe its covenants."[4] Wilson promised that there would be no secret deals among the allies to seize territory or carve up their conquests. Later in 1917, after the Bolsheviks took power in Russia, they published an array of secret agreements that the Allied powers had made shortly after the war began to plunder German, Turkish, and Austro-Hungarian possessions.

Faith in this "democratic peace" doctrine has revived in recent decades. President Reagan declared that "the surest guarantee we have of peace is national freedom and democratic government."[5] Clinton also embraced the doctrine and used it to sanctify his foreign policy time and again. As Thomas Carothers noted, "Clinton officials stock almost every general foreign policy speech with the argument that promoting democracy abroad advances U.S. interests because democracies tend not to go to war with each other, not to produce large numbers of refugees, not to engage in terrorism, to make better economic partners, and so on."[6]

But no president has been half as liberal with invoking the doctrine as George W. Bush:

- In his 2005 State of the Union address, Bush declared, "Because democracies respect their own people and their neighbors, the advance of freedom will lead to peace."[7]

- Calling in May 2005 for more foreign governments to assist U.S. efforts in Iraq and Afghanistan, Bush declared, "Democratic societies are peaceful societies—which is why, for the sake of peace, the world's established democracies must help the world's newest democracies succeed."[8]
- Bush explained why peace was the motive for encircling Russia with pro-U.S. governments: "But I did make it clear to President Putin . . . It really is in Russia's interest to have free countries and democracies on her border. The more democracies on the border of a country, the more peaceful the country will be."[9]

Wilson, Bush, and other presidents base their claims on a doctrine first enunciated by German philosopher Immanuel Kant. In his 1795 essay "Perpetual Peace," Kant declared:

> The republican constitution, besides the purity of its origin (having sprung from the pure source of the concept of law), also gives a favorable prospect for the desired consequence, i.e., perpetual peace.
> The reason is this: if the consent of the citizens is required in order to decide that war should be declared (and in this constitution it cannot but be the case), nothing is more natural than that they would be very cautious in commencing such a poor game, decreeing for themselves all the calamities of war.[10]

The fact that avoiding war seemed "natural" to Kant did not guarantee that subsequent generations of humanity would have the calm reasonableness of the Konigsberg philosopher. Despite history's failure to validate his theory, Kant's doctrine has been embraced in recent decades with the fervor of a religious revival meeting. One of the most vehement proponents of the doctrine of "democratic peace" is professor R. J. Rummel, who insists that democracy effectively guarantees peace because "Democracy is a method of nonviolence."[11]

The only way that history supports this doctrine is to exclude all the cases of wars between democracies. This theory can survive only as long as people look at history in a way that is so contorted that it makes the typical political campaign speech look honest. Some of the advocates of the "democratic peace" doctrine are slippery regarding categories, as if the fact that a nation starts a war proves that it is not a democracy.

There are plenty of cases to dismiss the democratic peace imperative. As professors Thomas Schwartz and Kiron Skinner noted, Britain, the mother of parliaments, "fought the United States in 1776 and 1812 and revolutionary France in its comparatively democratic years of 1793 and 1795. In 1848 the United States fought Mexico, not a perfect democracy but a good one for the times."[12]

The American Civil War was the biggest clash in the Western world between the Napoleonic Wars and the First World War. Both the United States and the Confederacy were representative governments with presidents purportedly bound by Constitutions.

Britain's Boer War, 1899–1902, involved the brutal crushing by one democratic government of another democratic government, as well as pioneering concentration camps and other methods of suppression that would become far more widespread in the twentieth century.

The First World War was by far the bloodiest conflict in human history up to that time. Schwartz and Kiner noted, "Woodrow Wilson proclaimed a war for democracy against 'Prussian dictatorship,' but that was propaganda. Germany had civil rights, an elected parliament, competing parties, universal male suffrage, and an unparalleled system of social democracy."[13] Germany was far more democratic than either the British or French empires.

Professor Joanne Gowa, author of *Ballots and Bullets,* examined "pairs of states between 1815 and 1981" and found "no statistically significant relationship between democracy and peace before 1946."[14] After World War II, democracies rarely fought each other because most of them were allied against a Soviet threat that was far more perilous than quibbles over trade flows or fishing rights. However, the fact that New Zealand and Switzerland have never fought each other is not sufficient basis for an iron law of international relations.

The "democratic peace" theory implies that there is latent wisdom in majorities—or some deep-seated love of peace that will triumph after a majority takes control of government policy. Or, perhaps once people are permitted to vote, they suddenly become immune to bloodlust. But Columbia University professors Edward Mansfield and Jack Snyder, in a 1995 study on "Democratization and War" published in *Foreign Affairs,* stressed that democratization can spur wars: "Formerly authoritarian states where democratic participation is on the rise are more likely to fight wars than are stable democracies or autocracies. States that make the biggest leap, from total autocracy to extensive mass democracy—like contemporary Russia—are about twice as likely to fight wars in the decade after democratization as are states that remain autocracies."[15]

Mansfield and Snyder analyzed data from 1811 to 1980 on wars and regimes classified as either democratic, autocratic, or a mixed regime, and viewed "democratization as a gradual process." They concluded that "an increase in the openness of the selection process for the chief executive doubled the likelihood of war. . . . States changing from a mixed regime to democracy were on average about 50 percent more likely to become engaged in war (and about two-thirds more likely to go to war with another nation-state) than states that remained mixed regimes." They warned: "This concoction of nationalism and incipient democratization has been an intoxicating brew, leading in case after case to ill-conceived wars of expansion."

Another key to the myth of "democratic peace" is to disregard the long record of democracies attacking nondemocracies. Bush, defending U.S. military action in Iraq, declared, "Free societies are peaceful nations. What we're doing for the long term, we're promoting freedom."[16] However, since World War II, the United States either attacked or invaded the following nations:

Korea 1950–53
Lebanon 1958
Vietnam 1961–73
Laos 1964–73
Dominican Republic 1965–66
Cambodia 1969–70
Lebanon 1982–84
Grenada 1983
Libya 1986
Panama 1989
Iraq 1991–2005
Somalia 1992–94
Croatia 1994
Haiti 1994
Bosnia 1995
Sudan 1998
Afghanistan 1998
Yugoslavia 1999
Afghanistan 2001–2005

Johns Hopkins University professor John Harper noted, "America's imperial career does little to support the view that the United States, by virtue of its democratic norms and institutions, is inclined to solve international disputes pacifically and to promote democracy abroad."[17]

Other democracies also lack pacifist resumes. Britain, which was a constitutional republic that became increasingly democratic as the twentieth century wore on, attacked many nations to expand or defend its empire. Since the government of Israel was established in 1947/48, it has attacked Egypt (1956), Egypt and Syria (1967), Lebanon (1982–2000), as well as engaging in more than 35 years of armed struggle against the Palestinians living in the Occupied Territories seized by Israel in the 1967 war. It also engaged in a defensive war in 1973 against Egypt and Syria.

Unless we assume that it is morally irrelevant when democratic governments kill people in nondemocratic countries, the bellicose record of democratic governments must be considered. The fact that democracies have been rare in history cannot whitewash democracies per se. The fact is that democracies attack.

Of course, the records of the worst authoritarian and totalitarian governments—Hitler's Germany, Soviet Russia, Red China, as well as other communist regimes—are far worse, and far more brutal, than those of Western democracies. But "not as bad as Stalin" is not the standard that democratic peace advocates invoke to deify their preferred form of government.

Majorities rarely succeed in thwarting rulers hungry for war. In the wake of the U.S. entry into World War I, author Randolph Bourne observed:

> Government, with no mandate from the people, without consultation of the people, conducts all the negotiations, the backing and filling, the menaces and explanations, which slowly bring it into collision with some other Government, and gently and irresistibly slides the country into war. For the benefit of proud and haughty citizens, it is fortified with a list of the intolerable insults which have been hurled toward us by the other nations; for the benefit of the liberal and beneficent, it has a convincing set of moral purposes which our going to war will achieve; for the ambitious and aggressive classes, it can gently whisper of a bigger role in the destiny of the world.[18]

Some democratic peace theorists sound as if the simple act of popular voting somehow makes government nonaggressive. And regardless of how much the government deceives people about the likely costs of a war, citizens will still demand peace. Bourne noted one reason why popular preferences could not rein in bellicose governments: "In the freest of republics as well as in the most tyrannical of empires, all foreign policy, the diplomatic negotiations which produce or forestall war, are equally the private property of the Executive part of the Government, and are equally exposed to no check whatever from popular bodies, or the people voting as a mass themselves."[19]

Democracies are especially susceptible to the mass gullibility that often follows a declaration of war. Bourne observed, "The moment war is declared, however, the mass of the people, through some spiritual alchemy, become convinced that they have willed and executed the deed themselves."[20] The higher the rulers raise the stakes, the more gullible many, if not most, people become.

The Democratic peace theory—especially in the Kantian classic version—presumes that people have a leash on the government, rather than vice versa. But there is nothing inherent in democracies to make people immune to the manipulation of war parties. Mansfield and Snyder observed in 1995:

> Although democratization in many cases leads to war, that does not mean that the average voter wants war. Public opinion in democratizing states often starts off highly averse to the costs and risks of war. In that sense, the public opinion polls taken in Russia in early 1994 were typical. Respondents said that Russian policy should make sure the rights of Russians in neighboring states were

not infringed, but not at the cost of military intervention. Public opinion often becomes more belligerent, however, as a result of propaganda and military action presented as faits accomplis by elites. This mass opinion, once aroused, may no longer be controllable.[21]

A similar pattern occurred in Germany before World War One, with the "German Navy League" (funded in large part by Krupps Steelworks) whipping up popular enthusiasm for creating a Navy that would end Britain's dominance of the seas.

The notion that democracy will end all mass killings implies that there is some nobility latent within the masses that merely requires a change in the process of selecting a nation's rulers to blossom. This would hold true if the only reason people sought blood was because they had not picked their own chiefs. The history of mobs does not indicate that popular selection of leaders assures nonviolence.

The "democratic peace" doctrine also assumes some level of soundness or comprehension on the behalf of the typical citizen. Yet citizens on average are far more ignorant of foreign affairs than they are of domestic events. The greater the ignorance, the more easily politicians can fan hatred and fear.

The ability of governments to connive nations into war is not limited to democracies. Nazi leader Hermann Goering commented in an interview during the Nuremberg trials: "Of course, the people don't want war. Why would some poor slob on a farm want to risk his life in a war when the best that he can get out of it is to come back to his farm in one piece. . . . But, after all, it is the leaders of the country who determine the policy and it is always a simple matter to drag the people along." Gustave Gilbert, the American intelligence officer who was interviewing Goering, retorted: "There is one difference. In a democracy the people have some say in the matter through their elected representatives, and in the United States only Congress can declare wars." Goering replied: "Oh, that is all well and good, but, voice or no voice, the people can always be brought to the bidding of the leaders. That is easy. All you have to do is tell them they are being attacked and denounce the pacifists for lack of patriotism and exposing the country to danger. It works the same way in any country."[22] The demagoging of critics of Bush's wars illustrates Goering's point.

The United States has gone to war many times since World War II, yet the U.S. Congress has not declared war since 1941. The right to bomb is now one of the presidency's most cherished prerogatives. In 1973, seeking to curb this power, Congress enacted the War Powers Act, which required the president to get authorization from Congress before committing U.S. troops to any combat situation that lasted more than 60 days. But the law has proved toothless. President Clinton in 1999 snubbed Congress before attacking Serbia. The House of

Representatives had voted on April 28, 1999, and failed to support Clinton's war effort. But the House vote did nothing to slow the onslaught of U.S. bombs. Thirty-one congressmen sued Clinton for violating the War Powers Act. A federal judge dismissed the lawsuit, ruling that the congressmen did not have legal standing to sue.[23] Even though Congress was controlled by the opposition party, Clinton paid zero price for flaunting both the law and the Constitution.

On September 18, 2001, Congress passed a resolution authorizing attacks on the perpetrators of the 9/11 attacks. Though this was not a formal declaration of war, Bush administration officials invoked it to justify the war against Iraq and any other country that could be accused of terrorist connections. In early 2005, the Bush administration greatly upped the potential targets when it announced that, henceforth, the war on terrorism would be broadened to a crusade against "extremism"—as if extremism anywhere is a threat to Americanism everywhere. This is reminiscent of Bush's bizarre comment in October 2001: "So long as anybody's terrorizing established governments, there needs to be a war."[24] Thus, any enemy of any established government almost automatically becomes an enemy of the United States—and Americans cannot be safe and secure unless the United States tries to prop up practically all the existing rulers in the world. This is another example of how the U.S. government grades the sins of governments far more leniently than the crimes of private groups.

Some advocates of democratic peace talk as if democratic governments are pacifist entities, almost incapable of militarism. Bush declared at a 2005 press conference that "a democracy reflects the will of the people, and people don't like war. They don't like conflict."[25] Yet during the 2004 presidential campaign, Bush constantly portrayed himself as a war president—though as a victim. As he told a carpenters' union in Las Vegas on August 12, "No President wants to be a war President. That was my last choice. And the enemy attacked us, and we got to respond."[26] Bush blurs categories, as if the 9/11 attacks authorized U.S. aggression against the entire world. But the ruse worked.

The democratic peace theory presumes that citizens are keenly aware of the potential costs, in blood and treasure, of their nation plunging into conflicts. However, nowadays, most Americans' primary experience of war is as something to alleviate the boredom during the off-season of their favorite sport. War is now free moral glory, a no-cost way to be a part of Bush's effort to save the world. As long as people attach a "Support Our Troops" sticker to their SUV, their sacrifice is sufficient. Thanks to massive deficit financing, no American has paid an extra dime in taxes to cover the $300 billion the U.S. government has already spent in Iraq. The cost of Bush's war simply does not exist in the minds of most Americans.

The doctrine of democratic peace is so potent that it can instantly rewrite history. Bush declared in April 2004 that "free societies do not threaten people or use weapons of mass destruction."[27] The U.S. attack on Iraq began with a massive "shock and awe" cruise missile and aerial bombardment of Baghdad and other primary targets, producing mushroom clouds rising above the Iraqi capital. A 1996 National Defense University study noted: "Theoretically, the magnitude of Shock and Awe . . . seeks to impose (in extreme cases) the non-nuclear equivalent of the impact that atomic weapons dropped on Hiroshima and Nagasaki had on the Japanese."[28] But Bush's benevolent intentions, not the mushroom clouds, defined the weapons.

Bush declared in early 2004: "Leaders around the world now know weapons of mass destruction do not bring influence or prestige; they bring isolation and other unwelcome consequences."[29] However, most of the nations known to have developed nuclear weapons are democracies, including the United States, Britain, France, India, and Israel. A few months later, Bush declared, "Free societies don't develop weapons of mass destruction to blackmail the world."[30] At that time, the Pentagon was racing ahead to create a new generation of nuclear weapons—known as the "Robust Nuclear Earth Penetrator."[31] Despite such brazen contradictions, Bush's claims on democracy and peace continue to be received with the same deference as political claims about motherhood and apple pie. The U.S. government will spend more than $500 billion for military operations in 2005—more than the combined military budgets of the next 21 largest militaries in the world.[32]

At the same time Bush orates about democracy guaranteeing peace, he is not shy about harping on the duty to spread democracy with an Iron Fist. The *Washington Post* noted in April 2005: "Increasingly, the president uses speeches to troops to praise American ideals and send a signal to other nations the administration is targeting for democratic change."[33] Does Bush believe that foreigners must consent to being democratized or the United States has the right to kill them? Who gave the United States the right to force foreigners to consent to their rulers? And who gave the U.S. government the right to define foreign consent?

The "democratic peace" mantra dulls some Americans' perception of the contradictions in U.S. foreign policy. While Bush pirouettes as a champion of peace, his administration's 2002 "National Security Strategy of the United States" profoundly alters U.S. military doctrine by invoking 9/11 to claim a nearly boundless right of preemptive attack against suspected threats. The report declared that the United States must "dissuade future military competition" from foreign nations: "Our forces will be strong enough to dissuade potential adversaries from pursuing a military buildup in hopes of surpassing or equaling the power of the United States"[34]—regardless of how the leaders of those countries are selected. This implies that military spending by some other countries could be viewed as an act of aggression against the United States. The current incarnation of the "democratic peace" is based on the United States alone having the right to attack anywhere in the name of democracy.

The theory of democratic peace provides a pretext for war. When he was asked on April 4, 2005, why the United States should continue suffering most of the casualties and paying most of the costs in Iraq, Bush replied, "the action is worth it to make sure that democracy exists, and because democracies will yield peace, and that's what we want."[35] In a late 2004 press conference, Bush declared, "The only way to achieve peace is for there to be democracies living side by side. Democracies don't fight each other."[36] Any government that is not a democracy is now simply a war waiting to happen. Because democracies never attack other democracies, democracies are entitled to launch unprovoked attacks on nondemocracies to force them to become democracies—and thereby ensure peace. Because democracy is the same as peace, then warring to spread democracy is the same as working for peace. The Bush administration is apparently confident that few Americans have read or remember Orwell's "war is peace" slogan from *1984*.

Bush's endless invocations of freedom and democracy shroud—at least for American eyes—anything the U.S. government does. In the weeks after Bush's re-election victory, U.S. Army soldiers and Marines smashed the city of Fallujah, Iraq, killing an unknown number of civilians, leaving the city a burnt-out ruin. Marine Col. Gary Brandl explained the U.S. holy mission: "The enemy has got a face. He's called Satan. He's in Fallujah and we're going to destroy him."[37] Yet, the carnage the U.S. forces were inflicting on the city (belated punishment for the killing of four U.S. contractors the previous March) was not portrayed as massive retaliation but the triumph of hope and freedom. Bush announced on December 1: "In Fallujah and elsewhere, our coalition and Iraqi forces are on the offensive, and we are delivering a message: Freedom, not oppression, is the future of Iraq. . . . A long night of terror and tyranny in that region is ending, and a new day of freedom and hope and self-government is on the way."[38] The survivors of Fallujah, who had been terrorized by U.S. aerial and artillery bombardments and by house-to-house raids in which soldiers seemed authorized to shoot practically anything that moved, might have failed to appreciate Bush's idealism.

And after all enemies and potential enemies of democracy have been exterminated (or incarcerated for life without trial), bliss and tranquility will reign forever and ever. There will be no more wars after "democracy" conquers the world. But the notion that there will be lasting, transcendent benefits from the next war(s) is a common canard of politicians and warmongers. Instead of Kant's "perpetual peace," we get "perpetual war for perpetual peace," in historian Charles Beard's apt phrase.[39]

The notion of warring to spread democracy ignores the profoundly corrosive effect of long-term war. "After each war there is a little less democracy to save," wrote journalist Brooks Atkinson in 1951. War spurs intolerance that undermines freedom. James Madison, the father of the Constitution, warned in 1795: "Of all enemies to public liberty war is, perhaps, the most to be dreaded because it comprises and develops the germ of every other. . . . No nation could preserve its freedom in the midst of continual warfare."[40] The following year, in his Farewell Address, President Washington warned of "those overgrown military establishments which, under any form of government, are inauspicious to liberty, and which are to be regarded as particularly hostile to republican liberty."[41] Washington, who helped found a nation in the same years that Kant developed his theory, would likely be the last politician to invoke the democratic peace theory. He observed that "the nation, prompted by ill-will and resentment, sometimes impels to war the government, contrary to the best calculations of policy." It took all of Washington's influence and reputation to restrain the new nation, hot with hatred of England and enthralled by some of the rhetoric of the French Revolution, from plunging into the European war. Washington was vilified far and wide for his refusal to satisfy the lust for war.

The popularity of the doctrine that democracies do not attack each other is another tribute to the historical illiteracy of both politicians and prominent commentators, as well as of many professors. The doctrine that democracies never fight each other should have been laughed out of existence after its first promenade. Yet, as long as Clinton, and later Bush, recited the "democratic peace" dogma, all contrary evidence vanished from the scales of respectable judgment. The theory serves the interests of the government—the ultimate test of truth in Washington. The primary effect of the doctrine of "democratic peace" has been to lower Americans' resistance to U.S. government foreign aggression.

Some advocates of forcibly spreading democracy talk as if this crusade is a unique combination of lofty vision and brute force. However, invading foreign nations on bogus idealistic grounds is one of the oldest tricks in the book. Nearly two thousand years ago, the Roman historian Plutarch commented that rivals Pompey and Julius Caesar could have devoted themselves to foreign conquest instead of civil war: "Scythia was yet unconquered, and the Indians too, where their ambition might be colored over with the specious pretext of civilizing barbarous nations."[42] The theory of democratic peace is simply the latest of a long series of such charades. But conquest is conquest, and killing is killing, regardless of the recitations by rulers.

INEVITABILITY INANITY

"The number of democracies in the world has been doubled within fifteen years," including Poland, Lithuania, Latvia, Estonia, Georgia, Armenia, and

Azerbaijan, crowed Lord Bryce, the British politician and historian, in 1921.[43] Democracy appeared to be the tidal wave of the future. Within 20 years, almost all of the new democracies had been destroyed from within or crushed from abroad. The democratic triumphalism that permeated the immediate period after World War I did nothing to protect new democracies from ruin.

Since President Woodrow Wilson proclaimed that democracy was the destiny of humanity, more than 100 democratic governments have crashed and burned around the globe, replaced by dictators, juntas, or foreign conquerors. Yet, we continue to be assured that democracies are inevitable, and that universalizing democracy will solve almost all of the world's political problems.

History has seen the rise and fall of many democracies and republics. Athens was very democratic, at least by the standards of the fifth century B.C., but fell prey to the Gang of 30 dictators during the Peloponnesian War (after Athens brutally crushed the second-best known democracy of its time, Syracuse). Carthage was one of the most respected republics in the Western world—until it was razed and salted over by the Romans. The Roman republic eventually collapsed under the stress of civil war and too many temporary dictators.

During the late Middle Ages, limited representative government flourished in many places, thanks in part to the sheer weakness of most monarchs. As Thomas Babington Macaulay noted in 1828, "In all the monarchies of Western Europe, during the middle ages, there existed restraints on the royal authority, fundamental laws, and representative assemblies. In the fifteenth century, the government of Castile seems to have been as free as that of our own country [England]. That of Arragon was beyond all question more so . . . Sweden and Denmark had constitutions of a similar description." The tide of history appeared clear, especially with the spirit of individualism that the Renaissance exuded.

But freedom and representative government were crushed by one rising despot after another. Macaulay adds: "Let us overleap two or three hundred years, and contemplate Europe at the commencement of the eighteenth century. Every free constitution, save one, had gone down. That of England had weathered the danger, and was riding in full security."[44] Macaulay objected to the blind optimism of his times: "It is the fashion to say that the progress of civilization is favorable to liberty. The maxim, though in some sense true, must be limited by many qualifications and exceptions."[45]

The notion that representative government is inevitable is one of the most striking differences between contemporary thought and that of the era of the Founding Fathers, when pessimism permeated political expectations. King George III and his ministers were seeking to assert absolute power over Americans. The Declaratory Act of 1766 announced that Parliament "had, hath, and of right ought to have, full power and authority to make laws and statutes of sufficient force and validity to bind the colonies and people of America, subjects of the crown of Great Britain, in all cases whatsoever."[46] The fact that Britain was supposedly a free country did not diminish the fetters foretold in such language. If the Founders had assumed that representative government was inevitable, many of them would not have risked their necks in the cause.

A century and a half later, at the 1919 peace conference at Versailles, new democracies were all the rage. But democracies collapsed like houses of cards in the following decades. The rise of fascism occurred partly because people had lost faith in the value and viability of representative government.

The current cult of "democratic inevitability" was jump-started by Francis Fukuyama, whose 1989 article (later expanded into a book) on "The End of History" made him an instant intellectual cult figure. Fukuyama was a Reagan political appointee at the State Department and is currently on the Board of Directors of the National Endowment for Democracy. Fukuyama hailed the "unabashed victory of economic and political liberalism" and proclaimed that "we in the liberal West occupy the final summit of the historical edifice."[47] He announced: "What we are witnessing is not just the end of the Cold War, or a passing of a particular period of postwar history, but the end of history as such: that is, the end point of mankind's ideological evolution and the universalization of Western liberal democracy as the final form of human government."[48]

Fukuyama revealed that "the present form of social and political organization is completely satisfying to human beings in their most essential characteristics." Fukuyama is the Candide of political philosophy: liberal democracy is the best of all possible worlds, and we should all be happy because its triumph everywhere is fated. Fukuyama hailed German philosopher G. W. F. Hegel as the supreme "philosopher of freedom." But Hegel was as much a champion of freedom as Nietzsche was a champion of Christianity. Fukuyama reminds readers that Hegel "proclaimed history to be at an end in 1806. For as early as this Hegel saw in Napoleon's defeat of the Prussian monarchy at the Battle of Jena the victory of the ideals of the French Revolution, and the imminent universalization of the state incorporating the principles of liberty and equality." (In the book version three years later, Fukuyama clarified that this imminent universalization would be based on "the principles of liberal democracy.") Fukuyama stresses that the 1806 battle "marked the end of history because it was at that point that the vanguard of humanity (a term quite familiar to Marxists) actualized the principles of the French Revolution." Fukuyama notes that "the present world seems to confirm that the fundamental principles of sociopolitical organization have not advanced terribly far since 1806."[49] Fukuyama neglected to mention Hegel's rapturous comment after the battle of Jena—"I saw the emperor, this soul of the world, riding through the streets."[50]

To view the armies of Napoleon as engines of liberal democracy is peculiar. Napoleon, aside from crushing the Venetian republic, destroyed freedom of the press, had political opponents in France assassinated, brutally suppressed popular uprisings against French rule in Spain and elsewhere, and spawned wars that left millions of Europeans dead. Perhaps Fukuyama was merely ahead of his time, championing democracy being imposed by foreign conquests. But Napoleon's invasions did not create democracies; instead, they spurred a backlash of repressive reaction throughout Europe. Napoleon's wars profoundly stimulated efforts to unify Germany, which did not exactly advance liberty in Europe.

Fukuyama quotes Hegel's assertion that "the History of the World is nothing other than the progress of the consciousness of Freedom." But Hegel was not using freedom in the sense that Washington or Jefferson did. Hegel declared: "The State in-and-for-itself is the ethical whole, the actualization of freedom."[51]

G. W. F. Hegel was renowned as the "Royal Prussian Court Philosopher" at the University of Berlin. Far from being a champion of the individual against his rulers, Hegel stressed that "all the worth which the human being possesses—all spiritual reality, he possesses only through the State."[52] Hegel profoundly influenced modern political thinking by mystifying government, declaring that the State is "the shape which the perfect embodiment of Spirit assumes."[53] Hegel was the great liberator of political power: "The State is the self-certain absolute mind which acknowledges no abstract rules of good and bad, shameful and mean, craft and deception."[54] German philosopher Jakob Friedrich Fries, a contemporary of Hegel's, declared that his theory of the State had grown "not in the gardens of science but on the dunghill of servility."[55] German philosopher Ernst Cassirer observed in 1945 of Hegel: "No other philosophical system has done so much for the preparation of fascism and imperialism as Hegel's doctrine of the state—this 'divine Idea as it exists on earth.'"[56]

Roger Kimball, the editor of *The New Criterion,* observed that "in a footnote, Fukuyama acknowledges that Hegel overtly supported the Prussian monarchy. He nevertheless maintains that, 'far from justifying the Prussian monarchy of his day,' Hegel's discussion in *The Philosophy of Right* 'can be read as an esoteric critique of actual practice.'"[57] In other words, Hegel's reputation as a champion of freedom hinges on assuming that Hegel did not mean what he wrote.

No alarm bells went off in Washington, even though this theory of inevitable liberal democracy was deduced from a philosopher whose ideas were previously invoked to sanctify both communism and fascism. One eminent historian speculated during World War Two on "whether the struggle of the Russians and the invading Germans in 1943 was . . . a conflict between the Left and Right wings of Hegel's school."[58] Hegel's canonization as the hero of democracy is another example of how the historical record is not permitted to cast doubt on *theories* of history.

Fukuyama referred to "post-historical societies"—nations where democracy had already been established—as if there could be no turning back. Fukuyama takes his definition of the end of history from Hegel. As Cassirer noted, "To Hegel, the State is not only a part, a special province, but the essence, the very core of historical life. . . . Hegel denies that we can speak of historical life outside and before the State."[59]

Fukuyama's article concluded with profound lamentations: "The end of history will be a very sad time. . . . In the post-historical period there will be neither art nor philosophy, just the perpetual caretaking of the museum of human history. I can feel in myself, and see in others around me, a powerful nostalgia for the time when history existed."[60] The article was written at a time when the American Psychiatric Association had not yet established a recommended pharmaceutical regimen for woeful policy wonks. Fukuyama's assumption that life would have little or no meaning after the spread of democracy and freedom implies that political action, or political strife, is the primary source of life's meaning. This may be true in Washington, but happily, most people in the world do not take their life's mission from the government.

Fukuyama's article evoked thunderous praise. His thesis was fanatically embraced by many Washingtonians and much of the U.S. policy elite. The Fukuyama–democratic inevitability boom illustrates how Washington intellectuals react to pretentious obscurity with the same gullibility that many poor people react to Lotto advertisements.

Fukuyama's theory came at the perfect time—just as the Cold War was ending and a new rationale was needed for a massive U.S. military machine. Fukuyama's thesis sanctifies U.S. power the same way that Marx's law of history sanctified Soviet aggression to impose communism on foreign countries. His reading of Hegel provides an iron law of history in favor of the triumph of democracy. Karl Marx's interpretation of Hegel helped "prove" that communism was inevitable.

The democratic inevitability theory is also akin to the Marxist theory of the withering away of the State. Marx assumed that, after the creation of communism, the State would simply wither away, since there would be no need or incentive for people to exploit one another. Democratic inevitability implies that, once democracy is achieved, politicians will no longer seek power to violate the rights and liberties of citizens. For some unexplained reason, after democracy becomes universal, voting will turn politicians into choir boys.

Hegel declared that the Prussian State is the best of all possible governments. Nearly 200 years later, Fukuyama concluded the same thing about liberal democracy. He implicitly sanctifies existing democratic governments, as if they inherently serve people and respect rights. There is little or no recognition that the seeds of their destruction could be lurking within.

In a preface to his administration's 2002 National Security Strategy, Bush practically canonized Fukuyama's view: "The great struggles of the twentieth century between liberty and totalitarianism ended with a decisive victory for the forces of freedom—and a single sustainable model for national success: freedom, democracy, and free enterprise."[61] The Bush administration effectively invoked historic inevitability for its preferences and values—in the same document in which it proclaimed the right to launch preemptive attacks on practically any nation on Earth.

G. W. Bush uses God instead of G. W. F. Hegel to sanctify his foreign policy. Bush proclaimed at a 2004 fundraiser that "the Almighty has—believes that every person should be free. It's a gift from the Almighty, regardless of their religion or the color of their skin. I believe that as the torchbearer of freedom, the United States must lead and must never shirk our duty to lead."[62] (Bush routinely uses democracy and freedom interchangeably.) If nothing else, promising to spread freedom abroad consoles some Americans for its loss at home.

Nothing has happened in the last century—or millennium—to make politicians less dangerous. Those who pursue power remain the predator class. There is no magic in a proclamation that "democracy has now been officially achieved everywhere" that will change human nature.

Why would history stop after democracy was achieved? The experience of many countries has, instead, been "one person, one vote, one time." Yet, we are supposed to assume that the parade ceases after democracy is reached and will not proceed over any nearby cliffs.

Encouraging people to view democracy as inevitable lulls people to dangers posed by their rulers and other ambitious politicians. If democracy is inevitable, then political progress is on automatic pilot. The Founding Fathers believed that freedom would always be in danger from power—that there would always be politicians and tyrants and tyrant assistants conspiring against freedom. "Eternal vigilance is the price of liberty" was a common American saying in the nineteenth century. The contemporary version of that slogan appears to be: "Eternal sloth is the luxury of democracy."

Why would democracy be inevitable? Not because of human genes—since most of the human race has gotten along without it for 99.9 percent of its recorded history. Not because of technological destiny: the tools for surveillance (and thus, central control) are spreading far more quickly than the average citizen's defenses against external intrusions.

Some people insist that democracy is inevitable because it is the only just form of government. Since when is justice inevitable? "Would be nice if true" is not a good test of probability. Democracy is inevitable only if one assumes that almost all history is the "exception that proves the rule" about what the future will be.

The more that democracy is assumed to be inevitable, the more likely democracy will self-destruct. Faith in inevitability deadens the sense of peril—and people blithely acquiesce to one power seizure after another by the ruling class. Attention Deficit Democracy breeds habits that can doom democracy.

Since democracy is superior to dictatorship, people are obliged to swallow any and all hogwash about democracy. The fact that democracy is usually less oppressive than authoritarian governments somehow proves that democracy is perfect, self-sustaining, and tamper-proof. Because something is a lesser evil does not prove that it is the greatest good. The issue is not whether democracy is good, but whether it is a panacea. And unless it is a panacea, then spreading democracy at all costs will almost certainly do more harm than good.

CHAPTER 10

Big Picture Myopia

In considering the idea of the State, one must not think of particular states, nor of particular institutions, but one must contemplate the idea, this actual God, by itself.
—G. W. F. Hegel[1]

GOVERNMENT HAS VASTLY EXPANDED AT THE SAME TIME that government power has become largely non-controversial. Attention Deficit Democracy intellectually anaesthetizes Americans to the failures of government and the abuses of their rulers. The dearth of popular understanding of politics may lead some people to believe that government should be controlled by academic experts and the policy elite. But popular ignorance is no proof of elite wisdom.

Politically empowering the elite has long been popular with some intellectuals. British philosopher John Stuart Mill was for many years a patron saint of liberals. In his 1862 *Considerations on Representative Government,* Mill advocated a system of "plural voting," by which people with "instructed minds" would, by receiving two or more votes each, achieve "Superiority of influence" to counterweigh popular ignorance. Mill stressed, "The only thing which can justify reckoning one person's opinion as equivalent to more than one is individual mental superiority, and what is wanted is some approximate means of ascertaining that." Mill advocated a system by which the number of votes a person received would hinge upon their job: "Wherever a sufficient examination, or any serious conditions of education, are required before entering on a profession, its members could be admitted at once to a plurality of votes." Mill urged that "the same rule might be applied to graduates of universities." He envisioned a tiered system in which a person would receive extra votes according to his certification, stressing that the number of votes each elite member receives "is not in itself very material, provided the distinctions and gradations are not made arbitrarily, but are such as can be understood." Mill derided anyone who opposed awarding extra votes: "No one but a fool, and only a fool of a peculiar description, feels offended by the acknowledgment that there are others whose opinion, and even whose wish, is entitled to a greater amount of consideration than his."[2]

Mill's values were heartily embraced by subsequent generations of advocates of Big Government. University of Pennsylvania professor Michael Delli Carpini observed that "much of the power behind progressive-era arguments in favor of government-by-experts derived from the belief that average citizens lacked the ability to govern themselves."[3] As Professor Dorothy Ross noted, "The old Progressive faith in the educability of the people turned into the need for scientific techniques by which leaders could lead and the public could be trained into accepting the correct path."[4]

While members of the media, academia, and "public intellectuals" may be more learned than average voters, this group often has their own mental blinders that deter them from recognizing or admitting the dangers of government power. The political delusions and self-interest of the elite are a primary reason why Leviathan is thriving.

POLITICALLY CORRECT THOUGHTS ON GOVERNMENT

Why is it that the vast majority of government abuses and failures either never show up on the intellectual radar screen, or are merely one or two blips and then forever gone? Many intellectuals have long disdained the specific details of government policies—refusing to notice the screws, levers, and threats that government officials apply to compel people to submit. The more coercive government becomes, the more gauche it is to admit that government coerces. Looking at the actual details of government policy is left to the auditors and accountants, the congressional staffers, or perhaps the interns.

A decade ago, there was a hullabaloo to denounce "politically correct" mandates and imperatives. But the biggest beneficiary of "politically correct" thinking may be political power itself. The politically correct attitude looks beyond the government's past failings and current botches, and focuses instead on the *idea* of government.

The incarnation of this attitude is the Big Picture. The Big Picture is a type of abstraction—or pseudo-abstraction—that might be more appropriate in theology than in politics. The Big Picture mind set ensures that hard facts rarely enter one's conscious mental orbit—or, if they do, only as shooting stars. People are urged to "look beyond" or above banal political reality, and encouraged to keep their eyes on the clouds so they don't see how many government-made potholes endanger their path.

Politicians, pundits, and others perennially invoke the "Big Picture." Recognizing the role of the Big Picture is vital to understanding how contemporary democracies are going off the rail. The Big Picture provides preemptive exoneration for almost anyone who wants to kowtow and cheerlead for political power.

Big Picture myopia is partly the result of the arrogance and narrowness of the elite. The Big Picture easily becomes the mirror image of the day-to-day plundering and blundering by government agencies. Big Picture Statists rely on "transcendental math," which always proves that no matter how much government appears to be bumbling it is actually a glorious success.

This is no novelty. It is the same spiel courtiers used for centuries: the king is much greater than he appears to be, his bad judgments are not his fault, and veneration cures all. Throughout history, political power has rarely had a shortage of intellectuals happy to hail its achievements and disparage all who doubted its majesty. Writers who place government on a pedestal have been far more likely to raise themselves.

For many political commentators, the details of government programs don't matter because the actual performance of government is almost a moot issue. In recent years, neoconservatives have been the most prominent champions of government power. Their absolutism is clearest on foreign policy. Bill Kristol, the most prominent neoconservative, called in 1996 for the United States to exploit its "military supremacy and moral confidence" to achieve "benevolent global hegemony."[5] But in order for the U.S. government to maintain credibility with the American people for conquests abroad, it is vital to make government revered at home.

In 1997, David Brooks, a commentator on the PBS *NewsHour with Jim Lehrer* and a frequent contributor to the nation's top editorial pages, promulgated a new political theology in the *Weekly Standard*, where he was senior editor. Brooks, widely known as liberals' favorite conservative, began with a paean to the Library of Congress: "The building just overpowers you with its exuberance and grandeur."[6] Brooks conceded: "When you get down to looking at the details, you find that the craftsmanship is actually mediocre: You can travel around Europe and find a hundred buildings with better paintings and better sculpture. Nonetheless, there is something about the energy of the building that makes it more than the sum of its parts, that makes it not so much an artistic wonder as a spiritual artifact."[7]

This is the essence of the Big Picture view of government—that government is far more than the sum of its parts—and it should be judged on spiritual terms, not on the prosaic win-loss records of its interventions. Brooks, invoking a favorite Hegelian term, hailed the 1897 edifice as symbolizing that "America was emerging as a world-historical force." Brooks saw the government building as a politico-theological achievement: "The library represents a coherent system of belief: A divine order created by God. A view of history in which man makes long progress toward that order. A series of great nations which contribute to that progress."[8]

Brooks experienced the Library of Congress as a starry-eyed spectator, not as a frustrated user. At the time of Brooks's gushing over the appearance of the library, the library itself was riddled with employee theft, as well as pilfering by members of Congress and their staff. The library's atmosphere was becoming more jail-like each passing decade, with layer after layer of "security" that did little other than reducing the unemployment rate of surly people in the District of Columbia. Service to patrons was stymied by rules seemingly designed to protect government clerks from sweating.

Brooks grieved that Americans no longer "engage in grandiose hero-worship," are "suspicious of hierarchies," and lack "any sense of a transcendent order." Brooks disparaged conservatives who claimed to oppose Big Government on principle and those who succumbed to "Populism": "They have taken a healthy distrust of elites and turned it into a blanket hostility to establishments. . . . Many of today's conservatives . . . use phrases like 'inside the Beltway' to condemn those who have risen to high positions in public life. They support term limits on the grounds that experience in government is corrupting, rather than a form of public service." Brooks proclaimed that "ultimately, American purpose can find its voice only in Washington." Brooks did not explain where exactly in the memos, meetings, and machinations which engross the capital that "American purpose" arises. Brooks warned that Americans' mental health depends on the federal government proclaiming a purpose for the people: "Without vigorous national vision, we are plagued by anxiety and disquiet."

After the government proclaims a "national mission," Brooks explained, "individual ambition and willpower are channeled into the cause of national greatness. And by making the nation great, individuals are able to join their narrow concerns to a larger national project." This makes sense only if political efforts are inherently superior to private lives—if individuals are most valuable when serving as cogs in their rulers' schemes.

Brooks concluded by hailing government action as a supreme good:

It almost doesn't matter what great task government sets for itself, as long as it does some tangible thing with energy and effectiveness. The first task of government is to convey a spirit of confidence and vigor that can then *spill across* the life of the nation. Stagnant government drains national morale. A government that fails to offer any vision merely feeds public cynicism and disenchantment.

But energetic government is good for its own sake. It raises the sights of the individual. It strengthens common bonds. It boosts national pride. It continues the great national project. It allows each generation to join the work of their parents. The quest for national greatness defines the word "American" and makes it new for every generation.[9]

Brooks's notion of the purpose and role of government in people's lives could have vindicated East Bloc regimes. The key for Brooks is the overwhelming need of people for the government to give meaning to their lives. No matter how badly government flops, lacking faith in government is worse.

Brooks's vision had more in common with Benito Mussolini than with Thomas Jefferson, the founder of the Library of Congress. In a 1932 essay, Il Duce declared: "The State is the . . . custodian and transmitter of the spirit of the people, as it has grown up through the centuries in language, in customs and in faith. . . . And the State is not only a living reality of the present, it is also linked with the past and above all with the future, and thus transcending the brief limits of individual life, it represents the immanent spirit of the nation. . . . It is the State which educates its citizens in civic virtue, gives them a consciousness of their mission and welds them into unity; harmonizing their various interests through justice, and transmitting to future generations the mental conquests of science, of art, of law and the solidarity to humanity."[10] But fascist ideas are not tolerated in Washington—if they are labeled fascistic. Brooks and other neoconservatives would likely heartily agree with Mussolini that the State "leads men from primitive tribal life to that highest expression of human power which is Empire."[11]

A few months later, Brooks and Bill Kristol, the editor of the *Weekly Standard,* elaborated on the theme in a *Wall Street Journal* editorial page article entitled, "What Ails Conservatism."[12] They derided the "antigovernment, 'leave us alone' sentiment that was crucial to the Republican victory of 1994." It was as if Republicans should have been smart enough to realize that their antigovernment message was simply a ruse to help them seize power. They lectured: "An American political movement's highest goal can't be protecting citizens from their own government. Indeed, in recent years some conservatives' sensible contempt for the nanny state has at times spilled over into a foolish, and politically suicidal, contempt for the American state."[13]

Brooks and Kristol stressed that the "American understanding of greatness . . . isn't unfriendly to government, *properly understood.*"[14] They stressed: "National greatness conservatism does not despise government. How could it? How can Americans love their nation if they hate its government?" This was the same line that President Clinton used in 1995, when he sought to make critics of government appear to be co-conspirators with Oklahoma City bomber Timothy McVeigh.[15] But there is a vast gap between attacking federal office buildings and expecting politicians and bureaucrats to provide meaning for one's life.

Brooks and Kristol were not assuming that these national values, this lofty national tone would emanate from a hearing of the House Subcommittee on Capital Markets, Insurance, and Government-Sponsored Enterprises. Instead, the values would be established by the intellectuals who had the ear of the rulers. When they talk of "national greatness," they mean more power and prestige for intellectuals. This is another variation of the Platonic theme that "the wise should rule."

The Brooks–Kristol national greatness vision works only if one views government as an abstraction. The more blurred the abstraction, the more idealistic the vision. "National Greatness" becomes a magician's trick to draw people's eyes away from the real action.

The "national greatness" doctrine is profoundly un-American. It looks for greatness to come from people obeying their rulers—from the nation falling into line behind Washington. It is a Napoleonic recipe for greatness, not a prescription for free people. The American version of national greatness, at least in the Founders era, looked to the noble actions and great achievements of free citizens. If people are unchained and unoppressed, they can soar. As Henry David Thoreau commented in 1848, "The character inherent in the American people has done all that has been accomplished; and it would have done somewhat more, if the government had not sometimes got in its way."[16]

Brooks and Kristol concluded with a final Statist gush, declaring that "a key to that [American] greatness is our system of government—a government that must be improved, but one that remains, to quote Lincoln once more, 'an inestimable jewel.'" The Founding Fathers respected the government they created as a means to protect individual rights and to secure individual liberty. Brooks and Kristol venerate the government simply because it is government. Perhaps government is so attractive because it is a way for some people to find meaning in life by forcibly imposing their values on others.

These essays did not get Brooks and Kristol laughed off the national stage. Instead, they subsequently became more prominent and respected. Brooks was anointed a *New York Times* op-ed page columnist a few years later, and Kristol's work appears frequently on the editorial page of the *Washington Post.*[17]

SKEWED SCORING

"Mulligan" is a golf term used when someone disregards a bad first shot and simply tees up again, takes the shot over, and pretends the initial goof never happened. Though such scoring is prohibited in golf tournaments, this is the standard perennially used to evaluate government interventions.

Washington policy debates are often like a criminal trial in which all the evidence of the defendant's past offenses is ruled inadmissible. The disdain for past failures is the key to Leviathan's continued intellectual credibility. Faith in Big Government probably cannot survive without a Big Picture mentality. Unless people choose to ignore the grisly details of what government is doing and costing, then people cannot sway others to support perpetuating nearly boundless government power.

Though many people mocked George W. Bush for taking America to war against Iraq based on little or no sound information, such decisions are practically business as usual in Washington. It is rare for advocates of new government programs or new foreign wars to stop and consider the evidence of the past. Whether it is a question of sifting through Inspector General and General Accounting Office reports or bluntly facing the evidence of previous U.S. interventions in the same country, Washingtonians avoid soiling their minds with the records of past debacles. The purity, genius, and good intentions of advocates of expanding government power or launching new wars make all prior experience irrelevant.

Foreign aid, for instance, retains its prestige with the media and the establishment after being completely disdained by most Americans since the 1960s. The continuance of foreign aid is a tribute to the power of elite opinion and interests—and to administrations that want to ensure that the secretary of state and president receive red-carpet welcomes when they travel abroad. As University of Pennsylvania professor Walter McDougall observed, "Our half century of experience with foreign aid has been almost a total loss, and the reason is not hard to find. It resides in the contradiction inherent in programs whose purpose is to demonstrate the superiority of the free market model but whose methods are entirely statist."[18] McDougall derided efforts in the mid-late 1990s to "attempt to teach ex-Soviet peoples how to be good capitalists through the medium of government grants administered by government agencies for the benefit of our own and foreign bureaucracies."[19] A comprehensive study of the effects of foreign aid on 92 developing countries by the London School of Economics found that "no relationship exists between the levels of aid and rates of growth in recipient countries." But the aid did result in "increasing the size of recipient governments and lining the pockets of elites."[20] Such pocket lining occasionally catches the attention of prosecutors. In August 2005, Harvard University paid the federal government $26 million for false claims made to the U.S. government regarding Harvard's involvement in a massive foreign aid debacle in Russia.[21]

THE BIG PICTURE ON CAPITOL HILL

In 1999, the *Journal of Personality and Social Psychology* published a study that explained why "the incompetent will tend to grossly overestimate their skills and abilities." The article concluded that "those with limited knowledge in a domain suffer a dual burden: Not only do they reach mistaken conclusions and make regrettable errors, but their incompetence robs them of the ability to realize it."[22] The article quoted the apt saying by Charles Darwin that "ignorance more frequently begets confidence than does knowledge." While the study focused largely on people scoring in the bottom quartile on intelligence tests, the same pattern of overconfidence and incompetence characterizes many members of Congress.

One of the biggest Big Picture delusions in Washington is that congressmen understand what they are doing most of the time. However, many congressmen blunder through their days as haplessly as a Nebraska tourist wandering downtown Washington fruitlessly searching for the Washington Monument. For instance, on March 23, 2004, a dozen members of Congress attended a ceremony in a Senate office building at which the Rev. Sun Myung Moon was crowned as "humanity's Savior, Messiah, Returning Lord and True Parent." Rep. Danny Davis (D-Ill.) wore white gloves as he placed an ornate gold crown on Moon's head. Moon announced during the event that "Hitler and Stalin have found strength in my teachings, mended their ways and been reborn as new persons."[23] Moon, the founder of his own religion, was previously renowned for a tax evasion conviction and for conducting mass wedding ceremonies for strangers who were members of his church. When the news media began asking why congressmen attended Moon's coronation, Davis explained, "I see people crowned. I go to parades quite a bit—[and see] the queen of the homecoming parade, queen of the festival."[24] (He neglected to say that a Moon organization had organized a fundraiser for Davis before the event.) Rep. Roscoe Bartlett (R-Md.) commented on his attendance: "I remember the king and queen thing. But we have the king and queen of the prom, the king and queen of 4-H, the Mardi Gras and all sorts of other things. I had no idea what he was king of."[25] One senator had sponsored the event, and thus allowed the coronation to occur in a federal building; however, the Senate Rules and Administration Committee refused to disclose the name of the sponsoring senator. All of the congressmen queried by the media stressed that they did not personally believe that Moon was the Messiah.

The behavior of congressmen at a typical hearing is what would get a juror fined and jailed for "contempt of court" at a trial. Most congressmen do not show up for most hearings, and those who do show up attend sporadically, wandering in and out and paying scant attention to witnesses. Most hearings, especially in the House, showcase congressmen often awkwardly reading questions written out by their aides. An intelligent, spontaneous, piercing follow-up question is as rare as a federal agency requesting a reduction in its budget.

Because congressmen are assured that grasping the Big Picture gives them all the information they need, they are prone to both negligence and incorrigibility. Legislators base their own votes not on what they have read, but instead on their dread of controversy. Eric Sterling, former chief counsel of the House Judiciary Committee and the director of the Criminal Justice Policy Foundation, observed, "There's a saying on the Hill that if you have to explain the vote, it's a bad vote."[26] Whatever a politician cannot explain in 15 seconds doesn't get done—or, in the case of previous bad legislation, doesn't get fixed. Often, the title of a piece of proposed legislation is all that members of Congress consider it necessary to know. A single punchy phrase absolves almost all those who repeat it from knowing what they are voting on.

An example of such institutionalized negligence is the 1996 "Freedom to Farm Act," still portrayed as a crowning achievement of the Republican Revolution that commenced with the GOP takeover of Congress in 1994. Several conservative and libertarian Washington think tanks, and even the *Wall Street Journal* editorial page, bought into the phrase.[27] "Freedom to farm" was widely assumed to mean the end of federal farm subsidies. Most of the supporters of free market policies made little or no effort to understand the legislation. The act increased, rather than eliminated, subsidies. Farmers made out like bandits at the same time conservative congressmen preened about ending one of the feds' biggest boondoggles. The arcane details of the program were crafted by the congressional agricultural committees, who ensured that their donors would retain freedom to farm the U.S. Treasury.[28] The program provided vastly more handouts to large farmers than to small farmers; the top one percent of farmers collected an average of more than $500,000 in federal payments each thanks to "Freedom to Farm."[29]

Congressmen are renowned for rarely reading the hefty bills they vote upon. Yet, even though congressmen often have little or no idea what they are voting on, as long as they occasionally invoke the Big Picture, they are presumed to be sufficiently competent to continue controlling other Americans' lives.

Most congressmen judge most government programs simply by whether they deliver the goods. They use a standard akin to the tracking system of

United Parcel Service—the issue is not whether the product is any good but simply whether it arrived—and thus made voters grateful. The lack of oversight by Congress means that it is far easier to launch new programs than to rein in abuses. Politicians show far more enthusiasm for policing the lives of private citizens than for policing the use of government power.

NO-COST KILLINGS

Big Picture Myopia makes it easy for the U.S. government to kill large numbers of innocent foreigners while paying no cost at home. Often, the government need merely enunciate a lofty goal or disparage the victims to exonerate all the policymakers for the deaths of innocent people. The vast deference that the intelligentsia and the pundit class pay to government permits politicians to seize far more power and do more damage than most Americans recognize.

Presidents, defense secretaries, and other policymakers are rarely held to the same standard that applies to U.S. soldiers. According to the U.S. Army, a homicide is "a death that results from the intentional (explicit or implied) or grossly reckless behavior of another person or persons."[30] The Army specifies: "Homicide is not synonymous with murder (a legal determination) and includes both criminal actions and excusable incidents (i.e., self-defense, law enforcement, combat)."[31] But this standard is only used for assessing individual or small numbers of deaths. It is inapplicable for policies or actions that result in hundreds of thousands of deaths. In such cases, the issue is not homicide, but whether proper political or bureaucratic procedures were followed, and whether politicians and government spokesmen uttered phrases that absolved the government, either before or after the deaths.

One of the clearest examples of Big Picture absolution is the political and public response to the effects of the economic sanctions that the United Nations imposed on Iraq (largely at U.S. government behest) in 1990 and continued through the fall of Saddam's regime in 2003. The original purpose of the sanctions was to compel the Iraqi army to withdraw from Kuwait. After the United States and its allies expelled Iraqi forces from Kuwait, the formal purpose of the sanctions was revised to compel Iraq to cease its efforts to develop Weapons of Mass Destruction. However, shortly after the United Nations formally reconsecrated its blockade, U.S. Secretary of State James Baker announced that the sanctions would continue until Saddam Hussein surrendered power.[32] This purpose was reinvoked by President Clinton and by his secretary of state, Madeline Albright. The sanctions were micromanaged by the UN Security Council, which was dominated by the United States and, to a much lesser degree, Britain, on this issue. The French and the Russians opposed the punitive policy but did not have the votes to end the blockade.

The sanctions became an economic noose, a blockade around most of the country (excepting the Kurdish area in northern Iraq, which was considered friendly to the United States). From late 1990 to late 1996, the United Nations, acting at the United States' behest, banned all oil exports—even though oil had been the source of almost all of Iraq's foreign currency prior to the war. By banning exports, the sanctions also effectively banned almost all imports. Iraq had imported most of its food and almost all of its medical and pharmaceutical supplies. Iraq's economy collapsed, with national income falling by more than two-thirds.

The blockade wrecked Iraqis' health. A 1995 article in the Air Force's *Airpower Journal* noted that the 1991 bombing of Iraq's civilian infrastructure, combined with the blockade, had the result that "epidemics of gastroenteritis, cholera, and typhoid broke out, leading to perhaps as many as 100,000 civilian deaths and a doubling of the infant mortality rate."[33] A doubling of the infant mortality rate would have resulted in far more than 100,000 deaths. A team of doctors (including a representative of the Harvard School of Public Health) visited Iraq in 1995 and estimated that the sanctions resulted in the deaths of 567,000 children in the previous five years. (Most later studies made lower estimates of fatalities.) A 1999 United Nations Children's Fund (UNICEF) report estimated that the sanctions had thus far killed half a million Iraqi children.[34] Colombia University professor Richard Garfield, an epidemiologist and an expert on the effects of sanctions, estimated in 2003 that the sanctions had resulted in between 343,900 and 529,000 infant and young child fatalities.[35]

The U.S. government knew that, as of 1995, Iraq had destroyed all its chemical and biological weapon stockpiles and that Iraq had ceased efforts to develop or acquire nuclear bombs shortly after the first Gulf War. Perpetuating the sanctions based on Saddam's failure to abandon WMDs was dishonest. The U.S. government quickly recognized that the blockade of Iraq was having catastrophic public health consequences. Hundreds of thousands of Iraqi children died as a result of the U.S. government's refusal to publicly admit that the Iraqi government had complied with the sanctions' original justification. By the mid-1990s, Saddam was using the sanctions to tighten his grip on power, making Iraqis far more dependent on government rationing of food and other goods. The U.S. government knew that the blockade was killing Iraqis without fatally undermining Saddam's power; yet, because being "tough on Saddam" was good domestic politics, the blockade continued.

Most of the American Establishment never showed the slightest interest in how many Arabs were dying because of the blockade. The carnage from the sanctions on Iraq almost never popped up on the American radar screen, except on the far left and momentarily in one *60 Minutes* interview. CBS correspondent Lesley Stahl asked U.S. ambassador to the United Nations Madeline Albright: "We have heard that a half million children have died. That's more children than died in Hiroshima. And—and you know, is the price worth it?" Albright answered: "I think this is a very hard choice, but the price—we think the price is worth it."[36] (Among the items that the United States vetoed importing into Iraq were ambulances, tires, car batteries, soap, pencils and other education supplies, and dental and medical equipment, including dialysis units.)

The U.S. government exonerated itself by pointing out that Saddam built himself new palaces during the years the sanctions were in place. However, the cost of constructing a dozen new ornate buildings is dwarfed by the cost of providing food and health care for 25 million people for a dozen years. Even after the oil-for-food program began in late 1996, Iraq's oil revenue was far less than it would have been without the UN restrictions on its oil sales. As long as the U.S. government could claim an idealistic, Big Picture motive for the sanctions—removing Saddam from power—it escaped blame for policies that knowingly killed hundreds of thousands of Iraqis.

The sanctions' toll was a major issue with Al Qaeda and Osama Bin Laden, and was a profound grievance with Arab populations from the early 1990s onward. But, after the start of the second Iraq war, the only thing necessary to completely exonerate the U.S. government (and to damn all the critics) was the "discovery" that bribes were paid to evade the blockade. The vast majority of such bribes occurred after the so-called Oil for Food program began in late 1996. The program permitted Iraq to export some oil but the U.S. government effectively had veto power over the spending of all oil revenue. At that point, hundreds of thousands of Iraqis had already perished because of the blockade. As of mid-2002, the U.S. government was exploiting its position on the UN Security Council to block the delivery of $5 billion in humanitarian imports into Iraq that Iraq had already paid for and that the UN monitors had already approved.

The selective indignation over the oil-for-food bribes exemplified Big Picture myopia. There was no sense that any U.S. government official should be held responsible—or even obliged to answer questions—on the carnage the sanctions inflicted on the Iraqi people. Instead, the only issue to hold Washington's and America's attention was the fact that some people profited from kickbacks. But wherever there is a blockade, there will be bribes: prohibition breeds bootleggers. There was probably a hundred times more coverage in the U.S. media in late 2004 and early 2005 of the oil-for-food corruption scandal than of the catastrophic loss of life that resulted from the blockade.

Most Americans—if they had any awareness or recollection of the sanctions policy—looked only at the proclaimed intent. There was little or no curiosity about what the U.S. government was actually doing or whether the program was succeeding. There was no concern about collateral damage. Instead, it was as if the fact that the United States and its allies had defeated Saddam's forces in 1991 conferred the right to inflict perpetual capital punishment on the Iraqi people for failing to overthrow their dictator.

The history of the Iraqi sanctions illustrates how easily the U.S. government can perpetuate policies that knowingly kill hundreds of thousands of innocent people. What matters is what the president says the United States intends to do. The president has a monopoly on defining good and evil, thus ensuring that the government will do no evil. The more people who take their "moral values" from the president, the more people government can kill with impunity.

Many academics and intellectuals who favor government intervention have the same attitude toward "collateral damage" as do Pentagon spokesmen discussing the latest U.S. bombing of a foreign city. Collateral damage is by definition irrelevant, since it was not what the government officially intended. Permitting politicians and bureaucrats to define their victims out of existence—to relegate them to asterisk status—is vital to maintaining faith in the benevolence of Leviathan.

The Big Picture promotes the habit of sweeping government victims under the rug. All that is necessary is for government spokesmen to announce some lofty motive or pious formula and the government is automatically exonerated from blame. The standards the government uses to whitewash itself are far lower than those permitted citizens defending themselves in government courts.

The easier it is to shift blame for the dead, the less incentive the government has to avoid killing innocent people. The government's ability to use propaganda to commit "no-cost killings" further undermines any semblance of democratic control over government.

AUTOMATIC IMMUNITY

The Big Picture immunizes policymakers from history. The Vietnam War was one of the clearest illustrations of the mental incorrigibility of "the best and the brightest." Government policymakers became mesmerized by a few phrases and became impervious to real-world evidence that the phrases and theories did not apply. The CIA debunked the "domino theory" explanation for intervening in Vietnam by 1964, and assured Nixon in 1969 that there was no threat of communist takeovers throughout the region as a result of a precipitous U.S. withdrawal. Yet, as the *Pentagon Papers* noted, "only the Joint Chiefs, Mr. [Walt]

Rostow [Johnson's chief intellectual advisor] and General [Maxwell] Taylor appear to have accepted the domino theory in its literal sense."[37] These were the individuals who had vast influence in raising U.S. troop levels in Vietnam to half a million. Similarly, as Hannah Arendt noted, "The divergence between the facts established by the intelligence services—sometimes by the decision makers themselves (as notably in the case of McNamara) and often available to the informed public—and the premises, theories, and hypotheses according to which decisions were finally made is total."[38]

In 1967, the Pentagon ordered top experts to analyze where the war had gone wrong. The resulting study contained 47 volumes of material exposing the intellectual and political follies that had, at that point, already left tens of thousands of Americans dead. After the study was finished, it was distributed to the key players and federal agencies. However, the massive study was completely ignored. At the time the *New York Times* began publishing excerpts in 1971, "the White House and the State Department were unable even to locate the forty-seven volumes."[39] *New York Times* editor Tom Wicker commented at the time that "the people who read these documents in the *Times* were the first to study them."[40]

One of the most important lessons of the *Pentagon Papers* was how the war strategists became misled by fixating on the battle "to win the people's minds." Arendt noted, "What is surprising is the eagerness of those scores of 'intellectuals' who offered their enthusiastic help in this imaginary enterprise, perhaps because it demanded nothing but mental exercises." It was easy for the intellectuals "to remain unaware of the untold misery that their 'solutions,' pacification and relocation programs, defoliation, napalm, and anti-personnel bullets, held in store."

Three decades after the publication of the *Pentagon Papers*, another president launched a "crusade" to win "the hearts and minds" of the world. Unfortunately, once again, the lessons of history were not permitted to stymie the salvation campaign. The *Pentagon Papers* revealed how "sheer ignorance of all pertinent facts and deliberate neglect of postwar [World War II] developments became the hallmark of established doctrine within the Establishment."[41] Three decades later, America has a president and top advisers who appear to adamantly refuse to permit reality to enter either their plans or their favorite phrases. The Bush administration appears to have devoted far more effort to propaganda than to understanding the impediments to its crusades in the Middle East and elsewhere.

THE WASHINGTON INTELLECTUAL MILIEU

The Big Picture helps Washington intellectuals define issues in ways that buffer the federal government from any damage it inflicts. Much of the

Washington establishment is devoted to maintaining the prestige of government as the single most important fount of their own personal prestige.

Many Washington think tanks are becoming little more than "cash machines for power" for politicians. Clifford May, the president of the Foundation for Defense of Democracies, commented in 2005: "It is the job of think tanks to create political capital. It is the job of politicians to spend it."[42] The pretense of ideas sanctifies the pursuit of power. (May's think tank lavishly praises the Bush administration and politicians who favor military aggression against Arab and Muslim nations.)

While idealists hoped that the surge of intellectuals into Washington in recent decades would raise the tone of the government, the result is often merely one more group beseeching favor, funding, and recognition. Appearances by government officials at think tank events are trumpeted much as the visits of saints' bones were heralded at cathedrals 800 years ago. There is nothing like a grip 'n' grin photo with a prominent politician to adorn a think tank's annual report. This creates a vicious cycle: think tanks prove their clout (and worthiness for donors) by heaping accolades on politicians, and politicians use the accolades to seize more power.

Think tanks are sometimes fronts for political operatives. Jack Abramoff, the most powerful lobbyist in Washington, placed an aging beach lifeguard at the head of American International Center, a think tank he created to funnel money to himself and his favorite causes.[43] Because of the aura that surrounds think tanks, the scam was fruitful, at least until Abramoff's other machinations hit the papers.

The respect with which think tanks are often treated in Washington is another sign of the city's memory deficit. Think tanks tied to the Pentagon played a major role in the "defactualization" of policy that helped create the quagmire in Vietnam. As Arendt observed, "No ivory tower of the scholars has ever better prepared the mind for ignoring the facts of life than did the various think tanks for the scholars and the reputation of the White House for the President's advisers. In this atmosphere, defeat was less feared than admitting defeat."[44] The more financially ambitious Washington think tanks become, the more vigilant they must be to prevent their thinking from impeding their fundraising.

The intelligentsia is perhaps the ultimate partner in power—given all the government consulting contracts, all the tenured gigs at government-subsidized universities (including private universities that depend on federal research grants and subsidized loans to students). As Professor David Ciepley noted, "Starting in the First World War, and much more so during the New Deal and World War II, American social scientists became part of the autonomous state themselves, helping staff the mushrooming government agencies."[45] Much of the expert class, including academics, editorial writers, and public intellectuals—are swayed by their aspirations for government. Advocating a reduction of government power is akin to reducing the size of the playpen for all intellectuals. Many intellectuals' advocacy for government is as credible as someone hustling people to jump onto an old rug, claiming that it is a magic carpet.

The Big Picture is the great labor saver for intellectuals. There is no need to exert themselves understanding what the government does since they already know what it means. Their disdain for mere details proves their profundity. Regrettably, it is often the intellectuals who are in the forefront, encouraging intellectual negligence toward public policy.

The Big Picture also perennially triumphs in the work of Washington journalists. The Washington press corps has long been derided as "stenographers with amnesia."[46] Actually, this epithet is going out of fashion, in part because fewer people know the meaning of *stenographer.*

In Washington, there is a surprising lack of curiosity about government. There is passionate interest about the latest budget proposals for government agencies, passing new laws, or creating new programs. But the actual operation of government, the details of what specific government programs achieve or inflict, is considered mundane. The less a journalist understands an agency's policies, the more gullible he is for its propaganda.

Washington journalists' reality is largely defined by government press releases. The media rarely looks beyond the government's proclaimed purpose for a program or policy. "Pack journalism" predominates—and the pack rarely strays from the government reservation. When they do stray, it is often in a group—after something has occurred or some pronouncement has been made signaling that it is okay to temporarily deviate from the official line. There is almost never any liability for a Washington journalist who peddles false information received from the government, but they risk their careers if their criticisms of government turn out to be unsubstantiated. Sam Donaldson, the legendary ABC White House correspondent, observed of the Washington media: "As a rule, we are, if not handmaidens of the establishment, at least blood brothers to the establishment. We end up the day usually having some version of what the White House . . . has suggested as a story."[47]

What responsibility does the media have for trafficking false government claims? In recent decades, federal prosecutors have continually expanded the definition of "conspiracy." The Drug Enforcement Agency prosecutes individuals for passing on information—even without any profit or personal stake. Even if someone at a concert merely points an undercover federal agent in the general direction of someone rumored to be selling drugs, the person can be convicted for conspiring to distribute illicit drugs and be sent to prison for ten years.[48]

By the same standard, most of the news media would be guilty of conspiring with the federal government to deceive the American people. The media effectively stamps its seal of approval on the vast majority of government assertions and presidential proclamations it delivers to the American people. The fact that prominent media personalities profit massively from their coziness with government doesn't annul their responsibility.

THE BIG ABSOLUTION

When folks tacitly accept that the Big Picture is all that matters, they are practically forswearing trying to understand specific federal policies. The Big Picture is the Big Absolution. People forfeit their own judgment to those who define the Big Picture, like PBS commentators or post-speech analysts, who tell people the meaning of what they just saw.

With the Big Picture, the danger of government power is usually permanently kept off the radar screen. The Big Picture can be calibrated to perceive threats from everything except the government.

The Big Picture, by minimizing or preemptively defusing controversy about government abuses, helps propel the growth of government power. People suffice with the Big Picture in part because they are convinced that government by nature does good things—and thus they need not trouble their little heads about the details. Yet, Statism is the most dangerous elitism of our times. And still it advances year after year, decade after decade, president after president. Openly talking about putting government on a pedestal would get some people riled. Instead, there is an endless profusion of laws and edicts and executive orders that raise the government above the people. The people are becoming legally inferior to the government, but it is not a problem, because the government denies it and the Establishment talks about other things.

Today's intellectuals maintain their Statism the same way that earlier generations maintained their socialism. The persistent faith in socialism was one of the starkest triumphs of the Big Picture: intellectuals knew capitalism was evil, and everything else became irrelevant. Economist Robert Skidelsky observed that "the collectivist belief system existed independently of the facts of modern life."[49] Since the socialists occupied the moral high ground, they had no need to consider or explain how government ownership of the means of production would produce prosperity or justice. Instead, the dogma was treated as a revealed truth to which all refined minds must assent.

Similarly, well-educated intellectuals today intuitively know that vast government power is necessary to protect people from themselves. Leviathan today receives the same deference that socialism received in the 1930s. Except that few people injudiciously use the "L-word" in a positive sense.

The Big Picture is often the ultimate deduction. It is not as if commentators and "public intellectuals" and editorial writers are reaching sweeping conclusions based on a careful study of the evidence. Instead, they possess the Revealed Truth—and the "facts" about government and government programs are deductions from the Big Picture. The goal becomes simply to apply the Big Picture—the Big Truth—so that, in each specific case, people are made to realize that government is benevolent and trustworthy.

As long as government power expands—as long as government and political leaders are glorified—it really doesn't matter whether government programs succeed or fail. Or, more accurately, the programs are a success because their advocates and defenders and champions are well compensated and often treated regally.

Those who invoke the Big Picture often have a vested interest in discouraging people from looking at grisly details. The Big Picture becomes the enabler of the Big Lie. The studied avoidance of the details of government policy makes it far easier for politicians to manipulate and deceive the public. The Big Picture allows governments to do as they please, confident that few people will pay attention to the details. And even when hundreds of thousands of people are killed, the government need only redefine the issue.

The Big Picture ensures that people learn little or nothing from the past and ignore the problems of the present. The Big Picture is the higher truth—and everything else is mere ephemera. Big Picture Myopia empowers those whose schemes and ambitions would be thwarted if people understood their plans. Attention Deficit Democracy creates a vacuous atmosphere in which Big Picture advocates can dominate political discussions regardless of the illogic or imbecility of their doctrines.

CHAPTER 11

Democracy vs. Liberty

Perhaps the fact that we have seen millions voting themselves into complete dependence on a tyrant has made our generation understand that to choose one's government is not necessarily to secure freedom.

—Friedrich Hayek, 1979[1]

Your Government's not going to let people destroy the freedoms that we love in America.[2]

—George W. Bush, May 8, 2002[2]

MODERN DEMOCRACY IS FAR MORE EFFECTIVE at unleashing government than at protecting individuals. The Founding Fathers believed that governments were created to secure rights. Subsequent generations of politicians have disparaged such a constrained vision of their own prerogatives. Yet, regardless of how often popularly elected governments trample people's rights and liberties, many people continue to equate democracy with freedom.

There is nothing inherently liberating about majority rule. From the history of American slavery and Jim Crow to the history of the Serbs, the Croats, the Tutsis in Rwanda, and other contemporary groups, majority rule is no recipe for peace or justice.

People are taught that, thanks to democracy, coercion is no longer dangerous because people get to vote on who coerces them. Because people are permitted a role in choosing who will be in charge of the penal code, they are free. Being permitted to vote for politicians who enact unjust, oppressive new laws magically converts the stripes on prison shirts into emblems of freedom. But it takes more than voting to make coercion benign.

In the first half of the twentieth century, democracy lost much of its credibility as popular governments collapsed or became oppressive or brutal. The reputation of democracy was redeemed by default by the obvious depravity of the Soviet bloc and other totalitarian countries. The fact that other forms of government failed catastrophically made democracy a comparative success story. Because democracy was usually not as oppressive as other forms of government it came to be equated with liberty.

The notion that democracy is the same as liberty is as absurd as the doctrine of the "democratic peace" and as dubious as the pending universal triumph of democracy. The fact that it would even be necessary to explain the difference is a sign of the political illiteracy of our times—a delusion fostered by those who seek to unleash the State in the name of the people.

THE FATAL CONFUSION

Throughout Western history, tyrants and tyrant apologists have sought to browbeat citizens into obedience by telling them that they are only obeying themselves—regardless of how much the subjects disagree with the government's edicts. Thomas Hobbes explained in 1652 how *Leviathan* is blameless:

> Because every subject is . . . author of all the actions and judgments of the Sovereign Instituted; it follows, that whatsoever he doth, it can be no injury to any of his subjects; nor ought he to be by any of them accused of injustice. For he that doth any thing by authority from another, doth therein no injury to him by whose authority he acted: But by this Institution of a commonwealth, every particular man is author of all the sovereign doth; and consequently he that complaineth of injury from his sovereign, complained of that whereof he himself is author.[3]

Hobbes sought to achieve domestic peace via obliging people to submit to almost anything the government inflicted. Hobbes sanctified the duty to submit by absurdly claiming that people are responsible for whatever government inflicts. Thus, government can never do the people wrong—and people never have a right to resist the government.

Hobbes' absolutism mortified friends of freedom in the late 1600s. However, later political philosophers used Hobbes' doctrines as foundations for new systems to glorify government. Jean-Jacques Rousseau made Hobbes' ruse a standard part of the mythology of democracy. Rousseau wrote: "Each man, in giving himself to all, gives himself to nobody. . . . Each of us puts his person and all his power in common under the supreme direction of the general will, and, in our corporate capacity, we receive each member as an indivisible part of the whole."[4] The general will is "infallible," and "to express the general will is to express each man's real will," Rousseau asserted and many people believed him. Rousseau taught that people need not fear a government animated by the general will because each citizen would be "obeying only myself."[5] And because the people's will would actuate government, the classical warnings on the danger of government power became null and void. The horrors of the French Revolution cast Rousseau's doctrines into temporary disrepute, but Rousseau's intellectual contortions permeated nineteenth- and twentieth-century thinking on democracy and government.

The growing passion for democracy helped devalue individual freedom. Lord Bryce noted in 1921 that "the idea of Liberty has been, though not renounced, yet forgotten or ignored. This is not merely because political Liberty, in the sense of the exercise of power by the people, has been won and needs no further thought, but also because the rights of the individual man to lead his life in his own way, work at what he will, take his pleasure as he will, save and spend for himself, are no longer . . . deemed to be a part of Liberty."[6] Freedom to vote was presumed to be the supreme freedom. As long as government permitted people a role in selecting rulers, governments became entitled to dictate how people must live.

Some U.S. presidents who have been most enthusiastic on seizing power have exonerated themselves by claiming that "the people did it." FDR declared in 1938, "Let us never forget that government is *ourselves* and not an alien power over us,"[7] and Bill Clinton declared in 1996 that "The Government is just the people, acting together—just the people acting together."[8] Invoking "the government is the people" is one of the easiest ways for a politician to shirk responsibility for his actions. This doctrine makes sense only if one assumes that government's victims are subconscious masochists and government is only fulfilling their secret wishes when it messes up their lives.

At the time when government power was soaring—in the 1930s and 1940s—American political thinking systematically disregarded the danger from government. Democracy became the purported champion of freedom in part because people were taught that democracies were inherently non-oppressive. Professor David Ciepley observed, "round the time of World War II, just as the American state was acquiring new levels of capacity for autonomous action, the State was dropped from American social science, as part of the reaction to the rise of totalitarianism. All traces of state autonomy, now understood as 'state coercion,' were expunged from the image of American democracy."[9] Professor Gabriel Almond explained the sanitized view of government power in 1960: "Instead of the concept of the 'state,' limited as it is by legal and institutional meanings, we prefer 'political system'; instead of 'powers,' which again is a legal concept in connotation, we are begging to prefer 'functions;' instead of 'offices' (legal again), we prefer 'roles'; instead of institutions,' which again directs us toward formal norms, 'structures.'" Ciepeley explained that "the emergence of Hitler and Stalin as the ultimate social engineers led American political scientists to forget their erstwhile Progressive allegiance to elite guidance, and what is more, to fall silent about all such activities in the American governmental system. If totalitarianism means elite social engineering, then American democracy must mean popular control."[10]

This doctrine has prospered more in the halls of academia than it has in the courts and legislatures of the nation. Courts, intended as a check on tyranny, routinely roll out red carpets for politicians and government agents to pointlessly subjugate American citizens.

For instance, in June 2005, the Supreme Court, by a 5-to-4 vote, gave government officials unlimited power to confiscate private land to give to other private citizens or entities. The case of *Kelo vs. New London* involved 15 Connecticut homeowners who were objecting to government plans to seize their homes to turn over their property to a private developer. There was nothing wrong with the homes being seized—the government did not even attempt to allege blight. Instead, it was simply a question that the government had a comprehensive plan that it believed would provide more revenue for itself and more economic stimulation than permitting people to continue residing in their homes.

The eminent domain case turned on the Fifth Amendment, which declares, among other things, "nor shall private property be taken for public use, without just compensation." While the Founding Fathers understood "public use" to mean land for post offices, forts, or government roads, today's new, improved constitutional thinking is all-inclusive. Justice John Paul Stevens, writing for the majority, declared that "public use" really meant "public purpose"—and, apparently anything that helps the government serves a public purpose. Stevens declared that even cases in which the government seizes one person's land to directly give it to another private citizen could meet this standard because, "Quite simply, the government's pursuit of a public purpose will often benefit individual private parties." Stevens declared that the Court would avoid "intrusive scrutiny in favor of affording legislatures broad latitude in determining what public needs justify the use of the takings power."[11] Thus, the Court frowned upon examining rationales or motives of politicians seizing private property—as if requiring evidence for the use of blunt force is "intrusive." His comment illustrated how the Court is often far more protective of politicians' prerogatives than of citizens' rights. The Court assumed that this seizure power would be used prudently—despite the long record of federal, state, and local officials using eminent domain for "Negro Removal" in the 1950s and 1960s.[12] Law professor Richard Epstein observed that, according to the Court's majority opinion, "New London had made its case when it asserted, without evidence, that the new projects would both increase tax revenues and create new jobs. It hardly mattered that its projections had been pulled out of thin air and were already hopelessly out of date when the case reached the Supreme Court."[13] The Court chose to sacrifice real rights for a will-of-the-wisp—any chance that government confiscation and expulsion of owners might provide a "net social benefit."

Justice Sandra Day O'Connor dissented to the *Kelo* decision, warning that "the specter of condemnation hangs over all property. Nothing is to prevent the State from replacing any Motel 6 with a Ritz-Carlton, any home with a shopping mall, or any farm with a factory." O'Connor explained how the decision would breed corruption, because "the fallout from this decision will not be random. The beneficiaries are likely to be those citizens with disproportionate influence and power in the political process, including large corporations and development firms."[14]

The Kelo decision was hailed by the editorial pages of both the *New York Times* and *Washington Post* and by law professors such as Harvard's David Barron, who gurgled that "The Supreme Court empowered cities to confront the next phase of urban development with imagination and energy."[15] The Supreme Court effectively decided that it is government revenue that makes the citizen free. Thus, whatever boosts government revenue—such as massive redevelopment plans—is a triumph of freedom, regardless of how many citizens' lives are ruined in the process, and regardless of whether the redevelopment plan flops. The fact that the homeowners in New London had the chance to vote for local officials did nothing to stop the government from razing their homes.

The notion that democracy guarantees liberty presumes that elected representatives cherish—or at least give a damn about—the rights of individual citizens. But there is scant evidence of such a class prejudice.

The Founding Fathers, having experienced the depredations of British customs agents, recognized the need to protect Americans from the arbitrary power of petty government officials. Thus, the Fourth Amendment "guarantees the right to be free from 'unreasonable searches and seizures,'" as Justice O'Connor noted in a 2001 dissent on the case of *Atwater v. Lago Vista*. This case began in 1997 when a policeman in Lago Vista, Texas, stopped Gail Atwater's pickup truck after he noticed that her two young children riding with her did not have their seatbelts fastened. Atwater had been driving 15 miles per hour through a residential area. Atwater never posed any threat to anyone; however, the policeman arrested her, handcuffed her, loaded her into his patrol car, and, Atwater's seatbelt unfastened, drove her to the police station where she was briefly jailed.

A majority of Supreme Court justices recognized that "Atwater's claim to live free of pointless indignity and confinement clearly outweighs anything the City can raise against it specific to her case"—but upheld the arrest anyhow.[16] As O'Connor summarized the case, police officer Bart "Turek was loud and accusatory from the moment he approached Atwater's car. Atwater's young children were terrified and hysterical. Yet when Atwater asked Turek to lower his voice because he was scaring the children, he responded by jabbing his finger in Atwater's face and saying, 'You're going to jail.'"[17] Turek failed to inform Atwater of her right to remain silent.

The provision of the Texas code that Atwater violated contained no provision for arresting violators. Atwater settled the charge by paying $50, after which she filed a lawsuit claiming that her constitutional rights had been violated. The seatbelt law Atwater violated may have been enacted by the Texas legislature under federal duress. Congress, seeking to maximize its own power, dictated that states that failed to enact laws penalizing drivers with unfastened seatbelts would lose much of their federal highway subsidy. Local and state law enforcement priorities are often driven by federal grants, rather than by any expressed popular opinions. In 1998, the Colorado legislature prohibited the state police from making traffic stops based solely for seatbelt violations; the Colorado State Police, fattened by a $500,000 federal grant, ignored the legislature.[18]

The Supreme Court declared that "If an officer has probable cause to believe that an individual has committed even a very minor criminal offense in his presence, he may, without violating the Fourth Amendment, arrest the offender."[19] The Court explained that if arrests were limited to only offenses for which the statute book includes arrests as punishments, the result could be a "systematic disincentive to arrest." Instead, the Court's ruling created a systematic bias in favor of accosting and handcuffing citizens. The Court also worried that putting any limits on police's right to arrest people for petty offenses could result in "personal liability" for officers who make such arrests. O'Connor, in a stout dissent, warned that "such unbounded discretion carries with it grave potential for abuse." O'Connor also mocked the Court majority for stressing that there was little evidence of "an epidemic of unnecessary minor-offense arrests." The fact that governments did not keep statistics on such abuses somehow justified entitling government agents to commit more abuses. O'Connor also noted that "If the State has decided that a fine, and not imprisonment, is the appropriate punishment for an offense, the State's interest in taking a person suspected of committing that offense into custody is surely limited, at best."[20]

It would be difficult for a Court verdict to more loudly trumpet the legal inferiority of private citizens vis-à-vis government enforcement officers. According to Capt. Steve Powell of the Colorado State Patrol, "Ninety percent of the cars out there are doing something that you can pull them over for. There are a jillion reasons people can be stopped—taillights, windshields cracked, any number of things."[21] There is no way to reconcile individual liberty with empowering the government to arrest almost everyone based on vague or all-expansive laws. The fact that legislators at some level of government voted on a law (which they may or may not have read) before enacting new penalties does nothing to loosen the handcuffs around citizens' wrists. The fact that people had the chance to vote for a member of Congress or a state legislator does nothing to lighten their subjugation when they encounter a government agent hungry to fill his quota for arrests. Legislators rarely rein in overzealous police or other enforcement agents when their aggression boosts government revenue.

The notion that democracy automatically produces liberty hinges on the delusion that "people are obeying themselves." But, as Sheldon Richman, the editor of *The Freeman,* commented, "When you rushed to finish your income tax return at the last minute on April 15, were you in fear of yourself and your fellow Americans or the IRS?"[22] People who exceed the speed limits are not "self-ticketed." People who fail to recycle their beer bottles are not self-fined, as if the recycling police were a mere apparition of a guilty conscience.

If the citizen is the government, why are there far harsher penalties for any private citizen who pushes, threatens, or injures a federal employee than the punishment for similar actions against private citizens? Why are governments allowed to claim sovereign immunity when their employees injure or kill private citizens?[23] Why is it perfectly acceptable and routine procedure for politicians and government employees to lie to citizens, but a federal crime for citizens (such as Martha Stewart) to lie to the government?[24] Many state government vehicles have license plates declaring, "For Public Use." But if a private citizen assumes that the license plate means what it says and drives off in the car, he will be charged with grand larceny. Yet, by assuring people that they are the government, this makes all the coercion, all the expropriation, all the intrusive searches, all the prison sentences for victimless crimes irrelevant.

DEGRADING LIBERTY IN THE NAME OF DEMOCRACY

In the era of the founding of the United States, Americans understood that liberty meant lack of coercion—especially lack of government coercion. "The Restraint of Government is the True Liberty and Freedom of the People" was a popular motto of the times.[25] John Phillip Reid, in his seminal work, *The Concept of Liberty in the Age of the American Revolution,* observed that liberty in the eighteenth century was largely thought of as freedom from arbitrary government.... The less a law restrained the citizen, and the more it restrained government, the better the law. Stated positively, the rule was that the 'Society whose laws least restrain the words and actions of its members, is most free.'"[26] This concept of freedom continued early into the twentieth century. The Supreme Court noted in 1923 that liberty "denotes not merely freedom from bodily restraint but also the right of the individual to contract, to engage in any of the common occupations of life, to acquire useful knowledge, to marry, to establish a home and bring up children, to worship God according to the dictates of his own conscience, and generally to enjoy those privileges long recognized as common law as essential to the orderly pursuit of happiness by free men."[27] A small amount of coercion—enough to secure respect of other people's rights and safety—is necessary to minimize coercion. The fact that some government coercion occurs does not mean that the citizen has no freedom.

Unfortunately, rising enthusiasm for democracy has clouded thinking on liberty. The Founding Fathers did not share the contemporary adoration of democracy. The word "democracy" was mentioned only twice in annual State of the Union messages between 1789 and 1900. But the word was invoked 189 times between 1901 and 2000.[28] Political scientist Elvin Lim noted that "Franklin Roosevelt was blatantly wrong when he claimed in his third inaugural that 'democratic aspiration is no mere recent phrase in human history.'"[29]

The more vehemently a president equates democracy with freedom, the greater the danger he likely poses to Americans' rights. President Abraham Lincoln was by far the most avid champion of democracy among nineteenth century presidents—and the president with the greatest visible contempt for the Constitution and the Bill of Rights.[30] Lincoln swayed people to view national unity as the ultimate test of the essence of freedom or self-rule. That Lincoln suspended habeas corpus, jailed 20,000 people without charges, forcibly shut down hundreds of newspapers that criticized him, and sent in federal troops to shut down state legislatures was irrelevant because he proclaimed "that this nation shall have a new birth of freedom, and that government of the people, by the people, for the people shall not perish from the earth."[31]

Praising democracy has long been among the best ways for presidents to aggrandize power. President Wilson pioneered democracy-as-salvation bosh. Yet his administration had the worst civil rights record since the Civil War— imposing Jim Crow restrictions for federal employees that resulted in the mass firing of black civil servants. After taking the nation into World War I, Wilson rammed a Sedition Act through Congress that empowered the feds to imprison anyone who muttered a kind word for the Kaiser or General Ludendorf.[32] Wilson pushed conscription through Congress—as if his goal of having "a seat at the table" at the post-war peace conferences entitled him to dispose of hundreds of thousands of American lives.

After World War I, Prohibition should have been the most valuable public education lesson of the early twentieth century, vivifying how an activist minority could capture the machinery of government to torment the majority. And yet, the pervasive abuses, dishonesty, and corruption of the federal war on alcohol made little or no impact on Americans' political thinking. H. L. Mencken commented on the presidential election of 1932: "Very little was heard during that campaign of the argument that Prohibition was essentially tyrannical and infamous. All the politicos were afraid to raise the point. They confined themselves to the contention that resuming brewing and distilling would make farmers rich. What they really had their eyes on, of course, was the revenue from Excises and licenses."[33] The abuses of Prohibition did nothing to make Americans wary of FDR greatly increasing the government's coercive power.

In his 1841 inaugural address, President William Henry Harrison declared, "The spirit of liberty is the sovereign balm for every injury which our institutions may receive."[34] But in the twentieth century, Americans came to expect more from government than from liberty. President Franklin Roosevelt, in a 1937 speech on the one hundred and fiftieth anniversary of the signing of the Constitution, declared that "even some of our own people may wonder whether democracy can match dictatorship in giving this generation the things it wants from government."[35] FDR's comment was part of his attack on those who opposed his seizure of power over property, wages, and contracts. Earlier that year, in his second inaugural address, he bragged, "In these last four years, we have made the exercise of all power more democratic; for we have begun to bring private autocratic powers into their proper subordination to the public's government."[36] When the Supreme Court found that many of Roosevelt's power grabs were unconstitutional, he announced plans to wreck the power of the Court by stacking it with new appointees—showing his contempt for any limits on his power.

FDR's presidency was the clearest turning point in the American understanding of freedom. In his 1941 State of the Union address, FDR announced the "four freedoms"—"freedom of speech and expression—everywhere in the world;" "freedom of every person to worship God in his own way everywhere in the world;" "freedom from want, which, translated into world terms, means economic understandings which will secure to every nation a healthy peacetime life for its inhabitants—everywhere in the world"; and "freedom from fear, which, translated into world terms, means a world-wide reduction of armaments to such a point and in such a thorough fashion that no nation will be in a position to commit an act of physical aggression against any neighbor—anywhere in the world."[37] FDR's revised freedoms ignored most of all the specific limitations on government power contained in the Bill of Rights. Now, instead of a liberty for each to live his own life and go his own way, Roosevelt offered freedom from fear and freedom from want—"freedoms" that require omnipresent government surveillance and perpetual government intervention. Roosevelt perennially invoked freedom as a pretext to increase government power. Roosevelt's promises of freedom for the entire world distracted attention from how his administration was subjugating Americans.

Freedom became increasingly bastardized in the decades after FDR. President Nixon, like most of his predecessors, encouraged Americans to be complacent about their liberty. In 1973, in his second inaugural address, he declared: "Let us be proud that our system has produced and provided more freedom and more abundance, more widely shared, than any other system in the history of the world."[38] Americans later learned that, at the time of Nixon's statement, the FBI was involved in a massive campaign to suppress opposition to the government and to the Vietnam War, and Nixon himself was involved in obstructing the investigation of the Watergate break-in and related crimes. But Nixon may not have seen such actions as a violation of liberty because, as he explained to interviewer David Frost in 1977, "When the president does it that means that it is not illegal." Frost, somewhat dumbfounded, replied, "By definition?" Nixon answered, "Exactly. Exactly."[39]

President George H. W. Bush, in a June 29, 1992, speech dedicating a new Drug Enforcement Agency office building, gushed, "I am delighted to be here to salute the greatest freedom fighters any nation could have, people who provide freedom from violence and freedom from drugs and freedom from fear."[40] Bush oversaw a vast expansion of the drug war—multiplying the number of no-knock raids, seizures of property from innocent people, and other incursions by federal drug agents.[41] Americans have gone from achieving freedom via kicking out the British army to being liberated by urinating into a federally approved cup. And yet, because Bush proclaimed that the goal was "freedom from drugs," all the DEA's violence was a triumph of freedom.

President Clinton openly scapegoated freedom for many problems caused by government (such as welfare programs). In a 1994 interview with MTV, he declared,

> When we got organized as a country and we wrote a fairly radical Constitution with a radical Bill of Rights, giving a radical amount of individual freedom to Americans, it was assumed that the Americans who had that freedom would use it responsibly. . . . What's happened in America today is, too many people live in areas where there's no family structure, no community structure, and no work structure. And so there's a lot of irresponsibility. And so a lot of people say there's too much personal freedom. When personal freedom's being abused, you have to move to limit it.[42]

The Bill of Rights did not give freedom to Americans; instead, the Bill of Rights was a solemn pledge by the government that it recognized and would not violate certain pre-existing rights of individuals. The Bill of Rights was not "radical" according to the beliefs of Americans of that era; instead, it codified rights both long recognized in English Common Law and purchased in blood during the Revolution. The Founding Fathers had difficulty getting the Constitution approved in many states not because it was "radical" in giving people rights—but because it was perceived as concentrating too much power to violate rights within the federal government.

Clinton often praised freedom at the same time that many of his policies unleashed government. In a 1997 brief to the Supreme Court, the Clinton administration asserted that "it is ordinarily reasonable for police officers to dispense with a pre-entry knock and announcement."[43] In other words, the Clinton administration sought to create a presumption of the legality of no-knock raids—despite hundreds of years of judicial precedent against such surprises. Perhaps from the Clinton administration view, government agents barging in on people with no warning was not a violation of people's freedom because government is the source of freedom.

President George W. Bush uses freedom and democracy interchangeably, as if they were two sides of the same coin. Bush explained to a Dutch journalist in May 2005: "Holland is a free country. It's a country where the people get to decide the policy. The Government just reflects the will of the people. That's what democracies are all about."[44] Later that day, he was questioned by another Dutch journalist:

Q. How do you define freedom?
The President. Freedom, democracy?
Q. Freedom as such.
The President. Well, I view freedom as where government doesn't dictate. Government is responsive to the needs of people. . . . That's what freedom— government is of the people. We say "of the people, by the people, and for the people." And a free society is one if the people don't like what is going

on, they can get new leaders. . . . That's free society, society responsive to people.[45]

In other speeches and comments, Bush mentions the need for governments to respect freedom of religion and women's rights, with other provisos sometimes tossed in. The periodic recitation of such laundry lists is supposed to inoculate him against criticism from his other comments on liberty.

Bush freedom is compatible with nearly unlimited power. Bush tosses freedom accolades to some of the world's most oppressive governments. Uzbekistan was among the most barbaric of former Soviet republics, renowned for vicious prosecutions of anyone who attended private Muslim prayer groups or distributed literature not preapproved by the government; the government boils alive dissidents and other suspected enemies of the regime.[46] Yet, in September 2002, Bush sent Uzbek President Islam Karimov a letter proclaiming his readiness "to work together to create a world which values people and promises them a future of freedom and hope."[47] Karimov may have used some of the U.S. aid he received to slaughter 500 peaceful demonstrators in 2005.(The Bush administration blocked international efforts to condemn Karimov for the massacres.)[48] The U.S. government is helping cover up Karimov's abuses because it wants to perpetuate U.S. military bases on Uzbek territory—which are vital for the U.S. vision of spreading freedom around the world.

The government of Kazakhstan, another central Asian tyranny, has collected more than $100 million in U.S. government handouts since George W. Bush became president, despite the government's record of torture and "extrajudicial killings," in the State Department's euphemism.[49] Yet Bush issued a joint statement with Kazak ruler Nursultan Nazarbayev pledging to "reiterate our mutual commitment to advance the rule of law and promote freedom of religion and other universal human rights."[50] Shortly after Bush hailed the Kazak government, it shut down 30 newspapers and television stations and roughed up and arrested journalists because the media had reported the Kazak president's billion-dollar Swiss bank account. U.S. aid to the Kazak government soared after it destroyed the independent media.

Sometimes, a government is certified as pro-freedom simply if its ruler does not object to Bush's warring at the United Nations Security Council. In a 2003 speech to the Australian parliament, Bush declared, "We see a China that is stable and prosperous, a nation that respects the peace of its neighbors and works to secure the freedom of its own people."[51] At that time, the Chinese government was brutally suppressing the Muslims in western China, razing mosques, and conducting mass arrests and detentions, as well as crushing freedom of speech, locking up or killing Christian missionaries, and torturing prisoners. Perhaps Bush was not aware that the Chinese Communist

Party leadership was not popularly elected. Bush portrayed the Chinese government as "securing the freedom of its own people"—even though the Chinese government itself was by far the biggest threat to the rights and liberties of these people. Bush may have presumed that everyone the government did not shoot or imprison had been freed. Or perhaps Bush sees China as an example of his top-down vision of how freedom originates. In a January 29, 2004, interview with the Middle East Television Network, Bush declared, "Now, I recognize not every government is going to fashion a free society in the vision of America."[52]

Nations whose governments kowtow to the U.S. government are by definition free. On May 10, 2005, Bush visited Tbilisi, the capital of Georgia, and told an adoring crowd that "Georgia is today both sovereign and free and a beacon of liberty for this region and the world."[53] Georgia had become a democracy a mere year and a half before. The government had yet to reach Jeffersonian standards, due to pervasive torture, killings of dissidents and potential opponents, and jailing people without charges.[54] Human Rights Watch reported that Georgia's government is "one of the most corrupt in the world . . . and has a record of persistent and widespread human rights abuses."[55] But, because the government sent troops to Iraq and permits U.S. troops to base themselves in the country, Georgia is a "beacon of liberty."

While gushing praise of freedom at almost every opportunity, Bush, like Clinton, has also scapegoated freedom. In a November 29, 2001, speech to federal attorneys, Bush proclaimed that "we must not let foreign enemies use the forums of liberty to destroy liberty itself. Foreign terrorists and agents must never again be allowed to use our freedoms against us."[56] But the record of federal investigations show that the government had more than enough power and resources to detect the 9/11 terrorists before they wreaked havoc. The fact that numerous government agencies botched their duty to defend the American people became, in Bush's eyes, a failure of freedom itself.

Bush portrays unchecked executive power as the bulwark of liberty. In 2001, a congressional committee sought to subpoena documents on the more than 30-year involvement of the Federal Bureau of Investigation with a killing spree by Boston's Irish mafia that left 20 people dead. (The FBI obstructed justice to block the prosecution of its favored killers and to send innocent men to prison for life in their place.) Bush invoked executive privilege to thwart the subpoena, declaring: "The Founders' fundamental purpose in establishing the separation of powers in the Constitution was to *protect individual liberty.* Congressional pressure on executive branch prosecutorial decisionmaking is inconsistent with separation of powers and *threatens individual liberty.*"[57] Perhaps the highest freedom is that of the executive branch to continue covering up its involvement in mass murder. Bush could make such an invocation only because so many peoples' minds have gone blank on the subject of freedom.

Bush exploits and twists the word *freedom* to provide cover for whatever policy he is pushing at that moment. Perhaps Bush's clearest corruption to the meaning of liberty is his endless invocations of the word to sanctify his foreign aggression and war on terrorism. Bush declared in July 2003 that, because of the U.S. invasion of Iraq, people are "going to find out the word 'freedom' and 'America' are synonymous."[58] Freedom is equated with U.S. military triumphs—with the imposition of the will of the U.S. government on foreign peoples. In his second inaugural address, Bush invoked freedom and liberty more than 40 times. But none of these comments were in reference to restrictions on U.S. government power. Instead, they sanctified the president's right to forcibly intervene abroad wherever he believes necessary. In a televised speech from Fort Bragg, North Carolina in June 2005, Bush invoked freedom and liberty more than 20 times to sanctify the U.S. occupation of Iraq.

Bush Freedom hinges on government as the savior of freedom. Debates over the Patriot Act provided further opportunity for degrading the American vocabulary. Attorney General John Ashcroft titled the August 2003 launch speech of his national Patriot Act promotion tour "Securing Our Liberty: How America is Winning the War on Terror." Earlier in 2003, Ashcroft characterized Justice Department antiterrorist deliberations this way: "Every day we are asking each other, what can we do to be more successful in securing the freedoms of America and sustaining the liberty, the tolerance, the human dignity that America represents."[59] In a July 2002 Senate Judiciary Committee hearing, in response to pointed questions about federal law enforcement procedures, Ashcroft babbled: "I believe what we are securing is liberty. And if what we are securing is liberty, there has to be that serious attention to the freedoms involved, and I want to give that in every respect."[60] Ashcroft's pious rhetoric and meaningless tautologies succeeded only because few listeners had their brains switched on. Ashcroft's successor as Attorney General, Alberto Gonzales, used the same rhetoric to sanctify the Patriot Act: "Congress did a good job in striking the appropriate balance between protecting our country and securing our liberties."[61] The Patriot Act authorized confiscations of travelers' money (in violation of a Supreme Court ruling), the use of new surveillance software that could vacuum up millions of people's e-mail without a search warrant, nationwide "roving wiretaps,"[62] and seizing library, bookstore, and other business and financial records based solely on subpoenas issued by FBI field offices on the flimsiest of pretexts.[63] The act also greatly increased the power of the so-called Foreign Intelligence Surveillance Court—a kangaroo court that meets in secret, never permits any defense attorney to appear to challenge the government, and approves 99.9 percent of all the wiretaps the

FBI requests.[64] After the Patriot Act was signed, there was a hundredfold increase in the number of emergency spying warrants issued solely on the Attorney General's command—and later rubber-stamped by the Foreign Intelligence Surveillance Court.[65] But all the violations of Americans' rights and liberties by federal agents are irrelevant because the proclaimed intent of the Patriot Act is to "secure liberty." There is no freedom without security, and no security without absolute power. Thus, if you favor freedom, you must support permitting the president to lock people away forever without any evidence, to order torture, and to lay waste to foreign lands based on whatever bogus claims he invokes. And anyone who advocates maintaining the old-time limits on government power is a "September the Tenth" American—and not "with us, but against us."

Bush's power grabs have been far less controversial than Clinton's—in part because most of the conservative media continue to be enthralled by their man. The ease with which Bush, Ashcroft, and others defined the war on terrorism as a crusade for freedom is proof of the political illiteracy and docility of both American citizens and most of the American media.

Freedom has become merely another invocation to sanctify power. The more often he invokes freedom, the more deference Bush expects to receive. Bush uses the word "freedom" as an incantation to lull people to sleep—to douse any concerns about his latest expansion of government power, his latest deployment of U.S. troops, his most recent executive order. Bush maximizes confusion over freedom in order to minimize resistance. In ancient Rome, as long as the emperor praised the Senate, the republic was presumed to be safe. In contemporary America, as long as the president gushes over freedom, then the people's rights are considered safe. And the more a politician praises freedom, the more leeway he has to destroy it.

"Open the door to freedom! Put a strong man at the helm!" was the campaign slogan for National Socialist candidates in the 1932 *Reichstag* elections.[66] The fact that Nazi politicians invoked freedom to win votes did nothing to protect people from their subsequent tyranny. "Strong leader" is also a favorite Bush invocation. The *Washington Post* noted in September 2005, "The term 'strong leader' appears in at least 98 speeches [Bush] has given during his White House years . . . and was the subtext of his 2004 campaign strategy."[67] Simply because Bush used the same "freedom and strong leader" theme used before the collapse of the Weimar Republic does not prove that vultures of doom are circling Washington. But it is a warning that illiteracy on liberty and craving for a strong leader can be a fatal combination.

Surprisingly, Bush's bastardizing of freedom has stirred no controversy. Instead, people who should know better have embraced his Orwellian distortions. R. J. Rummel, professor emeritus at the University of Hawaii, is the most vocal proponent of the "democratic peace." In early 2005, Rummel urged the destruction of American freedom to prevent any loss of support for Bush's military crusade to spread democracy. Rummel bewailed, "One has to be pretty far on the left not to see the media as biased against freeing Iraqi from tyranny. The bad news is generally highlighted, and the good news ignored. . . . Obviously, this is an attempt to repeat the glory days of the Vietnam War when the media turned military victory into defeat." Rummel hectored that "we cannot afford to have the media freely providing aid and comfort to the enemy. The stakes are too high." Rummel justified censorship because, if the media did not cease undermining Bush's war, terrorists would launch an attack on U.S. cities and "survivors will violently attack reporters, commentators, and the offices of the media they believe to be partly responsible."[68] Censorship thus becomes necessary to save democracy, which will save freedom, except for the censorship.

Just because a president's comments are insipid does not mean they are innocuous. Americans cannot expect to preserve their rights if they take their political reality from the words of the person with the most to gain from subverting freedom. When people take their political reality from their rulers, they are already more than half way to servitude.

The more confused people's thinking becomes, the easier it is for rulers to invoke freedom to destroy freedom. The issue is not simply Clinton's or Bush's absurd statements on freedom but a cultural–intellectual smog in which politicians have unlimited leeway to redefine freedom. If politicians can redefine freedom at their whim, then they can raze limits on their own power.

A MODERN MYSTERY

It is difficult to understand why intelligent Americans continue to complacently assume that being permitted to vote will provide all the protection their rights and liberties need. Country singer Merle Haggard observed: "In 1960, when I came out of prison as an ex-convict, I had more freedom under parolee supervision than there's available to an average citizen in America right now . . . God almighty, what have we done to each other?"[69] Haggard might overstate the loss of liberty slightly; however, few politicians and pundits who assure Americans that they have ample freedom today experienced parole in the early 1960s.

How is democracy supposed to protect liberty these days? Today's Americans demonstrate little of the passion for freedom that their forefathers showed. How many young people and college students would happily permit the government to monitor all their e-mail in return for unlimited free music downloads? How many Wal-Mart gift certificates would it require for a typical citizen to forfeit all his Fourth Amendment rights, entitling government agents to search his car, house, and himself whenever they chose without a warrant? How many McDonald's gift certificates would it take to sway a person to pledge never to publicly criticize the president? How many Americans would agree to cease reading newspapers (and their pesky editorials) in return for free cable television (including HBO, Showtime, and other premium channels)? How many senior citizens would agree to support the ruling party in perpetuity in return for a 20 percent boost in their Social Security benefits? How many people would happily surrender most of their constitutional rights in return for a president's promise that he will thereby make them safe?

Many Americans are far more interested in being cared for than being left alone. This is why American democracy is becoming one of caretakers and cage keepers, instead of representatives with narrowly prescribed duties.

How many people today value democracy primarily as a means to forcibly live at someone else's expenses? In contrast, how many people value democracy as a way to deter government from exploiting or abusing any individual or group? How many people value democracy as a meal ticket, and how many value it as a bulwark for rights and liberty? Dick Meyer, editorial director of CBSNews.com, observed that voters "see the government like a pharmaceutical company. They feel entitled to cheap if not free access to products and services, they want everything to be risk-free, and they want compensation if something goes wrong. Politicians of both parties have been perfectly willing to pretend the world can work that way."[70]

Many voters don't understand or don't care about freedom. Many don't recognize that permitting government to seize boundless power negates liberty. Many voters don't grasp how government surveillance is a threat to liberty. Most politicians don't appear to care about liberty either, except when they are in opposition and periodically invoke it to score points against the ruling party. Most of the media are government dependents, so they are not going to champion restraints on government, either.

It is as if the mere invocation of the word *democracy* will provide liberty with all the defense it needs—or deserves. Democracy will supposedly guarantee freedom even if most people don't care about freedom. This is the same kind of wishful thinking that props up the "democratic peace" argument.

America's political future is imperiled by the loss of a clear concept of freedom that provides a boundary line between the citizen and the State. The more clearly Americans understand freedom, the more constrained presidents will be. Politicians and government propaganda sway people to lower their resistance—at the same time that rulers invoke a popular sanction to stretch their power.

The majority has no right to dispose of the minority's freedom. Poet and political pamphleteer John Milton wrote, "It is just that a less number compel a greater to retain their liberty rather than all be slaves."[71] Milton wrote those words in the heat of the English Civil War, when the Cavaliers sought to crush resistance to Charles I, despite his oppression. If most people are so apathetic or deluded by political speeches as to not object to the shredding of their liberties, is the minority obliged to surrender their liberties as well? Is the minority entitled to liberty only if the majority shares the minority's valuation of independence? Are some people obliged to let other people drag them to political ruin?

Yet, at the current time, the tyranny of the majority is not the primary peril to liberty. Tocqueville warned in 1835, "If ever freedom is lost in America, that will be due to the omnipotence of the majority."[72] However, freedom in America is being lost not primarily because of majority demands, but because of people's acquiescence to one political ploy after another. Attention Deficit Democracy has made it far easier for rulers to exploit presumed majority approval to raze limits on government power. Mass ignorance permits politicians to pick off rights one by one, until citizens wake up one day to find themselves defenseless against their masters.

It is better that government be representative than non-representative. But it is more important that governments respect people's rights than fulfill some people's wishes to oppress other people. The rules that a person must obey are more important than the identity of the nominal rulers. The existence of democracy does not change the meaning of individual liberty. A person is free or not free, regardless of how many people approve his fetters.

The Founding Fathers fought for a government that would respect their rights, not for a government that would allow them to forcibly micromanage the lives of their fellow citizens.

The only way to claim that democracy automatically protects liberty is to say that the only freedom that matters is "freedom for the government to rule in the name of the people."

Democracy promised to release the chains on people that kept them in their place, subject to despots, aristocrats, or other successful power-grabbers. However, if democracy becomes merely another means to pull people down, then it has destroyed its promise and become a menace. It is not a question of whether democracy is preferable to dictatorship. Instead, it is a question of whether democracy lives up to its billing—whether democracy deserves the adulation politicians claim. Coercion is coercion, regardless of who approves or who suffers or who profits.

The fact that democratic governments violate liberty does not prove that democracy is uniquely or inherently evil. Instead, this is simply what governments do. In the same way that a political candidate's lies don't create a presumption that his opponent is honest, the fact that democracies routinely violate rights and liberties creates no presumption that other forms of government would not be worse.

CHAPTER 12

Conclusion

Self-government is flattered to destroy self-government.
—John Taylor, 1821[1]

The magic word democracy has become so all-powerful that all the inherited limitations on governmental power are breaking down before it.
—Friedrich Hayek, 1976[2]

IN THE 1770S, AMERICANS WON THEIR FREEDOM from foreign rule thanks to the "de-sacralizing" of the British monarch.[3] The mists before Americans' eyes dissipated and they recognized that King George III was a mere mortal and often a dangerous buffoon. Rather than being awed by the titles of the king's ministers and appointees, they saw them as power-mad individuals determined to make Americans kowtow. Instead of continuing to genuflect toward London, they recognized that the claims by the British parliament to absolute power over the colonies were the death of their own rights and liberty. Instead of swallowing the "virtual representation" myths by which the British government sanctified itself (claiming that Americans were magically represented in Parliament), they recognized tyranny for what it was and revolted. This de-sacralizing was part of what Sen. John Taylor described in 1822 as the American people's "commission to overturn political idolatry."[4]

It is time to de-sacralize democracy. Being crowned a winner by the Electoral College does not give one American the right to dispose of all other Americans' lives and liberties. If we want a new birth of freedom, we must cease glorifying oppressive political machinery. Most of what the government does has little or nothing to do with "the will of the people." The combination of ignorant voters and conniving politicians is far more likely to ruin than rescue this nation. In the same way that our forefathers in the 1770s refused to be grabbed off the streets and pressed into His Majesty's navy, so today's Americans must cease permitting politicians to impose one scheme and fraud after another.

Democracy is merely a form of government. It is not a mode of salvation. It is not a catapult to the Promised Land. It is not a penicillin that cures all politically transmitted diseases. It is good for some things—especially for peacefully removing bad rulers. But the ability to remove bad rulers provides no assurance that good rulers will take their place.

When Georgia governor Lester Maddox was criticized in the late 1960s for the abysmal conditions in his state's prisons, he blamed the problem on the poor caliber of the convicts. Similarly, with contemporary democracy, many people talk as if the system's failures are simply the result of the poor quality of today's politicians. People exonerate themselves by pointing at the people they voted for. But the problem is far deeper than the current crop of rascals in Washington. If Americans want less venal politicians, there is no substitute for a higher class of citizens.

"We must count upon a progressively critical, skeptical public opinion, incapable of degradation. . . . Such a popular mind does not of course exist, but it is for us to determine whether we shall increase or decrease the possibilities of that mind. Some of us aspire toward a state where you can fool fewer and fewer of the people less and less of the time," wrote Gertrude Besse King on the eve of the United States entry to World War I.[5]

Americans' thinking has not become "incapable of degradation"; it has not become more difficult to fool most of the people at crucial times; and the emergence of a "critical, skeptical public opinion" now seems as likely as 25-cent-a-gallon gasoline. Americans proved as gullible regarding the 1999 U.S. bombing of Serbia and the 2003 invasion of Iraq as they were with Wilson's "make the world safe for democracy" antics.

Most of the lofty hopes of democratic theorists from a century ago have long since been shattered. Citizens have not risen up to rein in rulers or to demand an end to their oppression. Instead, people have tacitly accepted the defining down of democracy. Most citizens appear satisfied with the biannual invitation to visit polling places and register a preference between officially approved candidates. Many citizens are unable to recognize foul play regardless of how brazenly politicians betray their oaths of office. Liberty has been at the wrong end of the shooting gallery for decades, and the political assaults have intensified during the past two presidencies.

Have we passed the point where the people can rein in the government? Has the government amassed enough power, established enough precedents, and squelched enough opposition that its further growth is unstoppable? What is the tipping point to tyranny, and have we passed it? At what point can American democracy be considered a failure? Unless there are profound and widespread changes in how Americans view government power, any hope for a revival of individual rights will be lost.

What will it take to awake Americans to the rising political peril? When the government spends the nation into ruin? When the government launches dishonest, unjustified wars around the world? When the government persists in torturing people, and lying about the torture? How many people does the government have to imprison without charges before Americans recognize the threat? How many people must the government victimize before Americans recognize the predatory nature of the State?

Why do people continue to expect elections to produce saviors, or at least quasi-saviors? Consider a private job application process in which applicants were effectively encouraged to tell as many lies as possible—the gaudier, the better; to viciously smear all other job applicants; and to repeatedly offer to bribe the people in charge of the hiring decision. Few people would expect such a process to result in good people being hired. It would be especially re-grettable if the person selected could not be fired for four years. And yet—this is how Americans now fill purportedly the most important job in the country.

If we accept most voters' ignorance, politicians fanning mass fears, and government's nearly boundless power, then what sort of political system are we left with? Sticking the label "democracy" upon it comforts and reassures peo-ple. But it is an oppressive sham nonetheless.

It is unrealistic to expect the typical American to become a devoted reader of both the *Congressional Record* and *Federal Register,* or even to consistently check the footnotes in dissenting Supreme Court opinions. There are no signs that Americans are on the verge of becoming Super Citizens, more enthralled by federal budget estimates than by baseball batting averages.

What is needed is a political system that will not self-destruct in spite of the ignorance or laziness of common citizens. There are basically two alterna-tives. We can either embrace paternalism and openly admit that the govern-ment must protect people from themselves (and from their foolish political opinions), or we can reduce the size and scope of government to something that the average citizen can better understand.

It is possible to have a far better political system even if citizens do not immerse themselves in the arcana of government. Changes in the size of government and reversals in the mental defaults that people bring to the political arena are the keys.

Following are a few points that can help curb Leviathan and revive liberty.

RECOGNIZING GOVERNMENT FORCE

Expunging delusions about government is the first step to restoring Americans' rights. Idealism on liberty demands brutal realism on the nature of power. Government is not some well-meaning abstraction. Citizens must recognize the daily peril they face from the power of a traffic cop to handcuff them for a seatbelt violation, the power of an IRS agent to seize their bank accounts based on a wrongful suspicion of tax evasion, the power of the City Council to seize their home and render the land underneath it to a campaign contributor, or the power of a president to immerse the nation in endless foreign conflicts. The question is not how many citizens are being coerced or wronged by the government at any specific time. The issue is the constantly growing arsenal of legal penalties the State can deploy against the citizen.

The fact that government is coercive must be revived as the first truth of political thought. Governing means, more often than not, compelling submission by threat of force. History offers endless lessons on the dangers of dictators, both petty and grand. Yet, the perils of arbitrary power vanish again and again in the mists of official propaganda and intellectual confusion. The more that philosophers cloak the nature of the State, the more their systems are biased in favor of servitude.

The most dangerous illusion is that government has been tamed once and for all. As long as humans are humans, coercion can be deadly. Coercion is far more effective at repressing than at uplifting. It is time to recognize the limits of coercion as a tool for individual and social salvation. This was something recognized in theological circles hundreds of years ago, but the political realm is lagging behind.

No institutional changes will help if there are not profound changes in the attitude of tens of millions of Americans toward government. The prerequisite to the revival of liberty is for Americans to take government off the pedestal in their own thinking. Many Americans are far more craven to officialdom than they realize. The more deference government receives, the more damage politicians can inflict.

REVIVING REPRESENTATIVE GOVERNMENT

Myths about democracy make citizens unfit for self-government. The more hokum people swallow about democracy, the less likely they are to harvest the benefits of representative government.

America was born as a republic—with limited government powers, carefully crafted checks and balances, and distinct roles for the people, for legislators, for judges, and for the executive branch. Americans these days are supposed to be content with "democracy"—regardless of how much of the strength and safeguards of the original Constitution have been lost.

"Representative government" is a phrase far less prone to induce mass delusions than is democracy. "Democracy" sounds like automatic pilot—that the government will serve the people simply because that is part of the mission statement. In contrast, the term "representative government" sounds more hit and miss. There is no transcendence in the term "representative government"—nothing to make people believe that government bureaus magically fulfill the rhetoric of presidential speech writers. Representatives are merely representatives, not incarnations of the General Will or the voice of God. Instead, they are usually simply people who preferred the pursuit of power to other ways of making a buck. Even when representative government works tolerably well, it is difficult to inspire the representatives to do much more than hustle for their own reelection.

To recognize the benefit of representative government, merely consider the alternative—despotism. And it will not matter if the despotism is blessed by theology, or by the most respected graduate schools in the nation, or by the collusion of the media and the Establishment. Despotism will deny people any voice on basic public policy issues that impact their lives.

RESTORING THE RULE OF LAW

The Founding Fathers viewed the Bill of Rights as a sacred compact between the government and the people. Presidents and members of Congress take an oath to uphold the Constitution—and thus to respect the rights recognized and guaranteed by the Bill of Rights. Insofar as the feds trample the Bill of Rights, the government is illegitimate. Insofar as the government perennially violates the Bill of Rights, it becomes an aggressor against the American people.

The Founding Fathers sought to craft a structure in which government would be forever subservient to the law. If the rulers are above the law, then law becomes merely a tool of oppression, not a bulwark of the rights of the people. As long as rulers are above the law, citizens have the same type of freedom that slaves had on days when their masters chose not to beat them.

The Founding Fathers sought to boost the odds of good presidents by carefully confining the power of the nation's chief executive officer. Almost all the reforms since 1933 have loosened or severed those binds.

Americans cannot expect to have good presidents if presidents are permitted to make themselves czars. At this point, every president is more likely to be corrupted by power than his predecessor, since he inherits more power than his predecessor did upon his inauguration.

The president and his top officials should face the same perils and procedures common citizens face when they are accused of breaking the law. To investigate the president and his top aides is not to imperil the American people. In fact, seeing a president answer for his actions—if not his crimes—would be uplifting. But this is something that happens less than once a decade in this nation, and even then, recent presidents have paid no lasting price. It is interesting to consider the subsequent course of American foreign policy if Lyndon Johnson or Richard Nixon had been tried, convicted in federal court, and publicly punished for committing war crimes.

RECOGNIZING THE LIMITS OF LEGITIMACY

"Democratically elected" should mean something more than "successfully conned." Would Bush have been reelected president if his administration had opened the files and disclosed what it knew and when it knew it regarding the Iraqi weapons of mass destruction, Saddam's non-role in 9/11, and the administration's determined effort to go to war with Iraq by falsifying a threat?

Insofar as Bush was reelected as the result of lying about or withholding evidence of his first term as president, his power is illegitimate. The same was true of Clinton's second term and Nixon's second term—election victories gained in part by deceit and suppression of information. Of course, if John Kerry had won the 2004 election via deceit, his power would also have been illegitimate. Bush's illegitimacy should, at a minimum, create an overwhelming presumption against permitting the federal government to seize new powers or start new wars.

Americans must recover sufficient self-respect to become intolerant of official lies. With the current docility to pervasive deceits, "good government" is when politicians lie to the people for the public good, and "bad government" is when politicians lie for their own selfish interest. And how can you distinguish between the two? You have to trust politicians to tell you which is which.

The easiest way to stack the deck in favor of honesty is to reduce the number of cards politicians can hold. The smaller the government, the fewer dead bodies it will likely need to hide. The less power government possesses, the more difficult it will be for rulers to exploit people's ignorance.

In politics, "positive thinking" is often a slave's virtue, something people do to delude themselves about the burdens and chains being placed upon them. It is as foolish for citizens to congratulate themselves for thinking well of the typical president as it is for workers to think well of a CEO who is looting their pension fund.

Instead of asking, "Whom should we trust with all this power?' Americans should ask, "How much power can any politician be personally trusted with?" The issue is not whether Republicans or Democrats are more trustworthy, but whether any politician with nearly boundless power is trustworthy. Does a politician become more trustworthy as he snares more power to suppress the evidence of his falsehoods?

Legitimacy must be earned via honesty and obedience to the law and to the Constitution. Americans can trust the Constitution, or unquestioningly trust their rulers. If they trust rulers who blatantly violate the Constitution, then they place themselves on the political chopping block.

RECOVERING A HEALTHY DISDAIN

There will be scant political progress in the United States until enough Americans recover their forefathers' disdain for Washington. The more things Washington has screwed up, the more powerful and respected Washingtonians have become. In the past decades, there has never been any penalty or liability for the federal government as a whole, regardless of how many of its salvation schemes blew up on the launch pad. Nor has there been any cost paid by the Washington establishment that embraced and championed intervention after intervention. Instead, this Establishment looked at each question through the prism of maintaining its own prestige and power. "Do no harm to government power" is the Washington version of the Hippocratic oath. Policies can be amended, and on very rare occasion, programs abolished—but Leviathan must continue its advance.

Americans must be wary of fixes that merely distract attention and breed docility. One of the clearest examples of a bait-and-switch Washington solution is the Bipartisan Campaign Reform Act (BCRA) of 2002. For the prior decade, much of the media and many politicians howled about the pox of "money in politics." The BCRA purportedly fixed the problem. In reality, the law prohibited most issue ads on television or radio in the months before a presidential or congressional election. As Justice Antonin Scalia noted in a dissent to the Supreme Court decision upholding the law, the BCRA "cuts to the heart of what the First Amendment is meant to protect: the right to criticize the government."[6] The 2002 legislation became simply another in the long history of Incumbent Protection Acts. Republicans exploited the law in 2004 to seek to intimidate groups, such as Rock the Vote, whose ads criticized the president.[7] BCRA illustrates why politicians cannot be trusted to reform politics. Congressmen railed about the danger of special interests—and then crafted legislation to suppress opposition. Campaign finance reform continues to be one of the great false hopes of our time. Power will corrupt, regardless of the rules politicians concoct to collect money from government beneficiaries.

Politicians have no incentive to learn from their mistakes if the clearest lesson is that their power should be reduced. There is no reason to assume that "the system" itself will hit the brakes and announce that it possesses too much power. This is simply not how Leviathans work. Remorse is a trait of individuals, not bureaucracies and political parties. The default now is for expansion of government power. There is no automatic self-correcting mechanism in a political system in which so many people profit from other people's subjugation.

REPELLING LEVIATHAN

Leviathan is premised on government's need to control the people. Democracy rests on people's right to control the government. The conflict between these two principles generates much of the deceit that permeates contemporary politics. One result is the continual defining down of democracy to allow Leviathan to stake ever more claims over the daily lives of the American people. Yet, regardless of how much sway government captures over people's lives, it will supposedly still be a democracy because the government continues to permit people to vote.

The more Leviathan, the less democracy. Leviathan inherently raises government above the people. Government power becomes the great insulator, shielding the rulers from the citizenry. Nowadays, "in the name of the people" is close enough for democracy. The more subservient contemporary democracies become to Leviathan, the more they resemble Soviet-era "People's Democracies."

The larger Leviathan grows, the more irrelevant popular preferences become. If the majority voted that lions should no longer bite people, that would not make it safe to open the zoos and let lions wander down Main Streets. Similarly, a majority vote that Big Government should not be oppressive does not make Big Government benign. The issue is not what ignorant people want: the issue is the momentum of coercive power. For instance, on torture,

the question was never whether 51 percent or more of Americans favored brutalizing detainees. Because of widespread public fear of more terrorist attacks
after 9/11, the president was able to seize absolute power and keep almost all
of his interrogation rulings and policies secret. The checks-and-balances completely failed, as neither the legislative nor the judicial branch showed the will
to stop U.S. government agents from violating the Anti-Torture Act.

Americans must recognize the contempt for the common man upon
which Leviathan is built. It is cynical to expect salvation from coercion and
subjugation, rather than from incentives and innovation. It is cynical to expect
that humanity's problems will be solved by finding better masters, rather than
by removing the burdens and binds on common citizens. Multiplying the
number of people receiving a Masters of Public Administration is no recipe for
nirvana.

George Orwell observed in 1944, "The sin of nearly all left-wingers from
1933 onward is that they have wanted to be anti-Fascist without being anti-
totalitarian."[8] Similarly, the sin of most political activists today is that they
want to be anti-conservative or anti-liberal, anti-Republican or anti-Democra-
tic, without being anti-Leviathan. But it will take more than changing the
names and party affiliations of the people violating the Constitution to revive
American liberty. It will take more than denouncing and demonizing opponents to restore the Bill of Rights.

American society and the American media may be so addicted to government that no evidence of political incompetence or treachery can discredit
Leviathan. It is as if the need for Leviathan is so far beyond questioning that
all we can do is lament that our rulers are often knaves. Are we reduced to the
medieval practice of merely hoping and praying that the next king will not
slaughter en masse?

We must cease expecting government to be better than it has been. No
one can redeem Leviathan. No one can reconcile government supremacy and
individual liberty. There is no way to revive self-government without slashing
government power.

No matter what political changes are made, vesting coercive power in
some people—even elected ones—will usually work out badly. In the near
term, the goal of political efforts should be to reduce the harm government inflicts. Minimizing damage, rather than attaining utopia here and abroad,
should be the target. Because political action will routinely be both inefficient
and deceitful, private effort is far more reliable for forward progress.

Once government expands beyond a narrow confine, people will be badly
governed, regardless of whether the masses or elites are making decisions. The
answer to the problems of democracy is not to crown a monarch or to install
an aristocracy. Instead, the answer is to radically decrease the power of gov-

ernment—any government. Democracy is a poor way to run other people's lives.

REVIVING THE SPIRIT OF LIBERTY

Many Americans no longer value freedom enough to make any effort to understand government or political action. If people choose not to think, then they have chosen to submit. If people choose to make no effort to understand the machinations of government, then they have chosen to be political victims. If people choose to disregard past lies and abuses, they choose to sacrifice themselves to the next liar and abuser.

It is unclear whether liberty can be revived in America. It is unclear how many Americans still give a damn about freedom—still give a damn about the chance to carve out their own lives according to their own values. It is unclear how many people would suffer any inconvenience or notoriety for voicing or supporting unpopular views. It is unclear how many Americans have the courage to decry government abuses that the majority tolerates or applauds.

The failures of Attention Deficit Democracy are a reminder to Americans to place their faith in themselves and in liberty. There is no reason to continue expecting some "Great Leap Forward" in the caliber of government and the integrity of politicians. Instead, the government in the coming years will be like the government in preceding years—often oppressive, chronically inept, and frequently deceptive. The success of recent power grabs, the reelections of two profoundly dishonest presidents, and the collapse of intelligent oversight or opposition in Congress illustrate why the high road and politics will rarely, if ever, intersect.

Is American democracy in a death spiral? The belief in American uniqueness blinds many people to the growing political decay. We must recognize that mankind has not yet devised stable, lasting institutions that can safeguard rights without spawning oppression. Almost all the previous solutions have eventually failed. No surefire means has been found to assure that coercive power will be used to protect, rather than oppress and exploit. It is folly to trust politicians with any more power than the bare minimum.

If we cannot have honest politicians, at least we can have rulers with fewer levers to destroy private lives and livelihoods. If we cannot have honest elected officials, at least we can have less dangerous liars. It is far easier to reduce politicians' power than to raise their characters.

America needs a higher grade of patriotism. It is not patriotic to ignore violations of the Constitution. It is not patriotic to "look the other way" when politicians ravage rights. It is not patriotic to pretend that politicians are entitled to all the power they can grab, at least until they get impeached or indicted. It is not patriotic to give the benefit of the doubt to people trying to shackle you.

Americans must begin to think again as free citizens, and not like wholly owned subsidiaries of Washington. We will know that Americans have regained the right perspective toward Washington when a negligent congressman dreads a public meeting with his constituents the same way the average citizen anticipates an IRS audit.

Government is far more likely to destroy us than to raise us. Americans have long been taught to count on their rulers to protect and rescue them. But a bogus panacea is worse than no panacea at all. And Leviathan is the most bogus panacea of them all.

Acknowledgments

OVER THE YEARS, DISCUSSIONS AND EXCHANGES WITH MANY people have helped me gain some insight into the problems of democracy, mass ignorance, and Leviathan. I would like to thank James Petersen, Jacob Hornberger, Claire Wolfe, Robert Meier, Nebojsa Malic, Brian Wilson, Jeff Tucker, and one friend who requested anonymity and a waiver of liability. My research and thinking on some of the issues in this book were aided by excellent websites, including Antiwar.com, FFF.org (the website of the Future of Freedom Foundation), and LewRockwell.com.

At Palgrave MacMillan, I much appreciated Editorial Director Airie Stuart's enthusiasm and her ideas on structuring and broadening the book. Production Director Alan Bradshaw did his usual masterful job of "bringing order out of chaos." He made many excellent comments and suggestions in the final laps; I appreciated his ideas, his long, late hours on this project, and his keen eye and sharp ear for the English language. Copy editors Bruce Murphy and Meg Weaver each bagged the season's limit of glitches and also made many helpful suggestions.

Updated information on this book and my commentaries on current developments and controversies are available at *www.palgrave-usa.com/blog/bovard* and www.jimbovard.com.

Notes

CHAPTER 1

1. Quoted in John Phillip Reid, *The Concept of Representation in the Age of the American Revolution* (Chicago: University of Chicago Press, 1989), p. 115.
2. Ilya Somin, "When Ignorance Isn't Bliss: How Political Ignorance Threatens Democracy," Cato Institute Policy Analysis, September 30, 2004.
3. "Shocking Poll: A Majority of Americans Cannot Name a Single Department in the President's Cabinet," The Polling Company, November 4, 2003.
4. William Penn, *Some Fruits of Solitude,* 1693. Text available at http://etext.lib.virginia.edu/toc/modeng/public/PenSoli.html.
5. "President's Remarks at a Victory 2004 Rally in Poplar Bluff, Missouri," White House Office of the Press Secretary, September 6, 2004.
6. Deborah Caldwell, "Did God Intervene? Evangelicals Are Crediting God with Securing Re-election Victory for George W. Bush," Beliefnet.com, November 14, 2004.
7. Greg Mitchell, "Public Remains Poorly Informed On Reasons for War," *Editor and Publisher,* August 26, 2004.
8. "The Separate Realities of Bush and Kerry Supporters," The PIPA/Knowledge Networks Poll / University of Maryland, October 21, 2004.
9. Jim VandeHei and Peter Baker, "President Struggles to Regain His Pre-Hurricane Swagger," *Washington Post,* September 24, 2005.
10. Kate Santich, "Politics on the Brain," *Orlando Sentinel* (Florida), October 27, 2004.
11. Stephen Earl Bennett, "Another Lesson about Public Opinion during the Clinton-Lewinsky Scandal," *Presidential Studies Quarterly,* June 2002.
12. "A Pedigree of Presidential Prevarication," Associated Press, September 30, 1998.
13. Accessed at http://www.democrats.org/blog/comment/00010947.html.
14. Robb Willer, "The Effects of Government-Issued Terror Warnings on Presidential Approval Ratings," *Current Research in Social Psychology,* September 30, 2004.
15. "The President's Inaugural Address," *Public Papers of the Presidents,* January 20, 2005.
16. From a statement Washington wrote on "An Act to establish an Executive Department to be denominated the Department of War, 7 August 1789." Posted at http://www.army.mil/cmh-pg/books/RevWar/ss/repdoc.htm.
17. Quoted in H. L. Mencken, *Prejudices,* 2nd ser. (New York: Knopf, 1924), p. 221.
18. Tom Jackman, "U.S. a Battlefield, Solicitor General Tells Judges," *Washington Post,* July 20, 2005.

CHAPTER 2

1. Accessed at http://etext.virginia.edu/jefferson/quotations/jeff0350.htm.
2. Harley Sorensen, "Vote For Me, Suckers," *San Francisco Chronicle,* October 25, 2004.
3. James Bryce, *Modern Democracies,* vol. 2 (New York: Macmillan, 1921), p. 113.

4. Ibid., p. 115.
5. Stephen Earl Bennett, "Is the Public's Ignorance of Politics Trivial?" *Critical Review*, 2003, Nos. 3–4, p. 311.
6. Ibid., p. 312.
7. Seba Eldridge, *The New Citizenship* (New York: Thomas Crowell, 1929), p. 3.
8. Ibid., p. 19.
9. "Pretensions or Clues," *Manas Journal*, October 25, 1978.
10. Eldridge, *The New Citizenship*, p. 22.
11. Michael Delli Carpini, "In Search of the Informed Voter," paper presented at Middle Tennessee State University / Murfreesboro and Nashville, Tennessee, November 12, 1999.
12. Ibid.
13. Michael Delli Carpini and Scott Keeter, *What Americans Know About Politics and Why It Matters* (New Haven: Yale University Press, 1996), p. 70.
14. Richard Morin, "Who's In Control? Many Don't Know or Care," *Washington Post*, January 29, 1996.
15. Richard Morin and Dan Balz, "Americans Losing Trust in Each Other and Institutions," *Washington Post*, January 28, 1996.
16. Louis Menand, "The Unpolitical Animal," *New Yorker*, August 30, 2004.
17. "Is Voter Ignorance Killing Democracy?" *Salon*, November 22, 1999.
18. Christopher H. Achen and Larry M. Bartels, "Blind Retrospection Electoral Responses to Drought, Flu, and Shark Attacks," Department of Politics and Woodrow Wilson School of Public and International Affairs, Princeton University, January 27, 2004.
19. Ibid.
20. Ilya Somin, "When Ignorance Isn't Bliss: How Political Ignorance Threatens Democracy," Cato Institute Policy Analysis, September 30, 2004.
21. Jeff Jacoby, "The Ignorant American Voter," *Boston Globe*, October 24, 2004.
22. Menand, "The Unpolitical Animal."
23. Delli Carpini, "In Search of the Informed Voter."
24. Stephen Earl Bennett, "Americans' Exposure to Political Talk Radio and Their Knowledge of Public Affairs," *Journal of Broadcasting and Electronic Media*, March 2002.
25. Hillel Italie, "Johnny Won't Read: Report Shows Big Drop in Reading," Associated Press, July 7, 2004.
26. "John Stacks, "Hard Times for Hard News: A Clinical Look at U.S. Foreign Coverage," *World Policy Journal*, December 2003.
27. Alexis De Tocqueville, *Democracy in America* (Garden City, NY: Doubleday, 1969), p. 91.
28. Stephen Earl Bennett, "Another Lesson about Public Opinion during the Clinton-Lewinsky Scandal," *Presidential Studies Quarterly*, June 2002.
29. Phrase quoted in Elvin Lim, "Five Trends in Presidential Rhetoric," *Presidential Studies Quarterly*, June 2002.
30. Richard Morin, "The Dumbed-Down Presidency?" *Washington Post*, September 26, 2004.
31. Elvin Lim, "Five Trends in Presidential Rhetoric," *Presidential Studies Quarterly*, June 2002.
32. Ibid.
33. Jean Jacques Rousseau, *The Social Contract and Discourses* (New York: E. P. Dutton, 1950), p. 291.
34. Bennett, "Is the Public's Ignorance of Politics Trivial?," p. 308.
35. Ibid.
36. Somin, "When Ignorance Isn't Bliss."
37. Ibid.
38. Ibid.
39. John Mueller, "Democracy and Ralph's Pretty Good Grocery: Elections, Equality, and the Minimal Human Being," *American Journal of Political Science*, Vol. 36, No. 4, November 1992, p. 983.
40. Ibid.
41. Accession Number 1609822, Public Opinion Online, Roper Center at University of Connecticut.
42. Ken Blake, "Tennessee Poll Analysis: Summary of Election Findings, Fall 2004," Middle Tennessee State University, Fall 2004. Available at http://www.mtsusurveygroup.org/mtpoll/f2004/MT-SUPoll_Election_Report.htm.

43. Robb Willer, "The Effects of Government-Issued Terror Warnings on Presidential Approval Ratings," *Currents Research in Social Psychology,* September 30, 2004.

44. Bob Woodward and Dan Eggen, "Aug. Memo Warned Of Attacks Within U.S.," *Washington Post,* May 19, 2002.

45. "Harris: 43% Believe Bush Admin Failed to Take Steps It Should Have Taken to Prevent 9/11," *The Hotline,* April 29, 2004.

46. "News Conference with Robert Borosage, Campaign for America's Future; and Stanley B. Greenberg, Democratic Party," Federal News Service, November 5, 2004.

47. Accessed at http://www.nationalgeographic.com/geosurvey/highlights.html.

48. "Text of a Letter from the President to the Speaker of the House of Representatives and the President Pro Tempore of the Senate," White House Office of the Press Secretary, March 19, 2003.

49. "Address to the Nation on Iraq From the U.S.S. Abraham Lincoln," *Public Papers of the Presidents,* May 1, 2003.

50. Bruce Morton, "Selling an Iraq–al Qaeda connection," CNN.com, March 11, 2003.

51. Frank Davies, "Poll: American Public's False Beliefs About Iraq War 'Striking,'" *Pioneer Press* [Twin Cities, Minnesota, June 22, 2003.

52. Accession Number: 0456128, Public Opinion Online, Roper Center at University of Connecticut.

53. Eric Mink, "U.S. Intelligence on Iraq: Cheney Just Won't Let It Go," *St. Louis Post-Dispatch,* July 15, 2004.

54. Greg Mitchell, "Three Years After 9/11: More than 40% of Americans Still Think Saddam Did It," *Editor & Publisher,* September 10, 2004.

55. "The Separate Realities of Bush and Kerry Supporters," University of Maryland Program on International Policy Attitudes, October 21, 2004.

56. Lynn Sweet, "A Whopping 71 Percent Cared Most about Issues other than Moral Values," *Chicago Sun-Times,* November 11, 2004.

57. "President Says Saddam Hussein Must Leave Iraq within 48 Hours," White House Office of the Press Secretary, March 17, 2003.

58. Davies, "Poll: American Public's False Beliefs About Iraq War 'Striking.'"

59. "Kay: 'We Were Almost All Wrong,'" CBS News, January 30, 2004.

60. "The Separate Realities of Bush and Kerry Supporters."

61. Maureen Dowd, "Nuclear Fiction," *New York Times,* October 11, 2004.

62. "The Separate Realities of Bush and Kerry Supporters."

63. Ibid.

64. Ibid.

65. Ibid.

66. Ibid.

67. "Study Finds Widespread Misperceptions on Iraq," The PIPA/Knowledge Networks Poll, October 2, 2003.

68. Ibid.

69. Jim Naureckas, "O'Reilly Brags About Fox's Lack of Skepticism, Fairness and Accuracy in Reporting (FAIR)," December 2003.

70. "The President's News Conference with Prime Minister Tony Blair of the United Kingdom in Istanbul," *Public Papers of the Presidents,* June 28, 2004.

71. Rajiv Chandrasekaran and Walter Pincus, "U.S. Edicts Curb Power Of Iraq's Leadership," *Washington Post,* June 27, 2004.

72. "Remarks in Marquette, Michigan," *Public Papers of the Presidents,* July 13, 2004.

73. Edward Wong, "New Law in Iraq Gives Premier Martial Powers to Fight Uprising," *New York Times,* July 7, 2004.

74. "Majority of Americans Think New Iraq Regime Has As Much or More Power Than U.S. Has There, But Still Doubt Bush Plan, Annenberg Data Show," Annenberg Public Policy Center, July 9, 2004.

75. William Schneider, "Scare Tactics," *National Journal,* September 18, 2004.

76. Mark Danner, "Abu Ghraib: The Hidden Story," *New York Review of Books,* October 7, 2004.

77. Jim VandeHei and Howard Kurtz, "The Politics of Fear—Kerry Adopts Bush Strategy of Stressing Dangers," *Washington Post,* September 29, 2004.
78. Tom Engelhardt, "Ira Chernus on the Electoral Fear Factor," *Nation Institute,* December 14, 2004.
79. Ibid.
80. Christopher Hayes, "Lessons Learned about Undecided Voters," *New Republic,* November 17, 2004.
81. "How Can 59,054,087 People Be so Dumb?" *Daily Mirror,* November 8, 2004.
82. Mark Danner, "How Bush Really Won," *New York Review of Books,* January 13, 2005.
83. William Raspberry, "Change the Iraq Conversation," *Washington Post,* September 27, 2004.
84. "Civics Education," American Bar Association, August 8, 2005.
85. "Vast Majorities of American Adults Profess Support for Constitutional Concepts of Separation of Powers and Checks and Balances," American Bar Association, August 8, 2005.
86. Ibid.
87. Bennett, "Is the Public's Ignorance of Politics Trivial?," p. 323.
88. Martha Neil, "Members of Privacy and Civil Liberties Board Named," *ABA Journal,* June 17, 2005.
89. Caroline Drees, "Civil Liberties Panel Is Off to a Sluggish Start," Reuters News Service, August 8, 2005.
90. Paul Waldman and Kathleen Hall Jamieson, "Rhetorical convergence and issue knowledge in the 2000 presidential election," *Presidential Studies Quarterly,* March 2003.
91. Ibid.
92. "Remarks in Lakeland, Florida," *Public Papers of the Presidents,* October 23, 2004.
93. "State of the Union Address," *Public Papers of the Presidents,* January 20, 1996.
94. Accessed at http://www.yale.edu/lawweb/avalon/presiden/inaug/clinton2.htm
95. "Remarks at a Brunch for Hillary Clinton in Johnson City, New York," *Public Papers of the Presidents,* October 22, 2000.
96. Adam B. Lawrence, "Does it Matter What Presidents Say? The Influence of Presidential Rhetoric on the Public Agenda, 1946–2003," University of Pittsburgh, 2004.
97. "Acceptance Speech to the Democratic National Convention by Governor Bill Clinton from Arkansas," New York, NY, July 16, 1992.
98. "Remarks in West Allis, Wisconsin," *Public Papers of the Presidents,* September 3, 2004.
99. James Bovard, "Pork barrel prisons: who profits from the war on drugs?" *Playboy,* February 2002.

CHAPTER 3

1. Julie Hirschfeld Davis, "Presidential Candidates Play Politics of Fear," *Baltimore Sun,* October 21, 2004.
2. Dana Milbank, "Tying Kerry to Terror Tests Rhetorical Limits," *Washington Post,* September 24, 2004.
3. Baron de Montesquieu, *The Spirit of the Laws* (New York: Hafner, 1949), p. 26.
4. "President Discusses War on Terror at the National Defense University," White House Office of the Press Secretary, March 8, 2005.
5. H. L. Mencken, *In Defense of Women* (New York: Time Inc., 1963 [1918]), p. 43.
6. Thomas Fleming, *The Illusion of Victory* (New York: Basic Books, 2003), p. 465.
7. For a more detailed analysis of freedom from fear, see James Bovard, *Freedom in Chains* (New York: St. Martin's, 1999), pp. 78–82.
8. "The Whoppers of 2004," Factcheck.org, October 31, 2004.
9. Bruce R. Dold, "GOP Foolishness Overshadows Clinton's Errors," *Chicago Tribune,* July 25, 1997.
10. James Bovard, *Freedom in Chains,* pp. 78–82.
11. "State of the Union Address," *Public Papers of the Presidents,* February 2, 2005.
12. Jim VandeHei and Howard Kurtz, "The Politics of Fear: Kerry Adopts Bush Strategy of Stressing Dangers," *Washington Post,* September 29, 2004.
13. Beth Gorham, "War On Terrorism: Fear Plays Key Role in U.S. Election as Osama bin Laden Emerges," CNEWS, October 31, 2004.

14. Brian Knowlton, "Fear factor: Did Bush use it better than Kerry?" *International Herald Tribune*, November 19, 2004.

15. CNN exit poll data at http://www.cnn.com/ELECTION/2004/pages/results/states/US/P/00/ epolls.0.html.

16. "Bush's Re-Election Campaign Begins on a Positive Note," FactCheck.org, March 3, 2004.

17. Susan Schmidt and John Mintz, "FBI Seeks Tips on 7 Linked to Al Qaeda," *Washington Post*, May 27, 2004.

18. Ibid.

19. "Terrorism: Turf War Erupts," *The Hotline*, May 28, 2004.

20. Lisa Myers, "Terror Threat Source Called into Question," MSNBC.com, May 28. 2004.

21. Ibid.

22. Evan Thomas, Daniel Klaidman, and Michael Isikoff, "Enemies Among Us," *Newsweek*, June 7, 2004.

23. Ibid.

24. "Statement of Secretary Tom Ridge," U.S. Department of Homeland Security, July 8, 2004.

25. Ibid.

26. Michael Isikoff, "Election Day Worries," *Newsweek*, July 19, 2004.

27. "CNN Late Edition with Wolf Blitzer," CNN, July 11, 2004.

28. Brian Knowlton, "U.S. Officials Defend Terror Warning," *New York Times*, August 3, 2004.

29. "Intelligence: Let's Bank on Nothing Happening," *The Hotline*, August 2, 2004.

30. Jonathan Peterson and Josh Meyer, "Ridge Warns of Specific Threats," *Los Angeles Times*, August 2, 2004.

31. "Intelligence: Let's Bank on Nothing Happening," *The Hotline*.

32. Lydia Polgreen, "City Ponders Financial Costs of Terror Alert," *New York Times*, August 3, 2004.

33. Knowlton, "U.S. Officials Defend Terror Warning."

34. "The President's Radio Address," *Public Papers of the Presidents*, August 7, 2004.

35. Ted Bridis, "Official: No Evidence Attack Is Imminent," Associated Press, August 12, 2004.

36. Ibid.

37. John C. K. Daly and Martin Sieff, "UPI Intelligence Watch," United Press International, September 23, 2004. The controversy over this warning and the subsequent press spin is detailed at http://cryptome.org/oct-surprise.htm.

38. "Feds Concerned U.S. Terror Attack in Works," FoxNews.com, September 23, 2004.

39. Dan Eggen and Spencer S. Hsu, "Election Heightens Terrorism Offensive," *Washington Post*, September 27, 2004.

40. Ibid.

41. "Dayton Says Leaving Hill Staffers 'As Human Shields' Is Irresponsible," *The Hotline*, October 14, 2004.

42. Jim VandeHei, "Bush: Kerry Would 'Weaken' U.S.," *Washington Post*, October 7, 2004.

43. "Bin Laden: 'Your Security Is in Your Own Hands,'" CNN.com, October 29, 2004.

44. Thomas M. DeFrank, "Analysis: See Tape as Boost for Prez," *New York Daily News*, October 30, 2004.

45. Ibid.

46. "Text of Ashcroft's Letter to Bush," Associated Press, November 9, 2004.

47. Dan Eggen and Sari Horwitz, "As Jan. 20 Nears, Terror Warnings Drop," *Washington Post*, January 18, 2005.

48. Editorial, "Chiller Theater," *New York Times*, October 21, 2004.

49. Mimi Hall, "Ridge Reveals Clashes on Alerts," *USA Today*, May 10, 2005.

50. Matthew Yglesias, "War Profiteer," *American Prospect Online*, November 1, 2004.

51. Robb Willer, "The Effects of Government-Issued Terror Warnings on Presidential Approval Ratings," *Current Research in Social Psychology*, September 30, 2004.

52. Ibid.

53. Kevin Drawbaugh, "FBI Fumbled on Terror Financing, 9/11 Panel Says," Reuters News Service, August 22, 2004.

54. Dan Eggen, "FBI Backlogged in Translation of Counterterrorism Wiretaps," *Washington Post*, September 28, 2004.

55. John Mintz, "Cutbacks Threaten Work Of Homeland Security Unit," *Washington Post*, October 31, 2004.
56. Eric Lipton, "U.S. to Spend Billions More to Alter Security Systems," *New York Times*, May 8, 2005.
57. Ibid.
58. Accessed at http://www.steveclemons.com/GOPMailer.htm.
59. David D. Kirkpatrick, "Republicans Admit Mailing Campaign Literature Saying Liberals Will Ban the Bible," *New York Times*, September 24, 2004.
60. "Two Democratic Senators Demanding the Republican National Committee Apologize for their Recent Mass Mailing," *Morning Edition*/National Public Radio, October 1, 2004.
61. Dave Peyton, "Some People Think We're Really Dumb," *Charleston Daily Mail* (West Virginia), October 18, 2004.
62. Jim Rutenberg, "Scary Ads Take Campaign to a Grim New Level," *New York Times*, October 17, 2004.
63. Ibid.
64. "President Bush Television Ad: 'Wolves,'" Associated Press, October 22, 2004.
65. "Bush: A Wolf at the Door," *The Hotline*, October 22, 2004.
66. Deborah Frazier, "Wolf Ad Rubs Some the Wrong Way," *Rocky Mountain News*, October 28, 2004.
67. Ibid.
68. Fred Kaplan, "When Is a Cut Not a Cut?" *Slate*, October 22, 2004.
69. Quoted in "Clarke: 'White House is Papering Over the Facts,'" CNN.com, March 23, 2004.
70. Greg Hitt, "Fear Is Key as Election Nears," *Wall Street Journal*, October 19, 2004.
71. Lisa Trei, "Pollsters Dissect Bush Election Win," *Stanford Report*, November 17, 2004.
72. Mark Danner, "How Bush Really Won," *New York Review of Books*, January 13, 2005.
73. Jim Rutenberg, "Scary Ads Take Campaign to a Grim New Level," *New York Times*, October 17, 2004.
74. Dowd, "Cheney Spits Toads."
75. James Gerstenzang, Matea Gold, and Peter Wallsten, "Cheney Warns of Risk if Rivals Win," *Los Angeles Times*, September 8, 2004.
76. Maureen Dowd, "Cheney Spits Toads," *New York Times*, September 9, 2004.
77. Lisa Rein, "Cheney Is Voice of Fear on National Security," *Washington Post*, September 19, 2004.
78. Ibid.
79. James Gerstenzang, "Cheney Takes Race at Staid, Somber Pace," *Los Angeles Times*, October 20, 2004.
80. Dana Milbank, "U.S. Officials Make It Clear: Exile or War," *Washington Post*, March 17, 2003.
81. Walter Shapiro, "With Scare Tactics Aplenty, Election Rivals Halloween," *USA Today*, October 20, 2004.
82. Ibid.
83. "Remarks by Sen. Miller to the Republican National Convention," Washingtonpost.com, September 1, 2004.
84. Michael Powell and Dan Eggen, "A Tough Cop Tempered by 9/11 and Iraq," *Washington Post*, December 4, 2004.
85. Dana Milbank, "Tying Kerry to Terror Tests Rhetorical Limits," *Washington Post*, September 24, 2004.
86. Editorial, "An Un-American Way to Campaign," *New York Times*, September 25, 2004.
87. "Transcript for September 19—Meet the Press," MSNBC.com, September 19, 2004.
88. Bill Sammon, "Bush Camp Rips Kerry Rhetoric," *Washington Times*, September 29, 2004.
89. "Transcript: First Presidential Debate," Washingtonpost.com, September 30, 2004.
90. Judd Legum and David Sirota, "Vote for Bush or Die," *Nation*, September 27, 2004.
91. Jim VandeHei, "Daschle Angered By Bush Statement," *Washington Post*, September 26, 2002.
92. Frank Luntz, "Why Bush Won," *Washington Times*, November 5, 2004.
93. Dana Priest and Josh White, "War Helps Recruit Terrorists, Hill Told," *Washington Post*, February 17, 2005.
94. *The Political Writings of John Adams: Representative Sections*, ed. George Peek (New York: Liberal Arts Press, 1954), p. 32.

CHAPTER 4

1. William P. Alford, "Exporting 'the Pursuit of Happiness,'" *Harvard Law Review,* May 2000.
2. "President Sworn into Second Term," White House Office of the Press Secretary, January 20, 2005.
3. Tony Smith, *America's Mission* (Princeton: Princeton University, 1994), p. 43.
4. Frank Gibney, "Is President Bush Repeating McKinley's Mistake in the Philippines?" History News Network, July 28, 2003.
5. Ibid.
6. "Remarks to a Joint Session of the Philippine Congress in Quezon City, Philippines," *Public Papers of the Presidents,* October 27, 2003.
7. Smith, *America's Mission,* p. 70.
8. Ibid., p. 60.
9. Smith, *America's Mission,* p. 73.
10. Thomas Fleming, *The Illusion of Victory* (New York: Basic Books, 2003), p. 412.
11. Ibid., p. 246.
12. Irving Babbitt, *Democracy & Leadership* (Indianapolis: Liberty Fund, 1979; originally published by Houghton Mifflin, 1924), p. 232.
13. Fleming, *The Illusion of Victory,* p. 382.
14. Thomas Carothers, *Aiding Democracy Abroad* (Washington: Carnegie Endowment for International Peace, 1999), p. 7.
15. This 1933 speech is posted at http://www.fas.org/man/smedley.htm.
16. Thomas Fleming, *The New Dealers War* (New York: Basic Books, 2001), p. 326.
17. *The Public Papers and Addresses of Franklin D. Roosevelt, 1944–45,* vol. 13 (New York: Russell and Russell, 1950), p. 31.
18. Fleming, *The New Dealers War,* p. 283.
19. Smith, *America's Mission,* p. 198.
20. Ibid., p. 189.
21. Smith, *America's Mission,* p. 195.
22. Ibid., pp. 201–02.
23. President John F. Kennedy, "Address at a White House Reception for Members of Congress and for the Diplomatic Corps of the Latin American Republics," March 13, 1961. Accessed April 27, 2005, at http://www.jfklibrary.org/jfk_alliance_for_progress.html.
24. Carothers, *Aiding Democracy Abroad,* p. 22.
25. Carothers, *Aiding Democracy Abroad,* p. 27. The data on the number of rural leaders killed is from an USAID study conducted during the 1980s.
26. Ibid., p 36.
27. Norman Solomon, "Intervention Spin Cycle," *Baltimore Sun,* April 26, 2005.
28. Norman Solomon, "The Media on Iraq: Too Much Stenography, Not Enough Curiosity," Antiwar.com, February 5, 2005.
29. Todd S. Purdum, "Flashback to the 60s: A Sinking Sensation of Parallels between Iraq and Vietnam," *New York Times,* January 29, 2005.
30. Sami Ramadani, "The Vietnam Turnout Was Good as Well," *Guardian* (UK), February 1, 2005.
31. Available at http://www.mtholyoke.edu/acad/intrel/pentagon3/doc253.htm. The memo was reprinted in The Pentagon Papers.
32. Carothers, *Aiding Democracy Abroad,* p. 25.
33. Michael Dobbs, "Papers Illustrate Negroponte's Contra Role," *Washington Post,* April 12, 2005.
34. Ibid.
35. Carothers, *Aiding Democracy Abroad,* p. 34.
36. "Statement on the Election of Jose Napoleon Duarte as President of El Salvador," *Public Papers of the Presidents,* May 18, 1984.
37. Carothers, *Aiding Democracy Abroad,* p. 34.
38. President Ronald Reagan, "Promoting Democracy and Peace," United States Department of State Bureau of Public Affairs, June 8, 1982.

39. David Ignatius, "Innocence Abroad: The New World of Spyless Coups," *Washington Post,* September 22, 1991.
40. Accessed at http://www.ned.org/employment.html.
41. Walter Goodman, "Congress Assails Democracy Group," *New York Times,* August 15, 1985.
42. Ibid.
43. Ibid.
44. Norman Kempster, "Troubled Foundation; Democracy–Export Stirs Controversy," *Los Angeles Times,* February 6, 1986.
45. Robert M. Andrews, "House Members Urge Fund Cutoff for Democracy Endowment," Associated Press, April 8, 1986.
46. Gene Grabowski, "Payments to Political Parties Called Improper," Associated Press, March 22, 1985.
47. U.S. Code Sec. Title 22, Sec. 4414, (a) (1).
48. Barbara Conry, "Loose Cannon: The National Endowment for Democracy," Cato Institute, November 8, 1993.
49. Paul Webster, "Reagan Fund paid $830,000 to French Right-wing Union," *Guardian* (UK), November 28, 1985.
50. Stanley Meisler, "Allocation of Funds in France Embarrassing," *Los Angeles Times,* February 6, 1986.
51. Bill Beacon, "U.S. Defends Funds to Right-Wing Group," United Press International, November 28, 1985.
52. Carothers, *Aiding Democracy Abroad,* ftn. 26.
53. Ben A. Franklin, "Democracy Project Facing New Criticisms, "*New York Times,* December 4, 1985.
54. Beacon, "U.S. Defends Funds to Right-Wing Group."
55. Franklin, "Democracy Project Facing New Criticisms. "
56. "Agency Suspends Grant To Right-Wing Student Group," Associated Press, November 27, 1985.
57. Ibid.
58. Franklin, "Democracy Project Facing New Criticisms."
59. On the French menace, see Richard Perle and David Frum, *The End of Evil* (New York: Random House, 2004).
60. Bryna Brennan, "Endowment Cancels Program That Critics Say Favored Anti-Arias Forces," Associated Press, October 13, 1989.
61. Doyle McManus, "U.S. Fund Gives $433,000 to Opponents of Costa Rica Leader's Policies," *Los Angeles Times,* October 14, 1989.
62. Ibid.
63. Sidney Blumenthal, "Grantee of U.S. Endowment Funds Sandinista Opponents," *Washington Post,* March 19, 1986.
64. Robert Pear, "U.S. Allots $2 Million to Aid Anti-Sandinistas," *New York Times,* April 25, 1989.
65. "U.S. May Contribute $3 Million to Nicaragua Opposition Campaign," *Los Angeles Times,* September 9, 1989.
66. Jim Drinkard, "Bush Wants $9 Million to Aid Nicaraguan Opposition Candidate," Associated Press, September 20, 1989.
67. Sara Fritz, "U.S. Accused of Trying to Buy Election," *Los Angeles Times,* October 17, 1989.
68. Bryna Brennan, "Congressionally Funded Group Walks Fine Line In Foreign Policy," Associated Press, November 11, 1989.
69. John Spicer Nichols, "Electoral Meddling: Get the N.E.D. Out of Nicaragua," *Nation,* February 26, 1990.
70. Bart Jones, "U.S. Funds Aid Chávez Opposition," *National Catholic Reporter,* April 2, 2004.
71. Brennan, "Congressionally Funded Group Walks Fine Line In Foreign Policy."
72. "Address to the Nation on Panama," White House Office of the Press Secretary, December 20, 1989.
73. Quoted at http://www.addictedtowar.com/panama.htm. NED was not involved in Operation Just Cause.
74. Vladimir Bukovsky, "Drowning democracy," *National Review,* September 23, 1991.
75. Andrew Mollison, "Overseas political gifts? It's U.S. policy," *Austin American-Statesman,* February 23, 1997.

76. Stephen Engelberg, "U.S. Grant to 2 Czech Parties Is Called Unfair Interference," *New York Times,* June 10, 1990.

77. Ibid.

78. Janine Wedel, *Collision and Collusion* (New York: St. Martin's Press, 1998), pp. 98–99.

79. Ibid., p. 99.

80. Andrew Rice, "Congress-funded institutes export democracy," *The Hill,* October 20, 1999.

81. Lukáš Fila, "Foreign NGOs carried out pre-election activities in breach of rules," *Slovak Spectator,* November 18, 2002.

82. Ibid.

83. Joshua Kurlantzick, "The Coup Connection," *Mother Jones,* November 1, 2004.

84. Christopher Marquis, "U.S. Bankrolling Is Under Scrutiny for Ties to Chavez Ouster," *New York Times,* April 25, 2002.

85. Ibid.

86. Ibid.

87. David Corn, "Our Gang in Venezuela?" *Nation,* August 5/12, 2002.

88. George Gedda, "Bush Says Venezuelans Revolted after Losing Some Freedoms," Associated Press, April 18, 2002.

89. Scott Sherman, "When Is a Coup a Coup?" *Nation,* May 27, 2002.

90. Mike Ceaser, "US Tax Dollars Helped Finance Some Chavez Foes, Review Finds," *Boston Globe,* August 18, 2002.

91. Bart Jones and Letta Tayler, "CIA Papers on Venezuela Coup," *Newsday,* November 24, 2004.

92. Corn, "Our Gang in Venezuela?"

93. Marquis, "U.S. Bankrolling Is Under Scrutiny for Ties to Chavez Ouster."

94. "State Department Issues Report on U.S. During Venezuelan Coup; Inspector General finds U.S. officials acted properly during coup," U.S. State Department Press Release, July 30, 2002.

95. "Examining the Venezuela Coup—Gingerly," *Nation,* September 2, 2002.

96. Jones, "U.S. Funds Aid Chávez Opposition."

97. Bart Jones and Letta Tayler, "Venezuela; A *Newsday* Special Report," *Newsday,* May 1, 2005.

98. Ibid.

99. "Remarks by the President at the 20th Anniversary of the National Endowment for Democracy," White House Office of the Press Secretary, November 6, 2003.

100. Editorial, "Aristide's Record—Voodoo Democracy," *Virginian Pilot,* September 16, 1994.

101. "Radio Address to American Troops in Haiti," *Public Papers of the Presidents,* October 1, 1994.

102. Carothers, *Aiding Democracy Abroad,* p. 43.

103. Joshua Kurlantzick, "The Coup Connection," *Mother Jones,* November 1, 2004.

104. Matt Kelley, "U.S. Money Helped Opposition in Ukraine," Associated Press, December 10, 2004.

105. "President and Nigerian President Discuss AIDS, African Union," White House Office of the Press Secretary, December 2, 2004.

106. Ibid.

107. Ibid.

108. Rep. Ron Paul, "U.S. Hypocrisy on Ukraine," Antiwar.com, December 9, 2004.

109. Anders Aslund, "Betraying a Revolution," *Washington Post,* May 18, 2005.

110. "President Discusses the Future of Iraq," White House Office of the Press Secretary, February 26, 2003.

111. William Booth and Rajiv Chandrasekaran, "Occupation Forces Halt Elections Throughout Iraq," *Washington Post,* June 28, 2003.

112. Ibid.

113. Ibid.

114. Ibid.

115. Steven R. Weisman, "Iraq Exit Plan: New Obstacles," *New York Times,* November 29, 2003.

116. Linda McQuaig, "Iraqis Voted because They Want U.S. Troops Out," *Toronto Star,* February 6, 2005.

117. Ibon Villelabeitia, "In Armored Vehicles, Troops Tell Iraqis to Vote," Reuters News Service, January 29, 2005.

118. Steve Fainaru, "Blanketed by Security, Baghdad Grows Deserted," *Washington Post*, January 29, 2005.
119. Dionne Searcey, "Managing the Vote in Mosul," *Newsday*, February 4, 2005.
120. Colum Lynch, "U.S. Troops' Role in Iraqi Elections Criticized," *Washington Post*, January 27, 2005.
121. Ibid.
122. Dahr Jamail, "Some Just Voted for Food," Inter Press Service, January 31, 2005. The *Washington Post* referred to "rumors that food rations would be taken away if residents failed to vote." Anthony Shadid, "Iraqis Defy Threats as Millions Vote," *Washington Post*, January 31, 2005.
123. Ken Sanders, "Iraqi Elections: Bush's 'Resounding Success,'" *Politics of Dissent*, January 30, 2005. At http://politicsofdissent.blogspot.com/2005/01/iraqs-elections-bushs-resounding.html.
124. Ibid.
125. Searcey, "Managing the Vote in Mosul."
126. Brian Whitaker, "Fig-leaf Freedom," *Guardian* (U.K.), January 31, 2005.
127. "Transcript: 2005 State of the Union Address," Washingtonpost.com, February 2, 2005.
128. "Bush Demands Syria Leave Lebanon," BBC News, March 8, 2005.
129. Seymour M. Hersh, "Get Out the Vote," *New Yorker*, July 25, 2005.
130. Ibid.
131. Ibid.
132. Ibid.
133. Ibid.
134. Dafna Linzer, "U.S. Says It Did Not Carry Out Plans to Back Iraqis in Election," *Washington Post*, July 18, 2005.
135. Ibid.
136. Accessed at http://www.yale.edu/lawweb/avalon/washing.htm.
137. Ibid.
138. "Remarks by President Bush at International Republican Institute Dinner," White House Office of the Press Secretary, May 18, 2005.
139. Adam Smith, *The Wealth of Nations* (New York: Modern Library, 1937), p. 112.
140. For a discussion of contemporary U.S. aid to tyrants, see James Bovard, *Terrorism & Tyranny: Trampling Freedom, Justice and Peace to Rid the World of Evil* (New York: Palgrave, 2003), pp. 207–33.
141. Carothers, *Aiding Democracy Abroad*, p. 56.
142. James Bovard, "JFK's Baby at 25: Alive and Bumbling," *Reason*, May 1986.
143. Ibid.
144. *Congressional Record*, January 6, 2005, p. H115.
145. James Bennett and Thomas DiLorenzo, *Official Lies* (Alexandria, Va.: Groom Books, 1992), p. 260.
146. Jean Jacques Rousseau, *The Social Contract and Discourses* (New York: E. P. Dutton, 1950), p. 38.
147. Carothers, *Aiding Democracy Abroad*, p. 149.
148. Irving Babbitt, *Democracy & Liberty* (Indianapolis: Liberty Fund, 1979; originally published by Houghton Mifflin, 1924), p. 265.
149. Rep. Hank Brown, Letter to the Editor, "Poor U.S. Investment in 'Promoting Democracy'," *New York Times*, June 29, 1984.
150. Walter McDougall, *Promised Land, Crusader State* (Boston: Houghton Mifflin, 1997), p. 210.

CHAPTER 5

1. "President Participates in Social Security Conversation in New York," White House Office of the Press Secretary, May 24, 2005.
2. Milan Kundera, *The Book of Laughter and Forgetting* (New York: HarperCollins, 1978), p. 1.
3. Hannah Arendt, "Lying in Politics: Reflections on The Pentagon Papers," *New York Times Review of Books*, November 18, 1971.
4. Gordon Wood, *The Radicalism of the American Revolution* (New York: Vintage, 1991), p. 108.
5. Eric Alterman, *When Presidents Lie* (New York: Viking, 2004), p. 22.
6. Thomas Fleming, *The Illusion of Victory* (New York: Basic Books, 2003), pp. 17–20.

7. Alterman, *When Presidents Lie,* p. 17.
8. Ibid., p. 32.
9. David Corn, *The Lies of George W. Bush* (New York: Three Rivers Press, 2003), p. 5.
10. Arendt, "Lying in Politics: Reflections on The Pentagon Papers."
11. Ibid.
12. Scott Peterson, "In War, Some Facts Are Less Factual," *Christian Science Monitor,* September 6, 2002.
13. "Events in Lebanon and Grenada," *Public Papers of the Presidents,* October 27, 1983.
14. Elizabeth Wharton, "Carter Angered by Reagan's Remark," United Press International, September 27, 1984.
15. Philip Taubman, "House Committee Says U.S. Embassy Ignored Warnings," *New York Times,* October 4, 1984.
16. "President's Trip to the Far East," *Public Papers of the Presidents,* May 4, 1986.
17. "Iran-United States Relations," *Public Papers of the Presidents,* November 13, 1986.
18. Lizie Larsen, "Presidential Lies and Consequences," *Mother Jones,* October 6, 1998.
19. Peterson, "In War, Some Facts Are Less Factual."
20. Ibid.
21. Ibid.
22. Len Ackland, "Making Kuwait Safe for Oligarchy," *Chicago Tribune,* August 30, 1990; Harvey Morris, "Amnesty Alleges Kuwait Torture," *Independent* (U.K.), March 2, 1990.
23. James Bovard, *Feeling Your Pain: The Explosion & Abuse of Government Power in the Clinton-Gore Years* (New York: Palgrave, 2000).
24. "State of the Union Address," White House Office of the Press Secretary, January 27, 1998.
25. George Anthan, "Rural 'Inequality' Cited; Clinton Seeking a Program for the Future," *Des Moines Register,* April 25, 1995.
26. Clifford Alexander, "Clinton Lies About Race, Too," *Wall Street Journal,* September 2, 1998.
27. "Address before a Joint Session of Congress on the State of the Union," *Public Papers of the Presidents,* January 27, 2000. See also, James Bovard, "Truth Is the Casualty as Clinton Takes Aim at Guns," *Wall Street Journal,* June 25, 1998.
28. "Remarks at a Democratic National Committee Dinner in Portola Valley, California," *Public Papers of the Presidents,* May 14, 1999.
29. "President Bill Clinton News Conference White House Rose Garden," Federal News Service, April 20, 1993.
30. Keith B. Richburg, "Kosovo's Prime Minister Quits After Being Indicted for War Crimes," *Washington Post,* March 9, 2005.
31. "The President's Radio Address," *Public Papers of the Presidents,* March 27, 1999, p. 531.
32. "William Cohen Holds Defense Department Briefing," Federal Document Clearinghouse Political Transcripts, April 7, 1999.
33. "Transcript: Clinton Press Conference," U.S. Information Service, June 25, 1999.
34. Neil Clark, "How the Battle Lies Were Drawn," *Spectator* (U.K.), June 14, 2003.
35. "Remarks at Whiteman Air Force Base in Knob Noster, Missouri," *Public Papers of the Presidents,* June 11, 1999, p. 1,085.
36. "Massacres vs. Regrettable Accidents—Double-Standard for Coverage of Civilian Deaths in Yugoslavia," Fairness and Accuracy in Reporting, May 7, 1999.
37. David Ramsay Steele, "Why Clinton Bombed Yugoslavia," *Liberty,* August 1999.
38. "Videotape Address to the Serbian People," *Public Papers of the Presidents,* March 25, 1999.
39. Kristian Kahrs, "Divided by Distrust," *Christianity Today,* February 2003.
40. Matt Tiabbi, "US Propaganda Better than Soviet-Era Propaganda," *The Exile,* April 7, 1999.
41. "Interview with Wolf Blitzer of Cable News Network's 'Late Edition,'" *Public Papers of the Presidents,* June 20, 1999.
42. Carl Hulse and Philip Shenon, "Leaders of G.O.P. Try to Discredit a Critic of Bush," *New York Times,* Marcy 27, 2004.
43. "Rice under Oath (Part 4)," DailyHowler.com, April 17, 2004.
44. "Transcript of Rice's 9/11 Commission Statement," CNN.com, April 8, 2004.

45. Ibid.
46. "Rice under Oath (Part 4)," DailyHowler.com, April 17, 2004.
47. Ibid.
48. Staff Statement No. 10, "Threats and Responses in 2001," National Commission on Terrorist Attacks Upon the United States, April 2004.
49. "Transcript: Confirmation Hearing of Condoleezza Rice," NYTimes.com, January 18, 2005.
50. Ibid.
51. Editorial, "Was She Calling Ms. Rice a Liar?" *Hartford Courant,* January 20, 2005.
52. Editorial, "Confirming Secretary Rice," *Washington Times,* January 20, 2005.
53. Editorial, "Heckling Dr. Condoleezza Rice," *Chattanooga Times Free Press,* January 20, 2005.
54. Howard Manly, "Rice Hearings Didn't Focus on Merit," *Boston Herald,* January 27, 2005.
55. Sheryl Gay Stolberg and Joel Brinkley, "In Senate, Democrats Assail Rice and U.S. Policy in Iraq," *New York Times,* January 26, 2005.
56. Lori Robertson, "Campaign Trail Veterans for Truth," *American Journalism Review,* December 2004 / January 2005.
57. Howard Kurtz, "Ads Push the Factual Envelope," *Washington Post,* October 20, 2004.
58. "President Bush Thanks Americans in Wednesday Acceptance Speech," White House Office of the Press Secretary," November 3, 2004.
59. Walter Pincus and Dana Milbank, "Al Qaeda-Hussein Link Is Dismissed," *Washington Post,* June 17, 2004.
60. "Media Under Fire For 'Mischaracterization' of 9/11 Commission Findings," White House Bulletin, June 18, 2004.
61. Dana Milbank, "Bush Defends Assertions of Iraq-Al Qaeda Relationship," *Washington Post,* June 18, 2004.
62. "Cheney Blames Media for Blurring Saddam, 9/11," MSNBC.com, June 18, 2004.
63. Accessed at http://www.democraticunderground.com/articles/04/06/p/24_times.html.
64. Dan Eggen, "9/11 Panel Defends Intelligence," *Washington Post,* July 7, 2004
65. Milbank, "Bush Defends Assertions of Iraq-Al Qaeda Relationship."
66. James Gerstenzang, "Cheney Presses Hussein-Qaeda Link," *Los Angeles Times,* October 2, 2004.
67. "Transcript: Vice Presidential Debate," WashingtonPost.com, October 5, 2004.
68. Ibid.
69. Ibid. Italics added.
70. Liz Sidoti, "Meeting Was Not First for Cheney, Edwards," Associated Press, October 7, 2004.
71. Richard Reeves, "Bush, Cheney Deliberately Lied to Nation," *Press & Sun-Bulletin* (Binghamton, NY), October 21, 2004.
72. Edward Wasserman, "Reporting Lies Gives Them Weight," *Miami Herald,* October 20, 2004.
73. Richard Leiby, "The Reliable Source," *Washington Post,* October 7, 2004.
74. Peter Wallsten, "Cheney and Edwards Have Met Before," *Los Angeles Times,* October 6, 2004.
75. Bob Deans, "Cheney's Dig at Edwards Misses Mark," *Atlanta Journal-Constitution,* October 7, 2004.
76. David L. Greene, "Photos Show Cheney Met Edwards before Debate," *Baltimore Sun,* October 7, 2004.
77. Thomas Fitzgerald, "Cheney's Claim of Not Meeting Edwards Backfires on Vice President," Knight Ridder Newswire, October 7, 2004.
78. Adam Nagourney and Richard W. Stevenson, "In His New Attacks, Bush Pushes Limit on the Facts," *New York Times,* October 8, 2004.
79. Howard Kurtz, "Truth and Consequences," *Washington Post,* October 18, 2004.
80. Ryan Lizza, "Backward," *New Republic,* November 1, 2004.
81. Dana Milbank, "Bush Again Uses Selective Intelligence: Warning in Iraq Report Unread," *Washington Post,* July 19, 2003.
82. Dana Priest and Dana Milbank, "President Defends Allegations on Iraq," *Washington Post,* July 15, 2003.
83. Corn, *The Lies of George W. Bush,* p. 5.
84. Howard Kurtz, "News Quips Rile White House," *Washington Post,* April 27, 1996.

85. Alterman, *When Presidents Lie,* p. 26.

86. Flora Lewis, "Shine Light on the Lies Behind the Vietnam War," *International Herald Tribune,* August 20, 2001.

87. Dana Milbank, "The Minutes Waltz and a Skeptical Press Corps," *Washington Post,* July 16, 2002.

88. Howard Kurtz, "The *Post* on WMD: An Inside Story; Prewar Articles Questioning Threat often Didn't Make Front Page," *Washington Post,* August 12, 2004.

89. Todd Gitlin, "The Great Media Breakdown," *Mother Jones,* November/December 2004.

90. Alterman, *When Presidents Lie,* pp. 2–3.

91. Norman Solomon, "The Occasional Media Ritual of Lamenting the Habitual," Antiwar.com, September 23, 2005.

92. Paul Farhi, "Democrats Call Bush's Comedy Skit Tasteless," *Washington Post,* Marcy 26, 2004.

93. Greg Mitchell, "Bush's WMD 'Joke': Is the Media Still Laughing?" *Editor and Publisher,* June 18, 2005.

94. Mark Danner, "Secret Way to War," *New York Review of Books,* June 9, 2005.

95. "Text: Bush's 2003 State of the Union Speech," *Washington Post,* January 29, 2003.

96. Joe Conason, "A Press Cover-up," *Salon,* June 17, 2005.

97. Matt Wells, "Viewpoint: Has Katrina Saved US Media?" BBC News, September 5, 2005.

98. David Bauder, "NBC Anchor Says Reporters Feisty Again," Associated Press, September 12, 2005.

99. John Maynard Keynes, *Essays in Persuasion* (New York: Harcourt Brace & Co., 1932), p. 46.

100. Ibid., p. 48.

101. Alterman, *When Presidents Lie,* p. 306.

102. Quoted in Jim Lobe, "Leo Strauss' Philosophy of Deception," AlterNet, May 19, 2003.

103. Martha Derthick, *Policymaking for Social Security* (Washington: Brookings Institution, 1979), p. 232.

104. Friedrich Hayek, *The Constitution of Liberty* (Chicago: Regnery Gateway, 1972 [1960 first published]), p. 293.

105. "Outgoing Social Security Head Assails 'Myths' of System and Says It Favors the Poor," *New York Times,* December 2, 1979.

106. James Bovard, "Federal Job Training: Road to Nowhere," *The Freeman,* November 1987.

107. James Bovard, "The Failure of Federal Job Training," Cato Institute, August 28, 1986.

108. James Bovard, "Job Agency that Expects Employer to Call," *Wall Street Journal,* September 5, 1986.

109. James Bovard, "Clinton's Summer Jobs Sham," *Wall Street Journal,* March 5, 1993.

110. Lawrence A. Uzzell, "Education Reform Fails the Test," *Wall Street Journal,* May 10, 1989.

111. "Remarks at Highland Park Elementary School in Landover, Maryland," *Public Papers of the Presidents,* July 7, 2003.

112. James Dao and Eric Schmitt, "Pentagon Readies Efforts to Sway Sentiment Abroad," *New York Times,* February 19, 2002.

113. "Remarks by the President during Presentation of World Trade Center Bullhorn," White House Office of the Press Secretary, February 25, 2002.

114. "The Office of Strategic Influence Is Gone, But Are Its Programs In Place?" *FAIR,* November 27, 2002.

115. William Arkin, "The Military's New War of Words," *Los Angeles Times,* November 24, 2002.

116. Arkin, "The Military's New War of Words."

117. Ibid.

118. William James, *Pragmatism and Other Essays* (New York: Simon & Schuster, 1963 [1907]), p. 98.

119. Ernst Cassier, *The Myth of the State* (New Haven: Yale University Press, 1946), p. 267.

120. Ibid., p. 267.

121. Ibid., p. 258.

122. Ron Suskind, "Without a Doubt," *New York Times Magazine,* October 17, 2004.

123. Alterman, *When Presidents Lie,* p. 314.

124. Arendt, "Lying in Politics: Reflections on The Pentagon Papers."

125. Ibid.

126. Dave Eggen and Julie Tate, "U.S. Campaign Produces Few Convictions on Terrorist Charges; Statistics Often Count Lesser Crimes," *Washington Post,* June 12, 2005.

127. "TIME Poll: Campaign 2004," Time.com, September 24, 2004.
128. Todd S. Purdum, "President Seems Poised to Claim a New Mandate," *New York Times,* November 3, 2004.
129. Stephen Earl Bennett, "Another Lesson about Public Opinion during the Clinton-Lewinsky Scandal," *Presidential Studies Quarterly,* June 2002.
130. Danner, "Secret Way to War."

CHAPTER 6

1. "Statement on United Nations International Day in Support of Victims of Torture," *Public Papers of the Presidents,* June 26, 2003.
2. Mark Danner, "Abu Ghraib: The Hidden Story," *New York Review of Books,* October 7, 2004.
3. Timothy J. Kepner, "Torture 101: The Case Against the United States for Atrocities Committed by School of the Americas Alumni," *Dickinson Journal of International Law,* Spring 2001.
4. Gary Cohn, Ginger Thompson, and Mark Matthews, "Torture Was Taught by CIA; Declassified Manual Details the Methods Used in Honduras," *Baltimore Sun,* January 27, 1997.
5. Based on the number of American fatalities as detailed in the State Department's annual *Patterns of Global Terrorism* report.
6. Dana Priest and Barton Gellman, "U.S. Decries Abuse but Defends Interrogations," *Washington Post,* December 26, 2002.
7. "Remarks by the President on the Capture of Saddam Hussein," White House Office of the Press Secretary, December 14, 2003. Also, "Remarks by the President on Operation Iraqi Freedom and Operation Enduring Freedom," White House Office of the Press Secretary, March 19, 2004.
8. Seymour M. Hersh, "Torture at Abu Ghraib," *New Yorker,* April 30, 2004.
9. Seymour M. Hersh, "The Gray Zone," *New Yorker,* May 24, 2004.
10. Ibid.
11. Matt Welch, "The Pentagon's Secret Stash: Why We'll Never See the Second Round of Abu Ghraib Photos," *Reason,* April 2005.
12. "Interview with Alhurra Television," *Public Papers of the Presidents,* May 5, 2004.
13. "Testimony as Prepared by Secretary of Defense Donald H. Rumsfeld, Before The Senate and House Armed Services Committees," Friday, May 7, 2004. Posted at http://www.defenselink.mil/speeches/2004/sp20040507-secdef1042.html.
14. Lawrence DiRita, "'In the Company of Those Involved,'" *Washington Post,* May 15, 2004. [Letter to the editor]
15. "Statement of RNC Chairman Ed Gillespie on Democrat Politicization of the Iraqi Prisoner Issue," U.S. Newswire, May 10, 2004.
16. Charles Babington, "From GOP, Zero Tolerance For Democratic War Critics," *Washington Post,* May 16, 2004.
17. Ibid.
18. "Senator 'Outraged by Outrage' at Prison Abuse," Reuters News Service, May 11, 2004.
19. Karen Greenberg and Joshua Dratel, *The Torture Papers: The Road to Abu Ghraib* (New York: Cambridge University, 2005), p. 119.
20. Mark Danner, *Torture and Truth* (New York: New York Review of Books, 2004), p. 29.
21. Ibid.
22. Accessed at http://www.whitehouse.gov/news/releases/2004/05/20040525-3.html.
23. "The President's News Conference in Savannah, Georgia," *Public Papers of the Presidents,* June 10, 2004.
24. "Interview With Paris Match Magazine," *Public Papers of the Presidents,* May 28, 2004.
25. Helen Dewar, "Lott Defends Treatment of Iraqi Prisoners," *Washington Post,* June 3, 2004.
26. "Standards of Conduct for Interrogation under 18 U.S.C. §§ 2340–2340A," Department of Justice Office of Legal Counsel, August 1, 2002.
27. Dana Priest, "Justice Dept. Memo Says Torture 'May Be Justified,'" *Washington Post,* June 13, 2004.

28. "Standards of Conduct for Interrogation under 18 U.S.C. §§ 2340–2340A," Department of Justice Office of Legal Counsel, August 1, 2002. Following quotes from same source.

29. Accessed at http://texscience.org/reform/torture/dod-detainee-interro–6mar03.pdf.

30. "FBI E-Mail Refers to Presidential Order Authorizing Inhumane Interrogation Techniques," American Civil Liberties Union [press release], December 20, 2004.

31. "U.S. Officials Questioned Interrogations," MSNBC, June 24, 2004.

32. Adam Liptak, "Legal Scholars Criticize Memos on Torture," *New York Times,* June 25, 2004.

33. Jess Bravin, "Pentagon Report Set Framework For Use of Torture," *Wall Street Journal,* June 7, 2004.

34. Richard A. Serrano, "Prison Interrogators' Gloves Came Off Before Abu Ghraib," *Los Angeles Times,* June 9, 2004.

35. Dave Lindorff, "A First Glimpse at Bush's Tortureshow: John Walker Lindh, Revisited," *Counterpunch,* June 5/6, 2004.

36. Serrano, "Prison Interrogators' Gloves Came Off Before Abu Ghraib."

37. Lindorff, "A First Glimpse at Bush's Tortureshow: John Walker Lindh, Revisited."

38. "The President's News Conference in Savannah, Georgia," *Public Papers of the Presidents,* June 10, 2004.

39. Memo Says Bush Not Restricted by Torture Bans [Reuters/Yahoo]; Defense Department Regular Briefing, June 17, 2004 [Defenselink].

40. Editorial, "Torture Policy (cont'd)," *Washington Post,* June 21, 2004.

41. Ibid.

42. "Remarks Following Discussions With Prime Minister Peter Medgyessy of Hungary and an Exchange With Reporters," *Public Papers of the Presidents,* June 22, 2004.

43. "Press Briefing by White House Counsel Judge Alberto Gonzales, Dod General Counsel William Haynes, Dod Deputy General Counsel Daniel Dell'Orto and Army Deputy Chief of Staff for Intelligence General Keith Alexander," White House Office of the Press Secretary, June 22, 2004.

44. Ibid. (Italics added.)

45. Helen Dewar and Dan Morgan, "Senate Rejects Request for Abuse Documents," *Washington Post,* June 24, 2004.

46. James G. Lakely, "'Values' Guided Bush Torture Ban," *Washington Times,* June 23, 2004.

47. "Interview with Radio and Television Ireland," *Public Papers of the Presidents,* June 24, 2004.

48. T. K. Maloy, "On UN Day, Bush Denounces Prisoner Abuses," United Press International, July 5, 2004.

49. Accession Number 0455678, Public Opinion Online, Roper Center at University of Connecticut. (Poll released June 28, 2004, by CBS News and *New York Times.*)

50. Paul Richter, "U.S. Struggles in War of Ideas, Panel Says," *Los Angeles Times,* July 25, 2004.

51. "Bad Troops, Poor Leaders Responsible for Detainee Abuses," Department of Defense Press Release, July 22, 2004.

52. Ibid.

53. Josh White and Scott Higham, "Army Calls Abuses 'Aberrations,'" *Washington Post,* July 23, 2004.

54. Editorial, "An Army Whitewash," *Washington Post,* July 25, 2004.

55. "Public Rejects Nearly All Forms of Torture or Coercion Even in Face of Possible Terrorist Attack, Finds PIPA/Knowledge Networks Poll," U.S. Newswire Press Release, July 22, 2004.

56. Accessed at http://news.findlaw.com/hdocs/docs/dod/fay82504rpt.pdf.

57. Marjorie Cohn, "Bush & Co.: War Crimes and Cover-Up," Znet.com, September 20, 2004.

58. Accessed at http://news.findlaw.com/hdocs/docs/dod/fay82504rpt.pdf.

59. Ibid.

60. Alexander Cockburn, "Politicize the CIA? You've got to be kidding!" *Nation,* December 20, 2004.

61. James Schlesinger, "Trust and the Public Service," First Annual Elliot Richardson Lecture, American Society for Public Administrators and National Academy of Public Administration, Rutgers University, Newark, New Jersey, March 11, 2001. Accessed on April 19, 2005, at http://unpan1.un.org/intradoc/groups/public/documents/aspa/unpan002996.pdf.

62. "Guantánamo and Beyond: The continuing pursuit of unchecked executive power," Amnesty International, May 13, 2005.

63. Editorial, "No Accountability on Abu Ghraib," *New York Times,* September 10, 2004.
64. Accessed at http://www.defenselink.mil/news/Aug2004/d20040824finalreport.pdf.
65. Jackson Diehl, "Refusing to Whitewash Abu Ghraib," *Washington Post,* September 12, 2004.
66. Ibid.
67. Editorial, "No Accountability on Abu Ghraib."
68. Michael Isikoff and Mark Hosenball, "Has the Government Come Clean?" *Newsweek,* January 6, 2005.
69. Ibid.
70. Norimitsu Onishi, "U.S. Military Displays New Look for Abu Ghraib," *New York Times,* September 16, 2004.
71. Ibid.
72. "Remarks in St. Charles, Missouri," *Public Papers of the Presidents,* July 20, 2004.
73. "Remarks in Miami, Florida," *Public Papers of the Presidents,* October 31, 2004.
74. Mark Danner, "Abu Ghraib: The Hidden Story," *New York Review of Books,* October 7, 2004.
75. "The President's Radio Address," *Public Papers of the Presidents,* January 17, 2004.
76. Accessed at http://news.findlaw.com/hdocs/docs/dod/fay82504rpt.pdf.
77. Danner, "Abu Ghraib: The Hidden Story."
78. Rajiv Chandrasekaran and Scott Wilson, "Mistreatment of Detainees Went beyond Guards' Abuse," *Washington Post,* May 11, 2004.
79. John Hendren and Mark Mazzetti, "Army Implicates 28 U.S. Troops in Deaths of 2 Afghan Detainees," *Los Angeles Times,* October 15, 2004.
80. Douglas Jehl and David Rohde, "Afghan Deaths Linked to Unit at Iraq Prison," *New York Times,* May 24, 2004.
81. "U.S. Illegally Withheld Records on Abuses at Abu Ghraib and Elsewhere, ACLU Charges," American Civil Liberties Union [press release], June 2, 2004.
82. Neil A. Lewis, "Red Cross Finds Detainee Abuse in Guantánamo," *New York Times,* November 30, 2004.
83. Ibid.
84. Ibid.
85. Michael J. Sniffen, "Evidence Gained Through Using Torture OK, US Officials Say," Associated Press, December 3, 2004.
86. Richard A. Serrano, "Details of Marines Mistreating Prisoners in Iraq Are Revealed," *Los Angeles Times,* December 15, 2004.
87. Isikoff and Hosenball, "Has the Government Come Clean?"
88. Ibid.
89. Charlie Savage, "US Disclosures Signal Wider Detainee Abuse," *Boston Globe,* December 26, 2004.
90. Barton Gellman and R. Jeffrey Smith, "Report to Defense Alleged Abuse By Prison Interrogation Teams," *Washington Post,* December 8, 2004.
91. Letter from American Civil Liberties Union, Letter to the Senate Armed Services Committee regarding the Need for Accountability on Government Abuse of Detainees, June 21, 2005. Accessed at http://www.aclu.org/SafeandFree/SafeandFree.cfm?ID=18552&C=206.
92. "FBI E-Mail Refers to Presidential Order Authorizing Inhumane Interrogation Techniques," American Civil Liberties Union, December 20, 2004.
93. Dan Eggen and R. Jeffrey Smith, "FBI Agents Allege Abuse of Detainees at Guantanamo Bay," *Washington Post,* December 21, 2004. A Pentagon spokesman denied that Wolfowitz approved interrogation techniques.
94. Thomas E. Ricks, "Detainee Abuse by Marines Is Detailed," *Washington Post,* December 15, 2004.
95. Douglas Jehl and David Johnston, "White House Fought New Curbs on Interrogations, Officials Say," *New York Times,* January 13, 2005.
96. Neil A. Lewis, "Fresh Details Emerge on Harsh Methods at Guantánamo," *New York Times,* January 1, 2005.
97. Ibid.
98. Ibid.

99. M. Gregg Bloche and Jonathan H. Marks, "Doctor's Orders: Spill Your Guts," *Los Angeles Times*, January 9, 2005.

100. T. R. Reid, "Guard Convicted In the First Trial From Abu Ghraib," *Washington Post*, January 15, 2005.

101. T. R. Reid, "Graner Gets 10 Years for Abuse at Abu Ghraib," *Washington Post*, January 16, 2005.

102. Ibid.

103. Neil A. Lewis, "U.S. Spells Out New Definition Curbing Torture," *New York Times*, January 1, 2005.

104. "Transcript: Senate Judiciary Committee Confirmation Hearing," Posted at nytimes.com, January 6, 2005.

105. Jehl and Johnston, "White House Fought New Curbs on Interrogations, Officials Say."

106. Eric Lichtblau, "Gonzales Says '02 Policy on Detainees Doesn't Bind C.I.A.," *New York Times*, January 19, 2005.

107. "The President's Press Conference," White House Office of the Press Secretary, January 26, 2005.

108. Jane Mayer, "Outsourcing Torture," *New Yorker*, February 14, 2005.

109. David DeBatto, "Whitewashing Torture?" *Salon*, December 8, 2004.

110. R. Jeffrey Smith and Josh White, "Soldier Who Reported Abuse Was Sent to Psychiatrist," *Washington Post*, March 5, 2005.

111. DeBatto, "Whitewashing Torture?"

112. Ibid.

113. Will Dunham, "Video Shows U.S. Soldiers in 'Ramadi Madness' Abuse," Reuters, March 7, 2005.

114. Smith and White, "Soldier Who Reported Abuse Was Sent to Psychiatrist."

115. Ibid.

116. Josh White and R. Jeffrey Smith, "Abuse Review Exonerates Policy," *Washington Post*, March 10, 2005.

117. "Admiral Issues Report: 'No Policy Condoned Torture, Abuse,'" Department of Defense Press Release, March 10, 2005.

118. "Hearing of the Senate Armed Service Committee; Subject: Detainee Interrogation," Federal News Service, March 10, 2005.

119. Charlie Savage, "Admiral's Report, Document Differ on Detainee Plans," *Boston Globe*, March 11, 2005.

120. White and Smith, "Abuse Review Exonerates Policy."

121. "DoD News: Department of Defense Briefing on Detention Operations and Interrogation Techniques," Department of Defense, March 10, 2005. Posted online at http://www.defenselink.mil/transcripts/2005/tr20050310–2262.html.

122. Executive Summary, "Church—ISTF Report on Interrogation Operations," March 10, 2005. Accessed at http://www.defenselink.mil/news/Mar2005/d20050310exe.pdf.

123. Douglas Jehl and Eric Schmitt, "U.S. Military Says 26 Inmate Deaths May Be Homicide," *New York Times*, March 16, 2005.

124. "DoD News: Department of Defense Briefing on Detention Operations and Interrogation Techniques," Department of Defense, March 10, 2005.

125. Editorial, "More Excuses," *Washington Post*, March 13, 2005. Editorial, "Abu Ghraib, Whitewashed Again," *New York Times*, March 11, 2005.

126. Hanna Rosin, "On the Hill, Where It's Hot . . . or Not," *Washington Post*, January 7, 2005.

127. "Hearing of the Senate Armed Services Committee; Subject: Threats to U.S. National Security," Federal News Service, March 17, 2005.

128. Jehl and Johnston, "White House Fought New Curbs on Interrogations, Officials Say."

129. "Hearing of the Senate Armed Services Committee; Subject: Threats to U.S. National Security."

130. Douglas Jehl, "Questions Are Left by CIA Chief on the Use of Torture," *New York Times*, March 18, 2005.

131. Matt Kelley, "Army Investigation Reported Abuse, Possible Torture at Jail Near Mosul," Associated Press, March 25, 2005.

132. "Army's Own Documents Acknowledge Evidence That Soldiers Used Torture," American Civil Liberties Union, March 25, 2005.

133. Jim Spencer, "Good Guys? Military Logic Tortured," *Denver Post,* April 1, 2005.
134. Robert Weller, "Sergeant Recounts Severe Abuse at Facility where Iraqi General Died," Associated Press, March 31, 2005.
135. Spencer, "Good Guys? Military Logic Tortured."
136. Josh White, "Soldiers' 'Wish Lists' Of Detainee Tactics Cited," *Washington Post,* April 19, 2005.
137. "Army Memo Released By ACLU Suggests Perjury In Lt. Gen. Sanchez Sworn Testimony on Torture," American Civil Liberties Union, March 31, 2005.
138. Bob Herbert, "On Abu Ghraib, the Big Shots Walk," *New York Times,* April 28, 2005.
139. Editorial, "Impunity," *Washington Post,* April 26, 2005.
140. "Press Conference of the President," White House Office of the Press Secretary, April 28, 2005.
141. "Interview With Dutch TV NOS," *Public Papers of the Presidents,* May 5, 2005.
142. "President Bush Meets with Danish Prime Minister Rasmussen," White House Office of the Press Secretary, May 20, 2005.
143. Jeffrey Fleishman and Asmaa Waguih, "Iraqi Security Tactics Evoke the Hussein Era," *Los Angeles Times,* June 19, 2005.
144. James Hider, "West Turns Blind Eye as Police Put Saddam's Torturers Back to Work," *The Times* (London/UK), July 7, 2005.
145. John F. Burns, "10 Sunnis Suffocate in Iraqi Police Custody," *New York Times,* July 13, 2005.
146. Dana Milbank, "An Administration's Amnesty Amnesia," *Washington Post,* June 5, 2005.
147. "Cheney Offended by Amnesty Criticism," CNN.com, May 31, 2005.
148. Ibid.
149. "President's Press Conference," Office of the White House Press Secretary, May 31, 2005.
150. "Special Defense Department Briefing by General Richard B. Myers, USAF, Chairman of the Joint Chiefs of Staff," Federal News Service, August 26, 2005.
151. Eric Schmitt, "3 in 82nd Airborne Say Beating Iraqi Prisoners Was Routine," *New York Times,* September 24, 2005.
152. Ibid.
153. "New Revelations by American Soldiers of Abuse in Iraq," PBS Press Release, October 17, 2005.
154. "New Documents Contradict Army Report Denying Systemic Failures in Treatment of Detainees," American Civil Liberties Union, September 15, 2005.
155. Editorial, "Abu Ghraib, Rewarded," *New York Times,* June 22, 2005.
156. Tom Bowman, "Leader at Abu Ghraib Gets New Post in Ariz.," *Baltimore Sun,* March 11, 2005.
157. James Gordon Meek, "Gitmo Taunter Teaches Tactics," *New York Daily News,* March 16, 2005.
158. Marguerite Feitlowitz, "Torturer General," *Salon,* January 6, 2005.
159. Joseph L. Galloway, "On Torture, The Buck Stops in the Lowest Ranks," *The State* (Columbia, SC), March 18, 2005.
160. Liza Porteus, "Gitmo Detainee Allegations Cause Uproar," FoxNews.com, June 14, 2005.
161. Dave Sheinin, "Orioles Star Faces Inquiry for Testimony on Steroids," *Washington Post,* August 4, 2005.
162. Editorial, "The Vote on Mr. Gonzales," *Washington Post,* January 16, 2005.
163. "Federal Government Turns Over Thousands of Torture Documents to ACLU," American Civil Liberties Union [press release], October 21, 2004.
164. "Marine General's Blunt Comments Draw Fire," NBCSandiego.com, February 1, 2005.
165. Danner, "Abu Ghraib: The Hidden Story."
166. "Guantánamo Detainees Are 'Bad People', Says Cheney," *Guardian* (UK), June 13, 2005.
167. George Orwell, "Notes on Nationalism," in *The Collected Essays, Journalism, and Letters* (London: Penguin, 1970), p. 419.

CHAPTER 7

1. James Schlesinger, "Trust and the Public Service," First Annual Elliot Richardson Lecture, American Society for Public Administrators and National Academy of Public Administration, Rutgers University,

Newark, New Jersey, March 11, 2001. Accessed on April 19, 2005, at http://unpan1.un.org/intradoc/groups/public/documents/aspa/unpan002996.pdf.

2. Accessed at http://en.thinkexist.com/quotes/edward_abbey/.

3. William Simon, *A Time For Truth* (New York: Berkeley Books, 1978), p. 124.

4. "Notes for an Oration in Braintree, Massachusetts," Adams Electronic Archive, "John Adams diary 16, 10 January 1771—28 November 1772,"—online at http://www.masshist.org/digitaladams/aea/cfm/doc.cfm?id=D16.

5. Friedrich Hayek, *The Constitution of Liberty* (Chicago: University of Chicago, 1960), p. 246.

6. For a brief historical survey of how the American concept of government changed, see James Bovard, *Freedom in Chains* (New York: Palgrave, 1999), pp. 11–50.

7. Eric Foner, "The Education of Richard Hofstadter," *Nation,* May 4, 1992.

8. Richard Hofstadter, *The Paranoid Style in America Politics and Other Essays* (Cambridge: Harvard University Press, 1996).

9. Ibid., p. 5

10. Ibid., p. 90. Italics added.

11. Ibid., p. 119. Italics added.

12. Ibid., p. 44. Italics added.

13. Ibid., p. 45.

14. Thomas Hazlett, "The Fairness Doctrine Was Never Quite Fair," *Los Angeles Times,* October 4, 1987.

15. Tom Rhodes, "Kennedys Put Tax Squeeze on Foes," *London Times,* January 29, 1997.

16. Ibid.

17. Laurence H. Silberman, "Hoover's Institution," *Wall Street Journal,* July 20, 2005.

18. Ibid.

19. James Bovard, *Terrorism and Tyranny* (New York: Palgrave, 2003), pp. 147–154.

20. Mark Wagenveld, "25 Years Ago, Before Watergate, A Burglary Changed History," *Philadelphia Inquirer,* March 10, 1996.

21. Hofstadter, *Paranoid Style,* p. 102.

22. *Why People Don't Trust Government,* edited by Joseph S. Nye, Philip D. Zelikow, and David C. King (Cambridge: Harvard University Press, 1997), p. 81.

23. In congressional testimony, FBI Director Floyd Clarke stated that, "The destruction of the building was part of the ultimate plan which was included" in the briefing book given to Attorney General Reno on April 12, 7 days before the final assault. "Joint hearing of the crime subcommittee of the House Judiciary Committee and the National Security International Affairs and Criminal Justice Subcommittee of the House Government Reform and Oversight Committee subject: Review of siege of Branch Davidian's compound in Waco, Texas," Federal News Service, July 28, 1995.

24. David E. Sanger, "White House Chief of Staff Calls Attention to Waco a 'Diversion,'" *New York Times,* May 15, 1995.

25. Christopher Connell, "Treasury Secretary Defends ATF, Voices Concerns About Hearings," Associated Press, July 5, 1995.

26. Editorial, "'Callous Disregard,'" *Washington Times,* July 17, 1995.

27. "President Bill Clinton's Remarks to Directors of Federal Law Enforcement Agencies," Federal News Service, July 20, 1995.

28. Jacob Sullum, "The Fire Last Time," *Reason,* May 1998.

29. Ibid.

30. James Bovard, "Hearings Show Waco Defense is Wacky," *Wall Street Journal,* August 2, 1995.

31. "Reno Discusses Possible Bid for Florida Governorship," CNN.com, May 31, 2001.

32. Dan Eggen, "FBI Termed Uncooperative in Waco Probe," *Washington Post,* June 1, 2001.

33. James Bovard, "The Latest, Greatest Waco Whitewash," *American Spectator,* October 2000.

34. Huw Richards, "Fed up with the Feds; Perspective; Interview; Joseph Nye," *Times Higher Education Supplement,* January 23, 1998.

35. Ibid.

36. Ibid.

37. Ibid.

38. *Why People Don't Trust Government,* ed. Nye, Zelikow, and King, p. 91.

39. Ibid., p. 94.

40. Ibid., p. 200.

41. Ibid., p. 255. Italics in original.

42. Ibid., p. 257.

43. Joseph Nye, "In Government We Don't Trust; Declining Confidence of People in Their Governments," *Foreign Policy,* September 1997. Italics added.

44. Garry Wills, *A Necessary Evil* (New York: Simon & Schuster, 2000), p. 21.

45. Ibid.

46. James Bovard, *Feeling Your Pain: The Explosion and Abuse of Government Power in the Clinton-Gore Years* (New York: Palgrave, 2000), pp. 291–303.

47. U.S. Department of Justice, "Report Regarding Internal Investigation of Shootings at Ruby Ridge, Idaho During Arrest of Randy Weaver," 1994. (This report was never released by the Justice Department; *Legal Times* acquired the report and put it on the Internet in mid-1995.)

48. James Bovard, "Cover-up from Idaho to Waco?" *Washington Times,* January 18, 1995.

49. Henry Weinstein, "Court Blasts FBI Actions at Ruby Ridge," *Los Angeles Times,* September 26, 1997.

50. "*Washington Post* Poll: War on Terrorism," *Washington Post,* September 28, 2001.

51. Ibid.

52. R. W. Apple, Jr., "Big Government Is Back in Style," *New York Times,* November 23, 2001.

53. Al Hunt, "Government to the Rescue," *Wall Street Journal,* September 27, 2001.

54. Ronald Brownstein, "The Government, Once Scorned, Becomes Savior," *Los Angeles Times,* September 20, 2001.

55. Dana Milbank and Richard Morin, "Public Is Unyielding In War Against Terror," *Washington Post,* September 29, 2001.

56. "Post-9/11 Surge in Public Support of Government Reverses Course," Brookings Institution, April 17, 2005.

57. Ibid. Italics added.

58. Senate Select Committee on Intelligence, "September 11 and the Imperative of Reform in the U.S. Intelligence Community," December 10, 2002.

59. Sheryl Gay Stolberg, "Panel Members, Insiders All, Question Friends, but Too Gingerly for Some Viewers," *New York Times,* March 25, 2004.

60. Benjamin DeMott, "Whitewash as Public Service: How The 9/11 Commission Report Defrauds the Nation," *Harper's,* October 2004.

61. Ibid.

62. Carol Morello, "Conspiracy Theories Flourish on the Internet," *Washington Post,* October 7, 2004.

63. Ibid.

64. Ibid. Italics added.

65. William F. Jasper, "9–11 Conspiracy Fact & Fiction," *New American,* May 2, 2005.

66. Montaigne, *Complete Essays* (Palo Alto, CA: Stanford University Press, 1965), p. 265.

67. Attorney General John Ashcroft, "Memorandum on the Freedom of Information Act," Justice Department Office of Public Affairs, October 12, 2001.

68. "Further Implementation of the Presidential Records Act," *Public Papers of the Presidents,* November 1, 2001.

69. Scott Shane, "Increase in the Number of Documents Classified by the Government," *New York Times,* July 3, 2005.

70. Ibid.

71. Ibid.

72. Eric Alterman, *When Presidents Lie* (New York: Viking, 2004), p. 296.

73. Jim Hoagland, "The Limits of Lying," *Washington Post,* March 21, 2002.

74. Bob Herbert, "Truth and Deceit," *New York Times,* June 2, 2005.

75. Accessed at http://www.4president.org/speeches/carter1976announcement.htm.

76. David Corn, *The Lies of George W. Bush* (New York: Three Rivers Press, 2003), pp. 12–13.

77. Transcript, "Online Newshour," Public Broadcasting Service, December 18, 2000.

78. "The President's Inaugural Address," *Public Papers of the Presidents,* January 20, 2005.
79. James Bovard, *Terrorism & Tyranny* (New York: Palgrave, 2003), pp. 133–67.
80. Jack Douglas, "U.S. Security Memos Warn of Little Things," *Fort Worth Star-Telegram,* May 25, 2003.
81. See James Bovard, *Feeling Your Pain: The Explosion & Abuse of Government Power in the Clinton-Gore Years* (New York: Palgrave, 2000), pp. 109–127.
82. For an analysis of how public opinion and media credulity allowed the Bush administration to exploit 9/11, see James Bovard, *Terrorism & Tyranny.*
83. Michael Isikoff, "2001 Memo Reveals Push for Broader Presidential Powers," *Newsweek,* December 18, 2004.
84. Arthur Lionel Smith, "English Political Philosophy in the Seventeenth and Eighteenth Centuries," in *Cambridge Modern History,* vol. 6 (Cambridge: Cambridge University Press, 1909), p. 800.
85. James Bryce, *Modern Democracy,* vol. 2, p. 569.

CHAPTER 8

1. Katie Nguyen, "Ethiopia Frees Opponent, Amnesty Condemns Police," Reuters News Service, June 10, 2005.
2. John Phillip Reid, *The Concept of Representation in the Age of the American Revolution* (Chicago: University of Chicago Press, 1989), p. 30.
3. Ibid., p. 28.
4. Ibid., p. 2.
5. Ibid., p. 28.
6. Ibid., p. 9.
7. *Congressional Record,* January 6, 2005, p. H86.
8. Ibid., H118.
9. Ibid., H120.
10. Ibid., p. H87.
11. Ibid., p. H106.
12. Ibid., p. H109.
13. Ibid., p. H120.
14. Ibid., p. H113.
15. Ibid., p. H117.
16. Ibid., p. H122.
17. Ibid., p. S55.
18. Ibid., p. S56.
19. "Remarks at the Capitol after Signing the Voting Rights Act," *Public Papers of the Presidents,* August 6, 1965.
20. Elisabeth Bumiller, "The Voting; All Those Promises: Do They Really Matter?" *New York Times,* October 26, 2004.
21. "Farewell Address to the Nation," *Public Papers of the Presidents,* January 11, 1989, p. 53.
22. "Remarks to a Rally in Houston, Texas," *Public Papers of the Presidents,* November 2, 1992.
23. "President Holds Press Conference," White House Office of the Press Secretary, November 4, 2004.
24. Jesse Holland, "Gonzales Backs U.S. Assault Weapons Ban," Associated Press, January 18, 2005.
25. Dafna Linzer, "IAEA Leader's Phone Tapped," *Washington Post,* December 12, 2004.
26. Jim VandeHei and Michael A. Fletcher, "Bush Says Election Ratified Iraq Policy," *Washington Post,* January 16, 2005.
27. Benjamin Constant, *Political Writings* (Cambridge: Cambridge University Press, 1988; originally published, 1815), p. 264.
28. Marc Bloch, *Feudal Society,* vol. 1 (Chicago: University of Chicago, 1961; originally published, 1940), p. 261.
29. *Yick Wo v. Hopkins,* 118 U.S. 356, 369 (1886).
30. "Military Order—Detention, Treatment, and Trial of Certain Non-Citizens in the War Against Terrorism," White House Office of the Press Secretary, November 13, 2001.

31. Accessed at http://news.findlaw.com/hdocs/docs/hamdi/hamdirums61902gbrf.pdf.
32. Michael J. Sniffen, "Government Asserts Power to Keep Detainees," Associated Press, December 1, 2004.
33. "Letter to Secretary Rumsfeld on the 'Joint Doctrine for Detainee Operations,'" Human Rights Watch, April 7, 2005.
34. "Interview with Sir David Frost of BBC Television," *Public Papers of the Presidents,* November 12, 2003.
35. Tom Jackman, "U.S. a Battlefield, Solicitor General Tells Judges," *Washington Post,* July 20, 2005.
36. John Philip Reid, *The Concept of Representation,* p. 133.
37. *Complete Works of Tacitus* (New York: Random House, 1942), p. 139 (from the Annals 3.69).
38. Nguyen, "Ethiopia Frees Opponent, Amnesty Condemns Police."
39. John Philip Reid, *The Concept of Representation,* pp. 37, 39.
40. Gordon Wood, *The Radicalism of the American Revolution* (New York: Random House, 1993), p. 179.
41. William W. Beach, "The 2005 Index of Dependency," Heritage Foundation, June 13, 2005.
42. For a breakdown of the numbers, see James Bovard, *Freedom in Chains* (New York: Palgrave, 1999), pp. 125–129.
43. James Bovard, *Feeling Your Pain* (New York: Palgrave, 2000), pp. 67–83.
44. James Bovard, "FEMA Money! Come & Get It!" *American Spectator,* September 1996.
45. John Mintz, "Report Calls Payments By FEMA Questionable," *Washington Post,* May 19, 2005.
46. Martha Derthick, *Policy-making for Social Security* (Washington: Brookings Institution, 1979), p. 360ff.
47. Al Kamen, "Wanted: Stephanopoulos," *Washington Post,* May 3, 1996.
48. Eric Felten, *The Ruling Class* (Washington: Regnery Gateway, 1993), p. 63.
49. David Burnham, *A Law unto Itself: The IRS and the Abuse of Power* (New York: Random House, 1989). Also, James Bovard, *Lost Rights* (New York: St. Martin's Press, 1994), pp. 259–92.
50. Bovard, *Lost Rights,* pp. 227–44.
51. James Bovard, "Bankrupt Environmentalism," *New York Times,* July 9, 1985.
52. "Ronald Reagan: Remarks on the Occasion of 83rd Birthday Gala," February 3, 1994, accessed at http://www.americanrhetoric.com/speeches/ronaldreagan83birthday.htm.
53. Accessed at http://www.yale.edu/lawweb/avalon/alsedact.htm.
54. Nicholas Kittrie and Eldon Wedlock, *The Tree of Liberty: A Documentary History of Rebellion and Political Crime in America,* vol. 1 (Baltimore: Johns Hopkins, 1998), p. 89.
55. Thomas Carothers, "Democracy Promotion Under Clinton," *Washington Quarterly,* Autumn 1995.

CHAPTER 9

1. "Remarks at the Midwest Airlines Center in Milwaukee, Wisconsin," *Public Papers of the Presidents,* October 3, 2003.
2. "Address Before a Joint Session of Congress On The State of the Union," White House Office of the Press Secretary, January 25, 1994.
3. Jack Levy, "Domestic Politics and War," in Robert Rotberg and Theodore Rabb, eds., *The Origin and Prevention of Major Wars* (Cambridge: Cambridge University, 1988), p. 88.
4. Accessed at http://www.theamericanpresidency.us/warwilson.htm.
5. Tony Smith, *America's Mission* (Princeton: Princeton University Press, 1994), p. 273.
6. Thomas Carothers, "Democracy Promotion under Clinton," *Washington Quarterly,* Autumn 1995.
7. "State of the Union Address," WashingtonPost.com, February 2, 2005.
8. "Remarks by President Bush at International Republican Institute Dinner," White House Office of the Press Secretary, May 18, 2005.
9. "Interview With Lithuanian National Television," *Public Papers of the Presidents,* May 4, 2005.
10. Accessed at http://www.constitution.org/kant/perpeace.htm.
11. Accessed at http://www.hawaii.edu/powerkills/welcome.html.
12. Thomas Schwartz and Kiron Skinner, "The Myth of Democratic Pacifism," *Hoover Digest,* No. 2, 1999.

13. Ibid.

14. John M. Owen IV, "Ballots and Bullets: The Elusive Democratic Peace," [book review] *American Political Science Review,* June 2000.

15. Edward Mansfield and Jack Snyder, "Democratization and War," *Foreign Affairs,* May-June 1995.

16. "Remarks in Roswell, New Mexico," *Public Papers of the Presidents,* January 22, 2004.

17. John L. Harper, "The Dream of Democratic Peace," *Foreign Affairs,* May 1997.

18. Randolph Bourne, *War and the Intellectuals: Essays by Randolph S. Bourne,* 1915–1919, editor Carl Resek (New York: Harper Torchbooks, 1964), p. 66.

19. Ibid., pp. 66–67.

20. Ibid., p. 67.

21. Mansfield and Snyder, "Democratization and War."

22. Gustave Gilbert, *Nuremberg Diary* (New York: Farrar, Straus, 1947), pp. 278–279.

23. "War Powers Act Case Dismissed," *National Law Journal,* June 21, 1999.

24. "Remarks by the President in Roundtable Interview with Asian Editors," The White House Office of the Press Secretary, October 17, 2001. (The interview occurred on October 16, 2001.)

25. "Interview With Foreign Print Journalists," *Public Papers of the Presidents,* May 5, 2005.

26. "Remarks to the United Brotherhood of Carpenters and Joiners of America in Las Vegas, Nevada," *Public Papers of the Presidents,* August 12, 2004.

27. "The President's News Conference With Prime Minister Paul Martin of Canada," *Public Papers of the Presidents,* April 30, 2004.

28. David Von Drehle, "'Shock and Awe' Author Uneasy With New Fame," *Washington Post,* March 22, 2003.

29. "Remarks at a Bush-Cheney Luncheon in New Orleans," *Public Papers of the Presidents,* January 15, 2004.

30. "Remarks and a Question-and-Answer Session in Niles, Michigan," *Public Papers of the Presidents,* May 3, 2004.

31. Pamela Hess, "Pentagon Wants New Generation Of Smaller Cheaper Nukes," United Press International, April 2, 2004.

32. Dave Moniz, "Weapons Program Would Be Scaled Back," *USA Today,* February 8, 2005.

33. Jim VandeHei, "Marking 2 Years in Iraq, Bush Offers Thanks to Troops," *Washington Post,* April 13, 2005.

34. "National Security Strategy of the United States," White House National Security Council, September 2002. Available at http://www.whitehouse.gov/nsc/nss.html.

35. "The President's News Conference With President Viktor Yushchenko of Ukraine," *Public Papers of the Presidents,* April 4, 2005.

36. "President Holds a Press Conference," White House Office of the Press Secretary, December 20, 2004.

37. Robert H. Reid (Associated Press), "Insurgents Launch Deadly Attacks Across Central Iraq as US Prepares for Fallujah Attack," *Detroit News,* November 7, 2004.

38. "Remarks in Halifax, Canada," *Public Papers of the Presidents,* December 1, 2004.

39. James Philbin, "Charles Austin Beard: Liberal Foe of American Internationalism," *Humanitas,* No. 2, 2000, pp. 99–100.

40. Posted at the website of the Future of Freedom Foundation, www.fff.org/freedom/0893e.asp. Quoted from *James Madison, Letters and Other Writings of James Madison,* 4 vol. (Philadelphia, PA: Lippincott, 1865).

41. Accessed at http://www.yale.edu/lawweb/avalon/washing.htm.

42. Plutarch, *Lives of the Noble Grecians and Romans* (New York: Modern Library, 1935), p. 790.

43. James Bryce, *Modern Democracies,* vol. 2 (New York: Macmillan, 1921), p. 575.

44. Thomas Babington Macaulay, *Critical and Historical Essays,* vol. 1 (New York: Dutton, 1916), pp. 30–31.

45. Ibid., p. 31.

46. Gordon Wood, *The Creation of the American Republic, 1776–1787* (Chapel Hill: University of North Carolina, 1969), p. 348.

47. Francis Fukuyama, "The End of History?" *National Interest,* Summer 1989.
48. Ibid.
49. Ibid.
50. Ernst Cassirer, *The Myth of the State* (New Haven: Yale University, 1946), p. 272.
51. *The Philosophy of Hegel,* ed. Carl J. Friedrich (New York: Modern Library, 1953), p. 282.
52. G. W. F. Hegel, *Philosophy of History* (New York: Collier & Son, 1902), p. 87.
53. Ibid., p. 61.
54. Harold Laski, *The State in Theory and Practice* (London: George Allen & Unwin, 1935), p. 64.
55. Cassirer, *The Myth of the State,* p. 250.
56. Ibid., p. 272.
57. Roger Kimball, "Francis Fukuyama & the End of History," *New Criterion,* February 1992.
58. Cassirer, *The Myth of the State,* p. 249. The original comment was from German historian Hajo Holborn.
59. Ibid., p. 263.
60. Fukuyama, "The End of History?"
61. "National Security Strategy of the United States," White House National Security Council, September 2002.
62. "Remarks at a Victory 2004 Luncheon in New York City," *Public Papers of the Presidents,* April 20, 2004.

CHAPTER 10

1. G. W. F. Hegel, *The Philosophy of Hegel,* Carl Friedrich, ed. (New York: Modern Library, 1954), p. 283.
2. John Stuart Mill, *Utilitarianism, Liberty, and Representative Government* (New York: E. P. Dutton, 1951), p. 358.
3. Michael Delli Carpini, "In Search of the Informed Voter," paper presented at Middle Tennessee State University / Murfreesboro and Nashville, Tennessee, November 12, 1999.
4. David Ciepley, "Why the State Was Dropped in the First Place: A Prequel to Skocpol's 'Bringing the State Back In,'" *Critical Review,* 2000, vol, 14, Nos. 2–3, p. 162.
5. William Kristol and Robert Kagan, "Toward a Neo-Reaganite Foreign Policy," *Foreign Affairs,* July/August 1996.
6. David Brooks, "A Return to National Greatness; A Manifesto for a Lost Creed," *Weekly Standard,* March 3, 1997.
7. Ibid.
8. Ibid.
9. Ibid. Italics added.
10. Benito Mussolini, "The Political and Social Doctrine of Fascism," *Political Quarterly,* July-September 1933, Vol. 4, no. 3. This text is adapted from the 1932 edition of the *Encyclopedia Italiana.*
11. Ibid.
12. William Kristol and David Brooks, "What Ails Conservatism," *Wall Street Journal,* September 15, 1997.
13. Ibid.
14. Ibid. Italics added.
15. Jacob G. Hornberger, "Loving Your Country and Hating Your Government," *Freedom Daily,* September 1999.
16. Henry David Thoreau, *Civil Disobedience and Other Essays* (Mineola, NY: Dover, 1993), p. 2.
17. Brooks did not always place the federal government on a pedestal. Prior to moving to Washington, when he was Editorial Features Editor at the *Wall Street Journal* in 1994 and 1995, Brooks showed far more courage than most commentary editors in his willingness to run articles exposing federal abuses at Waco and Ruby Ridge.
18. Walter McDougall, *Promised Land, Crusader State* (New York: Houghton Mifflin, 1997), p. 209.

19. Ibid., p. 209.
20. Ibid., p. 210.
21. "Harvard Defendants Pay Over $31 Million to Settle False Claims Act Allegations," U.S. Agency for International Development, August 3, 2005.
22. Justin Kruger and David Dunning, "Unskilled and Unaware of It: How Difficulties in Recognizing One's Own Incompetence Lead to Inflated Self-Assessments," *Journal of Personality and Social Psychology,* December 1999.
23. James Kirchick, "Lawmakers Attend Moon 'Coronation'," *The Hill,* June 22, 2004.
24. Ibid.
25. Sheryl Gay Stolberg, "A Crowning at the Capital Creates a Stir," *New York Times,* June 24, 2004.
26. Jim Newton, "Long LSD Prison Terms—It's All in the Packaging," *Los Angeles Times,* July 27, 1992.
27. Editorial, "The Gang of Four," *Wall Street Journal,* September 26, 1995. The *Journal* also editorially endorsed the Freedom to Farm Act on September 20, 1995.
28. James Bovard, *Feeling Your Pain* (New York: Palgrave, 2000), pp. 187–205; and Bovard, *Bush Betrayal* (New York: Palgrave, 2004), pp. 95–107.
29. Editorial, "Prairie Plutocrats," *Wall Street Journal,* February 1, 2002.
30. Douglas Jehl and Eric Schmitt, "U.S. Military Says 26 Inmate Deaths May Be Homicide," *New York Times,* March 16, 2005.
31. Ibid.
32. Baker's May 1991 comment was quoted in Philip Shenon, "Washington and Baghdad Agree on One Point: Sanctions Hurt," *New York Times,* November 22, 1998.
33. Colonel John Warden III, "The Enemy as a System," *Airpower Journal,* Spring 1995.
34. David Leigh and James Wilson, "Counting Iraq's Victims," *Guardian* (UK), October 10, 2001.
35. Richard Garfield, "Excess Deaths Among Children In Iraq: How Many Children Have Died?," Working Paper, February 8, 2003.
36. James Wall, "Deadly Silence," *Christian Century,* October 25, 2000.
37. Hannah Arendt, "Lying in Politics: Reflections on The Pentagon Papers," *New York Review of Books,* November 18, 1971.
38. Ibid.
39. Ibid.
40. Ibid.
41. Ibid.
42. Richard Leiby, "Mary Cheney Sets Record Straight," *Washington Post,* March 30, 2005.
43. Gloria Borger, "Tales of Jack and Mike," *U.S. News & World Report,* July 4, 2005.
44. Arendt, "Lying in Politics: Reflections on the Pentagon Papers."
45. David Ciepley, "Why the State Was Dropped in the First Place: A Prequel to Skocpol's 'Bringing the State Back In,'" *Critical Review,* 2000, vol. 14, Nos. 2–3, p. 167.
46. Todd Gitlin, "It Was a Very Bad Year," *American Prospect,* July 2004. The phrase may have been coined by Jack Newfield, an author and *Village Voice* columnist.
47. Norman Solomon, "Let Us Now Praise 'Unfamous' Journalists," *Media Beat,* April 29, 1999.
48. James Bovard, "Narcs Should Let the Deadheads Be," *Newsday,* March 15, 1994.
49. Robert Skidelsky, *The Road from Serfdom* (New York: Penguin, 1995), p. 68.

CHAPTER 11

1. Accessed at http://www.onpower.org/quotes/h.html.
2. "Remarks at Logan High School in La Crosse, Wisconsin," *Public Papers of the Presidents,* May 8, 2002.
3. Thomas Hobbes, *Leviathan* (London: Penguin, 1974), p. 232.
4. Jean Jacques Rousseau, *The Social Contract and Discourses* (New York: Dutton, 1950), p. 14.
5. Ibid., p. 87.
6. James Bryce, *Modern Democracies,* vol. 2 (New York: Macmillan, 1921), p. 573.

7. *The Public Papers and Addresses of Franklin D. Roosevelt, 1938* (New York: MacMillan, 1942), p. 489. (emphasis added).

8. "Remarks to Business Leaders in Stamford, Connecticut," *Public Papers of the Presidents,* October 7, 1996, p. 1999.

9. David Ciepley, "Why the State was Dropped in the First Place: A Prequel to Skocpol's 'Bringing the State Back In,'" *Critical Review,* 2000, vol. 14, Nos. 2–3, p. 159.

10. Ciepeley, p. 200.

11. *Kelo V. New London* (04–108), accessed on August 18, 2005, at http://straylight.law.cornell.edu/supct/html/04–108.ZS.html.

12. See Steven Greenhut, *Abuse of Power: How the Government Misuses Eminent Domain* (Santa Ana, California: Seven Locks Press, 2004).

13. Richard Epstein, "Supreme Folly," *Wall Street Journal,* June 27, 2005.

14. *Kelo v. New London,* at http://straylight.law.cornell.edu/supct/html/04–108.ZS.html.

15. David Barron, "Ruling Empowers Urban Planners," *Philadelphia Inquirer,* June 29, 2005.

16. Accessed at http://straylight.law.cornell.edu/supct/html/99-1408.ZO.html.

17. Accessed at http://straylight.law.cornell.edu/supct/html/99-1408.ZD.html.

18. Ricky Young, "Cops Won't Buckle under on Seat-Belt Stops," *Denver Post,* November 29, 1998.

19. Accessed at http://straylight.law.cornell.edu/supct/html/99-1408.ZO.html.

20. Accessed at http://straylight.law.cornell.edu/supct/html/99-1408.ZD.html.

21. Young, "Cops Won't Buckle under on Seat-Belt Stops."

22. Sheldon Richman, "Government is not 'Us'," Future of Freedom Foundation, June 2, 2004.

23. James Bovard, *Freedom in Chains* (New York: Palgrave, 1999), pp. 188–196.

24. James Bovard, "Beyond Perjury: Thou Shalt Not Lie. Ever," *Playboy,* May 1999.

25. John Phillip Reid, *The Concept of Liberty in the Age of the American Revolution* (Chicago: University of Chicago Press, 1988), p. 65.

26. Ibid., pp. 65 and 114.

27. *Meyer v. Nebraska,* 262 U.S. 390 (1923).

28. Elvin Lim, "Five Trends in Presidential Rhetoric," *Presidential Studies Quarterly,* June 2002.

29. Ibid.

30. See Jeffrey Rogers Hummel, *Emancipating Slaves, Enslaving Free Men* (Chicago: Open Court, 1996), and Thomas DiLorenzo, *The Real Lincoln* (New York: Random House, 2003).

31. The Gettysburg Address, at http://www.law.ou.edu/hist/getty.html.

32. Thomas Fleming, *The Illusion of Victory* (New York: Basic Books, 2003), p. 382.

33. H. L. Mencken, *Minority Report* (Baltimore: Johns Hopkins University, 1997; [1956]), p. 193.

34. Accessed at http://www.law.ou.edu/hist/harrison.html.

35. *The Public Papers and Address of Franklin D. Roosevelt, 1937* (New York: Macmillan, 1941), p. 361.

36. Accessed at http://historymatters.gmu.edu/d/5105/.

37. Accessed at http://www.americanrhetoric.com/speeches/fdrthefourfreedoms.htm.

38. http://www.bartleby.com/124/pres59.html, accessed on August 17, 2005.

39. http://www.landmarkcases.org/nixon/nixonview.html, accessed on August 17, 2005.

40. "Remarks by President Bush at the Dedication of the DEA New York Headquarters," Federal News Service, June 29, 1992.

41. For details on the carnage of the first Bush drug war, see James Bovard, *Lost Rights: The Destruction of American Liberty* (New York: St. Martin's, 1994).

42. "Remarks by the President in MTV's 'Enough is Enough' Forum on Crime," Office of the Press Secretary, White House, April 19, 1994.

43. Craig Hemmens, "I Hear You Knocking: The Supreme Court Revisits the Knock and Announce Rule," *University of Missouri at Kansas City Law Review,* vol. 66, Spring 1998, p. 584.

44. "Interview With Dutch TV NOS," *Public Papers of the Presidents,* May 5, 2005.

45. "Interview With Foreign Print Journalists," *Public Papers of the Presidents,* May 5, 2005.

46. Opportunism in the Face of Tragedy, Repression in the Name of Anti-terrorism," Human Rights Watch, 2002. At http://www.hrw.org/campaigns/september11/opportunismwatch.htm.

47. "U.S. President Thanks Uzbekistan for Support to Fight Terrorism," BBC Monitoring Central Asia Unit, September 18, 2002.

48. R. Jeffrey Smith and Glenn Kessler, "U.S. Opposed Calls at NATO for Probe of Uzbek Killings," *Washington Post*, June 14, 2005.

49. "Kazakhstan," Country Reports on Human Rights Practices—2001, U.S. State Department Bureau of Democracy, Human Rights, and Labor, March 4, 2002.

50. "Amnesty International News Conference—2002 Annual Report on Global Human Rights," Federal News Service, May 28, 2002.

51. "Remarks as Delivered by President George W. Bush to the Australian Parliament," Federal News Service, October 23, 2003.

52. "Interview With Mouafac Harb of the Middle East Television Network," *Public Papers of the Presidents*, January 29, 2004.

53. Elisabeth Bumiller, "In Visit to Georgia, Bush Hails 'Beacon of Liberty,'" *New York Times*, May 10, 2005.

54. Frida Berrigan, "George in Georgia," *In These Times*, May 23, 2005.

55. Ibid.

56. "Transcript of Remarks by the President to U.S. Attorneys Conference," U.S. Newswire, November 29, 2001.

57. "Memorandum on the Congressional Subpoena for Executive Branch Documents," *Public Papers of the Presidents*, December 12, 2001 (italics added). For a discussion of this case, see

58. James Bovard, *The Bush Betrayal* (New York: Palgrave, 2004), pp. 148–50.

59. "Interview With African Print Journalists," *Public Papers of the Presidents*, July 3, 2003.

60. Gene R. Nichol, "Ashcroft Wants Even More," *Raleigh News and Observer*, February 20, 2003.

61. "Hearing of the Senate Judiciary Committee; Oversight of the Department of Justice," Federal News Service, July 25, 2002.

62. James Bovard, *Terrorism & Tyranny* (New York: Palgrave, 2003), pp. 81–103, 133–167.

63. Ibid., pp. 145–46.

64. Ibid., pp. 137–40.

65. Ibid., p. 144.

66. http://www.calvin.edu/academic/cas/gpa/posters/liste2b.jpg.

67. Jim VandeHei and Peter Baker, "President Struggles to Regain His Pre-Hurricane Swagger," *Washington Post*, September 24, 2005.

68. R. J. Rummel, "Censor the Media," posted at http://freedomspeace.blogspot.com/2005/02/censor-media.html. Journalist Anthony Gregory astutely analyzed Rummel's comments, posting his comments at http://blog.lewrockwell.com/lewrw/archives/007364.html.

69. John Derbyshire, "Attorney General Janet Ashcroft?" *National Review*, September 7, 2001.

70. Dick Meyer, "Look What the Tide Brought Back," *Washington Post*, September 18, 2005.

71. Arthur Lionel Smith, "English Political Philosophy in the Seventeenth and Eighteenth Centuries," in *Cambridge Modern History*, vol. 6 (Cambridge: Cambridge University Press, 1909), p. 795.

72. Alexis De Tocqueville, *Democracy in America* (Garden City, NY: Doubleday, 1969), p. 260.

CHAPTER 12

1. John Taylor, *Tyranny Unmasked* (Indianapolis: Liberty Fund, 1992 [1822]), p. 267.

2. *The Essence of Hayek*, edited by Chiaki Nishiyama and Kurt Leube (Palo Alto, Calif.: Hoover Institution, 1984), p. 352.

3. Gordon S. Wood, *The Radicalism of the American Revolution* (New York: Random House, 1993), p. 95.

4. Taylor, *Tyranny Unmasked*, p. 267.

5. Gertrude Besse King, "The Servile Mind," *International Journal of Ethics*, July 1916.

6. Justice Scalia's dissent. MCCONNELL V. F.E.C. (02–1674), December 10, 2003, at http://straylight.law.cornell.edu/supct/html/02-1674.ZX.html.

7. "GOP Pressures Rock the Vote to Stop Talking About the Draft," *Democracy Now!*, October 19, 2004.

8. George Orwell, *The Collected Essays, Journalism and Letters: Volume 3* (London: Penguin, 1970), p. 273.

Index